Education Empowered

amplify
an imprint of Amplify Publishing Group

www.amplifypublishinggroup.com

Education Empowered:
A Holistic Blueprint for Building Better Schools and a Better World

Creation of this book was financed by Sankalpa Education.

For more information, please contact:
Amplify Publishing, an imprint of Amplify Publishing Group
620 Herndon Parkway, Suite 220
Herndon, VA 20170
info@amplifypublishing.com

Library of Congress Control Number: 2024913388

CPSIA Code: PRV0125A

ISBN-13: 978-1-63755-679-5

Printed in the United States

*This book is dedicated to my parents and grandparents—
they paved the path I have walked on.*

*As pioneers who pushed boundaries, my grandparents
are a constant source of inspiration.*

*And I am forever indebted to my parents; their
sacrifices have opened the world for me.*

Education Empowered

A Holistic Blueprint
for Building Better Schools
and a Better World

SRINIVAS JALLEPALLI

amplify
an imprint of Amplify Publishing Group

Contents

Preface

Keep on beginning and failing. Each time you fail, start all over again, and you will grow stronger until you have accomplished a purpose—not the one you began with perhaps, but one you'll be glad to remember.

—ANNE SULLIVAN

As a child, I didn't fully appreciate the sacrifices my parents made to put my two sisters and me through school. As in most other lower-middle-class families in India, my parents struggled immensely to make ends meet. Still, they were determined to send us to one of the best private schools in the area. This was a very difficult decision with serious financial implications. It also went against the advice of several extended family members, especially my maternal grandfather. My grandfather, a former government school headmaster, repeatedly pointed out that my aunts' children were doing just fine in public schools. I find it remarkable that my parents, under these circumstances, were able to hold fast to their convictions.

Given this background, it isn't difficult to imagine the disappointment my parents must have felt at my lackluster academic performance. I was, at best, an average student. My mother's relentless prodding to do better fell on deaf ears. That is, until one day in the fall of 1979. I had just started the fifth grade. My mother sat me down and tried yet again to convince me that I was destined for a bleak future if I didn't drastically improve my grades. She insisted that only the top two or three students in a class could hope to be gainfully employed after completing their education.

My mother was determined to throw in all she had at her disposal. She promised to give me an allowance of ten rupees (about $1.25 in 1979 and $5.24 in 2023) every time I managed to come in first in my class, and five rupees whenever I placed second. Ten rupees was a lot of money at that time, especially for a ten-year-old. Perhaps these bribes did the trick. Or maybe I was finally old enough to pay attention. Whatever the real reason, my mother's entreaties finally resonated. Despite some trepidation about my own capabilities, I took all this to heart.

An opportunity to test my potential came within a month. Staying up late night after night, I prepared diligently for a set of comprehensive tests. Then I waited with bated breath over an interminable weekend for the results, which we finally received on Tuesday. While I did get a higher math score, there was little to celebrate as far as the other subjects went. I was crestfallen, and the reality slowly sank in. I came to believe that sheer application can only take you so far. I concluded that it's hard to perform at the highest levels if you are not naturally gifted.

To add to my frustration, our teacher announced that our class was going to be split up, with some of us moved to a new all-boys section. Before I'd even gotten to know some of my new classmates, it was time for yet another set of tests. Of course, my expectations had been well-tempered by then. So you can imagine my disbelief when our new teacher called my name at the top of the roll list. Apparently, I stood first in my class! It was customary at the time to publicly share the names of at least the top ten students in every class. It is an understatement to say that my performance was a surprise to everyone else as well. It did not make sense. Very few of my classmates even knew who I was. I was ecstatic, blown away by this new claim to fame. I felt like I was on top of the world.

This has been the most gratifying outcome I've ever experienced in my life. After I was able to repeat my performance a few times, I was convinced it wasn't a fluke. This episode also turned out to be an eye-opener. Over time, my understanding of what had occurred evolved. I came to believe that in grading tests, many teachers—at least in our school—relied more than they should have on their impressions of their students' abilities. This was feasible for the types of assessments we had at that time—ones that had a lot of subjective questions. The doomsday scenario my mother had portrayed for me, as well as her financial incentives, turned out to be a priceless gift.

As you might expect, this experience changed my perception of the capability gulf between frontbenchers and backbenchers. I was convinced that I stumbled onto a well-kept secret and that if I could turn my grades around, almost anyone else could as well. I was increasingly confident, as the years passed, that the achievement gap was largely a self-fulfilling prophecy, reinforced by the testing regime. In my case, and perhaps in many more, tests were not used to design classroom interventions. Instead, they were unwittingly used to pigeonhole children and condemn many to a life of low self-esteem and low expectations. I had witnessed, at close hand, those who benefited, the frustration of many who were weighed down by tests, as well as the fortitude of the few who managed to overcome failure and disappointment by the sheer dint of their character.

Personally, my own confidence steadily grew as I began to master test-taking skills. In fact, by the time I entered the seventh grade, I had developed a firm belief that my success no longer depended on the quality of my teachers. I distinctly recall my conviction then that teachers were simply stationmasters who kept the trains running on time. At the same time, like most students in my school and elsewhere, I did consider myself fortunate when I ran into truly gifted master teachers and was disheartened when I encountered those who were not at the top of their game. It was only much later that I came to see how my belief system distorted and diluted my expectations for schooling!

Years later, when faced with the task of picking a pre-K school for our daughter, my wife and I realized that, despite a large variety of choices, it was not easy to find a school with a small enough class size that the teachers could attend to the developmental needs of every child. As much as I was concerned about the inadequacies of the schools I attended as a child, the situation did not appear to have improved much over the years. Too many children seem to get lost in the system with too few advocates who really know them well enough. My wife and I began to toy with the idea of launching our own school.

Avner Goren, an Israeli archaeologist and an ardent friend of the Bedouins, once said, "I do believe very strongly that naiveté is a very good and important tool to accomplish dreams."[1] Perhaps it was such naiveté that led my wife and me to eventually start a primary school (Sankalpa Academy) in Austin, Texas, in 2018. It was a modest attempt to deliver holistic education through individualized learning plans (ILPs). The idea was to create a learning environment where every child was offered a program that best met his or her needs. We learned a lot from this experience about how much each child can benefit from such a personalized focus. However, the totality of our offering was more than what most of us could get our hands around. Despite the able guidance of Ali Ronder, our founding director, and the support of many passionate parents and educators, this school only lasted a year. The cold financial realities led us to make a few rookie mistakes and they took their toll.

But the journey continued. Sankalpa Academy was an enlightening experience that only deepened my interest in the search for a more meaningful educational approach. How can we help more young people reach their true potential, build self-esteem, and mature into independent, self-aware seekers? What does it take to dial down our excessive focus on testing and for schools to move past traditional academic achievements and gaps and understand the deeper learning that occurs in children's minds? What should we do to ensure that education becomes a journey of wonder and awe? How can we help children struggling to find themselves? Can we empower children so many more are able, as adults, to help shape a rapidly evolving world? How can learning from our collective history help us in this endeavor? Can we do all this without breaking the bank?

In the following pages, I try to bring these important issues and timeless aspirations into focus. I hope readers will gain a deeper understanding of how we can help our children reach their full potential regardless of the complexities facing our educational systems.

Introduction

> Destiny is no matter of chance. It is a matter of choice.
> It is not a thing to be waited for, it is a thing to be achieved.
> —WILLIAM JENNINGS BRYAN

For tens of thousands of years, humans have exercised almost complete domination over all other species. Over this period, with a steadily growing pace, we have also achieved remarkable mastery over our physical environment. Explorations into mining, agriculture, animal husbandry, music, philosophy, and the natural sciences have quickly distinguished us from the rest of the primates. We build homes in some of the most uninhabitable parts of the world and beyond. We build complex legal frameworks and institutions that allow billions of people to function cooperatively. We efficiently travel great distances and instantaneously communicate with people anywhere, on the planet and in space. We routinely send probes to other planets. We create masterpieces such as the *Mona Lisa* and produce musical geniuses such as Beethoven and Bach. We develop vaccines that can prime our bodies into creating their own cures. We know how to create designer babies. We can split the atom and use nuclear fission to fuel our world. We are now hard at work trying to replace humans with machines that can do most of this. Some say we have only barely started.

Undeniably, education has been a key enabler of this remarkable adventure. However, there is also a deeper story behind the headlines. Our ingenuity and technological and artistic prowess belie simmering discontent and growing unease about our future. It is nothing short of a tragedy, for example, that hopelessness among our youth has been on the rise in many countries. Indeed, it is shocking that 37 percent of high school students in the US expressed persistent feelings of hopelessness in 2019, an almost 50 percent increase since 2009.[2] While alarm bells have been going off for decades about the poor educational outcomes in the United States and elsewhere, we have not collectively focused adequate attention on the steady decline in our children's well-being. This is despite the fact that there have been many global innovations to improve the quality of education and student engagement. For example, a variety of progressive educational models, from Montessori to Waldorf to Sudbury to unschooling, have sprung up over the past century to address the diverse needs of individual learners. More recently, the International Baccalaureate (IB) and Advanced Placement (AP) programs have proliferated with a mission to instill rigor and foster richer student development. However, deeply entrenched challenges related to students' mental well-being, academic rigor, character development, access, and relevance have been proving too difficult to overcome. With few exceptions, these problems appear to be largely similar across the world. It is no wonder, then, that many parents and educators have long been deeply dissatisfied. In fact, the steady rise in the popularity of homeschooling, for instance, can be attributed to this situation. Despite this longstanding discontent, only a few studies have looked deeply enough at the challenges impacting education and student learning. Laurence Steinberg's rigorous survey suggested that there are in fact deeper and broader social and cultural issues at play in the US that can't be overcome by teachers and schools.[3] A more recent year-long study in the US also painted a similar, profoundly distressing portrait of crumbling public schools and disconnected and disengaged parents.[4]

In fact, for almost a century now, many thought leaders in our society have also been voicing similar concerns. If we are honest with ourselves, we cannot ignore the fact that although humanity has made incredible progress over the centuries across many domains, there is a wide range of severe and daunting problems that are far more threatening than inadequate student achievement. Some of these problems are new, while others have metastasized over a long period. For example, it is shocking that great numbers of people still perish through conflicts and wars. As of December 2024, over forty thousand Palestinians and Israelis have been killed in the most recent outbreak of war between Israel and Hamas. As the Russian invasion of Ukraine shows, these conflicts can erupt anywhere and with little warning. Beyond these pockets of devastation, there is also endemic suffering caused by poverty.

Almost 768 million people in the world faced hunger in 2020, an increase of 150 million in just five years.[5] At the same time, while too many countries still lack basic necessities, overconsumption elsewhere has led to a climate crisis that appears to threaten our very survival. A study by researchers at Oregon State and Harvard has shown that the rate of global warming in the last thirty years is unprecedented, compared to the pace over the last ten thousand years.[6] It is projected that the inundation caused by rising sea levels will lead to a massive loss of habitat. There is broad agreement that reversing global warming is a challenge unlike any that humanity has faced thus far. Overconsumption and the aggressive pursuit of material success seem to have resulted in other serious unanticipated consequences as well. A comprehensive study by Templin et al. reveals how obesity in poorer populations in 103 low- and middle-income countries rises as these nations develop economically.[7] It is perhaps not unexpected that obesity and attendant health issues have a strong positive correlation to a nation's prosperity. However, what is less understood is the apparent inverse correlation between financial success and sense of fulfillment and engagement. According to one study, levels of empathy declined by 48 percent between 1979 and 2009 among American students, and suicide rates among people between ten and twenty-four years old increased nearly 60 percent between 2007 and 2018 in the United States.[8] From the climate crisis to job loss due to automation, it is often the bottom 90 percent that unfortunately bear the brunt of the burden.

Many of us may not link these daunting challenges to shortcomings in our educational systems. Our lopsided progress and the persistence of inequities and internecine conflicts lay bare our failings as a species. They are first and foremost a stain on our legacy. However, as we live in an increasingly interconnected world, they are also a threat to our collective future and are not simply someone else's problems. Even the most affluent amongst us cannot be certain that their children can be insulated from these crises by the estates they inherit or the colleges they get into.

A key invariant over the course of recorded history has been the desire of most parents to secure a bright future for their children. As such, it's ironic that while we take great pains to give our children the best lives we can, not enough of us seem to link global well-being to our children's education and thus to our species' long-term welfare and prosperity. It is tempting to insulate our kids' education from these longstanding civilizational struggles. However, sitting at the intersection of our social, political, economic, cultural, and psychological aspirations, education is ideally positioned to help us address these challenges—provided we are brave enough to learn from our history.

We can begin by building a good understanding of the issues confronting us. For this, education should first create broad awareness. We should next seek to understand the common threads that run through some of these problems. For example, are stains on our collective conscience such as slavery and the Holocaust entirely different in their origins? Does the burden of racism implicated in cases of police brutality against African Americans have anything in common with the tribal warfare that has plagued many societies since time immemorial? Is it too far-fetched to link the climate crisis to the loss of fulfillment and engagement that economic success appears to engender? Our civilizational crises are rarely the work of only a few people. There is often an overt ecosystem that enables them or at least an absence of a mindshare that can anticipate and prevent them. Educating a few minds will not be enough. For example, our history is replete with pioneers such as Leonardo da Vinci and Copernicus from the past and futurist Hazel Henderson and others from more recent times who provided breakthrough knowledge that was simply too advanced for the broader populations of their era. To lay claim to a better future, we therefore need to ensure broader civilizational awareness, readiness, and engagement.

This is why, first and foremost, education should help us make sense of our legacy and build faith in the endless possibilities of human ingenuity. Education needs to target a lot more than the three R's. To foster meaning and purpose, it should seek to build broader and deeper awareness of our place in time, elevate our collective mindset, and take us to a higher ground. It is in this context that this book seeks to examine the universal, timeless challenges in education.

Structural Overview

We can't dive into pressing challenges in K–12 education or long-overdue reforms without stepping back to look critically at the purpose of education, namely, to equip students with the knowledge and skills they need to tackle societal and global challenges, both today and in the future. All of us—teachers, parents, and students—need to therefore intimately understand the challenges confronting us and their root causes. For this reason, part I of this book takes a deeper look at the big-picture arc of our journey and our educational objectives. It provides a historical perspective, analyzing how humankind's development over time is linked to educational practices, ascertaining which practices help and which harm, and laying the groundwork for an evidence-based approach to educational reform. This will clarify our current choices, challenges, and opportunities as well as the best next steps.

In part II, this learning is used to design a curricular framework of three pillars that best supports the high-level objectives identified in part I. These constitute the basis of a transformative and purposeful education.

Part III outlines some key operational aspects of this framework. It offers guidance on creating learning communities and experiences that can support the structure outlined in part II.

The discussion in the first three parts of the book will clearly demonstrate that we will not be able to meet our ambitious objectives without widespread participation. At the same time, history has demonstrated time and again that universal access to high-quality education is not easy. Part IV tackles this elusive goal: it investigates problems and solutions related to equity and scale.

However, first and foremost, as we embark on this journey, we should try to suspend our conventional expectations around what education entails. We can't truly embrace a new paradigm for education without fresh, bold thinking.

Using This Book

This book is a comprehensive resource that addresses many basic as well as advanced questions about human development and learning. Given its extensive scope, taking a moment first to reflect and plan can potentially help you gain a lot more mileage from your reading experience.

Importantly, this book is not an academic treatise; it is meant to serve as a practical guide for real-world use.

Reading slowly and taking copious notes will undoubtedly be beneficial. I'd also recommend that you consult the references often and critically consider the possibility of alternative explanations for the data presented.

The power of community and role models is a recurring theme throughout the text. As you wrap up your first reading of this book, consider engaging with other families from your child's school, sports team, book club, or place of worship who might be interested in joining you on this journey. Effective collaboration can be a force multiplier, whether you are a parent, teacher, or policymaker. But you must ensure early on that there is a meeting of the minds.

Think about who you would like to work with and how you would like to partner with them. Would you like to meet with them a few times to confirm or consolidate your understanding? Would you rather check in with them periodically to exchange notes on the results of your interventions and investments? Or would you like to collaborate with them on an ongoing basis, designing learning environments inside or outside of school?

Regardless of whether you are more comfortable working primarily as a family unit or partnering with others, it might be helpful to first identify the strengths and opportunities of your own family members. What are the growth areas for your children, and how can the adults support them? It would be helpful to ensure that all adults are reasonably aligned in their objectives and understanding.

It would be beneficial to focus on the learning environments at home and school as well. Add as much detail as you can and tweak it until you are comfortable. For adult education, consider concepts from the book that weren't intuitive to you and anything that seemed burdensome. Then break down these growth opportunities into discrete, achievable development items and associate them with measurements for success.

As you plan opportunities and experiences for your children, remember to think holistically. This might encompass not just your child's individual needs but also those of their broader learning community and potentially the school district.

Keeping a detailed log of your learning, interventions, and outcomes will help you periodically reassess your strategies and maintain momentum during challenging times. This log could also be valuable to others in your community.

Finally, I am eager to hear from you, whether it's a success story, a compliment, or criticism. Your feedback is invaluable and can help shape future editions of this book.

I

Finding Our Purpose

The Arc of Humanity's Journey

Education is simply the soul of a society
as it passes from one generation to another.
—GILBERT K. CHESTERTON

Ask any two people what the purpose of education should be, and it will be a miracle if you receive the same answer. Many will insist that it is to prepare students for productive careers. Development of the social and emotional skills of our youth may be its key objective for others. Some will be mortified if education does not help build children's character. There will undoubtedly be those who look to education as a process that helps children realize their highest potential. A large majority will likely list multiple purposes, and many may want all of the above.

It therefore makes sense that the debate on the purpose of education is longstanding. The lack of consensus on this subject is also reflected through the diversity in pedagogies and curricular objectives. Educational objectives determine whether schools embrace a holistic curriculum or focus on teaching to standardized tests. While some schools rely on direct instruction, others try to get children to take more ownership. Some schools tout unschooling while others are preparatory academies for colleges. Many cities typically also have half a dozen or so schools that defy easy classification. Their claims are often so tall that they seem like the answer to every parent's prayers.

Ironically, it is remarkable that while there is a proliferation of pedagogies and educational philosophies, many well-known educational approaches themselves have succeeded in remaining virtually unchanged over the course of a century or so. They are almost like religions. Even modest changes have often resulted in the birth of a brand-new system and have rarely come through the evolution of the original philosophy itself. And these new movements—Montessori, Reggio Emilia, Waldorf, Sudbury, or almost any of the other well-known educational systems—have, in turn, often produced only amazingly faithful adherents of the philosophies of their original founders. This rigidity manifests itself in both their overarching structure (the objectives of the curriculum, the organization of classes, the role of assessments and such) and their sustenance (teacher training and retention, parental involvement, and empowerment of children, parents, and teachers). How can multiple educational doctrines find it necessary to differ substantially from each other but then not find any opportunity for further evolution? A fuller understanding of the variety in educational objectives and the purpose they feed into is indispensable for any meaningful discussion on educational reform.

However, if we truly want to transcend the limitations of prevailing pedagogies, we must believe that our educational options can be more ambitious than what are currently available. We need to take several steps back and seek a deeper understanding of what makes us human and how exactly we shot past the other species. Prima facie, such a discussion may seem out of place in a book on education. However, a thorough understanding of our origins, how we distinguished ourselves, and where we are headed is essential for identifying the most optimal curricular objectives. Despite our best intentions and efforts, curricular aspirations that are inconsistent with the human condition are not likely to be very fruitful. Therefore, taking several steps back and peering deeply into our souls is essential for an appreciation of what matters for our long-term success, educationally and otherwise.

1

Unpacking Our Roots

Nature gives to every time and season some beauties of its own;
and from morning to night, as from the cradle to the grave,
it is but a succession of changes so gentle and easy
that we can scarcely mark their progress.
—CHARLES DICKENS

Over the last four billion or so years, more than a billion unique and fascinating species have called our planet home. Yet our accomplishments over the last ten thousand years put us, as humans, in a league of our own. Indeed it is remarkable that about 13.8 billion years after the birth of the universe, a *Homo sapiens* named Albert Einstein, standing on the shoulders of many great minds, formulated the structure of general relativity, aiming to unravel the profound secrets of our universe. It is equally remarkable that at around the same time, another group of *Homo sapiens* including Heisenberg, Niels Bohr, and their colleagues, described the microscopic world through quantum mechanics. The power of our collective is evident from the fact that the mind behind general relativity struggled to accept the implications of quantum mechanics. And just as many of the claims of general relativity have been experimentally proven over the years, so were the postulates of quantum mechanics. For instance, as predicted by quantum entanglement, particles in a system have been found to influence each other even at astronomical distances! Incidentally, quantum entanglement is increasingly seen as the fundamental basis for understanding the workings of the universe, casting space-time and all perceptions of separation and duality as an illusion and a consequence of entanglement within "one" fundamental projector reality.[1] There is no greater evidence of how *Homo sapiens* have painstakingly accumulated this knowledge over centuries, brick over brick, with each great mind contributing a piece to the edifice that was built by prior generations. We are now looking to the next generation of visionaries to reconcile these two breakthrough theories and to dig even deeper into the mysteries of our reality.

This chapter offers a deeper look at the origins of our journey, at how *Homo sapiens* came to reign supreme over all other species and at what makes *Homo sapiens* special and different from others. What quintessential human attributes support or constrain our full promise? We need a deeper understanding of the unique traits that define the human condition since education that is at odds with human development is not going to be very effective. Retracing our origins and unpacking the arrival of the genius of *Homo sapiens* will help us improve the alignment of our educational objectives with our core nature and traits.

The Lucky Break

For about a billion years, until about 2.5 to 3 billion years ago, prokaryotes are believed to have been the dominant life form on Earth. These are anaerobic cyanobacteria that used photosynthesis and produced large quantities of oxygen. The accumulation of oxygen in the environment led to the Great Oxygenation Event around 2.5 billion years ago and to mass extinction of the anaerobic bacteria. This event was a significant catalyst for fueling biodiversity.

The evolution of reproduction around 1,200 million years ago and cellular specialization in multicellular organisms around 900 million years ago have turned out to be significant breakthroughs that supported the eventual diversification of life on Earth. Other key milestones in the history of life on Earth are the appearance of cnidarians with an actual body, nerves, muscles, and eyes around 580 million years ago, the arrival of vertebrates about 500 million years ago, and the rise of dinosaurs around 260 million years ago. The dinosaurs reigned supreme on Earth for over 180 million years. Whether the long reign of the dinosaurs was truly due to their evolutionary advantages or was more a matter of luck, their long streak of domination didn't result in any notable increase in their mastery of the environment.

The extinction of the dinosaurs about 66 million years ago turned out to be an important catalyst for the proliferation of mammals and the ultimate emergence and dominance of *Homo sapiens*. Primates are believed to have appeared within 10 million years of that event. The era of humans came relatively rapidly thereafter with the appearance of the great apes about 15 million years ago, bipedalism and the first hominins between 4 and 7 million years ago, the arrival of *Homo erectus* around 1.8 million years ago, and finally the emergence of the first ancestors of both Neanderthals and *Homo sapiens* around 500,000 years ago.

The Hunt for the "Human Gene"

While the dinosaurs were unrivaled masters of the planet, 180 million years were not enough for them to domesticate plants and animals. How was *Homo sapiens* different? What capabilities and genetic traits enabled humans to leapfrog so far ahead? It may be challenging to arrive at a definitive answer as there are many possibilities, but this understanding is essential for us to chart an informed path forward.

The ability to fashion increasingly sophisticated tools was once believed to be a defining trait of our species and likely responsible for our triumph over others. However, growing research has laid to rest the notion that tool use is an exclusively human skill or that it is adequate to explain our superiority. Tool use has been observed in many primates. Capuchin monkeys have been seen inserting a stick into a tube containing viscous food, then extracting it and licking the food sticking to it. They have also been found using sticks as rakes to sweep up food and other objects. Chimpanzees, gorillas, and bonobos have been observed cracking nuts by placing them on a stone anvil and hitting them with a large stone hammer.[2] Chimpanzees are known to be capable of making spears for hunting. Tool use is not limited to animals on land either. Dolphins, for example, are regarded as the brainiacs of the seas and have been found to be prolific tool users. They likely spend more time hunting with tools such as basket sponges than any other nonhuman animal. In birds, too, tool use is apparent through the intricacies of their nests.

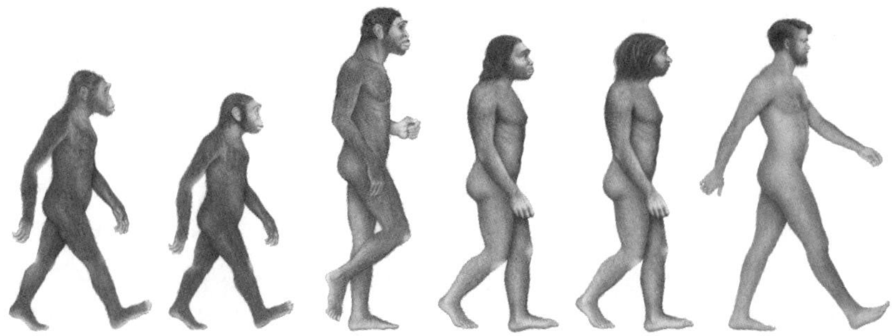

	Australopithecus afarensis	Homo habilis	Homo erectus	Homo neanderthalensis	Homo denisova	Homo sapiens
Height (cm)	104 - 165	100 - 135	145 - 185	152 - 168	Unknown	175
Brain Size (cm^3)	335-526	550-687	600-1250	1200-1750	Unknown	1350
Timeline	3.85 mya - 2.95 mya	2.4 mya - 1.4 mya	1.89 mya - 110 kya	400 kya - 40 kya	300 kya - 30 kya	200 kya - present

Figure 1.1. A brief timeline of key hominin species.

The first use of stone tools has long been attributed to our ancestors from the genus *Homo*, likely *Homo habilis* around 2.8 million years ago. However, an excavation conducted by the West Turkana Archaeological Project in Kenya has revealed substantive evidence that suggests that either ancient australopithecines like "Lucy" or *Kenyanthropus platyops* had begun fashioning stone tools as early as around 3.3 million years ago, long before the *Homo* genus emerged. Since research has shown that even bonobos are able to craft and use these kinds of stone tools when provided with the raw materials,[3] it is difficult to ascertain the original inventor. There was of course steady progress from the earliest Paleolithic stone tool industry, the Oldowan, around 2.6 million years ago to the more complex Acheulean industry that matured by around 250,000 years ago with a significantly higher quality of cores. It is therefore safe to say that *Homo sapiens* inherited a relatively well-developed, diverse template for making stone tools. As such, it is hard to understand how tool use can benefit humans more than any of the other hominins.

Like toolmaking, communication is another ability that was long believed to be the forte of humans and a likely contributor to human domination. Human language is thought to have emerged quite early. For example, cognitive scientist Kristian Tylén of Aarhus University and his team have investigated the possibility that 52,000- to 109,000-year-old markings found on rocks in South Africa could have been used as symbols by early humans.[4] This is one of the oldest records found for possible written communication by *Homo sapiens*. However, it is now known that communication, like tool-making, is not an exclusively human ability.

While animal communication continues to be an area of active research, much is already known. Many animals employ elaborate communication mechanisms through pheromones or vocal, visual, and tactile cues. Dogs, for instance, have a highly developed sense of smell that is about forty times sharper than our own. They are known to urinate on bushes and lampposts to mark their territory. While social groups such as wolf packs communicate extensively to facilitate cohesion, birds, monkeys, bullfrogs, and gibbons have been known to use auditory signals to communicate the presence of predators, warn competitors, or attract mates. Some animals such as chimpanzees and gorillas also use visual signals such as facial expressions, gestures, and posture to communicate anger, frustration, fear, or submission. Chimpanzees use so many gestures that we could spend a lifetime studying them.

Indeed, many animals employ communication technologies that surpass human capabilities. Elephants are known to communicate at frequencies lower than about 20 Hz. While these low frequencies can't be heard by humans, they can be picked up by other elephants up to 175 miles or so away! At the other end of the spectrum, we have animals such as bats and tarsiers that use very high-frequency sounds to communicate. Tarsiers use a high pitch that exceeds 20 kHz so they can send signals with little interference from the rumble of the jungle. Mantis shrimp communicate using a complex array of visual arrangements as they are equipped with sixteen color receptors compared to just the three that we humans have.

In fact, the conversations of some species are complex enough for them to be considered a language. A good example is the calls made by dolphins, which are quite elaborate and layered. Researchers from Tel Aviv University have used machine learning to map fifteen thousand different bat sounds to specific messages.[5] They have found that more than 60 percent were arguments about food, sleep positions, invasion of personal space, or unwanted advances.

Nonhuman animal abilities go far beyond basic communication. Research shows that many animals are also capable of relatively complex and nuanced behavior, socio-emotional intelligence, and cultural education. The firing of place cells in the hippocampus of rats demonstrates that rats in a maze consciously consider multiple options before deciding on the next step. Stanley Curtis of Pennsylvania State University has found that, with some training, pigs are able to rival primates in learning and playing simple computer games.[6] In a landmark 1959 experiment, researchers discovered that hungry rats refused food when it was only offered if they pulled a lever to shock their littermates.[7] In a subsequent study, Inbal Ben-Ami Bartal and colleagues from the University of Chicago showed that rats would repeatedly and almost impulsively free their cage-mates from closed containers when given an opportunity, even if there was no reward for doing so.[8] There are also many studies that show that great apes can plan and hide, anticipate peer and human reaction to their actions, learn and interpret human symbols, and engage in complex social skills including empathy, pretend play, and deception. There has also been a lot of research into the highly intelligent behavior of cetaceans. Dolphins, for example, have a remarkable memory and a knack for coming up with novel solutions to problems. They are also highly social and seemingly aware of the needs of others. In fact, they have been found to care for other species as well. There have been many instances of dolphins rescuing human swimmers from hammerhead sharks and even guiding stranded whales back to sea.

The more we dig, the more we seem to be learning about the complexity of animal interactions.[9] Researchers have also come across many examples of conduct that conveys a significant cultural value. Macaques in Thailand, for example, occasionally pull hair from visitors to use as dental floss. Closer observations have revealed that female macaques slow down and exaggerate their movements when they see their offspring watching them. It is now relatively common knowledge that adult elephants help groom young ones. They have also been known to mourn the loss of a member of their troop by burying the body with leaves and grass and keeping vigil over the site. In fact, they also keep revisiting these burial sites for years to come.

Incidentally, it is well known that chimpanzees in West Africa crack open hard-shelled nuts with rock hammers, but probably not as commonly known is the fact that chimpanzees in East Africa don't. While the East African chimpanzees are in principle capable and smart enough and do have the needed materials, they don't do it because they likely did not learn this from their elders. A study involving four groups of wild vervet monkeys living in the Mawana Game Reserve in South Africa's KwaZulu-Natal province serves as a great illustration.[10] The investigators gave each group two plastic boxes filled with corn, which was dyed blue in one box and pink in the other. In all four cases, the corn in one of the boxes was soaked in such bitter aloe leaves that the corn was extremely distasteful. The blue corn was bitter in two groups and the pink corn in the other two. It took about three months for the monkeys to learn to associate the bitterness with color and avoid the bitter corn. Normal corn that was not bitter but dyed blue and pink was again offered four months later to their offspring. Interestingly, adult monkeys now strongly preferred the same color as before and twenty-six of the twenty-seven infants ate only the corn preferred by their mothers.

The researchers made an even more interesting observation when male monkeys migrated between the groups during the mating season. Ten of the monkeys ended up migrating to a group habituated to corn of a different color. Nine of the ten monkeys seemed to have few qualms about eating the corn preferred by their new, adopted group, clearly demonstrating their ability to recognize the different preferences of the new group and placing a high value on assimilation into their new community. This illustrates the value these monkeys place on culture as well as their preference for conformity.

The discussion thus far shows that advanced tool use, ability to communicate, and cultural education were unlikely to be sufficient to lead to human supremacy. It's also clear that our human ancestors didn't acquire a magical gene or some other groundbreaking organ or attribute. While the sweat glands are one of the most effective cooling systems and the upright gait of humans has freed the hands to do more than help our ancestors move around, it's obvious that anatomical changes alone cannot explain the unequivocal dominance of our species.

How Fire Fueled the *Homo Sapiens*

Even though our arrival itself may have been fortuitous, it's hard to believe that our triumph has been an accident, so it's not surprising that there has been much speculation on the conditions that could have led to this exceptional mastery of the physical world. Some researchers argue that one of these conditions was fire. The earliest definitive evidence for the control of fire by a hominin is said to date as far back as one or two million years ago.[11] Richard Wrangham, a biological anthropologist at Harvard, presents an interesting thesis in *Catching Fire: How Cooking Made Us Human*.[12] He argues that fire led to the evolution and triumph of *Homo sapiens* and thus to modern humans. The ability to control fire would have completely transformed the lives of our human ancestors. For starters, it allowed them to move down from the trees and spend more time on the ground without as much fear of predators. Eating cooked food likely fueled anatomical and physiological changes such as the shrinkage of jaws, teeth, and guts and provided additional calories to support their expanding brains. As they were able to digest food faster, they would have been able to reduce the time spent on gathering and eating food. This freed them to pursue more creative activities. It also gave our ancestors the ability to make even more advanced hunting tools. Fire may have also helped our ancestors by reducing their stress levels. Chronic fear and stress caused by the need to constantly stave off predators and be on the lookout for the next meal would have previously led to round-the-clock mobilization of the hypothalamus-pituitary-adrenal (HPA) axis. Nourishment and growth would not have been prioritized in such a state of alertness. As a result, by helping lower fear levels and the need for constant vigilance, fire may have launched the acceleration of *Homo sapien* domination.

Shorter pregnancies might be another development that may have fueled our ancestors' intellectual development. A human fetus would require a gestation period of about eighteen to twenty-one months instead of nine if it were born at a developmental stage comparable to that of a chimpanzee newborn. There are several competing theories for why humans have relatively premature births. A popular theory says that the narrowing of the human pelvis due to bipedalism became problematic for childbirth when evolution led to larger brain sizes.[13] Another explanation is that the metabolic demands of the fetus begin to exceed the mother's ability to meet both the fetal energy requirements and her own at about nine months of gestation.[14] Relatively premature births might also have been genetically preferred since we are a socio-cultural animal that would benefit immensely from child development through environmental interactions outside the womb. Regardless of the reasons, the result is that evolution handed humans an increased opportunity for bonding and mentoring our young. Piantadosi and Kidd argue that since helpless infants require more intelligent parents for their survival, genetic selection of large brains and early birth can become self-reinforcing—that is, resulting in qualitatively superior cognitive abilities to other animals.[15] Interestingly, there is evidence that premature birth evolved late in human evolution, perhaps in the modern human/Neanderthal's last common ancestor. The fossil record of a 1.8-million-year-old *Homo erectus* child from Java suggests that a one-year-old child had about 80 percent of the typical *Homo erectus* adult brain size, more comparable to the great apes than to modern humans.[16]

It is fair to assume that any significant spurt in human ability would have registered in the morphology of the brain. Some have proposed that this advantage is implied by our larger brains. Surely an increase in brain size could support greater intellectual development and other advances. But humans don't have the largest brains, as elephants, dolphins, and many other animals come out ahead on this measure. This has led some to consider the brain-to-body-size ratio, though this is still a gross heuristic. While dolphins fare well by this metric, shrews are the ones with the largest ratio. Crows and other corvids are highly intelligent but have some of the smallest brains. Neuroanatomists designed an empirical parameter called Encephalization Quotient—through a more complex relationship between brain and body weights—that better mirrors our presumptions of the intelligence levels of different species. Regardless, most researchers have now come to believe that what matters more for the success of a species is neither the absolute brain size nor its relative proportion to body mass, but the complexity, structure, and organization of the brain and the various functions it supports.

There is also a school of thought that the hierarchical organization of the modern human brain is a result of the sequential acquisition of various brain structures and functions through evolution.[17] The basal ganglia or the reptilian brain—responsible for primal instincts—is believed to have developed first. The limbic system that's in charge of emotions came next. The neocortex, as the name suggests, is the most recent addition, around two hundred million years ago. The neocortex is responsible for our rational decision-making, and it first showed up in mammals.

However, advances in imaging suggest that physical separation of functions is an oversimplification. Brains mostly function through a complex system of communication between the various parts, rather than through a simple accumulation of parts that specialize in specific tasks. Only simple perceptual and motor functions are localized in different areas of the brain. Current learning says that most of the recent evolutionary development, in addition to dedicated areas such as the prefrontal cortex, is more prominent in the interconnecting network between the prefrontal cortex and the cerebellum. The cerebellum is the warehouse of memories, and the prefrontal cortex can handle complex reasoning and creativity. So, while high-level reasoning has been attributed to many other species as well as to ancestral humans, modern humans have a bigger warehouse and faster access to it.

A decade ago, in an insightful study, Matthew Rushworth of Oxford University's Department of Experimental Psychology and his team looked at the ventrolateral frontal cortex area and how it connects to the rest of our brain.[18] They obtained MRIs of this region from twenty-five human volunteers and twenty-five macaque monkeys. The researchers divided the ventrolateral frontal cortex into twelve areas that were consistent across all subjects, with each manifesting a unique pattern of connectivity with the rest of the brain. They noticed that eleven of the twelve areas connected to other brain areas in very similar ways in both species. However, one area of the human ventrolateral frontal cortex had no equivalent in the macaque: the lateral frontal pole prefrontal cortex. Interestingly, this area has been associated with strategic planning and decision-making as well as multitasking. Other research also shows that the right frontal insula and the anterior cingulate cortex have developed greatly and play a prominent role in certain higher-level functions such as empathy, metacognition, communication of homeostatic information to consciousness, and awareness of body states in humans and great apes.[19] More generally, the insular cortex has been found to play a significant role in the production of emotions, music, and language.

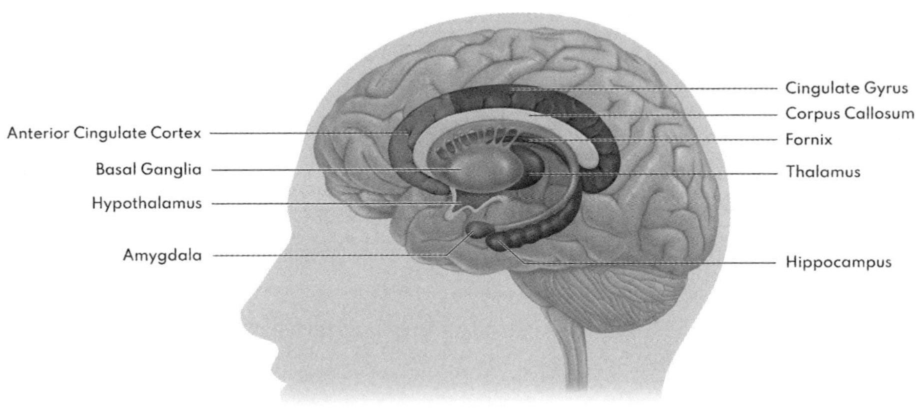

Figure 1.2. The human limbic system.

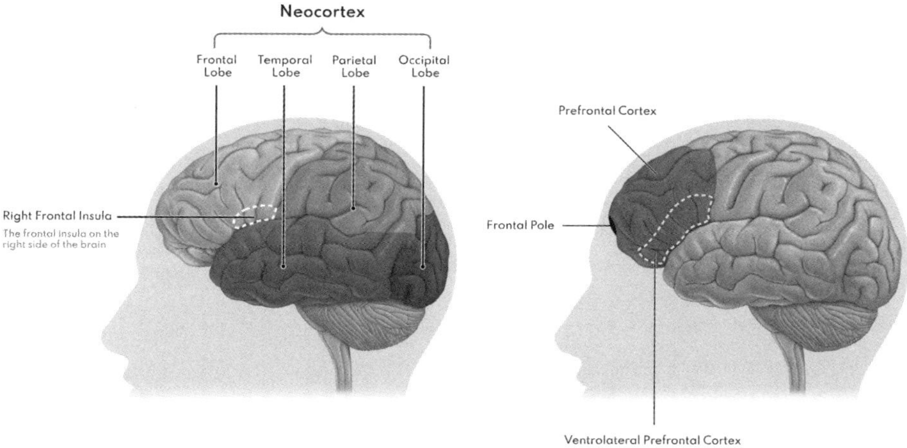

Figure 1.3. The neocortex and the prefrontal cortex in humans.

There is one important foot soldier that we need to acknowledge when we talk about the remarkable growth in brain power. The use of myelin as a sheath around an axon is a key evolutionary acquisition in hinged-jaw vertebrates. Axons and dendrites are two key conduits of neurons that facilitate information transfer. In addition to imposing a significant energy cost, the long lengths of axons limit the speed and amount of information transfer from a neuron. By reducing capacitive interference, myelin delivers a dramatic increase in the transfer speeds of up to 100 times. The evolutionary imperative of myelin can be inferred from the fact that it constitutes around 15 percent of the weight of a typical rodent brain and around 50 percent of a modern human brain. For example, neuronal activity caused by its excitation has been found to result in increased myelination and thus speed up access to new learning. In addition, as we practice new skills soon after their acquisition, our brains are able to grow new cells and pathways through additional dendrite connections and thus biologically consolidate the learning from our new experiences.

While all thoughts that cross our mind are physically recorded in the neurological pathways of our brain, many of them weaken over time. Only pathways reinforced by repetition will fire more readily as time goes on. With around 86 billion neurons (compared to about 100,000 in a housefly and around 75 million in a mouse), the human ability to process information appears limitless. We also now know that our neuronal budget is not fully determined by adolescence and that environmental enrichment and novelty can help these neurons thrive. By helping reduce energy costs, myelin plays a significant role in the human ability to host billions of neurons!

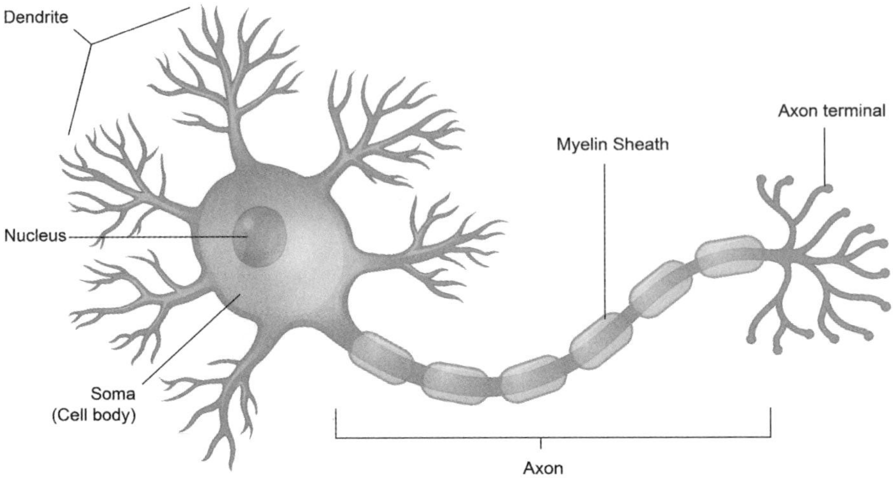

Figure 1.4. The myelin sheath in the overall neuron structure.

This discussion shows how our brain hardware could have supported our ancestors' evolution, as well as how it can support our ongoing development. Yet this does not tell us how seemingly gradual evolutionary changes resulted in such a revolutionary explosion in capabilities relative to other species, especially the other hominins.

The Pursuit of Possibility

As we have discussed, even though language skills, toolmaking abilities, and culture are quite advanced in *Homo sapiens*, these traits and skills are not exclusive to humans. What additional benefits then did larger and more capable brains bestow on *Homo sapiens* to result in such a remarkable divergence? One compelling explanation for human exceptionalism came from Thomas Suddendorf, professor of psychology at the University of Queensland,

Australia. He suggested that humans are unique in two respects.[20] The first is the ability to imagine. Humans use past experiences to envision a wide array of new future possibilities, real and fictional. Rushworth's findings on the development of the prefrontal cortex in humans—as discussed in the previous section—lend support to Suddendorf's claims about the role of imagination in our ancestors' success. We can also see the significant role of imagination in the lives of modern humans. For instance, it is our imagination that helps us design massive successes such as the Disney theme park or dismal failures such as the Iridium, Motorola's ambitious $3,000 satellite phone that managed to attract only ten thousand subscribers.

The second ability Suddendorf has identified is the sharing of the products of our imagination with one another so we can link our minds and build a force multiplier that can pursue larger goals. For example, we post safety signs, share useful information through blog posts and social media, and gossip at office water coolers. A visionary can dream up the concept of a theme park, but it is unlikely to materialize unless enough people buy into the prospect and its implications. We can imagine the implications for a species that excels in dreaming up new possibilities, sharing this vision with its group, and pursuing some of these prospects. If the size of the group is large or if there are many such groups, the accumulation of these adventures can soon add up. A larger population size can foster a proportionally higher number of experiences and these, in turn, have the potential to fuel a larger variety of conceptualizations of the future.

At the same time, cooperation in pursuing a shared objective is not unique to humans; it has been an evolutionary imperative. This has been seen within a species, across species, and between cells of individual organisms. Scientists hypothesize, for instance, that prokaryotic cells and early mitochondria developed a highly symbiotic relationship.[21] Mitochondria likely metabolized the oxygen and other waste products from the larger cell to produce enough energy for both. There is also speculation that mitochondria had likely even replicated inside the larger cell. Some such arrangement had possibly led to the development of early organisms. A similar symbiotic relationship might have also resulted from the ingestion of anaerobic bacteria by larger aerobic bacteria. Along with random variations that occur in nature, the universal tendency of life forms to decrease entropy or increase regularity and order has likely helped guide the survival and natural selection of organisms, especially in the early phases of the development of life on our young planet.[22]

Similarly, many animals such as bees, elephants, wolves, and dolphins also exhibit remarkable cooperation with others in their own group. Since any cooperation requires individuals to cede some of their independence, it is very likely that there is an evolutionary benefit to such cooperation. Similar cooperation can also be seen through the intelligence in cellular specialization that is manifested through the communication and coordination between our various organs and cellular functions and the higher-level consciousness. Take, for instance, the elaborate protection that our immune system provides. Millions of phagocytes stand guard around the clock as our vigilant foot soldiers. At the first sign of trouble, they telegraph the T cells for more frontline support and B cells to summon additional firepower through the antibodies. The affinity maturation process used by B cells to produce antibodies with rapidly increasing affinity for the identified antigens is remarkable. Our adaptive immunity system goes into a hyperactive mode and creates many variations in the antigen binding code sequences to keep improving the lock on the antigen. It is astonishing that the mutation rate that creates these variations is a million times greater than the mutation rate we typically see with cell lines outside the lymphoid system. The antibodies with the highest affinity are remembered so they can be quickly produced if the same pathogen were to attack later.

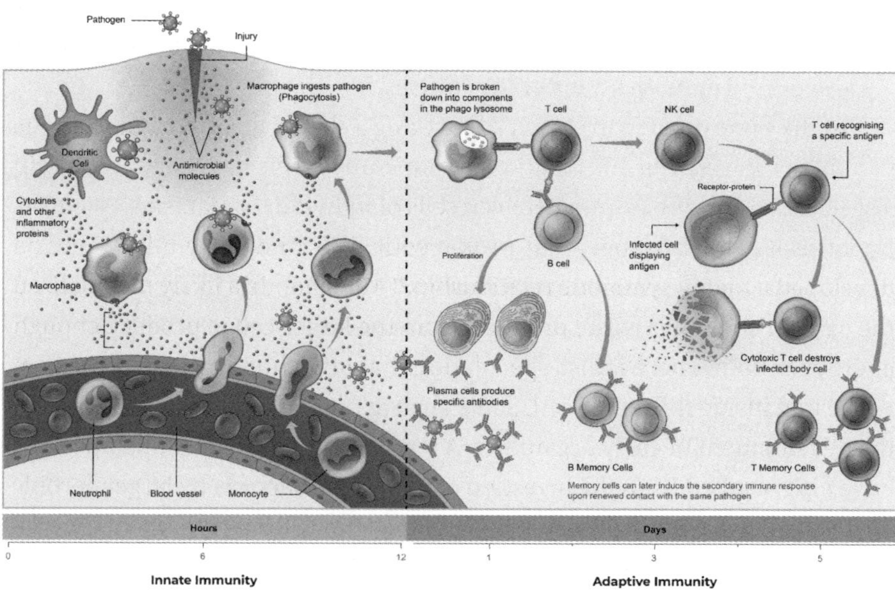

Figure 1.5. The various components of our elaborate immune system.

As Yuval Noah Harari explained, human collaboration operates very differently from biologically ingrained cooperation.[23] A key distinguishing feature of humankind is its ability to *flexibly* cooperate with an incredibly large number of fellow beings based on a mutually shared reality in a context-sensitive manner. While buffaloes may flexibly cooperate to stave off a threat from a lion, this cooperation is not based on an imagined reality. For example, many countries and companies trade and negotiate using the US dollar as they all *believe* in its valuation. We put our money in banks as we trust that we will be able to withdraw it when we want to. Many soldiers go to war and willingly risk their lives on behalf of a country as they believe in values and ideals that are larger than themselves. Bees and ants, on the other hand, cooperate along fixed, concrete templates. This context will help us understand why flexible cooperation across a canvas of dynamically changing shared imaginary realities would be even more powerful and could have led to our emergence as the dominant species. It is reasonable to expect that a society that tolerates risk-taking and experimentation would allow a richer vision of the future as it permits more flexible and versatile models of cooperation. But did these two abilities only emerge in *Homo sapiens*?

Rome Was Not Built in a Day

Given that our best understanding of the conditions that led to the eventual triumph of *Homo sapiens* also involves the control of fire, it's worth taking a closer look at *Homo erectus*, our hominin ancestor of that era. Despite their eventual extinction, *Homo erectus* holds many keys to our eventual rise to prominence. A zigzag engraving on a shell found in Indonesia in the late 1800s, for instance, has been attributed to *Homo erectus* and is the oldest abstract marking ever found; it has been dated to about 500,000 years ago.[24] Despite some controversy about whether it represents an intentional sculpture created by *Homo erectus*, the 250,000-year-old Venus of Berekhat Ram is believed by some to be a pebble shaped into the figure of a human female.

Homo erectus may also have been the first to fashion campsites as home bases. A small 1.75-million-year-old site made with volcanic rocks piled about 9 inches high at 2- to 2.5-foot intervals was discovered in Olduvai Gorge. British paleoanthropologist Mary Leakey speculated that these rock piles were likely used to hold poles supporting a hutlike structure.

At the 780,000-year-old Gesher Benot Ya'aqov campsite in northern Israel, researchers found evidence of the controlled use of fire, polished wooden objects, separate spaces for processing plant and animal foods, a hearth, toolmaking, and communal—but divided—living.[25] While the earliest evidence for the existence of campsites with hearths and shelters only dates back to about 780,000 years ago, it is possible that they have been in use for over a million years or more. This is supported by the evidence for woodworking in the artifacts found at the 1.7- to 1.5-million-year-old site in Peninj, Tanzania. It is also interesting that the brains of *Homo erectus* averaged around 58 cubic inches in volume. Even though this is smaller than the brain size of male Neanderthals (88 cubic inches) and sapiens (77 cubic inches), it is not much smaller than the typical brain size of a modern *Homo sapiens* female (69 cubic inches).

Figure 1.6. An artist's rendering of the prehistoric Gesher Benot Ya'aqov *Homo erectus* campsite.

Evidence of *Homo erectus* colonies has turned up in Africa, the Sinai Peninsula, Georgia in western Asia, China, and Indonesia. In a 2009 expedition, archaeologists from the American School of Classical Studies in Athens discovered rough axes and other stone tools—believed to be between 130,000 and 700,000 years old—close to shelters on the south coast near the village of Plakias on the Mediterranean island of Crete.[26] Since Crete has been an island for about five million years, *Homo erectus* must have found a way to travel the forty miles of open water. *Homo erectus* settlements in the island nation of Indonesia, Crete, and on Socotra in the Arabian Sea suggest they may have invented rafts to travel over water. Use of rafts, extensive migration, the high degree of organization seen in their campsites, and increased socialization also make it highly likely that *Homo erectus* spoke an early form of a protolanguage.

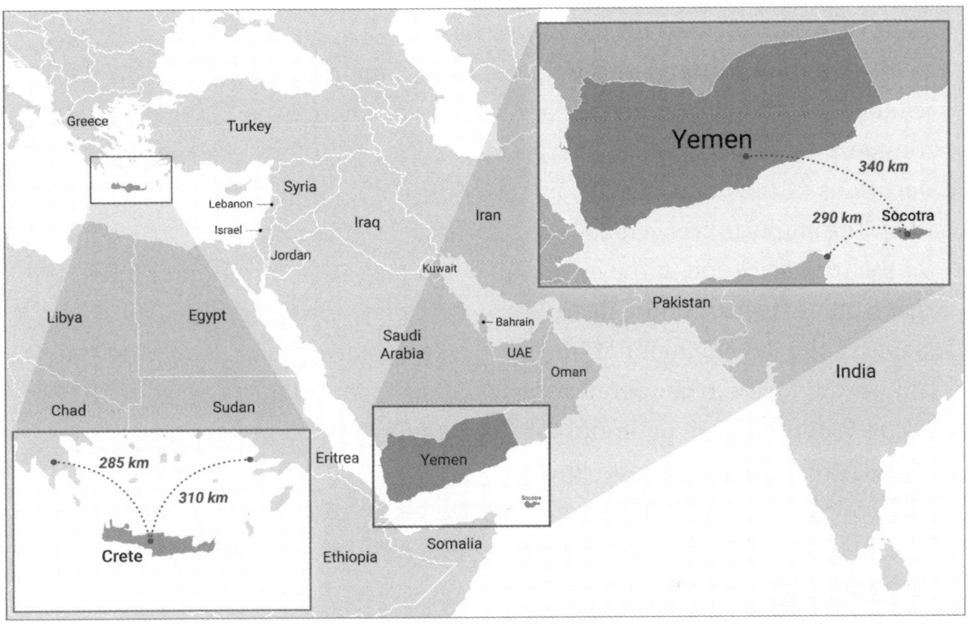

Figure 1.7. Crete and Socotra are about 300 km from the mainland.

While a 400,000-year-old *Homo erectus* hyoid bone from Castel di Guido, Italy, was found to be shaped more like the ones found in other *Homo* species than what we see in nonhuman apes, it did not have the telltale muscle impressions of modern humans. The hyoid bone enables modulation of the vocal tract so we can control pitch and volume. Researchers therefore feel that *Homo erectus* lacked the kind of vocal apparatus that supports speech in modern humans. Since cultural complexity likely provides the impetus for brain development and anatomical refinement, these would probably have taken more time to evolve. The protolanguage of *Homo erectus*, therefore, might have led to higher-order thinking and thus to more complex speech capabilities in *Homo heidelbergensis*, the common ancestor of Neanderthals and *Homo sapiens*. This is also supported by the fossil records of 530,000-year-old *Homo heidelbergensis* specimens from the Spanish Sima de los Huesos Cave.[27]

Daniel Everett, the trustee professor of cognitive sciences at Bentley University in Massachusetts, contends that while communication is transfer of information, language is the transfer of information using symbols. He feels that the lives of *Homo erectus* had all the characteristics of the use of symbols for communication.[28] Their tools, for example, seemed to represent culturally agreed-on meanings for time-displaced activities. Clearly, while communication skills help nonhuman animals navigate their daily challenges so they can survive and live to see another day, language helps humans do so much more! Pheromones help ants inform each other about locations of food and threats, but they cannot help with much more than that. The ability to create high-level conceptual representations is an example of the sophistication in the evolution of language that has differentiated us from other species. While flexible cooperation was a key enabler for *Homo sapiens*, the development of language was a critical tool and an important milestone for such cooperation. Baby steps toward language would have carried an immense potential for the rapid evolution of new capabilities. This is powerful evidence of how curiosity likely fueled the development of the biology needed to fuel even more curiosity and brain power. If *Homo erectus* were able to communicate using symbols, they would likely have broken a significant barrier.

With their extensive territorial expansion, control of fire, elaborate campsite organization, as well as sculpture and other types of art, *Homo erectus* had a significantly more advanced social structure than the societies of chimpanzees, australopithecines, *Kenyanthropus platyops*, or even *Homo habilis*. Their progress therefore set the stage for the eventual rise of *Homo sapiens*.

Restlessness Fuels Our Imagination

By all accounts, *Homo erectus* was a very adventurous species. Their remarkable progress suggests that the secret of our triumph lies in a deeper understanding of the abilities of *Homo erectus*. It is impressive that over a two-million-year period, *Homo erectus* and its subspecies have traveled the farthest of any of the hominins. Thousands of Oldowan stone tools made by *Homo erectus* were found in the Hadibo area in Socotra in 2008 and 2009 by three Russian archaeological expeditions. As mentioned earlier, Socotra is an island in the Arabian Sea, 150 miles off the Horn of Africa and 240 miles off the coast of Yemen. While learning how they traveled to Crete and Socotra is important, much more enlightening would be understanding why they chose to travel there. The risks in leaving the safety of land and venturing out into the open sea should have been very high for *Homo erectus*. It is difficult to say whether they have been driven by curiosity or if there was perhaps an existential threat. The number of tools found also suggests there may have been multiple expeditions.

The story of *Homo erectus* presents compelling evidence of their curiosity, risk-taking, creativity, and communication skills. But beyond all this, it is likely that they were restless. It takes a lot more than curiosity for them to be one of the first species to venture as far out as they did, to invent symbols, and to leave the safety of land and take to the seas. These actions suggest a growth mindset and a hunger for novelty and betterment. It makes sense that the capacity to imagine, to link our minds with others, and to flexibly cooperate with large groups is not sufficient. The brain hardware that generates multiple possibilities likely stems from the urge to do so. This restlessness is what primes *Homo sapiens* to repeatedly reach for a different reality and to sell that vision by engendering flexible cooperation within their group. This is what likely led to our emergence as the dominant species. At the same time, excessive restlessness can be detrimental to our well-being. If restlessness is caused by anxiety, insecurity, stress, or hyperactivity, the agitation of the brain can lead us to a state of constant vigilance. As we have discussed earlier, growth and nourishment are unlikely to be prioritized in such a state. Hence, it is reasonable to speculate that the safety provided by technological advancements, such as fire, as well as their growing population, played a pivotal role in their accomplishments. Our current understanding thus shows that *Homo sapiens* did not make an evolutionary leap; instead, their success arrived in small increments over a long period.

The Next Chapter in the Human Journey

Our discussion thus far shows that restlessness, imagination, and context-aware flexible sharing and cooperation likely led to the eventual emergence of *Homo sapiens* as the dominant species. This suggests that curiosity, creativity, persistence, risk-taking, and communication are probably what fueled the progress of *Homo erectus* and *Homo sapiens*. This understanding provides a window into the nature of our species and makes a compelling case for prioritizing these competencies through education. This learning affirms that educational objectives should, at a minimum, promote these skill sets and build further on the competencies that led to the triumph of *Homo sapiens*.

At the same time, there might also be a dark side to our success. While there is an abundance of evidence that our *Homo* ancestors contributed to the extinction of many species such as the woolly mammoths, mastodons, and many others, the reasons for the disappearance of hominins such as *Homo erectus*, Neanderthals, Denisovans, and *Homo heidelbergensis* are less clear. While there is some evidence of a potential role for climate change and poor adaptability in the extinction of *Homo erectus*, it is too sparse to be conclusive. The low population densities of *Homo erectus* and Neanderthals may also have played a role in their extinction. Our best estimates today suggest that there were no more than 56,000 *Homo erectus* individuals spread across the world 1.2 million years ago. Neanderthals had a slightly higher density with about 70,000 individuals in Europe. In comparison, there were supposedly ten times as many modern humans living alongside the Neanderthals at the time.

Of course, none of this absolves humans of complicity in the disappearance of the other *Homo* species, especially since chimpanzees and gorillas managed to survive. There has been a lot of speculation that our ancestors had a large role to play in their extinction. Perhaps they only aggressively outcompeted the other *Homo* species for food or other limited resources and did not physically slaughter them. We are learning more every day about what it means to be human. Given the intolerance we see between different races, tribes, ethnicities, and nations over the course of our recorded history, it's not inconceivable that early *Homo sapiens* did not countenance the peaceful coexistence of a different species that had a relatively close physical appearance and diet. The extinction of the other hominin species—our closest cousins—has therefore raised questions about our ability to peacefully coexist and collaborate with other groups. This is especially concerning since finding ways to divide ourselves into groups appears to be a propensity of modern day humans. However, regardless of what transpired in the past, we have come a long way. There is no reason to believe that through growing awareness we can't make steady progress toward a more harmonious coexistence.

It is gratifying that our hunger to grow and our ability to imagine and share a vision of a better future are at the heart of what differentiates us from other species. As such, these make up the essence of the human condition. At the same time, we should not turn a blind eye to the shortcomings and excesses of our species. As we will see in the remainder of this book, nurturing and cultivating all essential competencies is well within our reach. We should be mindful, though, that we face many challenges. Broad access to our best growth opportunities may not be easy. But if we're willing to truly learn the lessons of our history, we can hope to march forward in a more thoughtful and inclusive manner.

CHAPTER SUMMARY

- Our understanding of the contributors to human triumph over other species has evolved over time.
- For example, toolmaking, communication, and cultural education were long believed to be exclusively human abilities, yet they have all been observed among many other species as well.
- Many now believe that control of fire, significantly shorter gestation periods, and symbolic communication are among the list of key evolutionary milestones that likely led to the emergence of *Homo sapiens* as the dominant species.
- Over time, these developments primed the evolution of human brains into massively efficient processors that support increasingly complex learning.
- Ultimately, hunger for growth, the ability to imagine and share a variety of realities and to flexibly collaborate within larger groups, and the determination to persist in the pursuit of these shared realities are the unique traits that likely gave the edge to humans.

- At the same time, the extinction of the other hominin species—our closest cousins—has raised questions about our ability to peacefully coexist and collaborate with groups that are distinct from us.
- Educational objectives should first and foremost instill a deeper awareness of this story of our journey and arrival. Our long-term success requires that we learn from both the strengths as well as the shortcomings and excesses of our species.
- Education should prioritize the key skill sets that led *Homo sapiens* to seek growth, understanding, persistence, and communication. In other words, the value of our educational objectives should, at a minimum, be assessed in the context of their evolutionary relevance.

2

Back to the Future

Talent hits a target no one else can hit;
Genius hits a target no one else can see.
—ARTHUR SCHOPENHAUER

Mere history is not of much use. A critical analysis of the chronological record of events, on the other hand, can be quite valuable if it unpacks the lessons from our past. It is the tonic that quenches some of our curiosity about our roots while also shining light on the path ahead. It would be difficult to envision all the possibilities for any contemporary society without the benefit of the high vantage point created by history. The perspectives and context that history provides can be a tremendous asset. This kind of learning is also liberating. Only by understanding our roots well can we truly appreciate our choices, limitations, and potential. A reasonable forecast of our future is not possible without a thorough understanding of our past. In this chapter, we therefore continue our study of the past and use the lessons from this retrospective to project our best forecast of the future awaiting us. This understanding is essential for clarifying the educational objectives needed to secure the best version of our collective future.

The Arrival of Automation

As discussed in the last chapter, humans broke out of Africa over several waves of migration starting around seventy thousand years ago. Our ancestors largely foraged for food as hunter-gatherers until about ten thousand years ago before they began to adopt a more sedentary lifestyle, domesticating animals and plants and laying the groundwork for the birth of civilization. Over time, they organized themselves into city-states and empires. They experimented with various forms of government, produced a variety of cultures, and pursued increasing understanding and control of their physical environment. There was slow and steady progress over thousands of years. However, the advances in the last five hundred years are in a league of their own. Thanks to the explosion of innovation over this period, there is remarkably little resemblance between our lives today and those of our ancestors then.

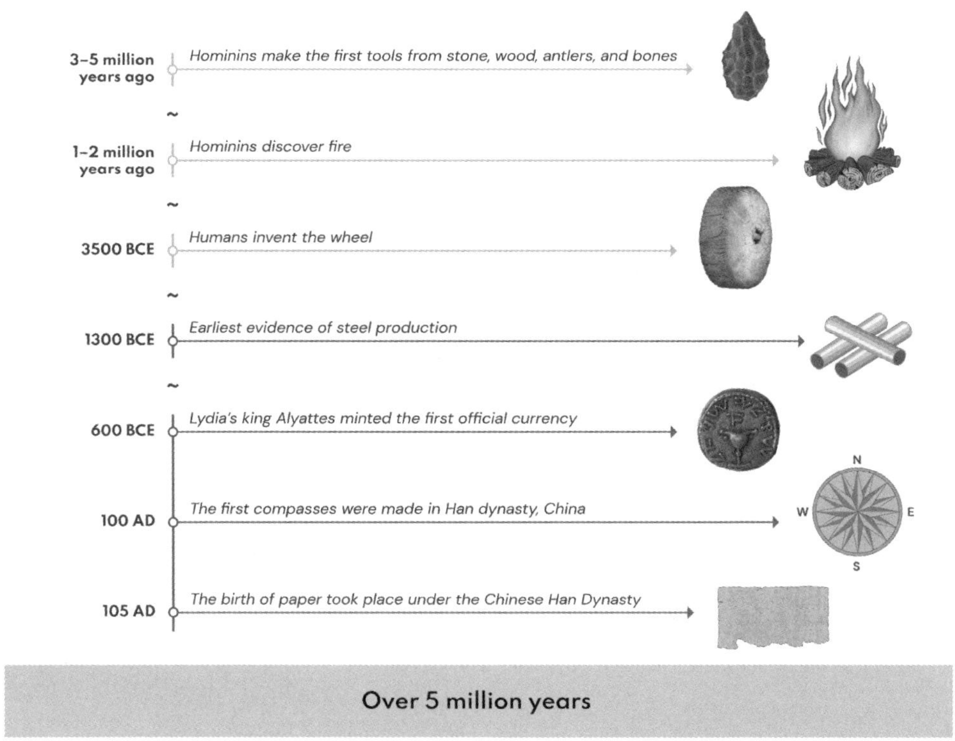

Figure 2.1. Key human and nonhuman accomplishments over a five-million-year period prior to 105 CE.

While the first book ever printed, the *Diamond Sūtra*, came out in 868 CE, it was only in the fifteenth century that books were mass-produced after the invention of the wooden press. The widespread use of the printing press enabled the democratization of knowledge sharing, the beginning of the decline of Latin as a lingua franca, the start of the Scientific Revolution, and eventually the onset of the Renaissance. Many small steps in the sixteenth and seventeenth centuries helped pave the way for the First Industrial Revolution in Britain in the eighteenth century. The rifle and printing press were the earliest noteworthy inventions in the fifteenth century. With the arrival of the flushable toilet, graphite pencil, spinning wheel, scissors, and compound microscope in the sixteenth century, we can see the first signs of a spurt in human ingenuity. The stream of inventions and discoveries continued in the seventeenth century with the pocket watch, mechanical calculator, first physical descriptions of bacteria, and a process for blood transfusion. However, all these advances only had a small impact on the quality of life of a typical family—for example, the flushable toilet was not available to ordinary people until the nineteenth century.

The eighteenth century was perhaps the first time in human history—after the Agricultural Revolution—that our innovations led to significant changes in how most people lived. There was a modest start to the century with the invention of the mechanized cotton spinning machine, commercial steam engine, and artificial refrigeration. However, with the invention of machines that aid machine tool development such as the gas turbine and hydraulic press, discovery of electricity, innovations in transportation such as the steam-powered automobile and manned hot-air balloon, and improvements in printing technology, the second half of the eighteenth century exploded with human ingenuity. These developments facilitated the birth of the modern factory through the creation of silk and cotton mills in Britain. And this burst of creativity laid the groundwork for much bigger changes to come in the nineteenth century.

The early nineteenth century saw the arrival of the first automobile with an internal combustion engine, general anesthesia, photography, the powered printing press, and the steam locomotive railway, among other innovations. It appeared as if the floodgates were suddenly thrown open. The electric motor, solar cell, pasteurization, telephone, incandescent electric bulb, wireless communication, and more showed up in the rest of the century. Each of these inventions had an outsized impact on daily life and productivity grew by leaps and bounds.

The sustained growth in the human population as well as household income due to this rise in productivity was unprecedented. The period beginning in the second half of the eighteenth century and lasting through the nineteenth century is often referred to as the First Industrial Revolution. This era is widely regarded as a major turning point in human history, second only to the domestication of animals and plants thousands of years prior. The power of water and steam was harnessed to improve mining as well as the manufacturing of low-cost iron and steel items and machines. The mechanized factory system that used these machine tools and large-scale manufacturing processes replaced slower manual production methods. With changes affecting almost every aspect of life for most people, a long period of improvements in the average standard of living began for much of the Western world.

Until the eighteenth century, many families worked together on small farms or as artisans and craftspeople in small cottage industries. Beginning with the second half of the eighteenth century, machines started to replace family units and fewer workers were now needed. This led to massive migration from the countryside to towns and cities. Subsistence farming increasingly yielded ground to larger farms, and use of machines and fertilizers led to dramatic increases in food production. For example, from 1800 to 1850, the population in British cities increased from 20 to 50 percent.[1] Family life was impacted by both the hectic work pace in factories as well as the increased use of child labor. The textile industry was the largest employer in most countries. Access to better medical care, conveniences such as refrigeration and canning, cheaper consumer goods such as storage bins and cooking utensils, and faster transportation resulted in more time spent at work to support the higher costs of living in the cities.

The improvement in medical care around this time was quite significant. While physicians and other healers have been exploring health and wellness at least since the period of ancient Mesopotamian, Egyptian, and Chinese civilizations, the nature of medicine changed almost beyond recognition in the eighteenth and nineteenth centuries. The invention of the microscope and the discovery of bacteria in the earlier centuries helped pave the way for the development of germ theory. Pasteurization suddenly made drinking milk far less life threatening. The invention of the syringe, stethoscope, and antiseptic surgical methods as well as the development of vaccinations played a huge role in fighting many infections and diseases such as smallpox, cholera, anthrax, and rabies.

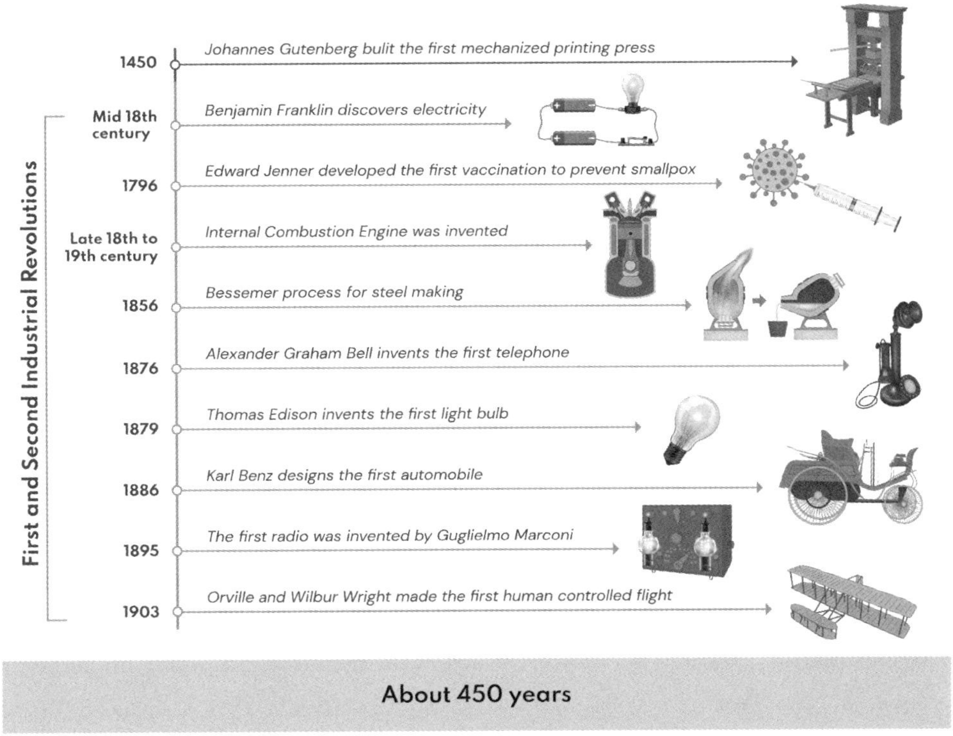

Figure 2.2. Key human accomplishments over a 450-year period between 1450 and 1905.

There was so much change that it would have been mind-boggling to someone who grew up in the eighteenth century. With the onset of automobiles, trains, and more capable ships, for example, long-distance travel suddenly became significantly easier. As a result, trade between distant nations flourished. The arrival of silk and cotton mills ushered in high-volume factory production of textiles and knitted and woven cloth that was a finer gauge than what could previously be produced by hand. Cheaper transportation also allowed for more competition between local and foreign manufacturers and resulted in a wider variety of more affordable clothing. The net result was that clothing suddenly became very disposable for the first time in history. To put this in perspective, most people—especially the lower classes—often either made their own clothes or sourced them from a local cottage industry prior to the Industrial Revolution. People would hem, sew, and dye their own garments and repair any clothes that were torn. As a result, clothes used to be expensive and greatly valued.

It is not a coincidence that washers and dryers, a major convenience that we often take for granted today, were also invented during the First Industrial Revolution. Clothes used to be largely washed at local rivers and streams prior to the nineteenth century; in fact, they still are today in some parts of the world. Clothes were submerged in running water, washed with abrasive stones, and beaten over rocks. Soap itself was not widely available until the nineteenth century. Interestingly, during both Roman times and in medieval Europe, human urine collected from public restrooms was used to wash clothes! Our ancestors figured out that the ammonia in urine was effective in dissolving grease and loosening dirt.

Perhaps more startling is the fact that nothing close to the toilet that we know today was in existence until well after the First Industrial Revolution. While the flush toilet was invented in 1596, it was not widely available until the 1850s. People either used communal outhouses, chamber pots, holes in the ground, or simply went into the woods when nature called. An underground network of pipes to carry away solid and liquid waste was not commissioned until the middle of the nineteenth century. In fact, they were not in use in most parts of Paris until well into the twentieth century. London also did not require indoor toilets in its building codes until after the First World War!

As human ingenuity mushroomed, innovations in one area led to insights in another, and the implications of the First Industrial Revolution were, not unexpectedly, multifarious and difficult to foresee. It produced many home conveniences, led to massive improvements in the medical field, expanded women's rights, and caused communication and transportation technologies to proliferate.

Scientific Breakthroughs Pack a Hefty Punch

The Agricultural Revolution, emergence of capitalism, increased use of steam power, and development of machine tools are some key factors that fueled the First Industrial Revolution. The groundwork for these innovations, however, was laid by the many fundamental breakthroughs in physics and chemistry that occurred in the sixteenth and seventeenth centuries. These, in turn, were a result of the Renaissance and ensuing Scientific Revolution. Led by thought leaders such as Francis Bacon and René Descartes, science was increasingly viewed as a utilitarian subject as opposed to an abstract intellectual exercise. As nature began to be studied more quantitatively, mathematical models emerged for testing the various theories. This development of an experimental, scientific method allowed researchers to attempt answers to the "how" questions rather than the "why" that had characterized the Greek method thus far. The success of these efforts also fueled increasing dissociation of humans from nature.

Over time, advances in manufacturing tools, machines, and practices led to a technological revolution extending from the mid-nineteenth to the early twentieth century. There was widespread growth of railways, telegraph systems, and utilities such as gas and water. This period of remarkable progress came to be referred to as the Second Industrial Revolution. While a few pioneers helped fund the innovations in the First Industrial Revolution, the second one saw the rise of a larger cohort of wealthy entrepreneurs who tapped into a growing pool of immigrants, colonial subjects, and migrants from rural heartlands to staff their new factories. Once again, there were tectonic shifts in the quality of life of many in the relatively short span of just half a century. The pace of progress was truly staggering and all-encompassing.

In a way, the story of plastic mirrors the story of the Second Industrial Revolution. After Leo Baekeland invented Bakelite, the first fully synthetic plastic, in 1907, plastics became very affordable and useful. They were exceptionally durable, heat resistant, and amenable to mass production. They helped more people afford previously expensive items, so they played a big part in fueling the consumer culture of the Second Industrial Revolution. Plastics took the place of ivory in combs, iron and wood in containers, steel in cars, and wood in furniture.

At the same time, the powered metal press, radio, and telegraph played a large role in the faster spread of news, ideas, stories, and political movements. The first mystery and detective novels, incidentally, were written only toward the end of the First Industrial Revolution. While motion pictures began to show up by the end of the First Industrial Revolution, it took until halfway through the Second Industrial Revolution for them to become a popular family pastime. Audio recording and playback revolutionized our ability to widely share music and news with many more people and over a longer period.

It makes sense, given this background, that a lot of the medical progress we take for granted today also originated during this era. The discovery of the benefits of vitamin D and insulin, X-rays, treatments for glaucoma and rheumatoid arthritis, and the invention of the bandage, cardiac pacemaker, and ultrasound are just a few examples. Collaboration between researchers also improved greatly with the help of conferences and journals. Discovery of vaccines for tetanus, diphtheria, typhoid fever, tuberculosis, influenza, polio, and many more led to a significant and long overdue victory over many diseases.

All this industrialization would not have been possible without a corresponding rise in agricultural productivity to feed the growing population. Human ingenuity rose to the challenge and crop yields doubled four times between 1820 and 1975.[2] While it first took a hundred years to double, it took only thirty, fifteen, and ten years respectively for the next three.

The momentum built toward the end of the nineteenth century continued to accelerate in the twentieth century. For example, the first half of the twentieth century produced the first powered and controlled human flight, audio recording and playback, the vacuum cleaner, television, liquid-fueled rocket, electron microscope, semiconductors, and much more. The invention and widespread acceptance of various contraceptives in the twentieth century perhaps represent one of the most significant developments in human history. While nature had designed procreation as a process for species to survive, adapt, and thrive, humans found a way to assume more direct control of their destiny. Even though this important objective is ostensibly now served by individual choice, it is highly likely that economic imperatives will increasingly compel many societies to start incentivizing birth.

Unfortunately, however, these advances have also created haves and have-nots. It is a tragedy of our history that the promise of the Scientific and Industrial Revolutions was not available to all sections of our society. For some, these centuries ushered in a deterioration in quality of life. First and foremost, the new factories generated substantial pollution and heralded our onslaught on the environment. All this progress and the higher cost of living also resulted in longer workdays for the labor force. Life became a lot more hectic for the factory workers, and the work was increasingly monotonous and stifling and lacked creativity. The displacement of workers who were previously engaged in manual labor brought forth exploitative labor practices and inflicted harsh living conditions upon those at the lower end of the social ladder. Consequently, slums and impoverished neighborhoods emerged as unfortunate consequences of the new economic order. Regrettably, these trends have endured over time, exacerbating social inequities and deepening the divides within society. The workers who served the system and enabled this productivity were not able to enjoy a higher quality of life than what their previous generation had experienced. However, they had little choice as the economic makeover eliminated their earlier means of livelihood.

The transition from rural, agrarian communities to urban, industrialized societies also had a profound impact on traditional social structures. The once close and interdependent relationships prevalent in rural areas gave way to individualistic and impersonal connections in urban environments, fostering a sense of disconnection and alienation. The communal bonds and shared identity that characterized pre-industrial societies were gradually replaced by feelings of social isolation and fragmented connections. Additionally, pursuit of employment often resulted in the separation of families, further disrupting the fabric of social life. There was also increased and indiscriminate use of child labor. This transformation thus hurt the family structure and children's rights.

In a broad sense, the Scientific Revolution also sanctioned and hastened the detachment of man from nature. The emergence of factory farming, for instance, can be traced to this mindset. Until around the end of the First Industrial Revolution, farmers were only fencing in their livestock. The discovery of vitamin D, however, enabled farmers to greatly reduce the outdoor time for farm animals. While chickens were the first to be factory-farmed in the late 1920s, factory farming of pigs and cattle was well established in many of the developed nations within the next few decades. Instead of being allowed to roam freely, pigs were now housed in tight quarters. Pregnant sows, for example, are still confined to 6.6 ft. x 2 ft. gestation crates to this day in most countries. These stalls do not allow them room to even sleep on their sides, as pigs typically prefer.

It should come as no surprise that progress is often accompanied by setbacks and unintended consequences, as science and technology ignite both our inclusive and exclusionary instincts. This is exemplified by the advancements of the first half of the twentieth century, which also gave rise to the atomic bomb and ballistic missiles. But there is more to come in this story, as we will see a little later in this chapter. We must remember, however, not to throw the baby out with the bathwater. It is imperative that we understand the drivers of both our progress as well as our failings. Only through awareness and vigilance can we ensure that our further development and actions are in line with the noblest aspirations of humanity.

The Digital Revolution

In the short span of less than two centuries, the world became far better connected, and a person living at the end of the Second Industrial Revolution may have reasonably assumed that almost all the progress that was feasible had already been made. Of course, we know now that nothing would have been further from the truth. Many refer to the following decades when personal computers, mobile phones, and the internet revolutionized our communications and commerce yet again as the Digital Revolution or the Third Industrial Revolution. There were of course other advances as well that were built on the insights gained during the Second Industrial Revolution. The video recorder, solar batteries, lasers, the artificial satellite, the Global Positioning System, nuclear power, manned space flights, and more are all very significant inventions in their own right.

The world's first "automatic electronic digital computer," for example, came at the height of the Second World War. John Vincent Atanasoff and Clifford E. Berry of Iowa State University developed and tested the Atanasoff-Berry Computer (ABC) in 1942. The ENIAC (Electronic Numerical Integrator and Computer), the first programmable computer, was designed in 1945 under the direction of John Mauchly and J. Presper Eckert of the University of Pennsylvania at a total cost of a little over $8.3 million in 2023 US dollars. A program on the ENIAC was mechanically set into the machine using patch cables and switches to represent a sequence of computations. A group of six women—widely referred to as the "ENIAC girls"—were initially trained in programming the ENIAC. By the end of its operation in 1956, ENIAC had 18,000 vacuum tubes, 70,000 resistors, 10,000 capacitors, 7,200 diodes, 1,500 relays, and approximately 5,000,000 hand-soldered joints. It weighed more than 27 tons, occupied 1,800 sq. ft., and consumed about 150 kW of electricity. Its first program was a study of the feasibility of the hydrogen bomb, the second-generation nuclear weapon.

The invention of the transistor in 1947 by John Bardeen and Walter Houser Brattain of Bell Labs triggered the digital tsunami. The successful fabrication of the metal-oxide-semiconductor field-effect transistor (MOSFET) by Mohamed Atalla and Dawon Kahng at Bell Labs in 1959 was one of the most significant breakthroughs. The MOS transistor was essentially a control switch and a logic unit; the voltage on its "gate" could be used to place it in an ON or OFF state. The ability to achieve high packing densities of MOS transistors at a low cost permitted their large-scale integration. In turn, this development heralded the miniaturization of computers. Semiconductor manufacturing technology was able to print hundreds of transistors on a single MOS chip by the late 1960s. This led to vastly more powerful and energy-efficient compute engines. And the personal computing era was officially launched in 1982, when instead of picking a Person of the Year, *Time* magazine chose the home computer as the Machine of the Year. By 1990, personal computers had become ubiquitous, with prices ranging from $1,000.

Separately, by April 1973, less than a hundred years after Alexander Graham Bell filed his patent for a telephone, Motorola's Martin Cooper made the first handheld mobile telephone call. This analog phone weighed 2.4 pounds, measured 9.1 x 5.1 x 1.8 inches, and boasted a talk time of 30 minutes on a 10-hour charge. The popularity of mobile communications fueled an increase in the number of base-station towers and battery technologies, and this, in turn, led to increasingly smaller and lighter handheld devices. IBM came up with Simon—the world's first-ever smartphone—in 1993. It included a pager, fax machine, calendar, address book, clock, calculator, notepad, email, and touchscreen with a QWERTY keyboard.

By 1990, advances in semiconductor manufacturing enabled the integration of up to a million transistors. This enabled significantly faster personal computers, more efficient cellphones, the arrival of the digital camera, and eventually ever more powerful smartphones. While a billion personal computers were sold by 2002, it took only six more years for another billion to be sold.[3] However, as many consumers moved most of their daily use to smartphones and tablets, the sales of PCs began to flatten out by 2013.

In parallel, the NSFNET project from the National Science Foundation in the US created a large network of local computer hubs by 1990. It gave many research and academic organizations in the US access to the supercomputing centers at other US universities. Eventually, with the decommissioning of NSFNET in 1995, acceptance of the Domain Name System, and the broad adoption of Transmission Control and Internet Protocols (TCP/IP) on existing networks, commercial use of the internet began to take root. The internet thus came with little fanfare but ended up having a revolutionary impact on our culture, commerce, and communication technologies. It led to almost instant email, the rapid rise of internet-based telephone and video call capability, and social media. Billions now have access to powerful machines and graphics cards that can enable rapid multiplayer virtual video games and high-speed internet connectivity for movies on demand!

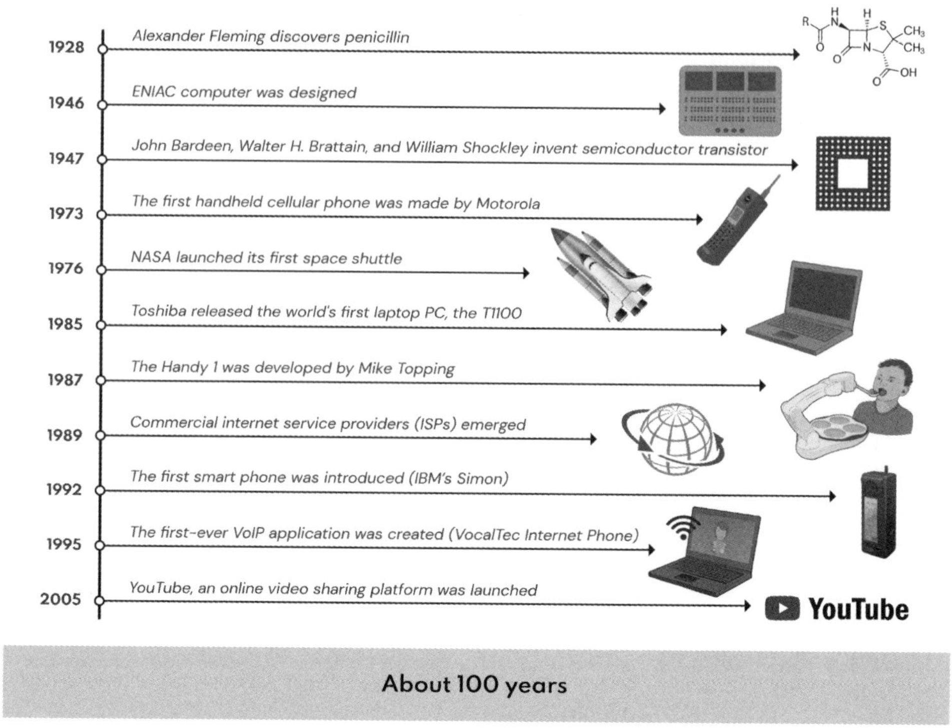

Figure 2.3. Key human accomplishments over a period of fewer than 100 years between 1928 and 2005.

The linchpin at the root of all this development is our success in packing an incredible number of MOS transistors on one chip. From one million transistors per chip in 1990, this number increased to about fifty million in 2000, one billion in 2010, and about fifty billion in 2020. By the 1990s, many high-level programming languages were developed to further simplify the encoding of algorithms through software. Complex commands that previously took hundreds or thousands of lines now took only a line or two. This greatly exploded the number of people who could write software. Over time, software led to technologies that enabled even faster computers. As software programs began to be used in real-world applications such as factory optimization, audio and video processing, or healthcare delivery, digital programs increasingly interfaced with the external analog world. Specialized analog-to-digital and digital-to-analog chips began to be designed to facilitate these interfaces between software algorithms and real-world applications. By 2000, Android and iOS operating systems also allowed simpler design of powerful applications (apps) for the cellphones.

As a result, the utility of smartphones grew exponentially since the mid-1990s. As of 2020, there are over 2.7 million Android apps in Google Play and 1.8 million iOS apps in the Apple Store. There are now apps for photography and videography, scientific calculations, alarms and reminders, communication, social media, education, music and other entertainment, travel, news, games, relationships, consumer services, and much more. These apps help us get a lot more out of the hours in a day. There is even an app to block other apps so they don't distract you from getting work done, and of course also an app to learn more about you based on your app usage!

In addition to personal computers and communication devices, semiconductors also transformed our healthcare delivery by enabling the general-purpose use of processors. They are used today in clinical diagnostics, medical imaging, low-power implantable devices, and portable as well as in-home patient monitoring. They have made possible magnetic resonance imaging (MRI) machines, computerized axial tomography (CAT), ultrasound machines, pacemakers, blood pressure monitors, electron microscopes, chemistry/blood gas analyzers, wireless wearables, and more. According to Cisco Systems, the number of connected wearable devices was expected to increase from around 325 million in 2016 to about 1.1 billion in 2022 and 10.5 billion by 2028.[4]

With the slowdown in the sales of personal computers and smartphones, it does seem like we are nearing the end of the Digital Revolution by the 2020s. However, we may have to wait a decade or more to be able to accurately characterize the developments of this era.

The Past Catches Up ...

The present moment certainly has been a long time in the making. Yet, given our exploding technological ingenuity since the late 1700s, it also seems that we may have been growing up too fast. In view of this accelerating pace of progress, it is extremely likely that even the wildest future projections will fall woefully short of what actually transpires. At the same time, the rapid advances of the last two centuries have also left several intractable problems and some ticking time bombs in their wake. Studying them should aid our understanding of the kind of future our children will inherit. It is also important to gain deeper insights into the reasons we were unable to anticipate these problems so we can try to avoid similar mistakes in the future. This learning is indispensable for our children to truly own their future.

A stark example comes from our fascination with plastics. After a significant quantity of plastic debris was found in the oceans in the 1960s, the environmental impact of plastic waste began to hit home. The same indestructibility that was its strength also turned out to be its liability. Recent research has also revealed the threat plastics, microplastics, and other forever chemicals pose to human health. In high doses, some of the additives used in plastics such as bisphenol A (BPA) and phthalates have been found to disrupt the hormonal system and cause developmental delays. Sensing the writing on the wall, the plastics industry began to champion recycling. There have been many campaigns against single-use plastic bags and straws. Despite concerted efforts, finding a replacement for plastic is proving difficult. While there has been active research on the development of biodegradable plastics and bioplastics, there is broad consensus now that complete elimination of plastics is unlikely.

As humanity gained increasing mastery over its environment, we also simultaneously pursued supremacy and control over each other. We constantly improved and developed new weapons to defend and to kill. With the use of chemical weapons in the First World War and long-range ballistic missiles and atomic bombs in the Second World War, the twentieth century has brought us weapons of mass destruction that have the potential to indiscriminately wipe out large population centers in a short period of time. While the use of artillery guns, mines, tanks, drones, and other conventional armaments continues in many small-scale conflicts around the world, the threat of a nuclear holocaust continues to hang in the background with advanced electronics in guidance systems enabling intercontinental ballistic and hypersonic missiles and second-generation thermonuclear weapons. The risk of nuclear or chemical weapons and biological agents falling into the hands of nonstate actors or deranged leaders—who may feel that they have very little to lose—has been a looming threat for some time. The threats of mass destruction and a nuclear accident have become far more relatable after Russia's invasion of Ukraine in 2022.

Perhaps the most ominous result of postindustrial human activity, however, is global warming.[5] A study by researchers at Oregon State and Harvard has shown that the rate of global warming in the last hundred years is unprecedented compared to what we have seen over the last ten thousand years.[6] This study relied on seventy-three sets of climate records, including some new analysis of fossil shell records from the ocean sediment cores. Moreover, two-thirds of the increase in the last hundred years has apparently come in the last thirty or so years!

While there are many stark reminders of the price we pay because of climate change and pollution,[7] there are few more visible examples than the suffering caused by air pollution in cities like Beijing and New Delhi. Starting around 2013, several wealthy private schools in China began purchasing expensive domes with purified air to protect students from the heavy smog. These domes cost anywhere from $150,000 to tens of millions of dollars. Besides contributing to climate change, air pollution, as a part of a vicious cycle, is also exacerbated by it. There are worries that global warming will seriously impact crop yields. There will likely be a massive loss of habitat due to the inundation caused by rising sea levels. In addition to severe droughts, floods, and other extreme weather events, scientists expect warmer temperatures to result in the extinction of many more species. Incidentally, several of these forecasts are already coming to pass. There is broad agreement that reversing global warming poses an unprecedented challenge. While there are about ten million environmental migrants in just the first half of 2020, current estimates project that there could be anywhere from two hundred million to up to one billion migrants by 2050.[8]

Some may lament the mechanization of science and its potential to disconnect us from nature and claim that nuclear weapons wouldn't have been possible if we were not on this downward spiral. Such claims are wishful thinking. As discussed in the first chapter, restlessness is inherent in our nature, and it is futile to attempt to halt the relentless march of scientific progress and technological advancements. Instead, we can hold onto the hope that heightened awareness and education will empower us to make more informed policy choices and cultivate societies that are inclusive, both for the current generation and those that follow.

We Gain a New Intelligence

Alongside crises such as climate change, there have also been other opportunities and challenges presented by our rapidly unfolding future. Some claim that we have just entered a Fourth Industrial Revolution, in which robotics, artificial intelligence (AI), and the internet of things are beginning to enable smart homes, virtual reality (VR), autonomous driving, and biotechnology. Many of these innovations will again be game changers, even altering our consciousness and fundamental experience of life! Just as previous cycles of innovation were beyond the wildest forecasts of most at the start of those roller-coaster rides, the destinations of current trajectories will likely seem implausible to many readers.

For decades now, most devices in our homes have had some degree of built-in intelligence. For example, electrical fuses trip and protect downstream circuit integrity if any devices in its network carry more than the prescribed current. Thermostats control the operation of home heating and air-conditioning systems based on preset temperature thresholds. The development of powerful smartphone apps and the shrinking costs of electronics have also allowed us to add an additional layer of convenience. We can now control thermostats, robotic vacuum cleaners, irrigation sprinklers, and even washing machines and home security systems remotely using an app. In fact, even before the advent of cellphones and mass electronics, the X10 modules had already envisioned some of this home automation back in 1975![9]

But what if the devices are also aware of what is expected of them? Perhaps the doors know who should be allowed in and who should not, and the windows know what they need to do to allow the right amount of light in. The kettle knows the steps it needs to take to prepare the right quantity and quality of tea at the right time. A home irrigation system is intelligent enough to be selective about what areas it waters and how often based on local soil needs. This is the objective of a smart home that relies on the internet of things. For some, such as the physically challenged, this kind of automation could be a life saver.

Autonomous self-driving cars are a great example of AI. To enable such autonomous functionality, complex software uses maps generated by various visualization technologies such as high-powered cameras, radars, arrays of lasers, and sonar to determine the inputs to be sent to the actuators for controlling acceleration, steering, and braking. Making sense of all the possible real-world scenarios is of course no easy task! Even so, we made tremendous progress. There are clearly demarcated regions where autonomous driving is already a reality. Since July 2019, for example, Lyft customers have been able to order a driverless Waymo minivan in certain Phoenix suburbs. Within its first year, Waymo clocked over 100,000 rides and covered twenty million miles on public roads. Of course, we are likely many years away from self-driving vehicles that can operate in any weather or road condition without human intervention. Given the staggering number of deaths due to traffic accidents and that numerous older people, disabled individuals, and others are unable or unwilling to drive, autonomous driving has immense potential to truly revolutionize local transport.

Figure 2.4. A driverless Waymo car uses electronic sensors to navigate Phoenix roads.

Many countries have also been turning to AI to compensate for a shrinking workforce. Since their employable population is likely to decline significantly over the next few decades, many aging nations such as Japan are facing a significant challenge in sustaining economic productivity and overcoming labor shortages. Automation has been a boon to these aging societies.

While the fruits of AI fueled by deep learning are very appealing, we also need to pay attention to growing worries about our newfound "intelligence." While the impact of automation on jobs is not easy to estimate, studies have suggested that between 25 percent and 50 percent of the jobs in the US are likely to be eliminated by around 2030.[10] An estimate by Andrew Haldane, previously the Bank of England's chief economist, suggests that as many as eighty million jobs in the US could be lost to automation by about 2040.[11] The impact will of course not be limited to the US. About 50 percent of the jobs within the thirty-two OECD (Organization for Economic Cooperation and Development) countries were found to be vulnerable to automation.[12] In the past, a labor force was often able to transition to emerging industries during a large-scale market upheaval. Typically, there was even a demand for a larger workforce from the new industries than from the older ones. However, there are many indicators that suggest that the current robotic explosion is different. As compared to the arrival of the automobile or personal computing, not only is its impact a lot more far reaching, but its maturation is also so much more rapid than past disruptions that the economy will likely find it difficult to adjust. As a result, we can expect a lot more political unrest than usual due to this rapid loss of employment.

Most of these forecasts were based on our initial expectation that robots would only replace us in tedious, algorithmic jobs that involve well-defined steps or in jobs that involve simple skills or routine information retrieval. Many thought, for instance, that doctors, nurses, and teachers could not be replaced. Professions that demand creativity, empathy, or complex intelligence were not believed to be under threat. However, as semiconductor chips shrank relentlessly and the increased processing power enabled more powerful machine learning algorithms and devices with growing AI, one cannot be as certain anymore that people in jobs that demand complexity and creativity are irreplaceable.[13] Deep machine learning is being increasingly coupled with AI to enable tools like Alexa and Cortina to adaptively learn a great deal about us. Similarly, our abundance of high-speed processing farms is fueling an unforeseen explosion in the maturity of AI models.

On a cold day in November 1997, pianist Winifred Kerner played three different classical pieces written in the style of Bach for a select audience—one by Bach, one by Dr. Steve Larson, professor of music theory at the University of Oregon, and one by a computer program called EMI (Experiments in Musical Intelligence). This was a Turing test for EMI; the audience was tasked with determining which was which. EMI was the brainchild of David Cope, the Dickerson Emeritus Professor at the University of California at Santa Cruz.[14] When faced with a composer's block in 1982, Cope decided to write a program that could analyze patterns in his music and come up with new pieces that could get him going. His program first deconstructed a piece and analyzed the patterns in the piece. Maintaining the same style, it then combined the pieces in a new pattern. Based on the insights he gained through this analysis, Cope was able to compose a new piece with a new style just two days after the program was complete. He then also went on to compose new music in the styles of other great composers like Bach, Beethoven, Mozart, Chopin, and Rachmaninoff. It was surreal when in the November 1997 faceoff, the audience picked the EMI music as the true Bach piece! It was a big shot in the arm to Cope, who decided in 2003 to begin work on Emily Howell, the successor to EMI that is now no longer limited to one style at a time. Emily creates her own style of music and has an intimate understanding of the works of thirty-six composers. Emily can also take feedback and modify her compositions. As one might expect, this has rattled many composers as well as music enthusiasts. There have been many questions about the production of music by a process that doesn't require an emotional investment—i.e., without the involvement of a heart or a soul. However, "the question," Cope says, "isn't if computers possess a soul, but if we possess one." It isn't clear, according to him, if the emotions exist within the notes or are ascribed to them by our experiences.[15]

This question will increasingly come up. Progress in many AI systems has exceeded most expectations. For example, after exchanging thousands of mind-bending messages with an AI-driven chatbot called LaMDA, Blake Lemoine, a software engineer who worked for Google's Responsible AI team, claimed in June 2022 that LaMDA had become sentient. If a chatbot can elicit this kind of understanding from an expert, we can only imagine its impact on the rest of us. Since language processing is one of the most difficult challenges, a Rome-based translation company called *Translated* developed a metric, Time to Edit (TTE), to calculate the time it takes for professional human editors to correct errors in AI-generated translations versus those in human-generated text. *Translated* estimates that AI systems can perform just as well as humans and thus show signs of Artificial General Intelligence by 2030. An AI system that passes the Turing test will transcend human ability and could transform society in unpredictable ways. In the process, Emily and other AI systems might help more of us understand what it truly means to be human!

Age Is Just a Number, or Is It?

From uncovering the true meaning of being human to discovering the origins of life and fighting aging and death, humans have increasingly confronted some of the most consequential questions over the last few decades. And, as we have discussed, the Digital Revolution resulted in powerful compute engines that can tackle increasingly complex machine learning and numerical simulation problems. This has allowed researchers to test novel theories in many health domains: stem cells and tissue regeneration, artificial organs, nanorobots for drug delivery, intelligent wearables, human-machine interfaces, faster detection of pandemics, cancer research, longevity factors, genetic engineering (for both disease prevention and trait selection), epigenetics, human and animal brain mapping, mental health, mind control and awareness, and even in unraveling the origins of life itself. While advances in each of these areas will greatly help overall human health, research in genetic engineering, longevity, brain mapping, and mental health has the potential to fight aging and death themselves, and thus to profoundly disrupt our centuries-long way of life.

For example, it's now possible to completely map the unique genome of an individual for under $1,000, with a partial readout of the most relevant parts available for as little as $200. The impact of eventual widespread use of DNA sequencing on our healthcare could be phenomenal.[16] A dramatic illustration of the power of genome sequencing came about when Michael Snyder, chair of the genetics department at Stanford University, learned he was at risk for Type 2 diabetes.[17] There was no obvious reason to believe it since he wasn't obese and didn't have a family history of diabetes. Despite his skepticism, he began monitoring his blood sugar out of an abundance of caution. To everyone's surprise, his blood sugar suddenly began rising until it spiked a few months later. He had turned into a diabetic in real time over the course of his observation. Fortunately, he managed to get it back under control through changes to his diet and lifestyle.

As exciting as knowledge and insights are, humans have never been satisfied with simply understanding how nature works, we have always wanted to tinker. For example, screening has been used since the 1970s to identify babies at risk of being born with Down syndrome. Then came the genome editing technologies in the late 1990s. The first clinical use of genome editing was for treating acute lymphoblastic leukemia in an eleven-month-old child in 2015. CRISPR-Cas9 has been used in research settings to investigate genetic diseases such as spina bifida, Down syndrome, cystic fibrosis, sickle cell anemia, diabetes, and more. In February 2019, Sangamo Therapeutics announced the first ever "in body" human gene editing therapy.[18] They succeeded in permanently altering the DNA of a patient to overcome Hunter syndrome. For now, most countries only allow somatic therapies that target nonreproductive cells. Changes made to these cells therefore cannot be passed through to later generations. It is worth pondering the implications if this were to change in the future.

Geeta Pandey of the BBC bureau in Delhi reported a fascinating story that's likely a harbinger of what is in store for us.[19] Abhijit was born with thalassemia major, a deadly disorder with no known cure that results in a dangerously low hemoglobin count and a life expectancy of only about twenty-five to thirty years. It badly compromised Abhijit's immunity and often made him sick. Blood transfusions were the only known remedy and by the time he turned six, he had received about eighty of them. When his father, Sahdevsinh Solanki, learned that a bone marrow transplant could be a permanent cure, he felt hopeful for the first time. But his joy was short-lived when he discovered that no one in their immediate family was a match as a donor. While a bone marrow tissue match from an unrelated donor was always a possibility, the cost for one such match they found in the US was about $68,000, a hefty sum that was beyond reach for them. Also, perhaps more importantly, the odds of success from a transplant from an unrelated donor were only about 20 to 30 percent. His hopes were lifted again when he came across an article on "savior siblings"—babies conceived solely for the purpose of donating organs, cells, or bone marrow to an older sibling. Solanki consulted Dr. Manish Banker, one of India's premier fertility specialists, to explore this option further.

About six months after Dr. Banker came on board, his wife was pregnant and ready to welcome Kavya Solanki, Abhijit's savior sibling. Using preimplantation genetic diagnosis, Dr. Banker first eliminated the disease-causing thalassemia gene from the embryo. After he screened it and ensured that it was a match for Abhijit, the fetus was planted in the mother's womb. About eighteen months after birth, when Kavya had grown to about twenty-five pounds, the bone marrow transplant was finally carried out. Kavya healed over the next few days and Abhijit's hemoglobin count also climbed steadily. The transplant was a success, and Abhijit was finally and permanently cured!

The creation of a savior sibling raises significant ethical dilemmas regarding the interests of both the child in need of medical assistance as well as the savior sibling. The decision-making process must meticulously consider the medical risks and rights of both children. There are serious concerns about a child being brought into existence solely for the purpose of providing medical assistance without being able to provide consent. Furthermore, normalization of savior siblings also raises questions about the potential knock-on impact on the likelihood of designer babies. The prospect of designing babies for specific purposes raises even greater ethical concerns. Perhaps cost, access, and awareness have been effective barriers so far. However, we cannot delay addressing these ethical considerations since designer babies may be here sooner rather than later. While gene editing and genetic therapies will undoubtedly be first used for fighting crippling diseases, it is difficult to imagine that they will not also be used to promote healthy genes and suppress "undesirable" traits. Those with means will likely have easier access to genetic therapies and life-saving organs.

Our fight against diseases and aging has included remarkable breakthroughs in the development of life support functions and artificial organs. Organ transplants, prosthetic limbs, pacemakers, neurostimulators, extracorporeal membrane oxygenation, and more have become increasingly sophisticated over the last few decades. And exciting advances in graphics tools, compute power, stem cell research, 3D printing, nanotechnology, and tissue grafts have opened up other unimaginable opportunities in recent years. There is advanced active research in neural prosthesis and artificial organs for the bladder, eye, ear, heart, testes, liver, ovaries, lung, kidney, and pancreas at various stages of development. For example, while the first artificial red blood cells (RBCs) were made in 1968, recent developments are paving the way for synthetic, coated artificial RBCs made from purified human hemoglobin proteins that are one-fiftieth the size of a real human RBC.[20] The new RBCs can capture oxygen when the blood pH is high, release it when the pH is low, take on the role of an antioxidant, and even prevent dangerous constriction of the blood vessels by not allowing the hemoglobin to react with the nitric oxide in the bloodstream. Complete replacement of almost every vital biological organ in our body by an artificial counterpart may well be within reach by 2050!

While hygiene and medical progress have steadily increased our average life expectancy, our maximum lifespan itself has been relatively unchanged so far. It is often considered a stable characteristic of a species. The maximum reported age at death for humans is currently believed to be 122 years, the age at death of a Frenchwoman named Jeanne Calment, who was born in 1875. This has prompted many to explore the mechanisms of aging and longevity more deeply. For example, the mission of Calico, an American research and development biotech company founded in 2013 by Bill Maris and backed by Google, is to deepen our understanding of the biology that controls lifespan. The inability of our cells to replicate, for example, is a key manifestation of aging. We have known for a while that this is often due to the damage to our DNA caused by the shortening of the telomeres, the protective caps at the ends of chromosomes. The buildup of these nondividing senescent cells is also known to curb cellular regeneration. Animal studies have shown that removing these nondividing cells can extend our remaining life by more than 30 percent. Many antiaging studies have therefore been focused on cleaning up these senescent cells and on increasing telomere lengths, the "holy grail" of youth. We have learned, for instance, that smoking, stress, and inflammation can accelerate the shortening of telomeres, and good nutrition and intense physical exercise, conversely, can have a modest beneficial impact.

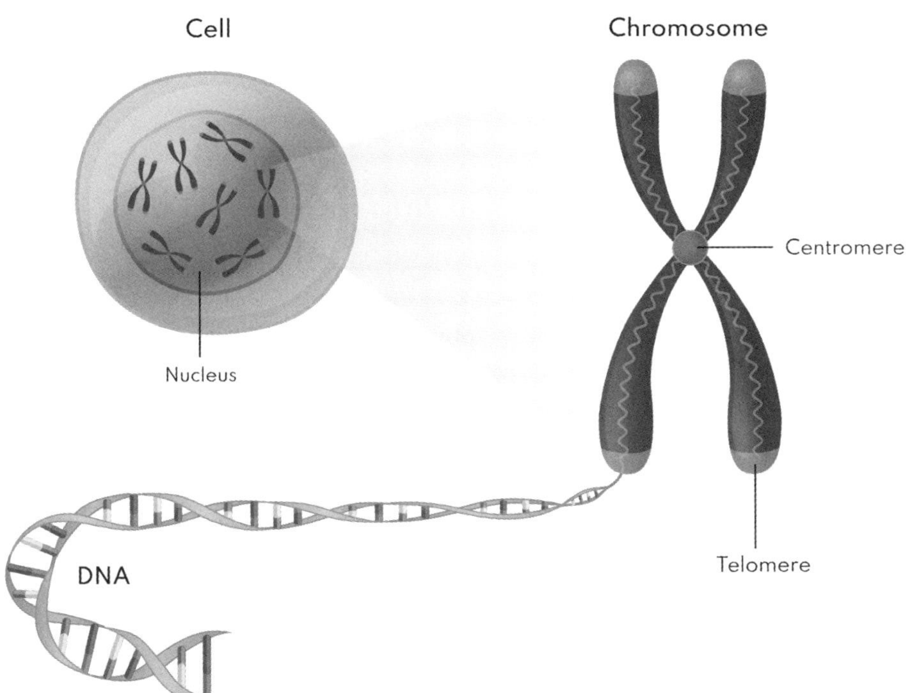

Figure 2.5. The telomere in a chromosome.

Scientists from Tel Aviv University have shown that providing pure oxygen to thirty-five healthy adults aged sixty-four and older in a hyperbaric chamber increased the length of their telomeres by 20 percent![21] This unprecedented result meant that the telomeres of the trial participants had regained the lengths they had twenty-five years earlier. Interestingly, the participants also saw a 37 percent reduction in their senescent cells. Each participant was given a mask with 100 percent oxygen in a pressurized chamber for ninety minutes a day, five days a week, for three months. It is believed that the pressurized chamber allowed more oxygen to be dissolved into the tissues and the resulting oxygen gradients likely helped with regeneration. In an unrelated initiative, about a year after embarking on an ambitious project called Blueprint, forty-five-year-old biotech entrepreneur Bryan Johnson reported measurements that showed that he had the heart of a thirty-seven-year-old and the lungs of a young adult.

It's hard to believe, but many are convinced we're inching closer toward immortality with every passing day. This is not unreasonable given the significant investments we've been making in the pursuit of this goal. The implications of this prospect in terms of the social, political, and economic impact are mind-boggling.

The New Intelligence Turns Its Focus on Us

In addition to the focus on conquering aging, researchers have long been interested in the power of the mind. This is just as well since a long life without an engaged mind can be beyond crippling. Yet, despite all manner of progress, mastery of our mind remains as elusive as ever. One key reason is that most of us experience an intangible ceiling for happiness. At a psychological level, our happiness is modulated by our expectations. When we get promotions or bonuses, we quickly pivot to the next opportunity and hang our happiness on the next big fix. Many of us find it difficult to get off the hedonic treadmill, and this has been a leading cause of most of our anxiety and despair. While peeling this onion can be a fascinating journey of discovery, individualizing the understanding of the human mind through the use of machine learning and AI can unleash unpredictable consequences.

Researchers have known for a while from invasive epilepsy research that some faces and events are associated with specific "tuned" neurons. As such, Seiji Ogawa's discovery in 1990 that tasks produced blood-oxygen-level dependent responses in neurons was a big breakthrough, as it gave us the ability to noninvasively locate brain activities to within a few millimeters through the clinical use of functional MRI (fMRI).[22] This gave researchers a tool to better understand the telltale brain activities of people with schizophrenia, addiction, and chronic depression, for example. As fMRI studies shed light on the neuroplasticity of our brains, there was a resurgence of interest in more direct brain stimulation.

A big breakthrough came in 2000 when scientists in Göttingen, Germany, showed that low-current "galvanization" can change brain function.[23] This technique, now referred to as transcranial direct current stimulation (tDCS), has gained widespread attention and popularity since then. The magnitude of the electrical current used in tDCS is high enough to enhance (with a positive current) or suppress (with a negative current) the probability of a neuron to fire, but not high enough to cause resting neurons themselves to fire. Numerous studies over the last twenty or more years have demonstrated significant improvement—often lasting—in behaviors, mood control, and cognitive tasks that require working language, memory, attention, executive functioning, and math with the use of tDCS.[24] For example, Vince Clark, director of the University of New Mexico Psychology Clinical Neuroscience Center in Albuquerque, used tDCS to help army recruits learn to detect hidden threats in complex images.[25] fMRI was first used to identify the regions in the brain that were active when the subjects played a video game that trained them in identifying concealed threats. These areas were then targeted by tDCS in a new group of recruits as they received the same training. While the control group only received a negligible amount of current, the other half was given the regular tDCS dose. In this influential study and in many others that followed, the subjects who received the prescribed dose were able to train about twice as quickly as the control group. While there has been growing evidence of the immense benefit that tDCS offers to those who suffer from chronic depression, the most dramatic benefits appear to be seen in the treatment of auditory hallucinations. About 70 to 80 percent of people diagnosed with schizophrenia, for example, are believed to hear voices. In addition to treatment of depression and schizophrenia, tDCS is also being used to improve cognitive performance and focus.

In fact, the experience of Sally Adee, the technology features and news editor at *New Scientist*, illustrates how the impact of tDCS on mental clarity can be a gamechanger for those afflicted by self-doubt. Adee was close to tears as she struggled to take down more than two dozen masked men with rifles and suicide vests who ran toward her one day in 2011.[26] For everyone she managed to kill, three new assailants showed up. She was unable to keep pace, and her struggles led to a vicious cycle of fear and failure and a sense of incompetence. Luckily for her, this was only a computer simulation in a lab in Carlsbad, California. After this round of marksmanship training ended, researchers placed the electrodes of a tDCS device at select locations on her head and a new simulation was launched. Her head felt so clear that she was now able to take down assailants as they appeared, with time to spare. Without the baggage of inner monologue dragging her down, she was suddenly an excellent shot. She did not fully realize what she went through until the simulation ended. The bewitching silence in her head lasted for three more days before self-doubt and mind-wandering caused by unbelieving voices gradually returned. Interestingly, Adee noted that she achieved a state that was closest to what tDCS gave her in a two-hour Iyengar yoga class.

Life might be very different if we all could be more in awe of all the wondrous things around us instead of being weighed down by the constant mental chatter produced by envy, competition, and all forms of conditioning. This raises a question about when we are closest to our truest self, with tDCS or without. Or whether one can even define "true self"? What is then the essence of reengineering our minds? Many Eastern religions have historically valued tools such as yoga and meditation that promote self-awareness through silence and reflection. There is a fine line between improving awareness through reflection, meditation, exposure, and judgment versus altering our perceptions through direct and selective coloring of experiences. When we have the tools, how can we draw the line?

It may take a while for us to fully process all the ramifications of suppressing voices in our heads or amplifying chosen thought patterns through tDCS, medication, or other means. Altering our perceptions through explicit or implicit mind control can have serious implications since all knowledge stems from our perceptions. When coupled with machine learning, targeted belief modification can be difficult to detect. Wu and colleagues published a study suggesting that machine learning models that solely rely on publicly available data such as Facebook "likes" can accurately predict personality profiles.[27] They tested their algorithm on more than seventeen thousand Facebook users utilizing a personality survey and information on their

Facebook "likes." The survey rated each subject on five OCEAN personality traits.[28] After the Facebook model was built on a training dataset to predict personality traits based on the "likes," it needed access to just ten "likes" to offer a more accurate prediction than a work colleague, seventy "likes" to do better than a roommate, a mere hundred and fifty "likes" to outperform a parent or sibling, and three hundred "likes" to even beat a spouse! Cambridge Analytica (CA), a British political consulting firm, used this algorithm to learn more about the voters on Facebook and to influence them. They used this capability to pursue hundreds of electoral consulting and marketing projects around the world. CA gained most prominence for its Brexit campaign and its work for Donald Trump's 2016 presidential campaign. The ability of technology to learn so much about us has dire implications. Machine learning and AI offer the ability to tailor and disseminate news—and possibly fake news—in a targeted manner. While fake news is not a new phenomenon, amplifying it, associating it with sources or facts we trust, and editing out other contradicting facts can be a powerful force multiplier.

There has also been a lot of research into the biological basis of influence and choice. Numerous studies over the years have established that there isn't a single self. We all have at least one experiencer or an initiator and a separate narrator who tries to make sense of the world for us. Pioneering work by American neuroscientist and Nobel Prize winner Roger Sperry and his colleague Michael Gazzaniga and others on "split-brain" patients (with their corpus callosum—the bundle of nerve fibers connecting the left and right hemispheres of the brain—severed) has shown that experiences perceived by the right hemisphere are only registered in one part of our body and invisible to the narrator in the left hemisphere. Some patients, for instance, had even reported incidents where "while their left hand was unbuttoning their shirt, the right hand would follow along behind and button it again."[29] Other studies have shown that our "narrator" often only summarizes key aspects of our experiences or even makes up stories to "explain away" certain observations and memories when unable to access a more detailed record. The fact that we have a distinct narrator that draws on other sources and can even make up stories is revealing. While our imagination and the stories we tell ourselves (and then others) have been key for the triumph of *Homo sapiens,* history is also replete with examples of how we have been led astray by them, both at an individual and a collective level.

In fact, verse 27 of chapter 3 of the *Bhagavad Gita*, a 6,000-year-old poem often viewed as a foundational treatise on Hindu thought, has also drawn attention to the interplay between the ego-driven "narrator" and the biology-based "experiencer." The *Bhagavad Gita* asserts that while ego is an essential tool, it can also limit our growth when it is given excessive prominence.

> prakṛiteḥ kriyamāṇāni guṇaiḥ karmāṇi sarvaśhaḥ
> ahankāra-vimūḍhātmā kartāham iti manyate
>
> *Even though all actions are a result of the qualities of our nature, the ego mistakenly identifies itself as the doer.*

If we can amplify or tune out debilitating voices in people with schizophrenia, we can also modulate voices in people not suffering from such auditory hallucinations. It is important to understand this deeply for it is our likely future. If tools and systems can be employed to understand and influence large majorities of our populations, those controlling such levers can wield disproportional influence on our collective future. As such, it is essential for education to build a deeper awareness of these key processes. Developing self-awareness into our 'narrators' should help us better understand our biological limitations and discern between the different shades of 'reality.' For example, insignia and dress codes, such as those worn by doctors and priests, have long been designed to secure our trust and allegiance by conveying to our subconscious that they are figures of authority. It is not uncommon for bad actors to attempt to influence us in a similar way, through subtle messaging and conditioning. Education serves as the only antidote that can safeguard and insulate us from the various forms of conditioning that we encounter.

Will Artificial Intelligence Claim Our Soul?

Given this history of our development, it is perhaps safe to assume that we are arriving at a time when we will soon have almost complete control and mastery over our physical and emotional environment. Algorithms will read us better than our own parents and spouses, and likely also better than we can read ourselves. Our ability to model and predict individual choices and behaviors is also fueling a massive interest in studies trying to get a deeper measure of what it even means to be human. As deep learning tools become more ubiquitous, they are poised to steadily take over our decision-making. And as we defer to these algorithms to make decisions for us, they will likely make it increasingly unnecessary for us to take on deeper analyses or to try something new.

Edison may have said that success is 99 percent perspiration and 1 percent inspiration. Growing automation, however, may make it increasingly difficult to choose perspiration and risk-taking. The genius of our work is typically best reflected in endeavors that take time and require planning. From painting masterpieces to fighting wars or pandemics, we are often guided by a larger-than-life purpose. Our sense of purpose is often rooted in religious convictions, but many also draw their moorings from a sense of identity or self-worth. As we increasingly cede control over decision-making and allow our minds to be placated and rewired, we run a growing risk of losing our sense of worth and meaning. These developments may even pose an existential threat. While we have been worrying about robots taking an increasing number of our jobs, we should perhaps also worry about an increasing number of humans being demoted to a more robotic life. Ironically, learning more about consciousness and our susceptibility to influence may shine a light on the presence of multiple voices, diminish our long-rooted notions of soul and identity, and thus negatively impact our sense of relevance and value.

The implications of tools capable of reshaping the thought patterns of large groups are undoubtedly serious. Throughout history, flexible cooperation based on a shared vision has served as a powerful catalyst for "progress." In the past, the ability to rally the largest group of individuals often increased the likelihood of success. However, we are now experiencing a unique shift in our history, as we become less reliant on the need to bring others along, at least through an overt effort.

The Promise of Our Journey

These are, of course, only tentative projections; the future has not yet been ordained. Some outcomes appear a lot more likely than others. Some will shock us and will perhaps be beyond our control. While recent events like the COVID-19 pandemic and the large-scale Russian invasion of Ukraine would have been unimaginable just a few years ago, even more significant upheavals are not unlikely over the course of upcoming decades. Slowly but surely, our capacity to learn from one another and from preceding generations has brought us here. It has allowed us to construct increasingly sophisticated tools, paradigms, and knowledge. Such perpetual learning has resulted in an acceleration in the pace of our "progress." In the past, change occurred relatively slowly, especially in the context of academic contracts and life events. However, in the early decades of the 21st century, it has become nearly inconceivable to assume that our children will have only one career throughout their lifetime.

Consider a farmer in 1650 Britain advising his son on farming challenges and strategies for a comfortable life. At that time, it would be reasonable to assume that the next generation would face similar challenges and circumstances. While a farmer in 1850 England might also follow in his father's footsteps and offer similar advice to his children, he would likely be less certain due to the unmistakable winds of change. There would have been increasing pressure to sell farms and migrate to cities. Nevertheless, throughout history, opportunities were relatively clear at most junctures, since even substantial changes have often extended beyond the lifespan of an individual adult. Consequently, families often acquired enough foresight to prepare for what lay ahead.

While elements beyond our control may impact the distant future, we have reached a point where human enterprise will clearly play a significant role in shaping our near-term and long-term prospects. Our progress seems to be also fueling our evolution in unexpected ways. The context of our evolution, our extraordinary history, the acceleration of our progress, and the unprecedented choices we face present a compelling narrative.

At the same time, even a cursory glance at our history showcases the immense scope of human curiosity and innovation. We have demonstrated remarkable tenacity, consistently renewing and replacing outdated technologies. It is genuinely astonishing how breakthroughs such as the landline telephone became obsolete in just over a century. As such, by gaining a deeper understanding of the problems we have generated in the wake of our progress, we can aspire to also engineer enduring solutions to them. The only thing that's more certain than the fog of the future is that thoughtful education can help us improve our odds for a more desirable destiny. As increasingly capable technologies proliferate, our children will be ill-served if they're not trained to leverage them judiciously as tools for foundational growth and avoid relying on them as crutches. Fundamental qualities and competencies such as curiosity, creativity, critical thinking ability, and communication skills should be key educational objectives. Failure to prioritize the development of these profound competencies through education would lead to a gradual erosion of our species' capacity for integrative complexity. As David Milch, Dan Meyer, and others have been exhorting, we need to reduce and reverse our growing penchant for quick fixes and our impatience with complexity and irresolution. It is also evident, in light of the discussion in this chapter, that empathy should be added to our list of key competencies. Only then will future generations be empowered to thrive.

In the next chapter—the final chapter in part I—we'll reconcile the learning from the first two chapters with our ongoing educational journey, so we have good clarity on available choices and the best next steps.

CHAPTER SUMMARY

- Humans experienced slow but steady progress for tens of thousands of years, until about three hundred years ago, when the accumulation of the knowledge of the physical universe over centuries led to a sudden spurt of breakthroughs and innovations. These have come to be referred to as the Industrial Revolutions.
- The innovations unleashed by these revolutions—such as mechanized textile weaving as well as the steam engine, printing press, electricity, vaccines, telephone, internal combustion engine, and automobile—have led to dramatic lifestyle changes for most people.
- The momentum of learning and progress only accelerated in the twentieth century, resulting in a Digital Revolution—with massive advances in computing technology, communications, healthcare, and more.
- While many of these developments have been positive (for example, advances in vaccine technology have led to the suppression and eradication of many diseases), some have caused great damage, in some cases even portending an existential threat.

- The confluence of machine learning, artificial intelligence, and advanced robotics is projected to result in a dramatically different future, potentially affecting even our sense of independence and self-worth.
- We should not be surprised if the next century turns out to be unlike any period we have experienced since the First Agricultural Revolution.
- In this uncertain climate, children cannot thrive without a significantly more thoughtful and inclusive education that showcases our journey and strengthens our unique abilities as *Homo sapiens*.
- For instance, competencies such as curiosity, creativity, critical thinking ability, empathy, and communication should be more front and center as key educational objectives.

3

Our Enduring Aspirations

To be what we are, and to become what we are capable of becoming, is the only end of life.
—BARUCH SPINOZA

Even though our biggest breakthroughs have often been a result of individual initiative, collective action has frequently been the silent partner that prepared the moment. For better or worse, education has been key in shaping this journey by moving every new generation a bit further along in its understanding of our place and time. And in the process, education itself has evolved from instructions on basic toolmaking to the modern-day behemoth. As such, while humans have long been passionate about preparing future generations to succeed in the world that is imagined for them, our understanding of what this *preparation* should entail has varied greatly across nations and over time.

While unfolding opportunities and challenges have been the primary driver of this evolution in educational practices, advances in our understanding of child development and the variety of belief systems and cultures have also played a large role. Thus, over the years, we have accumulated a rich legacy of educational approaches and philosophies from different cultures and eras.[1]

An examination of the motivations, practices, and results from this diverse slate of educational practices can help us assess how they align with the lessons from the previous two chapters. Have we ever attempted to anchor education on competencies such as empathy, ambition, and creativity? How often does education develop fluency with the big arc of our story? How well do leading educational philosophies leverage our individual strengths? To seek our fullest potential as a species, we therefore need to also heed the lessons from our educational journey.

The Birth of Organized Education

For more than a hundred thousand years after the arrival of *Homo sapiens*, children largely learned through self-directed play, exploration, observation of their peers, imitation of parents and other adults, and likely also through some coaching. They learned skills needed for foraging, toolmaking, and protecting themselves from predators. This may not have been too different from how chimpanzees and some of the other highly developed mammals reared their young. Life was challenging and short, but it was also likely interesting and unpredictable.

A paradigm shift occurred in children's lives around twelve thousand years ago when hunter-gatherer bands began to abandon their nomadic lifestyle and transition to more sedentary agricultural societies. The way of life of our ancestors shifted from being skill and knowledge intensive to one that was more labor intensive. A deep knowledge of toolmaking and the terrain and plants and animals on which they foraged was no longer as vital for a vast majority. Children were increasingly co-opted as laborers in the new societies. For many ensuing centuries, a large majority of children all over the world were employed as farm help.

The arrival of various writing systems in ancient civilizations during the Neolithic Revolution (around 3500 BCE) coincided with the earliest time in recorded history that demand grew for new skills. A small number of children trained as scribes, physicians, and civic and temple administrators. As societies developed more specialized professions, class structures, and other hierarchies, some of the privileged few were able to hire private tutors for their children. However, most of the others received minimal formal education, if any, especially in their formative years.[2]

Until the Middle Ages, no more than 1 to 5 percent of the children—largely boys from the upper echelons of society—have been estimated to receive this kind of education in most of Europe.[3] The curriculum varied greatly and was largely determined by private establishments. In contrast, China had a well-established formal education system by the time of the Han dynasty (~ 200 BCE), albeit still as a luxury mostly limited to boys in urban areas.[4] Its imperial education and examination system is believed to have been strongly based on the Confucian ideals of meritocracy that persist in Chinese education to this day. Education was typically focused on religion and morals, reading and writing, math, music, and a few vocational skills. There was also a focus on physical education, including archery and martial arts in some parts of India and China. The subjects reflected the needs and values of the societies. India had a residential gurukul system of education, in which children stayed in the homes of their teachers until their education was complete. In gurukuls, knowledge was largely passed on through oral traditions instead of through written texts.[5] For many centuries, while schooling was largely limited to boys elsewhere, the gurukul education was available to both boys and girls from all sections of society. However, with the passage of time, India's caste system effectively segregated the society into groups based on family professions and education began to be rationed.

While there still were some options for schooling, education was not prioritized in Europe in the Middle Ages after the fall of the Roman Empire and the rise of feudal societies. Bishops, priests, abbesses, and other religious scholars ran some classes in monasteries and convents to cater to a small percentage of the highly motivated children. But most common girls, peasants, and serfs had little chance of getting any education. Also, since most made a living either as a peasant or as a fighter, a majority did not have a practical use for education in mathematics, sciences, or the arts.

For the fortunate few, education typically began with reading and writing but the curriculum was also preoccupied with a study of grammar, rhetoric, dialectic reasoning, and logic. These consumed the first several years of a student's academic life. This was followed by instruction on the theoretical foundations of subjects like mathematics, music, and astronomy to prepare the student for an in-depth study of philosophy. While morality and religion were prioritized by the church, some children were also able to learn practical skills such as civic organization, defense, hunting, and weaving elsewhere. Education was focused more on rote memorization and less on understanding.

However, the social hierarchy changed significantly by the end of the medieval period. The gears of the society were turned more by clerks and bureaucrats and less by thinkers and clerics. There were also a small number of private, secular schools in larger cities by the fourteenth century, though enrollment was typically quite low. For example, there were no more than a few dozen scholars at the launch of The King's School in 1329—the same school Isaac Newton attended between 1655 and 1660. Only at the turn of the twentieth century did this school house more than a hundred students. Most children who were not employed on farms sought an apprenticeship that taught trades such as milling or felting cloth.

Injecting Passion through Meaning

Medieval education was anchored in the Socratic method of polemic exploration. It was originally a spiritual exercise to define the correct rules of morality and to shed light on transcendental truths. Debate was construed as an important vehicle of discovery and was not intended as a tool to match wits with someone else. While it was certainly a worthy pursuit at the time of Socrates, it had unfortunately degenerated over time into an empty academic exercise that was disconnected from everyday affairs or purpose.

By and large, there wasn't much fresh thinking in early education until the dawn of the Renaissance, with the notable exception of Ibn Sina. Ibn Sina, also known as Avicenna, was one of the very few thinkers from the medieval Islamic world (c. 980–1037 CE) who thought extensively about the significance of early education. This led him to promote a relatively streamlined program. He wanted children to be exposed to the Quran, literature, Islamic ethics, and some basic practical skills in a primary school between the ages of six and fourteen. He was not in favor of private tutors as he felt that children would benefit more in a group setting through emulation, competition, and group discussions. He trusted teachers to carefully design and customize empirical experiences so children could efficiently tease out universal concepts and develop a good foundation in reasoning and complex thinking. He viewed secondary education as a period of specialization for older students that should be personalized based on aptitude and interests. He was one of the first to pay attention to the complexity of students' chosen subjects, their competencies in these subjects, and their emotional development. This was a rather progressive view for his time. We don't find this level of customization in many schools even today, especially the emphasis on all-round development.

In Europe, the Renaissance ushered in the first serious challenge to medieval education. The poet John Milton (1608–1674) provided an interesting narrative on the prevailing educational issues in that era with his work "Of Education," though some vestiges of medieval concerns such as personal redemption remained. The growing gaps between entrenched pedantic educational practices and practical social needs fueled a lot of soul searching. Milton was quite alarmed that we were squandering the precious minds of children. He proposed drastic changes to both the content of the curriculum and its organization to promote greater engagement. Like Ibn Sina, Milton also felt that the study of philosophy and metaphysics early in a child's education was not appropriate. He believed that education should begin with sensorial pursuits such as the arts and literature and then progress to the more abstract disciplines such as logic and philosophy. The curriculum Milton proposed was quite vast. His list did include subjects that were traditional at the time, such as grammar, mathematics, astronomy, ethics, literature, logic, and theology. However, they also included other new and more practical subjects such as agriculture, geography, physics, economics, politics, and law. He was a humanist for whom education was a vehicle for realization of all the ideals contemplated by medieval thinkers.

John Locke (1632–1704), a contemporary of Milton, was arguably the most effective reformer of his time. He was a lot more successful than Milton in raising awareness of the need for extensive reform in education, with respect to both curriculum and teaching methods. His 1693 treatise, *Some Thoughts Concerning Education*, remained the most influential statement on educational philosophy through the end of the eighteenth century. In addition to English, several editions were also published in French, Italian, German, Dutch, and Swedish. It won critical acclaim from a broad array of contemporary thinkers across the political spectrum, including even from those who disagreed with various aspects of his philosophy. Interestingly, several of his ideas were not entirely novel. His emphasis on utilitarian subjects like the applied sciences and on challenges from the new world order and the changing economic conditions were borrowed from peers like Milton.

Locke's most prominent contribution was his advocacy of the "tabula rasa" (blank slate) model for the mind of a child. Like Ibn Sina, he firmly believed that a child's mind was like a blank slate that did not contain any innate ideas but was waiting to be defined and developed through experiences. He felt that education determined 90 percent of who we become. He was opposed to the religious view of human conception in sin as well as the premise behind the Cartesian dualism that we need to already "know" basic logic at birth to be able to connect mind and matter. In his view, infants are extremely impressionable, and we should take great pains to foster the correct association of ideas in them. His book, *An Essay Concerning Human Understanding*, is often cited as the foundational document of the "blank slate" or "empty pail" view. Locke warned against letting "a foolish maid" convince a child that "goblins and sprites" are associated with the darkness, for "darkness shall ever afterwards bring with it those frightful ideas, and they shall be so joined, that he can no more bear the one than the other."[6] Interestingly, even as he promoted his "tabula rasa" view of the mind, he did believe in some role for genetics. He advised parents to study the nature and aptitudes of their children so they could tailor an appropriate curriculum for them.

At a high level, Locke outlined three distinct objectives for education: the development of a healthy body, the building of a virtuous character, and the formulation of a customized academic curriculum. First, Locke, who was trained as a physician, viewed the physical health of children as at least as important as or even more important than their academic pursuits. He urged parents to carefully cultivate appropriate physical habits and training in their children and to pay the utmost attention to their physical health and endurance. Second, he valued virtue as our ability to prioritize the common good through a combination of self-control and delayed gratification. He repeatedly advocated reasoned thinking and habits over rules and authority. Locke's disciplinary system was founded on esteem and disgrace rather than on rewards and punishments. His thoughts closely resembled those of Confucius. Locke was also convinced that children can reason earlier in life than we give them credit for. Given the significance Locke attributed to education in determining who we become, it's not surprising that he also favored exposing children to knowledge of the real world to a degree that is both appropriate and educational. Thus, in his view, educational metrics and objectives should be designed to enable children to grow up into healthy, virtuous, responsible, and productive adults as quickly as possible. Also, despite occasional curricular suggestions, Locke was less focused on content and placed more emphasis on building a thirst for knowledge and instilling critical thinking and reasoning skills.

Locke's work was truly foundational and had an immense influence on many educational thinkers for centuries. Clearly, his reforms made education a lot more meaningful than what it was in the Middle Ages. Reorientation of educational priorities to rekindle passion for life's work and purpose is a familiar and recurring theme through the centuries, but it was during the Renaissance that it resulted in its biggest pivot.

The Arrival of the Factory

Modern, formal, classroom-based learning for all children only began in the early nineteenth century and has since spread around the world. The birth of this factory model of education came as an answer to the needs of the Industrial Revolution. It isn't commonly recognized that the factory model of uniform and structured education for about fifteen years of a child's life is a relatively new phenomenon. Historically, few outside the aristocracy were able to afford the personalized education provided by professional tutors. Most of the population in earlier periods received either some education at home or none at all, especially in their formative years. Older children would have trained as apprentices in various trades. Even the few who received formal education in reading, writing, and math spent time learning other skills and crafts. And when they attended a school, they were often in a single classroom with children of different ages. Until the Industrial Revolution, education was therefore somewhat responsive to the individual needs of children.

Using a relatively rigid curriculum, age-based classes, and metrics for progression from one grade level to the next, factory-style schools enabled efficient and affordable monitorial system schooling for most children. Most of these schools were initially available only to boys. Girls eventually began to be admitted during the early to mid-nineteenth century. In this system, efficiency and enrollment were increasingly valued more than the needs of individual children. The fact that these schools allowed both parents to work was a huge attraction. Factory-style classrooms offered an irresistible value for a large fraction of the population. For the first time, children had access to both a supervised environment and a structured curriculum at an affordable cost. Figuratively, the back door of the "cells and bells" school was expected to lead to the front door of the factory. Educational priorities have remained largely beholden to the needs of the business world since then.

Figure 3.1. An artist's rendering of a factory school in the mid-19th century.

While the duration of formal education varied significantly depending on factors such as geographic location, socioeconomic status, and cultural norms, many received only a few years of schooling until the end of the nineteenth century. The typical duration of compulsory education in most industrialized nations during the twentieth century ranged from six to twelve years, with some countries gradually increasing it to nine or ten years as the century progressed. Over time, technological and other forms of "progress" fueled a demand for increasing specialization and ever more advanced skills. Layers were added between the original "school" and the factory to extend the duration of education for those deemed qualified.

This was of course a gradual process that can be traced back to the development of universities as centers of advanced learning. One of the earliest such gatherings sprang up sometime before the sixth century BCE at Takshasila (in present-day Pakistan on the Indian subcontinent). Religious and philosophical studies made up a significant part of its curriculum, but various fine arts, archery, and hunting were also believed to have been taught in addition to law, medicine, and military topics. Takshasila even had courses on the art of discovering hidden treasures as well as encryption and decryption. It had Hindu, Buddhist, and Greek populations coexisting over the course of about ten centuries. The destruction of the city around the fifth century CE by the central Asian nomadic tribes led to the eventual demise of this protouniversity.

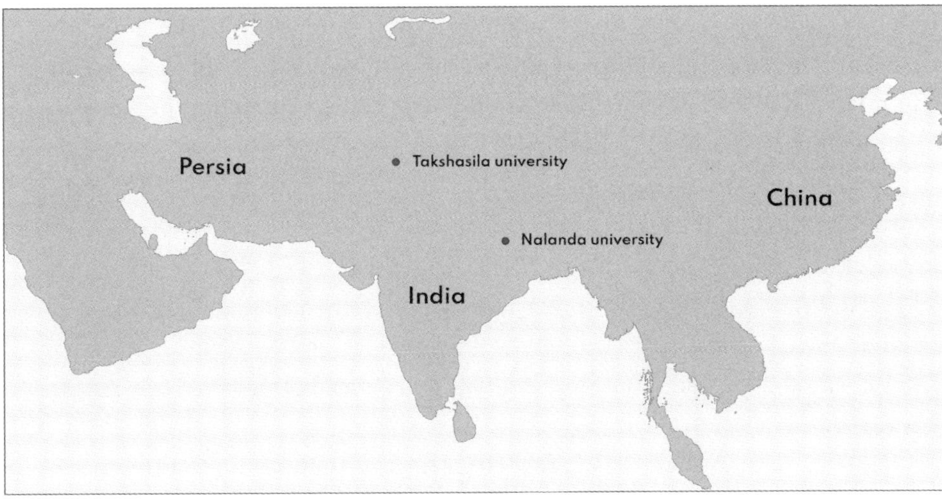

Figure 3.2. Takshasila is in present-day Pakistan; Nalanda is in northeastern India.

Around 450 CE, about the time of Takshasila's decline, a rather elaborate university was established by Kumaragupta, an emperor from the Gupta dynasty, at Nalanda, in today's state of Bihar in India. This university was a lot more representative of modern universities than Takshasila was. At one point, it is believed to have accommodated between three thousand and ten thousand students and fifteen hundred teachers, with pupils and scholars drawn from around India, today's Pakistan, China, the Tibetan and Korean regions, Japan, Iran, Turkey, and even Indonesia.[7] Even though Buddhist studies occupied a prominent place at Nalanda, it had a truly secular curriculum, and students pursued a broad range of subjects such as the fine arts, medicine, mathematics, astronomy, politics, and the art of war. The university itself was considered an architectural accomplishment. Within the grounds of the university, there were eight separate compounds, many temples, meditation halls, classrooms, lakes, and parks. One of its most notable buildings was a nine-story library, known as Dharma Gunj or Mountain of Truth. Librarians produced and maintained meticulous copies of its hundreds of thousands of volumes. In 1193, Nalanda was sacked by Bakhtiyar Khilji, a Turk ruler. This destruction led to a significant loss of ancient Indian scientific thought in mathematics, astronomy, alchemy, and anatomy.

The successes of Takshasila and Nalanda signified a healthy respect for the pursuit of all knowledge: domestic and foreign, secular and spiritual. Their patronage also signified broader recognition of the role a large university can play in social discourse and development. It's difficult to find a city in India today that does not have a school or college named after Nalanda, compelling evidence of its enduring legacy.

Other universities established in the five or six centuries after Nalanda's founding include the University of Karueein in Fez, Morocco, in 859 CE, the University of Bologna in Italy in 1088 CE, and Oxford University in England in 1096 CE. Many of these universities were centers of excellence in both religious and secular learning. Over the years, graduates of these universities became highly sought-after scholars and specialists across their respective regions.

As the demand for specialized careers grew, admission to universities became increasingly selective. Over time, universities also began to influence the curriculum and focus of the middle and high schools that prepared children for these higher studies. The requirements of these colleges (instead of the factories) increasingly became the guideposts for most K–12 schools.

The Child Is Given a Voice

Not surprisingly, the proliferation of factory education has led to criticism of the heavy emphasis schools placed on the employability of their students. Critics as diverse as Albert Einstein and Allan Bloom, the American philosopher and academic, have expressed concern that educational institutions have been unduly influenced by the forces of capitalism. They were quite critical of factory-style educational institutions that prioritize information acquisition over meaningful learning and growth, arguing that there is inadequate focus on the needs of individual children, deeper learning, and ethical considerations and conundrums. Frustration with traditional schools began to channel increasing energy toward alternative approaches. While factory-style education brought schooling to the masses, other, more innovative approaches began to sprout.

Friedrich Fröbel (1782–1852), a prominent nineteenth-century German educator, was one of the first to try to adapt education to the unique needs and capabilities of children.[8] He published *Die Menschenerziehung* ("The Education of Man" or "Human Education") in 1826 and is best remembered as the creator of the kindergarten. Fröbel was a big believer in the potential of a child. He felt that just as we let young plants and animals develop on their own, we ought to let children explore and flourish with agency and not treat them as pieces of clay or wax to be molded according to our priorities. He was a strong proponent of active learning through self-discovery. He believed that we need freedom of will as well as a passion for the task at hand to be able to truly engage and explore. This was one of the primary reasons he was so fascinated with play. He felt that children in typical classroom settings were too robotic, blindly followed orders, and didn't employ enough of their own inclinations and faculties. For Fröbel, the true purpose of education was to help children develop into perceiving and thinking beings.

Fröbel's insights into the importance of activity led him to the concept of "free work" (*Freiarbeit*) and to an emphasis on play as a dominant learning style in childhood. This understanding, in turn, led to the need to assess the educational worth of different kinds of play. Fröbel's passion and convictions propelled him to begin manufacturing educational play materials in 1836. These geometric building and activity blocks came to be known as "Fröbel gifts." In collaboration with Wilhelm Middendorf and Heinrich Langethal, Fröbel founded a Play and Activity Institute in 1837. In 1840, he coined the term *kindergarten* to describe his institute. Singing, dancing, gardening, and child-directed play with Fröbel gifts were often the curriculum at the first kindergarten. In Fröbel's view, these gifts should aid children in internalizing the external and externalizing the internal, helping them seek unity between their needs and the environment. Fröbel's kindergartens sprang up across parts of Europe and eventually spread to the US and the rest of the world. While kindergarten has become a familiar entity to most people around the world, its nature, however, varies greatly. It is limited to a few hours a day or a few days a week in some cases and is a full-fledged five-day program in others. While kindergarten is the first entry into a formal classroom outside the home for most children, a growing number are also entering kindergarten after having spent a year or two in a preschool.

Figure 3.3. An artist's rendering of Fröbel's gifts.

The concept of kindergarten has been well received almost from inception. In turn, the popularity of kindergartens fueled a spurt of innovations in early education over the next century. Rudolf Steiner (1861–1925), an Austrian philosopher, was one such innovator who is best known for the Waldorf system of schools. These schools were based on Steiner's understanding of the prominent developmental stages—an experiential stage from birth until about seven years of age, an imaginative stage until about twelve to fourteen, and the development of the intellect and a capacity for abstract thought thereafter. Steiner claimed that a young child is mostly driven by curiosity and has a strong impulse to imitate until about the age of seven. This child, according to Steiner, learns best from practical and sensory activities and needs a secure and healthy environment. At about age seven, Steiner felt that children desire the security afforded by the authority of a teacher and that they begin to be very imaginative. He also strongly felt that cooperation is a much more desirable behavioral trait than competition. According to him, abstract thought and the capacity for complex judgments and emotions required for compassion only begin to develop when young people enter adolescence at about twelve to fourteen. He also strongly believed that children's intellect and nascent notions of fairness and judgment should be appropriately supported and stimulated. Steiner was greatly influenced by Johann Wolfgang von Goethe (1749–1832)—Germany's literary genius and equivalent of Shakespeare—who argued that thinking is as much an organ of perception as the eyes or ears in the sense that we cannot correctly perceive ideas without good thinking capabilities.

Guided free play with simple toys that encourage multiuse and creativity, outdoor play time, group singing, story time, and celebration of local festivals are typical in a Waldorf curriculum for the experiential learners in the first stage. Access to recorded music, television, and computers is generally discouraged for these early learners. The Waldorf system employs various arts and crafts—the visual and performing arts such as singing, instrumental music, and drama—to channel the emotional development of the imaginative children in the second stage. Eurythmy, a form of artistic movement, is an important element in a Waldorf education. Most Waldorf schools also try to ensure that one teacher stays with a class through all the elementary years, at least for the primary subjects. Steiner believed that this promotes a productive relationship between teacher and students. Waldorf teachers believe that a child must be ready to receive before he or she can learn a new skill or master a subject. They therefore do not have goals for time-bound mastery of new skills.

In addition to the introduction of specialized teachers for different academic subjects, secondary education at Waldorf also emphasizes creative thinking and social responsibility. Students continue to take courses in the performing arts, music, and various crafts. They also begin to engage in some competitive team sports. Cultivation of the imagination and creative thinking abilities is an important component of a Waldorf education, not simply through its curriculum but also through its governance structures. Teachers are given considerable latitude to be agents of creativity. In fact, Waldorf schools are run by a college of teachers and a board of trustees, not by a principal or head teacher. The Waldorf schools are thus consistent in their promotion of individual empowerment, which can be helpful for the promotion of creativity.

Waldorf schools also have a reputation for cultivating the values of global citizenship such as compassion, tolerance, and social responsibility through their emphasis on collaboration and rational thinking. The pioneering work of these schools in building integrated communities in Israel and South

Africa, cutting across the Arab-Jewish and black-white divides in extremely challenging environments, attests to their focus on global citizenship and compassion.

Since the establishment of the first school in Stuttgart, Germany, for employees of the Waldorf-Astoria cigarette factory in 1919, Waldorf has steadily grown in popularity. There are now about a thousand independent Waldorf schools and fifteen hundred kindergartens in over sixty countries, in addition to other Waldorf-based public and private schools. The leap from Fröbel's humble kindergarten to the comprehensive Waldorf model illustrates how child-centered education began to garner a growing mindshare.

This movement toward child-centered education received a big boost with the arrival of Maria Montessori (1870–1952), the architect of the Montessori method. She is from a select group of educational thinkers with arguably the highest name recognition. She was an engineer, a psychiatrist, a philosopher, a passionate educator, a devout Catholic, and also the first female doctor in Italy.

As a student of psychiatry, Montessori was fascinated by the models of scientific education being pursued by French physicians Jean Itard and Edouard Séguin for educating children with special needs. Her subsequent investigations caught the attention of the Minister of Education in Italy and led to her appointment as the director of Scuola Ortofrenica, an institution responsible for the care of children with learning disabilities. Shocking many academicians and politicians alike, several eight-year-old "mentally disabled" students in her program managed to secure above-average scores on Italian State examinations. Fueled by her extraordinary success, her initial interest in educating children with disabilities quickly morphed into a deeper curiosity about the true potential of all children. Itard's observations on a child's natural activities and Séguin's exercises with self-correcting teaching materials stimulated Montessori's research into education for all children.

When she was asked to set up a daycare center for young children in a low-income housing project in Rome, she seized the opportunity. In 1907, she opened "Casa dei Bambini" (Children's House), her first school. Montessori soon saw something remarkable in her classrooms—children appeared to be transformed from their typical selves. They were engrossed in their work and the classrooms were very orderly and serene. Recognizing the amazing transformation in the behavior of these children, Montessori surmised that she had discovered the true nature of children. She saw a natural thirst for self-directed exploration. Montessori concluded that teachers should be unobtrusive observers who only have occasional interactions with the children to gauge their level of mastery, introduce new lessons, or address behavioral issues.

Montessori identified four different stages of development that she called "Planes of Development." These are very similar to the stages identified by Steiner. The first plane extends from birth to six years of age. Montessori believed that children are sensitive or receptive to sensory stimuli, the acquisition of language, and order and harmony in this plane. Typical lessons include Sensorial, Practical Life, Language, and Math subjects. In the second plane, children between six and twelve are capable of abstract reasoning, rich imagination, social sensibility, and compassion. Students are now exposed to more conventional texts and writing exercises, and they are believed to be less sensitive to physical stimuli. According to Montessori, the child is ready to fully appreciate the complex relationships in his or her environment in the third plane, extending from twelve to eighteen. The fourth plane involves the final integration and maturation of the adolescent in the adult environment.

Montessori believed that every child develops a capacity for self-discipline, independence, and social harmony through repeated episodes of deep concentration, focusing primarily on activities of their choice. She called this "Normalization" and believed that all children can achieve such an ordered mind by the time they turn six. A key driver for enabling this mastery, according to her, is young children's spongelike "Absorbent Mind."

While multiple strains of the Montessori method have evolved over time, several signature concepts are common to all Montessori methods. All Montessori classrooms are prepared environments that employ "autodidactic" teaching materials. They often have accessible furniture, utensils, work materials, and restrooms. The material in a Montessori classroom is organized by subject and level of difficulty. Aesthetics and order are important elements in a Montessori classroom. Montessori material is rarely revised, and many use the same apparatus that Maria Montessori originally developed. The Montessori method respects children's independence and lets them choose their own lessons, albeit with minor supervision to ensure that these lessons have been properly introduced.

Figure 3.4. An artist's rendering of a Montessori classroom.

Many Montessori parents believe that limited availability of objects of each kind in a classroom and the requirement that students can only use material that has been properly introduced help promote delayed gratification. In addition, the potential for frustration and disputes between children helps create opportunities for practicing peaceful conflict resolution.

Montessori schools also encourage parents to foster a Montessori environment at home that respects and enables a child's independence. To promote such independence, the Montessori system refers to most children's activities as "work," not "play." This is primarily to emphasize that their efforts are meaningful and rooted in purposeful reality. Finally, Maria Montessori believed children learn faster by watching and interacting with their peers and with those who are a little older. Hence, all Montessori classrooms are expected to be made up of mixed age groups: ages two to six in Plane 1 and six to twelve in Plane 2, for example.

About sixty years after Maria Montessori founded her first school, a new child-centered pedagogy took root in the preschools in the municipality of Reggio Emilia in Italy. Parents in the villages around Reggio Emilia began to adopt an innovative approach developed by pedagogist Loris Malaguzzi.

Malaguzzi's philosophy grew from his core belief that children construct new knowledge and understanding through experiences and relationships. The emphasis is therefore more on producing the right learning conditions than on producing learning. As such, exploration, play, and community interactions are key features of this methodology. As key stakeholders, Reggio Emilia children have a significant say in the direction of their learning. Another key tenet of this philosophy is the belief that children speak "a hundred languages" to express themselves. A primary goal of the Reggio Emilia approach is therefore to help the child fluently navigate between the many symbolic languages and modalities of communication (drama, art, poetry, and more). In addition, a lot of emphasis is placed on the environment and the climate.

Figure 3.5. An artist's rendering of children's hundred languages.

Interestingly, Malaguzzi even referred to the physical environment as the "third teacher"; he believed it was as important as the adults and other students. Abiding faith in the competence of children and in their potential and ambition and Malaguzzi's approach led to a proliferation of the Reggio Emilia schools in Italy.[9]

While teachers enjoy exceptional autonomy, Reggio Emilia schools also have a well-established tradition of close collaboration between teachers, parents, and children; the child is trusted as an active participant in the learning process. Thus, the transition from home to school is often seamless for preschoolers and their parents. In addition to being advocates for their children, parents are encouraged to take part in discussions on school policy, budgetary allocations, curriculum planning, and program evaluations. Most of the learning in Reggio Emilia typically takes place through child-initiated projects. And since Reggio Emilia teachers believe that the environment is a key ingredient in the education of a child, every aspect of the environment in a school is carefully curated. Most Reggio Emilia classrooms have clearly designated studio spaces for small- and large-group activities. Wall-sized windows, courtyards and other open spaces, open kitchen areas, welcoming entrances, accessible and interesting materials, and displays of children's project work are some of the common features of a Reggio Emilia school. The environment is expected to inform and engage the children as well as the adults. Finally, teachers in Reggio Emilia schools use a variety of tools to document the daily activities of their students and make learning as visible as possible. The children typically maintain a portfolio with samples of their work, which are often a source of great pride to them.

Figure 3.6. Strong relationships at Sankalpa Academy were the bedrock of learner empowerment.

There are also some interesting opportunities and challenges with the Reggio Emilia approach. One key difference versus other approaches is that a child's ability to negotiate in a peer group is a vital element of the learning process. Also, given the high degree of freedom and customization, it is not uncommon for teachers to begin projects without a clear understanding of where they might end. Finally, to authentically mimic true world learning, teachers are expected to embrace confusing experiences and to even intentionally allow mistakes to happen.

Much of the popularity of the Reggio Emilia approach can be traced to the touring exhibition titled "A Child Has 100 Languages: On Creative Pedagogy at Public Kindergartens in Reggio Emilia, Italy," which opened in 1981 at the Modern Museet in Stockholm, Sweden. Even by 1991, the Reggio Emilia approach had grown so much that *Newsweek* recognized it as one of the leading preschool systems in the world.[10]

One major difference between the Reggio Emilia and the Montessori and Waldorf approaches is that the Reggio Emilia philosophy, at least to date, has been largely limited to the preschool and kindergarten levels. A Schoolwide Enrichment Model (SEM) developed by Joseph Renzulli of the University of Connecticut can perhaps be considered a natural extension of the Reggio Emilia approach to the higher grades. Renzulli's approach is based on a novel three-ring model that looks at ability, creativity, and task commitment to measure giftedness.[11] Since he believes that all children can and should pursue more rigorous content, he argues that schools should provide all students with the opportunities needed to develop higher-order thinking skills and intelligences. SEM seeks to provide gifted education through enriched learning experiences and higher learning standards for all children. It also supports child-led exploration through enrichment clusters. SEM uses personalized talent development, a broad array of enrichment experiences, and targeted advanced follow-up opportunities based on children's strengths and passions to better engage the learners and educators. Many SEM schools have also been using technology to create individual profiles of each student's interests, strengths, and learning styles. This process also often identifies additional resources for extending and improving aspects of the regular curriculum.

Figure 3.7. At Sankalpa Academy, we actively sought to broaden the experiences of our children.

Since the Reggio Emilia approach has been largely limited to preschool and kindergarten children, its impact on long-term student outcomes has not been easy to assess. On the other hand, there have been numerous studies on Montessori and Waldorf children. Over the years, several studies have suggested that the Montessori approach to K–12 education can result in superior academic outcomes, relative to a traditional curriculum.[12] The Waldorf approach has also had a very positive reception. Many entrepreneurs and executives in Silicon Valley, for instance, are known to send their children to Waldorf schools that shun the use of gadgets such as laptops and tablets. Despite their commendable success and popularity in many countries, Montessori and Waldorf schools have struggled to gain mainstream acceptance in the United States beyond the kindergarten and early grade levels. On the other hand, while there is little data on the long-term educational outcomes of children from schools that have embraced SEM, it has been gaining significant popularity in recent years. As of 2019, SEM has been implemented in over four thousand schools across the US, and aspects of this approach have been implemented in Europe, Asia, and South and Central America.[13]

Catering to the Whole Child

The Montessori, Waldorf, and Reggio Emilia approaches give the child a larger-than-usual role in his or her education, but their focus is still on children's intellectual development. While these approaches often also benefit some aspects of a child's socioemotional development, they don't generally provide a targeted program for each child's physical, social, emotional, and ethical well-being.[14] There are, of course, isolated examples of schools that cater to the needs of individual children. The Students' Educational and Cultural Movement of Ladakh (SECMOL) Alternative School that Sonam Wangchuk and others helped create in 1987 is one from this select club.[15] While it is an outlier, if we broaden our search to include other cultures and time periods, we will likely turn up more examples of educational systems that had a stronger focus on the development of the whole child.

The gurukul system in ancient India is another good example (*gurukul* literally means the family of the teacher) of such a system. This tradition of residential study was the prevailing model of education in India by the sixth century BCE. The gurus, or the teachers in these schools, were expected to cater to each child's individual needs. Children typically arrived when they were as young as seven or eight and stayed for about twelve years at their teacher's house, often for months to years at a stretch. In addition to their studies, the children were expected to help with the household chores. Ancient texts placed the gurus at a much higher level of esteem than the biological parents of a child. These master teachers designed experiences that contributed to the physical, mental, intellectual, and spiritual growth of each child. In addition to studying religious texts, children were taught a wide variety of subjects—all primarily using an oral tradition. The gurukul system is a very revolutionary idea in today's social context. Delegating children's education was perhaps acceptable then since only a small percentage of the population was able to educate their children anyway. Interestingly, as education became more universal, most modern societies have increasingly taken a more parochial and insular view, seeking to shape children in their own likeness.

Figure 3.8. An artist's view of a morning in one Indian gurukul.

Plato (c. 428–348 BCE) and his student Aristotle (384–322 BCE)—two of the earliest known philosophers who expounded on the role of education—had also recognized the significance of individual needs and all-round development. Their view that the goal of education is social progress and justice through individual excellence prevails to this day. Plato, widely regarded as one of the pioneers in the field of basic education, felt that elementary education should be wholesome and include both known facts and practical skills, physical rigor through gymnastics, and sensitivity through music and art. Similarly, Aristotle believed that education must be cognizant of human nature and that it should help cultivate good habits and reasoning abilities. Aristotle also emphasized a balance between the theoretical and the practical to produce holistic development. While Plato's approach to taking children away from their parents was similar to the gurukul system in India, the objectives were very different. The gurukul system focused more on the needs of the individual children and on shaping and developing them, while Plato advocated investing in only those children who could further the needs of his republic.

Holistic development is vital since few would dispute that intellectual development alone is insufficient for success in life. This is why, for example, people have also been grappling with questions about the nature of intelligence for many centuries. Even though experts have long moved past unequivocal reliance on IQ and now believe that we need multiple intelligences to be successful in life, there is little consensus beyond this general recognition. Complex epistemological questions about the nature of intelligence will likely continue to be subjects of active research for a long time.

A name often associated with the idea that there are multiple intelligences is Howard Gardner (1943–), a well-known American developmental psychologist who argues that a child can be at very different stages of development in different areas at any given time. For example, she can be quite mature in grasping numbers, but still rather immature in visual perception. Gardner has come up with seven criteria for a behavior to be considered an intelligence.[16] According to him, any intelligence must show potential for brain isolation by brain damage, have a place in evolutionary history, be supported by the presence of core operations, show susceptibility to encoding (symbolic expression), be a distinct developmental progression, require the existence of savants, prodigies, and other exceptional people, and be supported by experimental psychology and psychometric findings. Gardner identified eight abilities that he feels would meet these criteria: musical - rhythmic, visual - spatial, verbal - linguistic, logical - mathematical, bodily - kinesthetic, interpersonal, intrapersonal, and naturalistic. However, several studies have found that at least some of Gardner's intelligences correlate with each other, implying that there are fewer streams of intelligence underneath some of these seemingly disparate abilities.[17]

Regardless, there is enough evidence for most researchers to now believe in multiple independent intelligences, the existence of individual differences, and a significant role for culture and environment in the development of intelligences. It is believed, for example, that language and music are indicative of an interplay between intelligence and the cultural context and that they are not simply indicators of cognitive abilities. This implies that there is both an empirical and an academic basis for investing in the development of the whole child. From ancient thinkers to modern thought leaders and reformers, and from the gurukul system to the Montessori, Waldorf, Reggio Emilia, and SEM philosophies, there have been several attempts, with varying degrees, at child-centered, holistic education.

The Reform of the Factory

While Montessori and Waldorf have demonstrated superior outcomes through approaches that give learners meaningful agency, they have not been able to significantly sway the juggernaut of mainstream factory education. Similarly, though there has been a lot of talk about holistic education, there hasn't been enough progress in its adoption. One likely reason for this is that most educational systems are too complex to accept large makeovers. This is probably why educators who have offered proposals for incremental reform have been more successful in improving the factory model. As a result, even though the high-level form and function have persevered, there have been many innovations in curriculum and education-delivery mechanisms during the last century that attempted to render traditional schools more efficient and relevant.

A key leader in this reform movement was John Dewey (1859–1952). Dewey attempted to strike a balance between the traditional social imperative for delivering knowledge and the larger need for experiential education through active learning. While he was opposed to the traditional authoritarian role for teachers, he also did not agree with some streams of progressive education that left almost no role for them. He believed that schooling was unnecessarily long and restrictive. Dewey had a gift for suggesting activities that captured the essence of what his students were expected to learn. He believed that the formation of an individual was an inextricably communal process and similarly that there could not be a community that was divorced from its citizens.

Dewey was a prolific writer who wrote on a variety of topics, including epistemology, psychology, aesthetics, democracy, logic, education, and humanism, over a forty-year-long career. While his views were broadly popular, they only gained limited traction in US public schools during his lifetime. His use of commonplace words to express uncommon and complex concepts, dense writing, and the length of his career made it easy for people to quote him on all sides of most debates. Also, since Dewey was focused on the educational challenges of the day, his writings from 1900 were occasionally at odds with his writings from 1940. However, over time, his writings succeeded in challenging the status quo and leaving a significant mark on mainstream education. His influence helped move schools away from recitation and rote memorization toward discussions, analysis, and problem solving. Dewey had argued that this was necessary to create an engaged community of learners.

Another pioneer whose research has had a wide-ranging impact on public education is Jean Piaget (1896–1980). Piaget was a Swiss epistemologist and a contemporary of Maria Montessori. He became interested in epistemology when he worked briefly at a street school in Paris run by Alfred Binet, creator of the Stanford-Binet Intelligence Scale. After his return to Switzerland in 1921 as director of the Rousseau Institute and after the birth of his own children, his interest in knowledge acquisition and the developmental stages of children deepened.

Piaget saw intellectual development as the result of harmonization between assimilation and accommodation. He came up with four different developmental stages to explain his observations: the sensorimotor stage from birth to age two, characterized by understanding and interacting with their environment in a purely physical manner; the preoperational stage from ages two to seven, marked by the development of language, symbolic thought, and imaginative thinking; the concrete operational stage from ages seven to twelve, recognized by the development of logical and literal thinking as well as some capacity for empathy; and the formal operational stage for those older than twelve, characterized by the capacity for abstract thought, deductive reasoning, and problem solving. Piaget's preoperational, concrete, and formal stages of development are based on a sequential model of development. He argued that children need to master skills at their level of mental ability before they can progress and build concepts and structures of higher order and complexity.

Piaget also explored questions of genetic epistemology through four separate models based on sociology, biology, formal logic, and figurative thought. As children became socially aware, he noticed, for example, that their answers to his questions changed from being intuitive to being factual and were eventually designed to be socially acceptable. This also mirrored their evolution from egocentrism to sociocentrism. Piaget believed that the biology of adaptation has a critical impact, through assimilation and accommodation, on intellectual development. As children assimilate new inputs, these can sometimes conflict with already-established schemas in their minds. They therefore constantly need to reconcile new learning with already established mental structures. This, Piaget claimed, is what fuels intellectual growth.

Piaget's work greatly influenced the evolution of modern Western education and helped encourage child-centered approaches. He repeatedly emphasized that the goal of education should not be to turn children into carbon copies of typical or even successful adults in contemporary society. For him, the mission was to empower children to become creators and innovators and not conformists. Piaget also made significant contributions to our understanding of the role of peers in the intellectual and moral development of children. He argued that children can learn more in cooperative groups as they impose fewer intellectual demands and constraints than in authoritative interactions, as with teacher-led instruction.[18]

While Piaget brought a much deeper understanding of children's developmental stages to the table than many of his predecessors had, several researchers questioned the simplicity of his claims, especially that knowledge hangs together in a structured whole at any given developmental stage. Also, Piaget did not sufficiently consider historical and cultural factors as he was more interested in the "epistemic" subject and not as much in individual differences. Moreover, since he believed that development was a universal process, he did not pay as much attention to sample size as he should have. For instance, his understanding of infant development was primarily based on observations of his own three children.[19] Regardless, Piaget's findings were a huge leap forward in our understanding of child development and were responsible for many improvements in our educational practices. His concept of developmental stages and biological maturation led to the acceptance of the notion of the "readiness" of a child for a lesson. This, in turn, led to increased understanding of windows of opportunity, use of formative assessments, and overall individualization. Piaget's concept of assimilation and accommodation also encouraged more active learning and group work.

The work of Dewey, Piaget, and numerous other epistemologists and child-development researchers has inspired the creation of numerous innovative curriculums. The Advanced Placement (AP) courses from the College Board, the Vienna-based International Baccalaureate (IB) programs, and the programs from Cambridge University are some notable examples of such curricular initiatives.[20]

AP classes initially focused on offering more advanced material and stressing information retention and memorization skills. However, the College Board revamped its approach and began to offer a more enriching Capstone program in 2014 that requires students to conduct independent research and present their findings and analyses. They now demand more engagement, intellectual rigor, and critical thinking than their initial offering.

At the same time, IB programs have emerged as an increasingly popular alternative to AP classes. They require in-depth understanding of subject matter through an inquiry-based approach.[21] IB offers three different programs: a Primary Years Program (PYP), a Middle Years Program (MYP), and a two-year Diploma program. The IB framework is known for its interdisciplinary units, personal and collaborative projects, deeper analyses, and global outlook. IB tries to pay attention to concepts as well as attitudes and actions. To promote academic rigor and international-mindedness, it has identified a learner profile with ten different attributes. IB encourages students to be inquirers, thinkers, communicators, risk-takers, knowledgeable, principled, caring, open-minded, well-balanced, and reflective. As of July 2022, this nonprofit educational foundation has worked with nearly two million students aged three to nineteen in over fifty-five hundred schools spread across about a hundred and sixty countries.

Mainstream factory education has indeed come a long way with more opportunities for critical thinking, deeper analysis, and need-based differentiation and interventions. This certainly represents progress. Even so, there is still a wide gap between the aspirations of programs like Montessori or Renzulli's SEM and systems like the gurukul on the one hand and what most modern public and private schools or programs like the AP and IB offer on the other. AP and IB programs lack a holistic curriculum and cannot fully cater to the needs of individual children. They are also expensive and hence not accessible to many students. Unfortunately, affordable and holistic child-centered K–12 education remains almost as elusive as ever.

The Rebels

Factory schools ushered in efficiencies that made it possible for millions of kids to get an education. For children with access, innovative approaches by Maria Montessori and Rudolf Steiner have been opportunities to take more ownership of their own learning, at least in the elementary grades. In addition to these well-known endeavors, there have also been pioneers and savants who championed significantly more ambitious programs. Their efforts have been focused not just on the needs of a child or community but on building a more harmonious and sustainable society for a broader set of stakeholders across generations.

The roots of these ambitious efforts run very deep. The sixth century BCE is one of the earliest such recorded periods of tremendous cultural revolution across much of the world. Evolution of our broader social priorities and educational objectives has been greatly influenced by the genius of many of the social thinkers, epistemologists, educational philosophers, and reformers of this period. The intellectual giants in this era include Pythagoras in Greece, Confucius in China, and Mahavir and Buddha in India. Socrates in Greece was also born just a century later.

Mahavir (born in 599 BCE as Vardhamana) was known for his ascetic lifestyle, his remarkable control over his thought, speech, and senses, and his role in the revival of Jainism, an ancient religion that predated Hinduism. Mahavir blamed excessive attachment to material possessions and worldly pursuits as the root cause of most human failing. Buddha (563 to about 483 BCE) was motivated by his thirst for understanding and desire to alleviate human suffering. He also concluded that attachment is one of the root causes of greed, envy, hatred, and other destructive tendencies. Buddha blamed our cognitive limitations for much of our suffering. He recommended a mindful analysis of our attachments so we can liberate ourselves from the clutches of everyday cravings. While both Buddha and Mahavir strongly advocated ahimsa—or nonviolence—and vegetarianism, the precepts of nonviolence toward all sentient beings and strict adherence to moral precepts such as truth and honesty took a stronger root in Jainism. Incidentally, both Mahavir and Buddha also believed that men and women are spiritual equals.

Confucius (551–479 BCE), one of the most remarkable and best-known Chinese philosophers, was born about a decade after Buddha. He was clearly a phenomenal social thinker and philosopher, whose thoughts on ethics, relationships, justice, and integrity have been the guiding force for Chinese society for many centuries. His life had striking similarities to that of Buddha. Both did not find peace in the life of a householder and left their young families. And both were more concerned about life on earth than about the hereafter. Confucius was fixated on the need for a just and harmonious society. He repeatedly emphasized the importance of knowledge and analysis and the need to think through difficult problems. Reflections on personal behavior, compassion, and self-control were much more important to him than any formal rituals. Confucius also had much in common with Socrates and Plato. He repeatedly pointed out that wisdom involved fully realizing what you know and what you don't. He encouraged flexibility and situational intelligence in ethical behavior in deciding what produces the greatest good for all. The Four Books and the Five Classics of Confucianism have been an important guiding force in Chinese education and thought across centuries.

Pythagoras (569–475 BCE), of the Pythagorean theorem fame, was a true rebel who left a significant impact on Western thought. He was also a close contemporary of Mahavir, Buddha, and Confucius. In *A History of Western Philosophy*, Bertrand Russell claims that Pythagoras should be considered the most influential of all Western philosophers. Pythagoras also ran an organization that represented a blend between a school and a monastery. His students (known as Pythagoreans) led a communal life that was remarkably austere, simple, regimented, and moral, with no individual ownership of property. They immersed themselves in ethics, philosophy, music, gymnastics, mathematics, and astronomy. Pythagoras was a leader and a pioneer in many respects; he had a profound impact on the prevailing social customs and belief systems. His efforts are all the more remarkable since the sixth century BCE was an era in which women were generally regarded as property. Yet, he insisted on and provided equal opportunities for men and women. Pythagoreans ate a primarily vegetarian diet for ethical and religious reasons. There is a strong parallel between the Pythagorean society and the gurukuls in India. Since the Pythagorean organization survived for hundreds of years and since Pythagoras and his followers are known to have traveled as far as India, it is also feasible that there was a deeper cultural exchange between these societies.

Another giant of this era and arguably one of the best-known philosophers ever is Socrates (469–399 BCE). Yet this pillar of Western philosophy is also one of the least understood and most enigmatic intellectuals of his time. The driving force of his life seems to have been his unflinching pursuit of understanding. Indeed, Socrates is known to have claimed that his self-awareness—especially of his ignorance—was one of the best indicators of his wisdom. He also strongly believed that everyone is virtuous at their core and that knowledge would help liberate this virtue and result in true happiness. This is, in fact, the basis for his Socratic method of investigation. The Socratic method has resulted in significant contributions to epistemology, logic, and scientific discovery. It is a practice that is still used in many classrooms today. It is also the foundation for most of the ensuing developments in Western philosophy. While the influence of Socrates can be felt even after all these centuries, his fearless pursuit of knowledge has unfortunately not been a common curricular objective, at least in recent decades.

Figure 3.9. An artist's rendering of a Pythagorean gathering.

Socrates, Pythagoras, Confucius, Buddha, and Mahavir had compelling life stories but limited success in shaping their own societies. However, they eventually came to be recognized as very influential thought leaders who made rich contributions to the foundations of philosophy, epistemology, ethics, culture, and education. Their explorations of human motivations and purpose have helped launch social belief systems that defined collective priorities for centuries to come. Yet, while Confucius's ideas about meritocracy have had a lasting impact on the educational system in China and the practices of Jainism and Buddhism have withstood the test of time, their teachings on ethics, morality, and personal exemplification rarely find a place in modern education. In fact, in many countries around the world, girls still cannot expect the same opportunities as boys. Further, while minimalists like Mahavir cautioned against overconsumption, messages such as these could not gain adequate traction in the broader society. Recent studies establishing a strong correlation between delayed gratification and positive life outcomes demonstrate the continued relevance of these teachings to our educational objectives.

Few others have held such sway over the broader social imagination as these giants from around the sixth century BCE. But it's not for lack of effort. Many have tried to impress on us the need for a more fulsome education, but with only limited success. Jiddu Krishnamurti (1895–1986), a contemporary and colleague of Rudolf Steiner, was one of the more recent thinkers who was able to create a bridge between his philosophy and the educational reform movement. Krishnamurti was adopted at a young age by Annie Besant, a British socialist, theosophist, and prolific author, as a protégé and eventually promoted as a messiah and world leader. At first, Krishnamurti's spiritual message greatly mirrored the worldview of the theosophists, but he began to come into his own as the years passed. Eventually, at an annual gathering in the Netherlands in 1929, he gave his famous Dissolution Speech in front of Annie Besant, three thousand odd followers, and an unknown number of radio listeners. He insisted that there cannot be a singular path to an absolute Truth and that everyone needs to find their own answers. He argued that any organized religion is therefore, by definition, inconsistent with a fearless search for Truth.

In later years, he turned his focus to school reform. Statements made by Krishnamurti in Ojai, California, in 1984 are very insightful and explain the crux of his message:

> Surely a school is a place where one learns about the totality, the wholeness of life. Academic excellence is absolutely necessary, but a school includes much more than that. It is a place where both the teacher and the taught explore not only the outer world, the world of knowledge, but also their own thinking, their own behavior. From this they begin to discover their own conditioning and how it distorts their thinking. This conditioning is the self to which such tremendous and cruel importance is given. Freedom from conditioning and its misery begins with this awareness. It is only in such freedom that true learning can take place. In this school, it is the responsibility of the teacher to sustain with the student a careful exploration into the implications of conditioning and thus end it.[22]

There are currently about twenty schools worldwide that are either managed by the Krishnamurti Foundation or claim to be inspired by his philosophy. Academic excellence, child-initiated learning, self-awareness, and a global outlook that promotes a deep affection between people everywhere are said to be the characteristics of his schools.[23]

While Krishnamurti and philosophers from the sixth century BCE advocated an overarching role for education that was cognizant of the broader social imperatives, there were others who favored a very limited, narrow role so the individual can even be a hermit if he or she so chooses. Jean-Jacques Rousseau (1712–1778), for instance, was one such extremely influential eighteenth-century educational thinker from Switzerland who, along with Locke, defined most of the discourse on childhood education in the eighteenth century. Rousseau described his educational methods in *Emile, or On Education*, an interesting portrayal of the education of a young boy. In *Emile*, Rousseau is very cynical of the corrupting influences of society on young children. He takes Emile to a country home to provide a healthy and idyllic environment for his education.

Rousseau insisted that our inclinations are our nature and that these should be held supreme above all else. He was a strong believer in universal and innate human virtues, ostensibly a prerequisite for objective morals. Rousseau limited the role of parents to creation and maintenance of the right environment and looked to children and their nature to solve the puzzles and problems presented in this environment, with little assistance from parents or tutors. Rousseau wanted the children to be more actively engaged and in charge of their own learning. They were expected to adapt to the presented environment. Rousseau had a minimalist vision of life that fell somewhat outside mainstream society and was focused more on the simple pursuits of the individual.

Like some of his peers, Rousseau recommended an age-appropriate education to make the best use of children's windows of opportunity. He was a proponent of a relevant, child-centered education. He believed that certain developmental processes were common to all humans, and accepted liberty, independence, and curiosity as the key drivers of the discovery process. He also regarded virtue as a key objective of education and valued critical thinking skills and reasoning over instruction by authority.

The clearest indication yet of the existence of strong dissatisfaction with the available educational options comes from the fact that a growing number of children are educated at home by their parents, private tutors, small networks of parents, and correspondence schools. In other words, the rebellion against prevailing state of affairs is not limited to individuals who might be considered outliers. Low educational standards in public schools, religious convictions, concerns over the environment and the peer culture in public schools, philosophical objections to teaching styles, lack of individual attention, and poor access are some commonly cited reasons for the popularity of homeschooling. While this is a universal phenomenon, interestingly, it appears to be more widespread in the developed world.

	ROUSSEAU		MONTESSORI		STEINER		PIAGET	
	Ages	**Characteristics**	**Ages**	**Characteristics**	**Ages**	**Characteristics**	**Ages**	**Characteristics**
STAGE 1	INFANCY (BIRTH – 2)	physical	EARLY CHILDHOOD (Birth - 6)	sensory practical early language early math	EXPERIENTIAL (Birth - 6)	practical sensory	SENSORIMOTOR (Birth - 2)	observant sensory
STAGE 2	CHILDHOOD (2 – 12)	sensory exemplary	CHILDHOOD (6 - 12)	abstract reasoning independence imagination empathy	ELEMENTARY (6 - 14)	language imagination empirical (through curiosity)	PREOPERATIONAL (2 - 7)	language symbolic thought imagination self-absorbed
STAGE 3	PRE-ADOLESCENCE (12 – 15)	empirical (through curiosity) intellectual imagination vocational	ADOLESCENCE (12 - 18)	emotional intelligence social sensibility building relationships	SECONDARY (14 - 21)	abstract reasoning emotional intelligence moral responsibility building relationships	CONCRETE OPERATIONAL (7 - 11)	logic literal thinking budding empathy
STAGE 4	ADOLESCENCE (15 – 20)	spiritual social moral (through experience) emotional	YOUNG ADULTHOOD (18 - 24)	fuller independence spiritual mooring self-concept identity			FORMAL OPERATIONAL (11 - Adulthood)	abstract thought deductive reasoning problem solving

Table 3.1. Key childhood stages as identified by Rousseau, Montessori, Steiner, and Piaget.

A key moment in its history came in the late 1960s when Raymond and Dorothy Moore investigated the validity of the claims made by the early childhood education movement.[24] They reviewed over eight thousand independent studies and came up with some startling findings. One interesting study, for example, showed that tribal children in Africa were socially and emotionally more mature, even by Western metrics, than typical Western children. Based on their observations, the Moores argued that formal education before the age of eight severely limited opportunities for emotional bonding with parents and siblings at home and led to juvenile delinquency, behavioral problems, nearsightedness, and a host of other problems. According to them, forcing children into restrictive formal environments when they are not yet ready for it often leads to emotional insecurity, frustration, and hyperactivity. This was a gap that could not be filled later as the children would have moved past the window of opportunity. They concluded that except for children in exceptional circumstances, most would fare better at home, even with mediocre parenting. With books such as *Better Late than Early*, *Home Grown Kids*, and *Homeschool Burnout*, they quickly became popular homeschooling advocates and consultants.[25]

Around the same time, in the mid-1960s, John Holt published two books, *How Children Fail* and *How Children Learn*, arguing that traditional schools subvert the natural learning processes of children and place an unreasonable burden on them.[26] While he had initially hoped to trigger a review and possibly an overhaul of our schools, he gradually realized that these institutions were a natural consequence of what society wanted and were unlikely to undergo any drastic changes. By 1980, he began to view homeschooling as intrinsically superior to even the best formal education, a claim that he first made in 1981 and expanded on with his coauthor in *Teach Your Own*.[27]

There are, however, concerns that adequate exposure to children from other ethnicities, religions, and socioeconomic or cultural backgrounds would be difficult for a homeschooled child. It would be a herculean task for parents to recreate the diversity of views that students typically encounter in a school. Regardless of these concerns, homeschooling appears to be increasingly legitimate in the eyes of many in mainstream society in the US and elsewhere. Interestingly, while Gallup polls in 1985 found that 73 percent of American voters opposed homeschooling, only 54 percent were opposed to homeschooling in 2001.[28] One study found that homeschooled children fare significantly better than children attending traditional schools.[29]

Another interesting study determined that while 50 percent of the children in conventional schools scored above the 50th percentile on the Piers-Harris Children's Self-Concept Scale, 89.7 percent of the homeschooled children scored at or above the 50th percentile.[30] Clearly, self-concept is a more pertinent metric for future success and a harbinger of positive socialization skills down the road than a measurement of the amount of early childhood social exposure. A study by the National Home Education Research Institute (NHERI) also found that homeschooled graduates exhibit significantly higher quality of life and levels of civic participation compared to those with traditional education.[31]

We can draw many lessons from the ambitious life stories of the trailblazers who sought to redefine education and social values. Through their deeply reflective lives, Buddha, Mahavir, Confucius, and Pythagoras exemplified delayed gratification. They taught us that a strong ethical mooring was essential in coping with the vicissitudes of life. Socrates emphasized the importance of the fearless pursuit of all manner of knowledge. Krishnamurti emphasized the importance of breaking free from the shackles of social conformity and conditioning. Rousseau insisted that every child should be allowed to blossom on his or her own terms. Incidentally, Krishnamurti's own transformational life story—his earliest tutors thought he was rather dim-witted—symbolizes the aspirations Rousseau had for all children. As growing numbers of homeschooling families treasure the freedom to pursue similar educational priorities, the lessons from these rebels represent an undeniable holy grail for mainstream education.

The Crosshairs of Education

For most of our history, education has largely been a vehicle for equipping the next generation with the skills needed to turn the gears of society. As a result, most educational objectives have been based on near-term market needs. The expectations for education therefore grew steadily as societies progressed, especially after the First Industrial Revolution. The growing need for economy, efficiency, and scale led to the cookie-cutter-style factory model for education. This model required a regimented structure and rigid, age-based grades and standardized tests so children could be efficiently assessed and advanced.

Over time and for the better part of the twentieth century, these expectations began to be set by universities in many parts of the world, as they emerged as the ultimate gateways to success. The growing demand for college admissions gradually turned schools into preparatory academies, largely focused on getting students into the most sought-after colleges. As the need to differentiate among students grew, so did the reliance on testing. In turn, this steadily eroded the relevance of individual passions and needs, whole-child development, and formative evaluations. The educational ecosystem increasingly relied on mastery of minutiae at the expense of big-picture understanding. Interestingly, Montessori recognized this evolving educational landscape and designed the Great Lessons as she saw that knowledge of our origins is vital for awakening a child's imagination and curiosity. Big-picture learning connects children to their roots and empowers them to engage with the world with a sense of awe and curiosity. In fact, excessive standardization also lowers the need for critical thinking and diversity of thought. This is a serious—albeit well-recognized—problem as it defeats a key objective of education: to produce confident, engaged, and inquisitive lifelong learners.

Race to Nowhere—the 2009 documentary directed by Vicki Abeles and Jessica Congdon—has articulated these concerns with education quite well.[32] Abeles was surprised when the pressures of school, homework, and extracurricular activities made her middle school daughter sick. This episode was a painful wake-up call; her subsequent research showed that this was in fact a widespread problem (perhaps with varying degrees across different countries). She found that while many parents detested this "pressure-cooker" culture, they could not afford to get their children out of the rat race—as acceptance into most good universities hinged on it. Abeles set out to showcase real-life stories of children and families that have been pushed to the brink by overscheduling, overtesting, and relentless pressure to succeed on a narrow set of measures. Even with little advertising and no large studio backing, her scathing indictment of our culture still managed to become one of the longest-running documentaries. Within just three years of its release, it had over six thousand screenings in schools, community centers, cinemas, and homes across forty-nine states and twenty-two countries. Using this film as the centerpiece of her campaign, Abeles has fueled a grassroots movement to fight this silent epidemic.

However, if someone watches this documentary and goes home thinking that all this stress is the price that has to be paid for a world-class education in the US, they're in for a rude awakening. Alarm bells have been going off for many decades about the poor educational outcomes in the United States. As far back as 2003, in his presentation to the Mathematics and Science Initiative, Michigan State University professor William Schmidt noted that many US students were two years behind their international peers in math by the time they completed the eighth grade. In fact, twelfth graders were closer to the bottom of the list in the Third International Mathematics and Science Study (TIMSS), the most extensive international comparative study of mathematics and science education ever attempted. Schmidt claimed that this was clear evidence that US schools were failing their students.

The publication of *A Nation at Risk: The Imperative for Educational Reform*, the landmark 1983 report issued by the National Commission on Excellence in Education during President Ronald Reagan's administration, was perhaps the first real wake-up call for the US.[33] The report claimed that the American education system was failing and that there was increasing acceptance of mediocrity. The commission recommended more rigorous content, higher standards, more school days in a year, and performance-based pay for teachers. Through the Improving America's Schools Act during the Clinton administration in 1994, the No Child Left Behind Act in 2002, Race to the Top in 2009, and the Common Core Standards Initiative in 2010, almost every US presidential administration since 1983 has come up with its own response to these recommendations. However, there is little evidence that all this funding and attention have significantly moved the needle. For example, the 2015 National Assessment of Educational Progress found that less than 25 percent of American twelfth graders were proficient in math and around 24 percent in science. It's no wonder then that 46 percent of the members of the American Association for the Advancement of Science felt that the level of K–12 STEM (science, technology, engineering, and mathematics) education in the US was below average.[34] It was therefore not a shock when the US came in thirty-eighth among the seventy-nine countries that took the mathematics literacy test administered by the Program for International Student Assessment (PISA) in 2018.

There is a widespread belief that the disappointing performance on the PISA is due to the fact that education in the US promotes creativity—a highly prized skill that can't be assessed well by these standardized tests. However, Ted Dintersmith in his documentary *Most Likely to Succeed* and William Deresiewicz in his book *Excellent Sheep* shattered this common misperception.[35]

Motivated by what he saw at his children's schools, Dintersmith, a successful venture capitalist, began cataloging his observations. He created one column for all activities that, in his view, prepared kids for life and one for everything that he felt was simply busywork that did not add much value. While he found way too many irrelevant items, the worst part of this exercise came when he saw a need to add a third column—experiences at school that hurt the curiosity and creativity of kids. He became a strong advocate for increasing the authenticity of a child's learning experiences by embracing project-based learning and eliminating passive acquisition of mundane information.

How should we reconcile these conflicting observations that children in the US are extremely stressed on one hand and that we have a culture of complacency and minimalist expectations on the other? This seems like the worst of both worlds. How do we distinguish between essential information that fosters deeper learning and forgettable facts? How can teachers sustain student engagement, passion, and creative thinking while meeting the expectations of standardized testing?

For better or worse, we are custodians of this planet and the most sentient beings around, at least per our best current understanding. To muster the needed courage for prioritizing long-term investments and not focusing disproportionately on short-term market needs, we need to learn the key lessons from our journey thus far.

We have accumulated a rich legacy of insights and learning. From no schooling to religious and preparatory schools to homeschooling, there is a very wide range of options available today. Some, like the Montessori schools, empower the learner through prepared environments. Others, like the IB, weave global perspectives into a reflective curriculum. A few, like the Reggio Emilia approach, greatly value parent input and participation. Several, such as Renzulli's SEM and Reggio Emilia, also go a step further and make provisions for incorporating learners' passions into their curricula. At the same time, from Pythagoras in the sixth century BCE to Jiddu Krishnamurti in the twentieth century to millions of homeschooling families throughout history, there have always been rebels who have sought to inspire children to reach a higher orbit and become part of something bigger than themselves. It is clear that our current expectations around what education should entail are not ambitious enough. We cannot hope to tackle our pressing civilizational crises until we collectively prize such education. There are many great examples to learn from; what we need most are intention, commitment, and investment.

CHAPTER SUMMARY

- For thousands of years, education largely consisted of learning from exploration of the environment.
- As societies evolved, education became more structured and centered around learning discrete facts and skills from knowledgeable adults so children could become productive contributors to society.
- Education has been key in shaping the human journey by equipping every generation with the skills needed to turn the gears of their society.
- The acute need for workers to staff the factories that sprang up during the Industrial Revolutions led to one of the largest increases ever in educational access, often through mandatory schooling. Using a relatively rigid curriculum, age-based classes, and metrics for progression from one grade level to the next, factory-style schools enabled efficient and affordable schooling for the vast majority of children.
- Plato, Locke, Bloom, Dewey, and Piaget are some of the many prominent thinkers whose philosophies have influenced the evolution of mainstream education over the past few centuries by repeatedly trying to harmonize the needs of learners with those of society.
- On the other hand, there have been other thought leaders (such as Socrates, Buddha, Confucius, Pythagoras, Rousseau, and Krishnamurti) and pathbreaking institutions (such as the gurukul and the Pythagorean society) whose revolutionary precepts on holistic child development have only had a marginal impact on mainstream practices.
- In fact, even less revolutionary innovations—Waldorf, Montessori, International Baccalaureate, Reggio Emilia, among others—also only had a modest influence on the factory model of education.

- At the same time, the growing demand for college admissions has increasingly turned schools into preparatory academies. Their outsized reliance on testing has led to excessive focus on minutiae at the expense of big-picture understanding. This has been inimical to student passion, growth, and engagement.
- The modern homeschool movement is one notable response to the problems seen with traditional educational institutions, though the concept itself has deep roots in hundreds of years of practice.
- While there is great variety in available educational philosophies and modalities, competencies such as curiosity, ambition, creativity, and empathy are typically not the explicit focus of many pedagogies.

II

Paving the Way

The Three Pillars

Our intention creates our reality.
—WAYNE DYER

We are at a pivotal point in our history. From the looming specter of a nuclear Armageddon to the dangers of climate catastrophe and the risks associated with AI takeover, the threats we face are undeniably real and ominous. Yet, at the same time, our insights and tools are unmatched. We know a lot more about ourselves: how we have arrived, our accomplishments and disappointments, our place in history, and the challenges and possibilities that are in front of us. This moment therefore presents a remarkable opportunity to shape our destiny and ensure that the promise of the human condition is more broadly accessible.

Our lessons from part I offer many valuable insights. Firstly, we must prioritize big-picture learning and strike a balance between our short-term need for efficient workers and the longer-term imperative of collective well-being through a passion for true learning and growth. Such engagement is possible only if we empower our children and make education more purposeful.

Secondly, it is essential that education enables us to dig deeper into the essence of being human. Living alongside AI advancements requires emotional resilience. Most rat races for the next big fix, for instance, only result in ephemeral happiness. Without an intimate appreciation of what truly brings us fulfillment, humanity risks self-destruction. Education that engenders this understanding in our children can help them strike a balance between restlessness and contentment. Therefore, a crucial objective of education should be to sharpen our focus on self-realization. The nuanced concept of happiness introduced in the curriculum of Delhi public schools in India, for example, could serve as an inspiration for other schools.[1] This curriculum cultivates mindfulness, critical thinking, and socioemotional growth by exploring happiness through learning, awareness, relationships, feelings, and active participation.

While these high-level educational objectives are essential for our future generations to thrive, part I has made it clear that we must, first and foremost, also meet the biological needs of children. Unfortunately, mainstream education has often been unable to sufficiently cater to the physical, mental, and emotional development of children. The rising rates of suicide in developed countries, for instance, may reflect an inability to cope with mounting disillusionment. We can't expect great learning outcomes when a child does not feel safe, secure, healthy, and connected. To cultivate purposeful, anchored, well-rounded, and healthy lives, educational objectives should be based on a holistic curriculum that addresses core human needs through a rich and diverse set of growth experiences.

As a species, we have seen that our progress came from our restlessness, our ability to imagine possibilities and share our vision, and to then flexibly cooperate with a large number of people in its pursuit. Restlessness is a manifestation of our ambition. To imagine new possibilities, people need understanding, curiosity, and creativity. Our survey of the outlook for the future in the second chapter made it abundantly clear that these competencies are indispensable for children to thrive in the decades and centuries ahead as well. Additionally, empathy and good communication skills are also essential for upcoming generations to protect our collective future through shared decision-making. In fact, the usefulness of fixed skillsets is diminishing fast in the face of the uncertainty of the rapidly unfolding future. There is therefore an urgent need for children to be adept at finding deeper patterns, taking measured risks, articulating their learning, and rallying support for their vision. In short, education needs to prioritize flexible learning and transferable skills. These must therefore be vital educational objectives.

At the same time, we cannot be oblivious to the fact that every child is unique. The village comprises a diverse set of talents and needs. While one child may need more help with mental health, another may benefit from support for intellectual or emotional development. One child may have a passion for music, while another may be fascinated by math. It is rare for a single individual to be gifted with multiple competencies. It's optimal for each child to focus on the development of the competencies that are most relevant to them. Individualization of educational experiences is therefore essential for us to fully harness our collective strengths.

Part II of the book details the philosophy, purpose, and structure of the three pillars of education that encompass these key lessons from our investigations in part I. A holistic curriculum that promotes physical, emotional, and spiritual resilience and mooring through big-picture understanding is essential to nurture the desire, freedom, and ability to explore and build a strong sense of purpose and engagement. This is then our first pillar. Our next objective is to prioritize transferable skills and fundamental competencies over mundane information and fixed abilities. These foundational competencies constitute our second pillar. Finally, to fully maximize their potential, this journey must be meaningful for every learner on their own terms. Individualization can help ensure that these educational objectives align well with the core of each child's makeup and experiences.

In the next three chapters, we explore how an education founded on these three pillars can help us achieve higher levels of empowerment, engagement, and fulfillment through greater access to our abilities, perceptions of reality, belief systems, and expectations.

4

Holistic Curriculum

Free the child's potential, and you will transform him into the world.

—MARIA MONTESSORI

As the COVID-19 isolation made it abundantly clear, life can be a lot harder for many of us when we are deprived of in-person social interactions. In fact, researchers continue to investigate the extent of the harm that the COVID-19 lockdowns have caused to many children. Our well-being relies heavily on both our physical health and our ability to interact fruitfully with one another. Our emotional health depends on our exchanges in the physical environment, the spoken and unspoken expectations of family and friends, and the depth of our relationships. As our brief review of the functioning of the human brain in part I shows, while our biology has evolved to adapt to our expanding needs, the need for meaning through social connections runs deep.

Russell Church's studies on rats, for example, were groundbreaking.[1] In one landmark experiment, hungry rats surprisingly refused food when it was only offered if they pulled a lever to shock their littermates. We have learned enough about animal behavior over the years to bear witness to the exceptional breadth of their social norms and structures. Wild boars, for example, are known to be highly curious and intelligent social animals that love to play. Elephants are renowned for exhibiting remarkable empathy and cooperative behaviors. They show compassion and care for injured or distressed herd members, often staying by their side and using their trunks to touch and comfort. Similarly, psychologist Harry Harlow's experiments with infant monkeys, though disgraceful and inhumane, were nevertheless insightful.[2] When given a choice between a metal-dummy mother monkey that had a milk bottle and a dummy monkey with a soft cloth but without any milk, infant monkeys chose the warmth of the dummy wrapped with cloth.

It is vital that for children to blossom to their fullest potential, their basic needs for social and emotional health are met. Education should first and foremost cater to these critical developmental needs so that every child can function well in his or her community. However, holistic health also encompasses the interconnectedness of our physical, mental, emotional, social, and spiritual well-being. For example, mental and emotional health also provide an essential foundation for intellectual growth. Our brain is unable to take the risks necessary for intellectual rigor and exploration when its bandwidth is taken up by anxiety or anger. Just as the different parts of the brain work together to support our cognitive abilities and overall functioning, attending to all dimensions of our health ensures that we can live a harmonious life, fully engage with the world, and reach our potential by shaping positive life outcomes.

Unfortunately, as we have discussed in part I of this book, the prospects for holistic development of our children often worsened as societies advanced. For a large part of our history, children were co-opted to work in farms and factories. They only began to attend schools in large numbers during the Industrial Revolution. Since then, education has largely been focused on preparing them to meet the needs of the supply chains of the factories. The factory model of education has historically been optimized to benefit factory owners and not the developmental needs of children. While this traditional model has seen various reforms over the years, few schools are yet able to truly cater to children's holistic development.

Inadequate support for a holistic curriculum can be traced to many factors. Of these, the costs involved, our expectations around the purpose of education, and the metrics used for assessing accountability and educational success have been the most prominent roadblocks. It takes significant motivation and resources for schools to be able to cater to the mental and socioemotional health of all children. This can be quite challenging as school districts are often starved for funds. Not enough of us appear willing to prioritize this among our many needs and challenges. Also, with the growing demand for college admissions, for instance, parents, legislatures, and school districts have increasingly turned to standardized testing to track progress. Test results have become a proxy for accountability for most oversight organizations. This presents another challenge since designing tests for progress in physical, mental, or emotional well-being is not trivial. Instead of empowering schools to focus on the specific needs and opportunities of each child, standardized tests have been pushing schools to prioritize narrow test-taking skills on a small range of subjects. The teachers, therefore, despite their best intentions, typically end up spending way too much time teaching for success on standardized tests in a small set of academic areas. While designing meaningful tests for the holistic development of each child is daunting, perhaps what is even less appreciated is how tests can also dilute and corrupt the curricular focus of even the so-called academic subjects. The damage caused by the testing regime cannot be overestimated.

In this chapter, we take a deeper look at some of the skills and capabilities children need to thrive and how education can meet the needs of their all-round development. We take a deeper look at children's holistic development in the context of their physical, emotional, intellectual, ethical, spiritual, and social abilities. While some educators may only refer to "nonacademic" subjects by "holistic" education, this is an arbitrary distinction. There is just as much need for children's true intellectual development as there is for their emotional and physical development. And given the outsized role of testing, it is important to also look at the impact of testing on the mainstream "academic" subjects. So, in this book in general—and in this chapter in particular—we will look at all dimensions (academic and nonacademic) of the balanced development of the whole child.

The Appetite for Physical Health

> Physical fitness is not only one of the most important keys to a healthy body, it is the basis of dynamic and creative intellectual activity.
>
> —JOHN F. KENNEDY

There has been widespread concern about the growing share of obese children in recent decades: from about 6.5 percent in 1980 to 19.6 percent in 2008 for children aged six to eleven and from 5.0 to 18.1 percent among adolescents aged twelve to nineteen, for example, in the US.[3] It is truly worrisome that this trend has persisted, with age-adjusted severe obesity rates in the US for adults over twenty years of age increasing from 4.7 to 9.2 percent between 2000 and 2018.[4] This phenomenon is also not limited to the US. A study has revealed how obesity in poorer populations in 103 low- and middle-income countries rose as these nations developed economically.[5] While there were cities where obesity rates were over 20 percent, the overall obesity rate in China was still below 5 percent as of 2003.[6] However, by 2019, the overall obesity rate tripled to about 16.4 percent.[7] Even as of 2005, 100,000 to 400,000 deaths per year in the United States were already blamed on obesity and, as of December 2010, obesity-related health costs were approaching about $300 billion per year.[8] For reference, in 2012, about 120,000 were killed in wars worldwide, 1.5 million died due to diabetes, and about 1.1 million died due to COVID-19 in the US as of January 2023. Increasing reliance on processed foods and other less than healthy dietary choices, increasingly sedentary lifestyles, genetic predisposition, and higher stress levels are believed to be some of the leading reasons for the obesity epidemic.[9]

The writing on the wall is clear. A holistic approach to the physical well-being of a child cannot be only a parental responsibility. An enduring solution to this crisis demands a more significant role for our educational institutions. Locke in the late seventeenth century was one of the first modern educational thinkers in the Western world to emphasize the importance of the physical well-being of a child. He even insisted that children's physical health was more important than their academic accomplishments. However, in most formal educational settings, physical education has only been a nominal part of the curriculum, though concerns about poor nutrition have led to reforms in many parts of the world. The revamping of lunch choices at school cafeterias in the United States, midday meal schemes in Indian public schools, and the introduction of five-course meals in French public schools are a few examples.[10]

Thomas Edison had reportedly predicted that (the exact source of this quote though is uncertain) "the doctor of the future will give no medication but will interest his patients in the care of the human frame, diet, and in the cause and prevention of disease." A key objective of a well-rounded education should be to build a keen awareness of the drivers of physical health. Curriculum should do more than simply showcase the science behind our physical well-being. Education needs to drive home the roles of heredity, nutrition, sleep, and exercise on overall health.

While the impact of heredity has been empirically observed from time immemorial, the discovery of the structure of DNA and its role in information transfer by James Watson and Francis Crick in 1953 has opened the door to unprecedented possibilities.[11] DNA sequencing holds great promise for individualizing healthcare delivery, especially as we make advances in decoding the genetic signatures of the various medical conditions. It is also very helpful that the unique genome of any individual can now be mapped for under $1,000. There are other aspects of individualization that ought to be explored as well. For instance, metabolic rates, allergy profiles, and endurance are all highly individualistic. Also, Ayurvedic practitioners claim that not all foods are suitable for all people at all times.[12] The Ayurvedic system recommends different foods for the vata (dry with perhaps a weak metabolism), pitta (excessive digestive fires), and kapha (excessive phlegm) body types. Similarly, many Eastern cultures assign heating and cooling attributes to food.[13] The potential benefits of personalizing diet in addition to medication and cure offers a promising avenue for further exploration.

Education should also bring awareness to the many obstacles that can frustrate people's desire to eat well. Globalization and opaque supply chains have complicated our dietary choices. In 2008, contamination of milk with melamine in China affected about three hundred thousand people and resulted in six deaths.[14] In the US, Beech-Nut paid $2.2 million in fines in 1987 for selling artificially flavored sugar water as apple juice.[15] While illegal food adulteration grabs a lot of attention, legal food additives and ingredients and high levels of processing can easily pose an even larger threat to our wellness.[16] Lack of adequate awareness of the ingredients in the foods we consume, widespread prevalence of forever chemicals, and inadequate research into the health risks of the various additives are some of the common culprits. Unfortunately, when our evolutionary predisposition to sugary foods is paired with poor access and low affordability of healthier options, the outcomes are not pretty. Not surprisingly, this issue has been disproportionately affecting low-income families in the US and exacerbating the prevailing health divide.[17]

There has also been growing recognition of the health benefits of plant-based vegetarian and vegan diets. Dr. Dean Ornish, Dr. Neal Barnard, Dr. Caldwell Esselstyn, and others claim that vegetarian diets can prevent or even reverse coronary artery disease, diabetes, and even some cancers.[18] A large twenty-year British study involving 44,561 people found that going meatless gives vegetarians a 32 percent lower heart disease risk than non-vegetarians.[19] According to Oklahoma State University economists Jayson Lusk and Bailey Norwood, vegetarian diets are also the most economical option for sustenance for many communities.[20] In her bestselling book *Diet for a Small Planet*, Frances Moore Lappé argues that a vegan diet can play a significant role in mitigating climate change.[21]

Even if we are blessed with great heredity and take good care of our diet, to keep our mind and body strong, we also need adequate sleep and exercise. Unfortunately, for cultural and other reasons, there isn't as much appreciation of the pivotal role that sleep plays in our overall health even though most of us can attest to the restorative benefits of good sleep. When we are not sufficiently rested, we become cranky, our brains are foggy, and we struggle to focus. Over the last few decades, scientists have obtained a deeper understanding of the significant role of sleep in learning consolidation.[22] Inadequate sleep is now believed to contribute to a whole host of problems ranging from poor mental health and weaker immunity to even more serious conditions such as coronary heart disease, diabetes, and obesity. There is even research that suggests that sleep deprivation in early years can manifest as attention-deficit/hyperactivity disorder (ADHD) symptoms later. A large six-year study of 11,000 children that began when they were six months old found that children whose sleep was affected by breathing problems were 40 to 100 percent more likely than those who slept normally to develop behavioral problems resembling ADHD.[23]

Our bodies take care of a lot of important restorative business during sleep. Most researchers recognize four distinct stages in every sleep cycle. The first three are nonrapid eye movement (NREM) and the last one is a rapid eye movement (REM) stage. This cycle repeats itself several times during a night of sleep with the REM stage lasting longer and going deeper in every successive cycle. The first stage is a transition between wakefulness and sleep that typically lasts about ten minutes. We spend about half of a typical night's sleep in stage two. In this stage, we become less aware of our surroundings, our heartbeat slows, and our body temperature drops. Our brains produce rapid, rhythmic activity (often referred to as sleep spindles) that correlates with the memory gathering and assessment activities of our brain. We file away many of our long-term memories during this stage. The third stage of our sleep cycle is associated with deep and slow brain waves known as delta waves. In this stage, our blood pressure drops, breathing slows, and our muscles are completely relaxed. This is typically one of the hardest times to awaken a person from sleep. Consolidation of memories associated with objective facts and personal experiences happens during this stage.[24] It is in this stage that our body also begins its physical repairs. It heals cuts, repairs cells, regrows tissues, builds new bone and muscle, and releases chemicals and hormones that strengthen the immune system. In the final REM stage of the sleep cycle, we breathe faster and our brain is more active. While this is also the stage where we dream, we will not be able to act on the dreams as our brain paralyzes our muscles. It is believed that the final consolidation of all our memories, especially our emotional learning, happens during this stage.[25] While adults typically spend about 20 percent of their sleep time in the REM stage, babies spend almost 50 percent of their sleep time in this stage.

Clearly, sleep plays a vital role in processing the information gathered during the day and consolidating our learning and memory. Some memories are moved from short-term to long-term and some experiences are simply deleted. This is critical given the fragility of our short-term memories (due to the limited storage capacity of the hippocampus). Some of our new memories are linked to older memories so they are etched deeper. In fact, it is when this kind of editing takes place that our life story is truly written. Since memory consolidation creates more room for short-term memories, sleep can also facilitate new learning. Research has suggested that REM sleep can also strengthen our creative thinking skills.[26]

In an interesting study, forty-four participants took part in two sessions of episodic learning, the first at noon and the second at 6:00 p.m.[27] All participants were tested right after these learning sessions. A randomly selected subset of twenty individuals were allowed to sleep for one hundred minutes between the two sessions. The researchers found that the group that napped between learning sessions had a modest 8 percent improvement in their learning ability while the group that did not nap saw an almost 11 percent decrease in retention. Given the significance of sleep, it is perhaps more important to use an alarm for winding up our activities and going to sleep than it is for waking up!

In addition to nutrition and sleep, for a high quality of life, we should also foster a healthy appetite for an active lifestyle from an early age. It is well known that exercise can reduce the odds of cardiovascular disease, diabetes, and depression. An optimum mix of aerobic and anaerobic exercise can also help us lose weight, slow down aging, and even help delay or prevent dementia. While individual sports such as swimming, cycling, and long-distance running can help build endurance and strength, team sports can be especially helpful for motivating us and building a sense of camaraderie and purpose. Clearly, there are many compelling reasons for pursuing a physically active lifestyle.

It is now believed that at least some of the beneficial aspects of exercise involve the molecular machinery of the brain itself. It is becoming increasingly clear that stimulation and exercise can help us sustain behavioral plasticity through structural changes in the brain at the cellular, molecular, and system levels.[28] Ongoing exposure to novelty and regular physical exercise are particularly essential as we age; they can minimize the odds of getting neurodegenerative diseases like Alzheimer's and other forms of dementia.

Figure 4.1. One of the creative ways the teachers at Sankalpa Academy fostered a love for physical well-being.

Incidentally, research suggests that there are also significant short-term benefits from exercise.[29] One study of twenty-seven healthy individuals found that novel vocabulary learning was 20 percent faster after high-impact anaerobic sprints relative to gains after low-impact aerobic running or a period of rest.[30] Besides investigating learning speed, researchers looked at retention after one week and eight months. They found that peripheral levels of brain-derived neurotrophic factor (BDNF) during learning after intense exercise were correlated with better short-term learning success. BDNF is believed to bind to receptors at the neuronal synapses along their dendritic branches and thus solidify learning through stronger associations with prior knowledge. On the other hand, dopamine and epinephrine levels were related to better intermediate and long-term retention of information respectively. We're learning more every day about the process of neurogenesis, the role of exercise in spawning new neurons, how learning takes place in the brain, and the role of BDNF.[31]

Beyond diet, sleep, and exercise, education should also make some room for lessons that help develop and refine our kids' senses—both the five physical senses that perceive concrete information from the environment and the subtler senses such as acceptance, balance, and equilibrium that perceive more intangible information. There are other opportunities as well. Some schools are more proactive than others in accommodating children with sensory processing disorders. And many schools also take vision and hearing screenings seriously, as they can have an outsized impact on children's confidence and learning. And while many schools have well-defined physical education programs, in most schools, these are often perfunctory and not adequate for instilling a serious enough appetite for physical health and well-being. Ultimately, education should help children gain greater ownership and agency in taking good care of their overall physical health.

Investing in Our Mental Health

Self-esteem is as important to our well-being as legs are to a table.

—LOUISE HART

A good appetite for physical health has long been a well-recognized marker of our overall well-being. Ominously, over the last several decades, mental health has increasingly become a greater concern.[32] On average, the annual

US suicide rate has increased about 41 percent, from 10.5 per 100,000 people in 1999 to 14.8 per 100,000 people in 2020.[33] It is nothing short of a tragedy that the percentage of high school students in the US with unrelenting feelings of hopelessness was nearly 37 percent in 2019, an almost 50 percent increase since 2009, with half of them seriously considering suicide.[34] While the prolonged isolation during the COVID-19 pandemic only made matters significantly worse (especially given that about two hundred thousand children have lost a parent or a caregiver), the deterioration of our children's mental health has been many years in the making.[35] In a metastudy, Sarah Konrath noted a 40 percent decrease in empathy in US college students between 1979 and 2009.[36] Konrath compiled data from fourteen thousand college students and seventy-two different studies. The costs of neglecting mental well-being are growing rapidly. For example, Simone Biles and Naomi Osaka—highly accomplished athletes in gymnastics and tennis respectively—made headlines recently for their courage in speaking up about mental health and advocating for self-care and well-being. The writing on the wall is clear. We will be facing significantly more tragic outcomes if we don't stem this tide quickly, especially given the discussion in the second chapter about the growing impact of AI and machine learning on our sense of self-worth.

There are many reasons for the rise in mental health issues, from environmental to biological. Chronic stress has been one of the largest contributors and it often stems from social or financial problems. It's typically the result of someone's perception that they're no longer in control of a situation. In some cases, the toxic achievement culture burdens kids and parents too heavily. Addiction to social media, for example, has also been widely recognized as a key contributor to increased rates of anxiety, depression, and low self-esteem. Such stress has been implicated in depression, high blood pressure, heart disease, and immune system disruption as well.[37] In some cases, self-focus mediated misregulation due to peer pressure and excessive competition can also lead to harmful stress and choking, especially if a person does not explicitly prepare for this. Sagvolden and colleagues have claimed that insufficient reinforcement of appropriate behaviors and/or insufficient suppression of some previously reinforced negative behaviors can result in impulsiveness, a need for instant gratification, difficulty in sustaining attention, hyperactivity in a familiar environment, and unpredictable behavioral swings.[38]

It therefore makes sense that an enriching life that is driven by purpose, empowerment, connection, and engagement is the best guarantor of mental health. For example, there have been studies that showed that a positive school culture has a strong correlation with improvements in students' mental health.[39] However, the approach to mental health issues in some families and most schools has been more reactive than proactive. A foundation of strong relationships built on trust, respect, and firm boundaries should always take precedence over reliance on time-outs and consequences. Most schools have limited budgets and only offer limited support to students' mental well-being. Often, the counselor's time is barely adequate to handle the most severe hyperactivity and other behavioral issues in children diagnosed with or prone to attention deficit disorders.

Interestingly, while ADHD has been on the radar since the 1970s, it has remained an unsettled medical condition. There are varying diagnoses and treatment protocols in different countries. According to Alan Schwarz in the *New York Times*, data from the National Survey of Children's Health (sponsored by the CDC) suggests that 11 percent of US children have been diagnosed with ADHD.[40] In France, the percentage of kids diagnosed and medicated for ADHD is less than 0.5 percent. While most of the children in the US with ADHD are prescribed stimulant medication, French psychiatrists, on the other hand, look at ADHD as a medical condition resulting from environmental causes. Hence, they often choose to treat ADHD with psychotherapy or family counseling. A survey by Faraone et al. suggests that apparent differences between countries in the prevalence of ADHD reflect differences in our understanding of the underlying causes and in diagnostic practices rather than true differences in the incidence of ADHD behavior.[41] While recent research helps clarify the genetic factors in ADHD, the root cause of the genetic expressions in early childhood remains a subject for further investigation.[42]

For example, as we discussed earlier, there is also growing suspicion that sleep deprivation early in life might result in symptoms that resemble ADHD. Also, a survey by Charach et al. suggests that parent behavior training is an effective intervention for preschoolers at risk of developing ADHD.[43] However, as noted earlier, the treatment of choice in the US for such hyperactivity is stimulant medication. Most medications typically seek to increase the availability of the neurotransmitter dopamine to children with ADHD.[44] This is based on the premise that the frontal lobes are underaroused and hence lacking in dopamine. Unfortunately, there are many serious concerns about the safety of the stimulant medications used to treat children.[45] Some studies also suggest that these stimulant drugs lose their efficacy over the long run.[46] Regardless, in many cases, medication may be the best or the only option, and an informed treatment option should always include the advice of a physician.

Research has shown that there are also other paths to alleviating mental health issues that don't necessarily go through medication. For example, there has been longstanding empirical research that argues for the mainstream clinical use of neurotherapy for attention deficit disorders.[47] Neurotherapy uses feedback from real-time quantitative EEG to guide computer-generated games that seek to stimulate and retrain the brain to produce more normal patterns of electrical activity. In a general sense, neurofeedback seeks to provide information about control of brain functions to subjects by monitoring brain waves. While some studies suggest that this approach is effective in helping those diagnosed with ADHD or other learning disorders, long-term benefits remain uncertain.[48]

Separately, a study by Bonhauser and colleagues found that regular exercise reduced anxiety scores in 198 Chilean high school students by about 13.7 percent.[49] Some studies also seem to suggest that a regimen of three days of exercise per week for thirty to forty-five minutes per day is the minimum amount of exercise required to receive any benefit.[50] While medication has long been used to combat depression, it is promising that some studies suggest that regular physical exercise is as effective as medication in reducing the level of depression in patients with major depressive disorders and more effective than medication in reducing the risk of subsequent relapse.[51]

As mentioned earlier, social media has been increasingly implicated in the rising levels of anxiety and depression. This is understandable given the picture-perfect lives projected by many on Facebook. In fact, Bryant and Veroff argue that humans attend more to real and perceived setbacks and adversities than to the many joys in our lives.[52] They argue that taking the time to savor life's many pleasures will help us stave off anxiety and depression better. The impact of our addiction to social media on mental health is so widely recognized that a small, remote village in the Indian state of Maharashtra adopted a rather drastic solution to this problem![53] The village council of Vadgaon voted to collectively stay away from television and internet for one and a half hours every evening. Vadgaon is a rural village with about three thousand farmers and sugar mill workers. Even though the digital detox was hard at first, many in the village reported a significant improvement in their social life after the switch. While we cannot expect that many communities will adopt such draconian measures, there is a vital lesson in this experiment for all of us as individual stakeholders.

Despite this recent focus on mental health, the emphasis on nurturing a healthy lifestyle and lowering stress are not modern developments. Meditation and pranayama exercises for the control and mastery of breath, for example, have been well established over many centuries as effective mechanisms for improving mental disposition and autonomic functions.[54] Many recent studies have confirmed that pranayama lowers stress and combats related ailments such as anxiety and depression.[55] The various asanas of Hatha yoga and the Chinese martial art of tai chi are two other disciplines that have become popular in the West for their health benefits. The Accelerated School—the 2001 *Time* magazine School of the Year—has published an extremely interesting report on their thirty-six-week yoga program for students who live in a war-zone-like violent environment in Los Angeles.[56] Their pilot study found that the 405 children who participated in their "Yoga for Kids" program experienced increased self-esteem in addition to improved physical health and fitness. Yoga helped these children learn to effectively understand, manage, and overcome their daily stresses. Their improved self-esteem resulted in fewer discipline problems and significantly better grades.

Meditation is another ancient practice for mental well-being that has its roots in the yogic system. A growing number of studies have found meditation very beneficial for overall mental and emotional health. The ordeal of a young soccer team in Thailand some years ago is a great testament to the potential of meditation. When soccer coach Ekapol Chanthawong and his twelve teenage soccer players were exploring an underground cave after their practice on June 23, 2018, the cave unexpectedly flooded with monsoon rain and quickly trapped them inside. It was eighteen days before the coach and young players were rescued by the Thai Navy SEALs. When the group was located by two British divers about ten days after their ordeal began, the soccer players were found meditating. It turns out that the coach, who had trained as a Buddhist monk, decided to teach his players meditation to help them conserve their energy and stay calm.

In simple terms, meditation is a practice that helps us observe our thoughts and gain increasing control of our minds. A key goal is to prevent our mind from excessive wandering. Specific brain structures that are collectively known as the default mode network (DMN) are active whenever we are not specifically engaged with a task or goal. Researchers have found that DMN becomes active whenever there is significant chatter in our mind.[57]

Figure 4.2. An artist's rendering of the Thai soccer team meditating after their cave's entrance was flooded.

Uddin et al. have also found that DMN was more active and less coherent in their ADHD subjects than in a control group.[58] It is therefore interesting that experienced meditators have been found to have less activation and greater coherence in their DMN than nonmeditators, both at rest and while engaged in a task.[59]

Meditation may be a tricky subject for the uninitiated as there are many kinds of practices and every type of meditation has its own attendant benefits. For instance, some strengthen our empathy, several help us increase our focus, and there are yet others that make us more mindful. There is loving-kindness meditation that requires us to focus our thoughts on compassion and love. Breath-awareness meditation, as the name suggests, requires us to focus on our breath. In transcendental meditation, we focus on a mantra. On the other hand, in mindfulness meditation, we don't constrain our thoughts. We pay close attention to them as detached external observers. Most kinds of meditation fall into two categories. We either focus on a chosen theme or object or we focus on the thoughts as they arrive. This helps practitioners achieve greater control over their thoughts and focus faster. Since all types of meditation are designed to cultivate self-awareness and improve concentration, they help calm the mind, reduce mental chatter, and promote learning.

A study by the US government found that over forty-six million US adults (about 14 percent of the population) had practiced meditation in the previous twelve months.[60] It was therefore not surprising when a study by Oman and colleagues concluded that meditation led to physiological health benefits through changes in neurological processes.[61] Some of these benefits include "effective functioning, including academic performance, concentration, perceptual sensitivity, reaction time, memory, self-control, empathy, and self-esteem."[62] Another study by Li Chuan Chu also found similar improvement in the overall psychological health and stress management of those who meditated.[63]

Incidentally, there has also been interest in more active and direct approaches to modulating our thought processes and lowering stress. As a contemplative practice that produces a relaxed state of consciousness, hypnosis is similar to meditation in many ways. Several researchers have therefore also been looking more deeply at the benefits of hypnosis and its neurological intersection with meditation.

Finally, it is also important to recognize that not all stress is bad. There is interesting research from Marios Kyriazis of the British Longevity Society, Suresh Rattan from the Laboratory of Cellular Ageing at the University of Aarhus, and others that suggests that seeking out moderate amounts of stress may actually be healthy for us.[64] Examples of such stress include frantic, time-bound activities such as home decoration or preparation for a trip. This is because of the house cleaning activities that take place in our bodies during short duration stressors. Internal repair mechanisms kick in when some of the cells in our body begin to break down due to stress. This process, referred to as hormesis, produces proteins that repair the damage and remove the harmful chemicals produced when cells break down. This makes our cells healthier than they were before the stress-producing event, since the response is typically greater than what is needed to repair the damage. Most inducers of helpful stress would likely be short-term activities that result in an immediate sense of accomplishment and are unlikely to lead to a chronic condition.

In summary, while there are several approaches for mitigating stress and promoting mental well-being, a proactive approach that focuses on a healthy lifestyle based on meaningful relationships and pursuits should form the foundation. We will explore this in greater detail in other parts of this book.

Building Capacity for Emotional Intelligence

There are moments in life, when the heart is so full of emotion
That if by chance it be shaken, or into its depths like a pebble
Drops some careless word, it overflows, and its secret,
Spilt on the ground like water, can never be gathered together.
—HENRY WADSWORTH LONGFELLOW

We can't be very successful if we're not able to distinguish between honest input, a message of tough love, ill-conceived or irrelevant feedback, and a malicious put-down. Poor emotional intelligence can wreak havoc with our overall happiness, learning ability, relationships, and more. Since people are predominantly creatures of emotion, it is not easy to build and sustain productive relationships with poor emotional skills. Similarly, it is not easy to shape behavior without understanding the emotions driving it. Bullying and other adolescent problems such as truancy, substance abuse, poor anger management, and teen pregnancies have all been traced to low self-esteem and emotional misregulation. Emotional difficulties have also been shown to have a direct impact on physical and mental health. For instance, poor emotional regulation has been shown to be a leading cause of chronic stress.[65]

Further, there is near unanimous agreement that IQ alone is not a particularly good predictor of job performance.[66] A forty-year study of 450 boys from Somerville, Massachusetts, and a study of eighty Berkeley graduate students are two great examples showing how emotional intelligence is a better indicator of life outcomes than IQ.[67] IQ has been estimated to explain only between about 4 to 25 percent of the variance of life outcomes. An experiment carried out at Yale by Sigdal Barsade, for example, is quite revealing.[68] Barsade created four teams of business students and gave each the task of allocating employee bonuses. She also secretly planted a professional actor on each team. Each actor was asked to play out a different emotion. One feigned enthusiasm, another hostility, the third was asked to be serene, and the fourth acted depressed. Students who picked up on an actor's positive emotions were perceived by themselves and others as more competent and successful (and so received a larger bonus) than those influenced by one of the negative emotions. Interestingly, students who were successful attributed their performance to their own skills and not to others' moods. Clearly, though the emotional contagion is very infectious, its role and impact are often poorly understood and attributed.

The growing need to recognize and negotiate through cultural, social, economic, and behavioral diversity requires empathy and emotional fortitude. Understanding each other's needs and constraints is clearly indispensable for meaningful success in life. Obviously, even while conflicts are not always undesirable or avoidable, our inability to fully appreciate the root cause of a dispute or to communicate and negotiate in an effective manner can lead to far worse outcomes than necessary. Emotional intelligence may sometimes require restraint and may at other times require an even more aggressive display of passion than what one is normally disposed to. As Aristotle said, "Anyone can become angry—that is easy. But to be angry with the right person, to the right degree, at the right time, for the right purpose, and in the right way—that is not easy."[69]

Much work has been done on unpacking emotional intelligence since the 1960s. The term first appeared in a paper by Michael Beldoch in 1964, but Wayne Payne's doctoral dissertation two decades later is widely accepted as the first substantive publication on emotional intelligence.[70] The next significant milestone came about when Stanley Greenspan in 1989 and Peter Salovey and John Mayer in 1990 published the first models for EI.[71] Finally, publication of Daniel Goleman's *Emotional Intelligence: Why It Can Matter More Than IQ* in 1995 showcased the significance of emotional intelligence, contrasted it with traditional IQ measures, and essentially brought it into broader social consciousness.[72] In Goleman's words, "If your emotional abilities aren't in hand, if you don't have self-awareness, if you are not able to manage your distressing emotions, if you can't have empathy and have effective relationships, then no matter how smart you are, you are not going to get very far."[73]

At the same time, humanity has been aware of the difficulties of emotional regulation for a very long time. Lengthy discourses on this subject can be found in many religious and philosophical texts. The *Bhagavad Gita* devotes several chapters to the significance of awareness and mind control.

Verses 62 and 63 of chapter 2 trace the source of emotional upheaval and turmoil. They point out that if we're not careful, cursory interest in something can take over our mental bandwidth through growing attachment. If left unchecked, it can transition into strong desire that can spiral into emotional turmoil and loss of intellect.

> dhyāyato viṣhayān puṁsaḥ saṅgas teṣhūpajāyate
> saṅgāt sañjāyate kāmaḥ kāmāt krodho 'bhijāyate
> krodhād bhavati sammohaḥ sammohāt smṛiti-vibhramaḥ
> smṛiti-bhranśhād buddhi-nāśho buddhi-nāśhāt praṇaśhyati
>
> *While contemplating the objects of the senses, a person can develop an attachment to them; this attachment can lead to lust and anger can sprout from such lust. Anger often gives rise to bias and delusion. Such bias and delusion can lead to poor memory and bad judgment. This is what often leads a person to his or her downfall.*

Scholars and scientists have been debating the precise definition of emotional intelligence, appropriate measures for its assessment, and possible instruments for its development.[74] The most widely accepted working definition is that emotional intelligence is the ability to perceive, understand, and manage emotions to improve the odds of a desired outcome. Emotions provide the affective component of our desires, so it makes sense to pay attention to the source of an emotion as well as the desired outcome and not just deal with the chips as they may fall.

Brain development, especially in the frontal lobes, has a direct impact on our emotional growth. It is also an ongoing process through much of adolescence.[75] In fact, selective pruning of unused synaptic connections and myelination continue even into early adulthood. Myelination in the frontal lobes is responsible for the development of our skills in planning, impulse regulation, social conscience, attention to consequences, risk assessment, judgment, and decision making, among others. Thus, while most cognitive development takes place by age fifteen, executive functioning and emotional development mature only past age twenty or so. This is one of the key reasons for the poor judgment and impulsive behavior we sometimes see in teens. In other words, the brains of teenagers are malleable and present great opportunities for strengthening the desired neuronal connections. Since incomplete myelination implies that skills and habits are not yet entrenched, intentional emotional intelligence education can pay rich dividends. Incidentally, as we can infer from recurring scandals in the news, emotional development may even remain unfinished in some adults!

Emotional intelligence requires self-awareness and understanding what makes us behave a certain way, but these can often take a lifetime. It is interesting, for example, that our peer referenced sense of fairness and entitlement are quite deeply ingrained. Frans de Waal, a Dutch primatologist and ethnologist, studied this behavior in the capuchin monkeys.[76] While some monkeys were initially quite happy with pieces of cucumber as a reward for handing a small rock to a lab worker, they were upset when other monkeys received a grape for the same task. Often, our happiness might depend more than it should on the fortunes of other people. In fact, in his influential work, Robert Cialdini has identified seven different principles of persuasion and influence: reciprocity, consistency (for which commitment is a reason sometimes), social proof (or peer pressure), authority, liking (requests from people you like), scarcity, and unity (the need to belong). We often think our decisions are driven by what's best for us or our loved ones. The reality, though, is more complex. Clearly, a good understanding of the dynamics of our emotions is an important first step toward further emotional development.

The responsibility for thinking, perception, information processing, problem-solving, and decision-making normally lies with the various regions in the cerebral cortex, often referred to as the neocortex or the gray matter. Under emotional stress, the amygdala takes over this role and thus short-circuits established protocols for information processing and decision-making. During this amygdala hijack, the emotional brain takes control away from the thinking brain. Research has revealed that amygdala nuclei, located deep in the medial temporal lobes of the brain in the limbic system, perform a primary role in the memory and processing of emotional responses.[77] The amygdala can send signals to the hypothalamus, thalamic reticular nucleus, ventral tegmental area, locus coeruleus, laterodorsal tegmental nucleus, and other nuclei for the explicit purpose of mediating a quick emotional response to incoming stimuli from the thalamus. Studies by Bickart et al. suggest that the size of the amygdala varies in direct proportion to the quantity and quality of a person's social network.[78] Interesting research by Hölzel et al. shows that mindfulness meditation produces changes in gray matter concentration in brain regions involved in learning and memory processes, emotion regulation, self-referential processing, and perspective-taking.[79] While other studies have observed differences between the MRI scans of brains of experienced meditators and those of the uninitiated, this is the first study to document brain changes occurring in real time as the participants practiced mindfulness meditation. In fact, research by Davidson's team has shown that Buddhist monks who practice rigorous selfless meditation focused on unquestioning love for all creatures can significantly modulate their amygdala volume.[80] This modulation is believed to result in an increase in a person's sociability and social connectedness.[81] Put simply, the size of our amygdala can affect our social outlook, our political persuasion, and thus the very fabric of our society. This understanding of the brain can explain why limiting the curriculum and IQ testing to an assessment of brain functions associated mainly with the neocortex can leave an obvious gap in children's emotional development.

While research has clearly established a central role for the amygdala in the evaluation and regulation of emotional responses,[82] a wider set of brain regions including the ventromedial prefrontal, insula, and anterior cingulate have also been shown to be critical for supporting a range of emotional abilities.[83] Complex intra- and interhemispheric functional interactions among these regions are likely associated with our emotional intelligence. We are learning more everyday about the various biomarkers that can help us better understand the underlying neural mechanisms of this form of intelligence.

As we discussed earlier, emotional development takes many years to mature and understanding this process can be quite valuable. It is well known, for example, that young children struggle to regulate their emotions. At the same time, we often notice that when a baby cries, many of the other babies in the vicinity begin crying as well. Clearly, development of empathy has its roots in infancy. Young children do not like to see another child hurt or upset. Most young siblings play together one moment and quarrel the next. Yet they typically pull together when one is hurt. They also seem able to recognize that circumstances that upset them could also upset other children. The catch is that these empathetic instincts often compete with their more selfish impulses. For example, it isn't easy for them to share their favorite teddy bear or toy car. We should therefore pay careful attention to all the forces that hold a child's world together: both their apparent inconsiderate behavior as well as their aversion to suffering. This suggests that emotional engagement can and should begin early.

Most of us may not pursue or even consider a structured program for our child's emotional development, but many, at some time or another, will at least perform a Google search or seek professional help when their child throws a difficult tantrum. We can't really escape the emotional roller coasters that our children present from time to time. They can throw a tantrum when they're very hungry, tired, sleepy, or otherwise frustrated with their inability to control their world. All creatures have a need for independence and control. Young children typically have little control over the world presented to them by the adults in their lives. Negotiations with other children and mastery of new skills will present their own set of frustrations. At the same time, they may not have the emotional capacity or even enough vocabulary to label and share their feelings. When children don't possess the tool set to deal with these emotional demands, they occasionally break into a tantrum. At such times, it helps to understand where they are coming from so we can offer solutions that give them some sense of control. Perhaps they get to pick the movie or the food for a party. Anticipating fears and conflicts can also help us proactively prepare them. Of course, acknowledging an issue does not mean we're going to solve the issue for them to their satisfaction.

Self-awareness is thus an essential step for enhancing emotional understanding. There are many vehicles for building this awareness and emotional capacity. Literature, drama, and other forms of artistic portrayal can be effective tools for self-awareness, so humanities programs are a great resource for facilitating deeper emotional learning. An understanding of the diversity and depth of our emotions and the aesthetics of the human condition, for example, is indispensable for any authentic artistic endeavor. As an effective vehicle for emotional development, art can help a child explore different possibilities through an imaginary world. It enables a process of discovery of oneself as well as one's relationship to the world. Artistic license is a time-honored vehicle for letting us construct imagery for an alternate reality—often a reality that may be difficult to acknowledge. Therefore, in addition to helping us understand the world as it exists today, art can be used to build a bridge to a different tomorrow. As such, art is clearly a natural language of creativity and emotional intelligence. In the words of Thomas Merton, the Anglo-American poet and mystic, "Art enables us to find ourselves and lose ourselves at the same time."[84]

Emotional development can also benefit from play. Friedrich Fröbel and Rudolf Steiner, among others, emphasized the importance of imaginative play.[85] Research has clearly documented the many benefits of fantasy play.[86] We find that children, with their fertile imagination, gravitate to themes that draw on some of their most recent or novel experiences, typically those that highlight social relationships. Their flights of imagination appear to be an attempt to internalize their learning. In this context, we can find many similarities between an accomplished adult artist and a child. Fantasy play is a valuable platform that gives children the artistic license to help validate and reinforce their daily experiences, thus strengthening their synaptic networks. This is not too different from the pursuits of an adult artist who wants to make sense of events in our society. Children and artists seek a remarkably similar end goal and they both need some artistic cover to succeed.

Children can also often gain valuable insights into their own behavior as they recognize it in other characters and scenarios. Many child psychologists of the twentieth century believe that fairy tales help children grapple with their inner fears, providing them with a greater understanding of the struggles in life. Fantasy play and fairy tales are thus valuable tools for emotional growth, allowing each child to find his or her own sense of meaning and purpose in these tales of triumph, often against great odds.

Sharing circles are yet another effective tool for facilitating greater emotional understanding and competency. These circles can be based on a daily or weekly theme and held at a place and time that provides the most uninterrupted attention possible for the group. These can be successful only if the attendees are able to share freely, openly, and equitably and with minimum interruption or criticism.

Emotional development can also be greatly facilitated by immersion. Children are typically quite efficient at soaking up their environment. Their natural curiosity, coupled with their strong need for order and stability, presents us with an excellent window of opportunity. Good role models can therefore go a long way in promoting the right behaviors and learning in a child. Role models also help children truly believe in the possibilities that the future holds for them. Every child can benefit from positive role models that look like them. Additionally, consistent behavior from teachers and parents would help children appreciate and develop a keen moral compass as young children can be led astray by mixed messages and unreliable adults. It would naturally be difficult for a child to accept that actions would have consequences if their everyday experiences don't bear that out. It is therefore important to not overlook or condone inappropriate behavior or be inconsistent in our response to transgressions. Of course, the nature of the consequences should be a strong function of both the actions and the age and emotional competence of the child.

Figure 4.3. Children at Sankalpa Academy exercising their artistic muscles.

Opportunities for promotion of emotional understanding present themselves all the time. For instance, children can send cards to friends and relatives as appropriate. These could be simple thank-you notes, sympathy cards, or notes of admiration or felicitation. While children learn most from incidental, everyday behaviors of their parents and teachers, adults can also, on occasion, engineer age-appropriate intentional experiences to stimulate deeper understanding. For example, it would be valuable to expose children to those lifting heavier burdens and those less fortunate than themselves. Some of these experiences can also turn into opportunities for service learning, volunteer work, and charity. Exposure to a modest amount of stress, perhaps by confronting a known fear repeatedly under a controlled environment, can similarly help build resilience and prepare us for a future emotional crisis.

Our history is also replete with outstanding examples of perseverance, compassion, and ethics from people such as Mohandas Karamchand Gandhi, Nelson Mandela, Mother Teresa, Martin Luther King Jr., Abraham Lincoln, and many others. Periodic exposure to such giants can help inspire and reinforce emotional learning and engagement. Of course, there are countless heroes right among us, people who strive for extremely high ideals despite onerous odds. It is important to not leave children with the wrong notion that outstanding integrity and leadership are somehow social anomalies. We can find remarkable individuals in every walk of life. Elinor Sauerwein from Modesto, California, for example, was someone who made it her mission to help people in need.[87] She never owned a clothes dryer, grew her own vegetables and fruits, never ate out, and never went to the movies or paid for cable television. Her extremely frugal life supported her mission to help as many people as she could. After she passed away, her estate was able to donate a little over $1.7 million to the Salvation Army, and her gift will keep on giving for decades to come. Emotional intelligence is about our ability to discern between a broad range of emotions and behaviors. It is therefore necessary, in an age-appropriate manner, to also expose children to historical figures who have not acted in the best interests of society. This kind of exposure is also helpful for stimulating critical thinking.

The discussion thus far has focused on the cultivation of a culture conducive to fostering empathy and emotional understanding. As children grow up, they need help in developing higher-order emotional skills. The first challenge for effective emotional engagement lies in the difficult art of listening. It's essential to be aware of the climate influencing a speaker such as the speaker's context, culture, and other circumstances, as well as our own dogmas and biases, to be able to understand both "what" is being said and the emotions behind the message or "why" it is being said. Logic may not always explain behaviors and motivations, and we may have to rely on emotion to bridge gaps.

Good listening skills also help us succeed in our second challenge: formulation of a good response. The end goal is to build proficiency in anticipating the potential reception and outcomes for different responses. Inaccurate perceptions can cloud our understanding of the real message more often than we might think. Therefore, refining our perception can improve our understanding and emotional response. Familiarity with a broad range of social, cultural, and economic contexts and emotions would give young people the necessary breadth and preparation to improve the accuracy of their perceptions.

We need an open mind to ensure that messages are not misread. This requires a high degree of self-esteem and comfort in one's own skin. These are therefore important prerequisites for accurate emotional understanding. Environments at home and school that respect the thoughts and opinions of children are clearly essential for their self-esteem and emotional health. It is therefore vital that every child has an emotionally supportive environment. Exercises to help showcase strengths or positive attributes can also help boost self-image and self-esteem. Role playing can therefore be an effective instrument for accessing and analyzing a broad array of emotions.

Managing emotional engagement to facilitate a desired outcome is a difficult but highly desired skill. This is especially critical in circumstances where it's necessary to choose from among many equally bad or good alternatives. Emotional management does not, of course, mean suppression of emotions. Suppression of emotions may be an optimum response under some circumstances, but it's not necessarily the best option in many cases. Lack of emotion might even be perceived as lack of empathy in some cases. It is difficult to be successful in negotiating a desired outcome to a dispute if a person either does not understand the stakeholders' interests and motivations or is unable to formulate or communicate an acceptable resolution. Mock conflict resolution exercises can therefore be a helpful tool for building this type of competency.

Even though emotional intelligence only concerns itself with the management of our emotions to ensure desired outcomes, children should also be able to appreciate the implications of the different outcomes and choices. This is not possible without a curriculum that also focuses on awareness, ethics, empathy, and cultural understanding. Given the large diversity in acceptable ethical behavior, one must be cognizant of prevailing cultural values and sensitivities in formulating such a curriculum or in prescribing standards for outcomes. Ethics is therefore another vital part of a holistic education.

Ethics as the Compass for Life

> Ethics is knowing the difference between what you have a right to do and what is right to do.
>
> —POTTER STEWART

The following passage is from the autobiography of Mohandas Karamchand Gandhi; it describes a memorable experience he had when he was about twelve:

> There is an incident which occurred at the examination during my first year at the high school and which is worth recording. Mr. Giles, the Educational Inspector, had come on a visit of inspection. He had set us five words to write as a spelling exercise. One of the words was "kettle." I had mis-spelt it. The teacher tried to prompt me with the point of his boot, but I would not be prompted. It was beyond me to see that he wanted me to copy the spelling from my neighbour's slate, for I had thought that the teacher was there to supervise us against copying. The result was that all the boys, except myself, were found to have spelt every word correctly. Only I had been stupid. The teacher tried later to bring this stupidity home to me, but without effect. I never could learn the art of "copying."[88]

This story continues to be a staple of many classroom discussions across India to illustrate Gandhi's character and his commitment to truth and honesty. The story has not lost any of its appeal over the last century and a half. Why would it? Cheating on tests is still as commonplace today as it apparently was generations ago. In a 2002 survey of high school students by the Josephson Institute, Michael Josephson found that the number of students who admitted to cheating on an exam at least once in the previous year soared from 61 percent in 1992 to 74 percent in 2002.[89] There is perhaps some reason for hope as only 51 percent of the students said that they had cheated on an exam at least once in a 2012 survey![90] This issue received significant media attention in 2019 when Operation Varsity Blues uncovered an undergraduate college admissions scandal that led to imprisonment for about two dozen prominent entrepreneurs, investors, executives, and actors.[91] About thirty-three parents of college applicants were accused of making illegal payments of more than $25 million between 2011 and 2018 to William "Rick" Singer. Singer was charged with inflating standardized test scores and bribing key college admissions staff at several top American universities. Singer confessed to fraud involving college admissions for children of more than 750 families and ended up with financial ruin, public shame, and a long prison sentence. The bottom line is that the irony in the appeal of Gandhi's story and, more importantly, its continued relevance should not be lost on us. Time and again, I have seen this story used to extol Gandhi's virtues, never to lament the low expectations we have of our teachers, young people, and educational institutions. What message would this story send to impressionable young people? Perhaps that what Gandhi did is not what's expected from a typical student, that Gandhi was more an exception to the rule?

We continue to hear the unending drumbeat of scandals in political, corporate, and financial circles. While these scandals cause irreparable damage to public faith in our institutions, the real tragedy is in their impact on our youth's impressionable minds. These incidents can sadly end up inspiring the next wave of unethical behavior. Even though the ramifications seem far higher now, it is difficult to argue that the dynamics underlying the moral failing of our civic leaders is a recent development. They are likely just symptomatic of a material world that has seen a rapid growth in opportunities for unethical conduct. Integrity and self-esteem do not appear to be universally valued and sadly, are sometimes even believed to impede social success.

Ironically, people who have been caught chasing power, influence, or riches with little regard to propriety and ethics are, in many cases, already well off and do not really need such aggravation. It is almost as if they simply had not taken the time to truly ponder the choices in front of them. One gets the sense that such people are sometimes on autopilot, chasing goals and dreams that don't add much to their quality of life. While these scandals are the bubbles that have surfaced, there are other ominous signs looming beneath the surface. There has been a significant rise, for instance, in the demand for management consultants as young executives struggle to cope with the allure and stresses of their professions.[92] Despite apparent career progress and oversubscribed lifestyles, there are many who seem to lack a coherent sense of purpose or a strong enough ethical mooring.

Instilling a high regard for integrity and character might appear especially difficult in today's environment. However, the ubiquity of social media and its long memory trail should perhaps make it easier to sensitize children to the possibility that even a single lapse in judgment can potentially ruin their reputation for years to come. Education should help them understand our interconnectedness and our shared purpose. Even if schools don't have a specific curriculum for ethics education, there are many opportunities as ethical concerns show up in everyday interactions as well as in discussions of history, civics, and science lessons.

From a young age, children develop their own sense of fairness and justice. At the same time, as Piaget noted, as children become socially aware, their responses to choices and questions change from being intuitive to being factual and are eventually dictated by social acceptance. Children do realize, as they grow older, that other children may have their own choices and preferences and that they may not align with their own values. One child may feel that loyalty is paramount and tattletaling is unethical, while another may feel that fairness demands that he reveal his friend's plans to the rest of the group. In addition, schools and other institutions often have written and unwritten rules for behavior and propriety that may not always align with a child's values. Navigating and understanding this web of information is essential for their holistic growth. Values are our own rules that we rely on to make personal decisions about what is right and what is wrong and what is good and what is bad. These values may or may not comport with the morals that society expects from us or judges us by. Ethics, on the other hand, are a set of rules that tend to be adopted by people as well as professions. Journalists and genetic researchers, for instance, may have their own written and unwritten codes of conduct. As our values evolve, so will our ethics. Often, when we ponder whether an individual's actions are ethical, we may be judging them using our own narrow set of values. In fact, given the widening polarization in our civic life, there is a growing need for children to engage more with those who hold opposing opinions.

We face many kinds of ethical dilemmas all the time. Do we only buy fair trade food? Do we only invest in net zero companies? The Ethics Institute at the all-girls Kent Place School in New Jersey and Ad Astra, Elon Musk's erstwhile exclusive private school in Los Angeles (and its successor schools, Astra Nova and Synthesis), are a few of the schools that have made open-ended discussions of ethical conundrums that require critical thinking, debating skills, and an ability to balance individual and community needs a central piece of their curricula.

While Astra Nova and Synthesis are relatively small schools that just got started, Kent Place School, on the other hand, has a comprehensive program on ethics including integration of ethics in all its disciplines and its summer program, exclusive ethics electives, ethics clubs, and ethics bowl competitions. They provide engaging challenges that are no doubt building a very engaged cohort of compassionate and wise student leaders. One of their case studies involves a woman who was thinking of leaving her disabled husband. Caring for his injuries had become challenging, and it was demanding all the woman's energy. With the passage of time, the couple's affection for each other had also diminished. The class had to debate if it was ethically wrong for her to leave him.

Huge ethics-related scandals grab headlines and might leave some with the false sense that only a small minority engage in unethical conduct. On the other hand, there are many obvious and not-so-obvious ethical questions that almost all of us have to contend with every day. Inevitably, there tends to be an ethical dimension to most decisions made in a democracy. For example, some of the companies that generate a lot of employment may also be exploiting tax loopholes or polluting the environment, or they may be large enough to unfairly manipulate the marketplace. It would be difficult to hold such companies to account unless ethics is a social priority. Similarly, low-cost imports from a country may be enabling human rights violations in the source country. It is vital that these important questions and the critical thinking skills to analyze them be woven into all subject areas of the curriculum, so that children can sharpen their awareness and develop fluency in making ethical choices.

The Wonders of Empirical Sciences

> It is paradoxical, yet true, to say that the more we know, the more ignorant we become in the absolute sense, for it is only through enlightenment that we become conscious of our limitations. Precisely one of the most gratifying results of intellectual evolution is the continuous opening up of new and greater prospects.
>
> —NIKOLA TESLA

Most science textbooks credit Nicolaus Copernicus (1473–1543) with establishing the heliocentric model of the universe. The contributions of Aristarchus of Samos (third century BCE), Seleucus of Seleucia (second century BCE), and Aryabhata of India (fifth century CE) are not as well recognized.[93] While Aristarchus, Seleucus, and Aryabhata had enough empirical data to substantiate their claims of a heliocentric universe, their work did not muster the credibility and exposure needed to bring along the larger scientific community. In a sense, the imagination of the world had not ripened enough to accept this reality. On the other hand, Copernicus, with his magnum opus *De revolutionibus orbium coelestium* (On the Revolutions of the Celestial Spheres), managed to turn the world upside down. As a result of the emotional toll that accompanied the demise of the earth-centric worldview and the scientific awakening that ensued, this watershed event even began to be referred to as the Copernican Revolution. Incidentally, Copernicus had anticipated this firestorm, at least to some degree. This is why he is believed to have delayed the publication of his book by over twenty-five years, almost until he was on his deathbed. He had confessed to his closest friends his morbid fear of scorn and ridicule from the clergy and the establishment, given the impact of his finding on the prevailing theological claims. The eventual publication of the treatise during his lifetime is likely a result of intense lobbying by Georg Joachim Rheticus, one of his most ardent students.[94]

History reminds us time and again that changing opinions and established order are never easy. The scorn faced by Copernicus and the opposition Charles Darwin faced to secure broader acceptance of his thesis on the origin of species illustrate the resistance from establishment and other believers and beneficiaries of status quo. These battles serve as reminders that progress does not come easily—it takes tremendous passion and perseverance. While almost all species seem to possess some level of mastery over their environment, *Homo sapiens* have come much further by standing on the shoulders of our predecessors. Yet, this is despite the fact that most of us also find it difficult to accept change. The more it disrupts the status quo or shakes the foundations of our beliefs and way of life, the harder it is to embrace it. For these reasons, new understanding often develops in fits and starts.

While new insights might take exceptional ingenuity and perhaps some fortitude, their broader acceptance depends heavily on the awareness and "scientific literacy" of the larger society. The larger the gulf, the greater the delay in reaping the benefits of any new understanding. While the wonders of science and the pursuit of knowledge should be reason enough for nations to aggressively pursue scientific literacy, the need to narrow the gulf between the scientific community and the general population makes it a critical imperative. It is not unreasonable that a nation's public policies are ultimately informed by the awareness and scientific temperament of its broader population, especially in a democracy. It is also often difficult to get beyond the short-term economics of issues such as global warming, space exploration, and even human and natural resource management. The cost of deficient or misinformed scientific policies can be staggering. In fact, poor scientific literacy is a major impediment to overall progress at every level. Individual self-esteem, employment opportunities, health of the economy and social institutions, equitable access to resources and justice, the well-being of future generations, and broader acceptance of public policies can all be adversely affected by poor scientific literacy.

According to Tan et al., we need to "rethink the epistemology and pedagogy in science classrooms today as the practice of science education needs to be proactive and relevant to students and prepare them for life in the present and in the future."[95] Peter Fensham, the Australian science educator, and many others have created a science, technology, and society (STS) movement within science education reform to address concerns around scientific literacy. They believe that students need to fully understand the significance of scientific discoveries, especially their impact on everyday life. They want students to engage with different voices and viewpoints on these issues and not be content with simply learning scientific facts and established theories—theories which are often far removed from everyday realities.[96] It is of course naive to expect that changes to the epistemology and pedagogy in science classrooms will be easy to implement or that they alone will deliver the change we are seeking. We also need to simultaneously prepare our children to be more empathetic, better critical thinkers, more amenable to change, and more ready to prioritize long-term needs.

By many accounts, the launch of Sputnik in October 1957 heralded a golden age in science education in the US.[97] Surveys have consistently revealed that there has been a general decline since then in interest in science and careers related to science among primary and secondary school students.[98] As we discussed earlier, Michigan State University professor William Schmidt interpreted results from TIMSS, the most extensive international comparative study of mathematics and science education ever attempted, to conclude that

US students steadily fall behind other countries with each advancing grade. While American fourth graders outperformed all other countries in science, they barely scored above the international average in the eighth grade and finished at the bottom by the twelfth grade. It is disappointing that the 2019 National Assessment of Educational Progress found that only 36 percent of fourth graders, 35 percent of eighth graders, and 22 percent of twelfth graders in the US scored at the proficient level or above.[99] Even so, waning interest in science education and science careers appears to be a universal problem that is not limited to specific geographies.

In many countries, classroom science is typically dominated by abstract theory or summaries of knowledge inherited from earlier generations.[100] We spend an inordinate amount of time learning known scientific facts, often trivial information such as distances and conversion scales, and too little on the process or the human adventure that led to discovery, or the implications of the various discoveries.[101] While proficiency in designing experiments and formulating and validating hypotheses should be an important goal of science education, experiments are, unfortunately, often time consuming and expensive. Consequently, there is typically a lot more discussion of active science research in the news media than in the classroom. And as meaningful assessments of experimental skills are challenging, many science competency tests also rely a lot more than they should on theoretical understanding. It shouldn't come as a surprise therefore that many children aren't adequately introduced to the vibrancy and excitement of the scientific discovery process, or the scientific skills associated with repeatability and peer review. To create future scientists, we need to cherish and nurture children's curiosity. Innovations and discoveries often flow from those who are skilled at proposing hypotheses, designing experiments, analyzing measurement results, and extracting the right understanding from this empirical data. The skills needed to validate, reject, or refine hypotheses can only be honed through practice and perseverance.

Carl Sagan, the well-known American astrophysicist and author, once said: "I am often amazed at how much more capability and enthusiasm for science there is among elementary school youngsters than among college students."[102] We appear to lose many children along the way to the higher grade levels. Significant delays in gratification that result from emphasis on knowledge over praxes can be taxing to young students. Given this context, it shouldn't be difficult to imagine why many of them become bored and disengaged. This loss of engagement might render even basic scientific skills and understanding inaccessible to many students, and they end up missing the forest for the trees. If a high school student doesn't experience awe and wonder, then we have greatly undermined our chances of winning her over to a scientific career. In fact, this is also responsible for poor scientific literacy rates and for society's inability to embrace new findings.

Figure 4.4. Children at Sankalpa Academy are fascinated by the lifecycle of butterflies.

It is therefore reassuring that the National Research Council convened a committee of distinguished scientists and science education experts to look at the challenges in science education in the US in the twenty-first century. The committee concluded that, to gain proficiency in science, children need to (1) know, use, and interpret scientific explanations of the natural world, (2) generate and evaluate scientific evidence and explanations, (3) understand the nature and development of scientific knowledge, and (4) participate productively in scientific practices and discourse.[103] To help educators, the National Research Council also compiled a list of instructional experiences and case studies for teaching science from kindergarten to eighth grade.[104] To do all this well, science education should instill a healthy respect for data and facts and train children to keep an open mind. As important as intuition is in the design of experiments and formulation of hypotheses, many discoveries often turn out to be counterintuitive. Until science is taught the way it should be, it is not reasonable to count on science education to foster true scientific literacy. Perhaps advanced video games, virtual reality, and other technological innovations can be called on to augment individualizing learning as well as testing. It is also critical that formative assessments test the competencies we desire and not proxies.

Going forward, the social impact of scientific prophecies will likely be increasingly dramatic. The growing symbiosis between science and technology and the potential impact on commercial interests implies that all science and practitioners of science are likely to be scrutinized even more closely.[105] Science metaphors have always been heavily colored by the cultural backgrounds of the scientists. Even so, national, economic, and political persuasions are all likely to increasingly influence and bias the formulation and prioritization of research initiatives. We cannot therefore ignore the cultural, social, economic, and political contexts of mainstream science research. This is another reason why scientific awareness is an increasingly compelling social imperative. There is also increasing recognition that sustainable development, equitable distribution of natural resources, and realization of efficiencies in overall resource management are more important than ever, so they too should be integrated into science education.[106] Students should be exposed to all these considerations, and science should not be presented as an agnostic pursuit that is completely objective and immune to the value systems of the researchers.

From the development of a scientific temperament to building fluency with technologies, science curricula around the world embrace a wide range of curricular objectives. At the same time, we might need out-of-the-box solutions to ensure that scientific experimentation is not sacrificed or unduly diluted due to economic considerations. While many schools do already incorporate available public resources such as research institutions and science or natural history museums into their lesson plans, we should consider increasing the breadth and depth of this engagement. Ambitious schools can also perhaps aspire to meet some of the civic needs of their region or city. These projects can address opportunities for efficiency in areas such as urban planning, agriculture, and public health. The opportunities for these win-win collaborations are almost endless.

Many innovators have pioneered science education approaches that are worth emulating. Inspired by Leon Lederman's work in the disadvantaged neighborhoods of Chicago, French Physics Nobel Prize winner Georges Charpak, with the support of the French Academy of Sciences, developed a new curriculum and pedagogy for elementary schools called "la main à la pâte" or "Hands-on Science."[107] In this program, children conduct experiments, study outcomes, and try to draw conclusions. While there is curricular guidance, they're also free to experiment on their own. There is some preliminary data to suggest that this hands-on methodology helps both in the acquisition of domain knowledge and in gaining fluency in the scientific method. Interestingly, children exposed to this pedagogy were also able to demonstrate more mature social skills and rational thinking, in addition to finding their path from simple observations to validated conclusions.

The spirit of la main à la pâte should not be difficult to emulate. I saw this, for instance, in one of my cousin's lesson plans. My cousin taught the fifth grade in a government school in a small village in India. One day, their discussion veered to the dangers posed by plastic debris to stray animals. Many stray cows and goats were ingesting flimsy single-use plastic bags while foraging for food in vegetable markets. This led to too many avoidable animal casualties in India. To educate and sensitize her students, my cousin took her class to the local vegetable market on a field trip. The kids fanned out and talked to the vendors and customers to get their understanding of the magnitude of this problem and what the vendors and shoppers were doing to help. It was already illegal for the vendors to offer plastic bags, but not everyone bought into the ban. This outing turned out to be a memorable science lesson for both the vendors and the children!

Like most subjects, ultimately, science is a human story. There is often a gripping tale of adventure and triumph behind many of our scientific breakthroughs. From Archimedes and Aryabhata to Copernicus and Galileo, the stories of each of the men and women behind scientific pursuits provide a powerful example of our curiosity, ingenuity, and resilience. Bardeen, the only person to have won the Nobel Prize twice in Physics, teamed up with Brattain in an intriguing patent battle against their co-winner of the Nobel Prize. The drama in most of these adventures is often an illustration of the timeless quest of humans for deeper understanding. While some have been fascinated by the material world, others have been captivated by the wonders of life. While some have focused on nourishing and restoring health, others have immersed themselves in exploring the amazing diversity of life around us. There is, in fact, evidence of dentistry in the Indus Valley Civilization as far back as 7000 BCE and cataract surgery in 600 BCE. Hippocrates made fundamental contributions to Western medicine around 400 BCE! Many have multiple interests. Avicenna (980–1037) was a Persian physician, astronomer, chemist, and philosopher, a man with a diverse set of passions and pursuits. Hypatia (born c. 350–370; died 415 CE) was a neoplatonist philosopher, astronomer, and mathematician. Leonardo da Vinci and Benjamin Franklin are widely recognized polymaths. Jagadish Chandra Bose is another more recent polymath who, in addition to breakthrough understanding in physics, biology, and botany, also wrote science fiction. Linus Pauling (1901–1994) was a leader in both quantum chemistry and molecular biology. Marie Curie was the first woman to win a Nobel Prize, the first person to win a Nobel Prize twice, and the only person to win a Nobel Prize in two scientific fields. Hermann von Helmholtz (1821–1894) was an eclectic researcher with contributions to physiology, psychology, physics, and philosophy! The life stories of these exceptional men and women present a wonderful opportunity for emotional engagement with the essential business of science and can help promote scientific skills and temperament in students. Exposure to their persistence and their trials and tribulations is often a more rewarding and enlightening experience than just a dry introduction to the fruits of their labor. Our pursuit of knowledge and understanding is both timeless and liberating. While Galileo, who made pathbreaking contributions to many sciences, was perhaps the most influential empiricist in history, there were numerous others before and after him who strongly believed that experience alone could help our minds evolve from a "tabula rasa" state. Fascination with the world and a passion for understanding its secrets are an essential hallmark of a scientific thinker. This is what science education should seek to foster.

Axioms and the Edifice of Mathematics

> The moving power of mathematical invention
> is not reasoning but imagination.
> —AUGUSTUS DE MORGAN

Over the years, our understanding of how the physical world operates has increasingly relied on the language of mathematics. In fact, mathematics plays a pivotal role in powering many aspects of our commerce, and math skills are essential for our financial well-being. Our mathematical vocabulary and the mathematical representations of the world often grow in lockstep with our understanding of the laws nature seems to obey. Even though math can never assign meaning to our conceptual understanding of why our world works the way it does, it can help us arrive at that understanding through models for its structure, form, and function.

There is great inherent beauty in mathematical relationships as they are built with bricks of self-evident axioms glued together with logic. Due to its inherent predictability, this subject of axioms and theorems is perhaps the most objective of all disciplines, so a proficient student can be confident in his or her knowledge (or lack thereof) independent of a book, guide, or teacher. This independence can be invaluable in the development of a child's self-confidence and self-esteem, which are, in themselves, the bedrock of all learning.

While mathematical prowess and education have been valued since the earliest of times, the International Commission on Mathematical Instruction (ICMI) in 1908 is perhaps the first formal assembly in the Western world for streamlining math education. There was a significant renewal of interest in math in the 1960s, and this led to the first International Congress on Mathematical Education (ICME) in Lyon, France, in 1969. Interest in math education has been growing exponentially ever since, especially taking off after the Second International Science Study (SISS) in 1984. In fact, in a landmark study, "The Toolbox Revisited," Clifford Adelman used federal data to follow students who were eighth graders in 1988.[108] Adelman discovered that students who completed an advanced math curriculum in high school were much more likely to go on to also earn a bachelor's degree, almost regardless of their ethnicity, family income, or even the educational background of their parents.

From basic skills needed to compare loans, do our taxes, or comparison shop to more advanced abilities that let us interpret and anticipate social trends, demographic shifts, career opportunities, or scientific data, math permeates almost all aspects of modern life. It's no longer solely the exclusive purview of the college-bound or those aspiring for careers in physics, engineering, or business; it's increasingly needed for a variety of basic transactions in everyday civic life. Lack of proficiency in math would likely be a major impediment, one that would inflict a significant toll on our self-esteem as well as our quality of life. The good news is that such aggravation is not needed. Math really doesn't have to cripple our lives, especially since math education, compared to subjects like physics and chemistry that typically require significant investments in expensive laboratory equipment, can be very affordable and accessible.

Even as far back as 1989, in *Everybody Counts: A Report to the Nation on the Future of Mathematics Education*, the Mathematical Sciences Education Board had recognized that the jobs of the future would increasingly need individuals able to think outside the box and to make accurate sense of chaotic data.[109] They foresaw that future generations would need to thrive in an environment of constant change and ambiguity. The authors issued a clarion call for help with the bold assertion that complacency resulting from a tradition of minimum math expectations had resulted in a crisis. They claimed that children were unprepared for even the jobs of the day, let alone the jobs of the future. They lamented that the character of the math curriculum and instruction had ended up filtering students out of promising careers and often out of schooling itself, resulting in almost a 50 percent or so dropout rate from math courses every year. Since alarm bells have been going off for many years now about the lack of quality in math education in the US, it was not a complete shock in 2018 when the US came in thirty-eighth among seventy-nine countries that took the mathematics literacy test administered by PISA.

It is an open secret that uninspiring teachers and teaching methods end up frightening many children away from math. While most forms of knowledge are cumulative in nature, math can be especially unforgiving if its basic concepts are not well understood. Students who fail to keep up with math in elementary school face a daunting task in middle school and beyond. It is therefore important to ensure that children are only advanced based on subject mastery and not to simply meet schedule requirements.

In this context, it is interesting to review the reform of the math curriculum that some countries undertook. Singapore rose to the top of the ladder in TIMSS in 1995 after coming in sixteenth among twenty-six countries in the Second International Science Study (SISS) in 1984. This success was attributed to the large-scale reforms that Singapore instituted in 1990. They introduced a differentiated curriculum that emphasized process skills and a focus on the development of a positive attitude. Singapore also began tracking students based on ability. China rolled out a similar reform of the standards for their math curriculum in 2005.[110] The emphasis was shifted from knowledge acquisition to processes and methods for the development of learning ability.[111] China supplemented this with changes in both teacher training and the methodology for student appraisal. The new curriculum also placed an emphasis on assessment of emotions and attitudes expressed by students, in addition to their proficiency in problem-solving and their ability to apply their knowledge to novel scenarios.

James Harper, in his travels in 1999 and 2000, discovered an extensive apparatus for social intervention in Japan.[112] He found that about 65 percent of the children in middle school and 85 percent of those in high school attend juku—cram schools for academic support and competitive test preparation. Harper also found that education was a significant priority in Japan and that many mothers were intimately involved in their children's education.

The Teaching Gap: Best Ideas from the World's Teachers for Improving Education in the Classroom by James W. Stigler and James Hiebert is an interesting read.[113] The authors try to understand why elementary school students from the worst Japanese schools routinely outperform students from the best American schools. According to Stigler and Hiebert, for the most part, the root cause for the performance gap lies not in the teachers but in their teaching methods. According to them, the math curriculum in Japan is coherent and designed around the development of an appreciation for various mathematical relationships. In contrast, most teaching in the US is focused on training in math procedures. Mathematical relationships are often presented as established facts. There is little time allocated to the joys of discovery and experimentation or to pursuits of mathematical proofs.

While the power of mathematics in enabling independent thought and in building self-confidence is well understood, it's extremely important to also recognize the harm that can be caused by real or perceived limitations in math proficiency. These problems can lead to lower self-esteem, higher reliance on authority, and even loss of interest in school itself. During my schooling in India, I witnessed some of the suffering that can be inflicted on children who are left behind. I saw many struggling students flock to cram schools for help with staying in the race. Understandably, given their preoccupation with test scores, these cram schools were almost always focused on training students in math procedures and not on strengthening their knowledge of the fundamentals. As a result, attendance at a cram school was almost always an acknowledgment of the failure of the traditional school system. While I have also encountered extremely motivated teachers who inspire amazing student participation and engagement, this was unfortunately more of an exception than the rule. In other words, there are several essential challenges with math education that are quite universal.

Given this state of affairs, it is important to gain a deeper understanding of what is ailing math education in the US and abroad. Since his 2003 presentation, Schmidt had repeatedly argued for greater coherence in math education, among other reforms.[114] While his observation on the decline in performance between the fourth and twelfth grades in the US is reminiscent of Torrance's famous observation of a "fourth-grade slump," it is hard to explain why this only happens to children in the US.[115] According to the authors of *Everybody Counts: A Report to the Nation on the Future of Mathematics Education*, most US schools consider math to be all about answers and the process of getting to those answers and not as much about creative thinking or the beauty of the underlying concepts and structure.[116] Teachers are frustrated and unable to establish a high-quality professional ethic as they lack control over the ends and means in the current educational hierarchy. Most students in public schools in the US can connect the dots and fully understand several of the basic concepts only when they gain meaningful retrospective understanding through an advanced vantage point years down the road. Often, the fog of confusion persists far too long and only students who take advanced courses see the light at the end of the tunnel. This approach is simply a recipe for frustration and failure for a majority of the students.

William Schmidt and others have also lamented that the math curriculum in the US often introduces relatively advanced content in the early grades before students have had an opportunity to truly master more basic concepts. Strangely, we also continue to circle back to basic numeracy skills all the way through eighth grade, and sometimes even beyond. Schmidt has characterized the US curriculum as a mile wide and an inch deep! In one study, he and his colleagues also found that US teachers scored at the bottom of the list on an algebra test of middle school teachers from six countries.[117] In addition, scorecards from the National Assessment of Educational Progress over the last two decades have documented the slow progress in closing the large achievement gap across socioeconomic levels.[118] The good news is that we have the necessary instruments to inform us of the magnitude and nature of the crisis.

Good math education requires that a child isn't rushed and that he or she has the time needed to make sense of a concept before moving on. This is especially important in the elementary grades. There is compelling evidence that children can make meaningful progress in understanding math only if they construct it for themselves, often through a hierarchical process of assimilation and accommodation.[119] Given how personal the process of knowledge creation is, we shouldn't simply hand children information for passive acceptance. There is substantial research that formative assessments that monitor comprehension of concepts are one of the most efficient vehicles for both student achievement and teachers' professional satisfaction.[120]

A good example is the Cognitively Guided Instruction (CGI) curriculum developed by education researchers Thomas Carpenter, Elizabeth Fennema, Penelope Peterson, Megan Loef Franke, and Linda Levi.[121] It seeks to assess the processes that students access for solving math problems. Formative assessments require testing within and between lessons and occasionally within and between units for the sole purpose of refining lessons and curricular goals based on real-time feedback from students. Such individualized attention can pay for itself many times over since we would not then need as much direct instruction or remedial work in high schools or colleges as we do today. In most cases, this would require small classrooms in the early grades and teachers with good domain knowledge as well as expertise in content-specific pedagogy.

To cater to these needs, the Association of Mathematics Teacher Educators (AMTE), the Association of State Supervisors of Mathematics (ASSM), the National Council of Supervisors of Mathematics (NCSM), and the National Council of Teachers of Mathematics (NCTM) have recommended the use of Elementary Mathematics Specialists (EMS professionals) in pre-K to grade 6 environments to improve student proficiency.[122] They have also identified a curriculum of content knowledge, pedagogical knowledge, and leadership skills for these EMS professionals. This is one of the clearest acknowledgments yet of the need for specialized intervention in the early years of a child. These specialists should of course also be adept at uncovering any underlying challenges with short-term memory, distractibility, grit, and so on that may be driving the more visible higher-level math proficiency concerns.

Figure 4.5. Individual support strengthened math understanding and engagement of Sankalpa learners.

In addition to math teaching, testing has also been a contentious topic. While math administrators and school boards are often enamored with the data that math testing can generate, educators have had many concerns about the impact of year-end summative testing, especially if the results are going to be used for decisions such as college admissions.[123] To keep children interested and engaged, it is important to ensure that testing is used to facilitate a child's math journey and not to rob them of their love of math. Given that most testing is designed to filter students, it is not surprising that there is tremendous pressure on teachers to teach to these tests. In addition, frequent use of multiple-choice questions on tests sometimes sends the wrong message that answers are more important than a student's understanding of mathematical relationships. Since testing values speed, domain knowledge often takes second place to the ability to handle stress well—to quickly prioritize and think clearly. While these are valuable skills, they should not be conflated with math ability. Tests are also known to encourage intensive short-term memorization, often heavily informed by the format of the test. Clearly, this culture and mindset is not helpful for either true learning or for long-term retention. For testing to be useful, it should be personalized, periodic, and based on pedagogical value, not driven by convenience.

In addition, it can be very helpful for parents and preschool programs to engage children in mathematical conversations from an early age. Seamless use of mathematical vocabulary in everyday activities at home, for example, can help children build math vocabulary and thinking. Paying attention to both pace and novelty is likely to keep children interested. Individualization can help educators ensure that a child's weakness in one area such as communication or test-taking does not derail their overall math learning and joy. In fact, one can tailor lessons to leverage a child's strengths to help develop opportunity areas and perhaps competencies such as risk-taking, delayed gratification, goal-setting, and planning.

While there is no shortage of tutors, academies, and strategies for math coaching, there appears to be a particular interest in abacus-based arithmetic lessons in recent years.[124] Many parents claim that proficiency in the use of the abacus has helped their children improve their focus, short-term memory, visualization, and processing speed. Some schools also offer advanced programs that eventually transition students to the use of mental representations of an abacus. There is some research that suggests that the mental activities associated with abacus mental addition result in a supramodal brain network with increased use of neural resources for visuospatial processing.[125] These observations and findings present a potential learning opportunity for many students, especially those who seek fluency in visual constructs. And, while there are many apps, games, and other math tools on the market, there aren't many that challenge children to engage their discovery and experimentation skills.

Some find pure mathematics to be an extremely rewarding pursuit, but for many, its attraction comes more from its applications in the real world. While there have been many cases where practical applications came up only several decades after the theoretical framework had already been in place, there have also been numerous instances where completely new mathematical constructs were inspired by discoveries in one of the natural science disciplines. The relationship between math and the natural sciences is quite symbiotic. Appreciation of the inherent beauty in mathematical relationships helps develop our understanding of the phenomena they seek to model, and our understanding of the phenomena in turn helps us develop new mathematical tools. Clearly, the insights needed for this kind of exploration require fertile and active imagination and a high level of passion and fluency. This is how math development and mathematicians work. It therefore helps if math instruction also mimics real-world applications and students are presented with relevant, real-life problems. In addition to a stronger emotional connection through a broader appreciation of the context and value, this can also give students a deeper understanding of sister subjects such as physics and chemistry. In fact, our lessons should also be designed to build empathy and cultural understanding through incorporation of meaningful ethical conundrums. This kind of an interdisciplinary approach is required for holistic development.

Many more children can develop these skills if they are empowered to explore and are unafraid to fail. To be able to solve real-world problems, they should develop the skills to decide what information is needed to solve a problem, what information is superfluous and what is missing, and to identify logical fallacies. They should therefore be given an opportunity to make sense of situations where there is superfluous information or where there is a need to supplement the information provided with additional research or back-of-the-envelope estimates. They should also receive only minimal scaffolding while they explore and experiment on their own. These skills are needed for the recognition of new patterns and to make full use of the opportunities presented by "big data." Also, the real world rarely requires us to apply the same learning repeatedly. While there is a need to commit some basic mathematical facts and conventions to memory, we also need to help children develop fluid reasoning and greater levels of comfort with novelty. Making up new conventions or rules (for example, *perten* instead of *percent*, etc.) and focusing on discovery would greatly help them build confidence. Learners should also be given opportunities to develop proficiency in designing new problems, recognizing the mathematical relationships inherent in real-world phenomena, and developing the art of mathematical communication.

Even without deviating significantly from current curricula, we can take large strides toward providing more opportunities for exploration. For example, the Pythagorean theorem that establishes the relationship between the lengths of a right-angled triangle is often introduced as a statement of fact in middle school. Few math classes even go into proof of this theorem, let alone its history. So, many may be surprised to learn that the theorem credited to Pythagoras was actually found on four Babylonian tablets from circa 2000–1600 BCE (about fifteen hundred years before Pythagoras's time). It was also mentioned in the Vedic texts in India, in the *Baudhayana Shulba Sutra* from the eighth to the fifth centuries BCE, and in the *Zhoubi Suanjing*, a Chinese text from the first century BCE. While Pythagoras's students made outstanding contributions to mathematics and helped shine a light on this theorem, there is in fact little evidence—given the secrecy of the school Pythagoras founded—that Pythagoras himself had even come up with any proof for this theorem! The Pythagorean theorem has fascinated so many people that it now has at least 372 unique proofs, including one by a twelve-year-old Einstein, one by the Arab mathematician-physician Thābit ibn Qurrah (c. 836–901), one by the Italian polymath Leonardo da Vinci, and even one by James A. Garfield, the twentieth president of the United States. In fact, two high school students from St. Mary's Academy in New Orleans, Calcea Johnson and Ne'Kiya Jackson, found yet another proof as recently as 2023 using trigonometry—an approach that at least one early twentieth-century mathematician thought was impossible! Not allowing children an opportunity to at least take a shot at proving theorems like this does them a grave disservice. It's not easy to develop the skills needed for building insights and pattern recognition if a person is not appropriately and adequately trained.

CHAPTER SUMMARY

- The holistic development of a child entails the development of his or her physical, emotional, intellectual, ethical, spiritual, and social abilities. Focusing only on academic abilities greatly limits a child's potential.
- Many studies show, for example, that emotional intelligence is a better indicator of life outcomes than IQ. Poor mental, physical, or ethical health can cause significant harm to a person's overall well-being.

- Yet, few schools are truly able to support the development of the whole child, especially through middle school and beyond. The investments needed appear to be beyond the capacity of most institutions.
- It should therefore not be surprising that our children's emotional and mental health have steadily worsened over the years, while their relevance to modern life has only increased.
- Our educational apparatus is geared more toward serving the supply chain of the marketplace. As a result, standardized tests have increasingly become a proxy for student success and accountability.
- Critical thinking and deeper understanding are often sacrificed as the emphasis on testing prioritizes mastery of a narrow selection of topics. Exploration, risk-taking, and resilience are not adequately nurtured.
- In addition to highlighting all the benefits, this chapter offers a roadmap for how we can pursue the all-round development of every child. It also suggests ways education can help more students internalize big-picture learning.
- As social and biological creatures, we can't ensure healthy outcomes unless adequate attention is paid to our nutrition, sleep, and physical exercise on the one hand and social and emotional health on the other. While moderate amounts of stress and discomfort can be beneficial, chronic fear and stress can lead to many negative outcomes.
- Practices like meditation and yoga have been shown to reduce mental chatter and promote long-term learning through improved memory, attention, and emotional well-being.
- Curricular reform, parent literacy, and teacher training are essential to ensure that there is widespread awareness and adoption of best-in-class research and practices.
- The mind shift necessary to prioritize holistic child development is an urgent civilizational imperative.

5

Foundational Competencies

The mind is the root from which all things grow.
If you can understand the mind, everything else is included.
—BODHIDHARMA

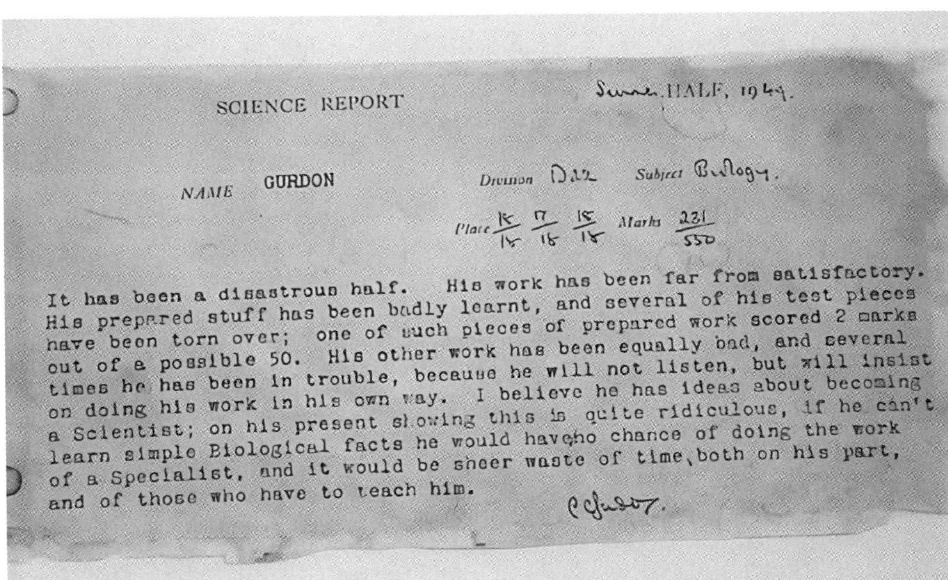

SCIENCE REPORT

Summer HALF, 1949.

NAME GURDON

Division D22 Subject Biology.

Place 15/15 17/18 15/18 Marks 231/550

It has been a disastrous half. His work has been far from satisfactory. His prepared stuff has been badly learnt, and several of his test pieces have been torn over; one of such pieces of prepared work scored 2 marks out of a possible 50. His other work has been equally bad, and several times he has been in trouble, because he will not listen, but will insist on doing his work in his own way. I believe he has ideas about becoming a Scientist; on his present showing this is quite ridiculous, if he can't learn simple Biological facts he would have no chance of doing the work of a Specialist, and it would be sheer waste of time, both on his part, and of those who have to teach him.

Figure 5.1. Comments of Mr. Gaddum, a science teacher at Eton College, on a student's science report.

> It has been a disastrous half. His work has been far from satisfactory. His prepared stuff has been badly learnt, and several of his test pieces have been torn over; one of such pieces of prepared work scored 2 marks out of a possible 50. His other work has been equally bad, and several times he has been in trouble, because he will not listen, but will insist on doing his work in his own way. I believe he has ideas about becoming a Scientist; on his present showing this is quite ridiculous, if he can't learn simple Biological facts he would have no chance of doing the work of a Specialist, and it would be sheer waste of time, both on his part, and of those who have to teach him.

These comments from Mr. Gaddum, an Eton College science teacher, were made on the 1949 report card of the joint winner of the Nobel Prize in Physiology or Medicine in 2012, John Gurdon.[1]

Is this an anomaly? Shouldn't we expect professional success to be largely correlated with scholastic excellence? What other factors are at least as consequential for our growth and progress as educational attainment?

As we have seen in part I, the triumph of *Homo sapiens* is a result of our competencies such as risk-taking, restlessness, empathy, and the ability to share our insights and imagination. It is reasonable to expect that these competencies would be correlated to academic success. But are they? More specifically, does one drive the other? To get a deeper understanding of the relevance of these competencies to modern day humans, it may be helpful to look at the lives of some of the changemakers, both those who were a force for our betterment and those who led us down a darker path by appealing to our worst instincts. It would be useful to understand what distinguished them from the rest of the population. To get a fair representation, it is essential to sample from a broad range of walks of life, cultures, and time periods. It also helps to look at people who are well known since their backgrounds would be more accessible and hence easier to scrutinize. For these reasons, we will take a close look at over two dozen inventors, statespeople, social reformers, polymaths, and also some who defy easy categorization.

The first person on this list is Louis Pasteur, an exceptionally successful French chemist and microbiologist. He found cures for chicken cholera, anthrax, rabies, and more and is considered the father of germ theory and immunology. Pasteurization, as we know, has saved millions of lives. Many may be surprised to learn that someone as accomplished as Pasteur was in fact regarded as a mediocre student in college. Pasteur's success and passion are primarily attributable to his ambition and curiosity and are not traceable to his academic accomplishments.

Let's look at Steve Jobs, Thomas Edison, and the Wright brothers next. They have a lot in common. Their inventions have revolutionized our lives. While Edison was a prolific inventor, Jobs was a perceptive designer. Edison and Jobs created solutions that others had not even envisioned. Edison came up with the electric lightbulb, power station, motion picture camera, and more. There is near consensus that Edison's success is largely due to his legendary self-confidence. He perceived no limits on what he could accomplish. As we discussed earlier, he was a huge believer in diligence and hard work. He said often that he knew how to benefit from the work of his predecessors and that he had the ability to persevere until he found a solution to a problem. Among Steve Jobs's many creations, the simplification of the user interface to personal computers and the reimagining of the "smart" phone are probably the most consequential. Steve Jobs was known for his ambition and creativity. The success of the Wright brothers, on the other hand, was driven more by their curiosity and their thirst for aviation history and science. It is not difficult to see that Edison, Jobs, and the Wright brothers were all very ambitious and laser focused on their pursuits. Interestingly again, they were all also self-made men who were misfits as far as formal schooling is concerned. While Edison had only three months of formal schooling, the Wright brothers dropped out of high school.

Let us consider Michael Faraday, Charles Darwin, Benjamin Franklin, and Albert Einstein next. None of these people need much of an introduction. With theories of evolution and general relativity, Darwin and Einstein revolutionized our understanding of the universe. Faraday and Franklin, on the other hand, along with numerous other contributions, helped us understand and benefit from electricity. All four men were known to be extremely curious, perceptive, and highly empathetic. Of the four, Faraday and Franklin were perhaps the most ambitious. They have also shown the most interest in sharing and communicating their learning and trade. For more than three decades, Faraday gave Christmas lectures to a young audience at the Royal Institution in London. As a philosopher, writer and statesman, Franklin's contributions to American society and transatlantic relationships are well known. Interestingly, however, none of these four were successful in school. In fact, Franklin and Faraday only had a few years of schooling each and

Einstein was, in fact, asked to leave school since authorities were worried that his indifference would be a negative influence on other students.

Unlike the men of science that we have considered so far, Harriet Beecher Stowe, Helen Keller, Leo Tolstoy, and Karl Marx were cut from a different cloth. Their claim to fame came from their writings. They were staunch advocates of an egalitarian society. Tolstoy and Marx had serious personal failings and many feel that Marxism has been a failure. Yet, we cannot deny the degree of influence that each of these people has achieved. Their reach was clearly due to their empathy, ambition, and communication. Stowe, the author of *Uncle Tom's Cabin*, helped wake up the collective conscience of her contemporary society. While Keller earned the respect of Alexander Graham Bell, Mark Twain, and Anne Sullivan, among countless others, Marx inspired many movements around the world. He even had at least some influence on Abraham Lincoln. Tolstoy similarly had a large following and a close relationship with Gandhi. Marx and Keller received no formal schooling, and Tolstoy was known to struggle as a student.

While there were leaders like Napoleon Bonaparte whose success was primarily due to their ambition, many more recent leaders also possessed an ability to communicate and connect. As discussed in part I, selling a vision for tomorrow is an integral part of the human story. So, whether it is driven by misguided intentions like in the case of Lenin or by empathy and egalitarian intentions like in the case of pathbreakers like Gandhi, Lincoln, Martin Luther King, and Ida B. Wells, we find that communication skills and single-minded persistence and ambition are unmistakable hallmarks of these leaders. While almost everyone on this list, except George Washington, Abraham Lincoln, and perhaps Ida B. Wells, had some formal education, their eventual calling in life and impact had very little to do with their schooling.

There are, however, two people on the list whose success could be attributed to their education, at least to some degree. Isaac Newton did very well in school, and this paved the way for his admission to Cambridge. Newton's success has been attributed to his curiosity, intelligence, and ambition. Sigmund Freud was another researcher who was also an outstanding student in school. His success there led him to the University of Vienna and thus to many collaboration opportunities. However, while his specialization was in nervous disorders, he had many other interests. He was a voracious reader of Darwin's findings, Nietzsche's philosophy, and more. His growth mindset, curiosity, and cognitive ability led him to explore, innovate, and eventually to develop his unique psychoanalytic methods.

Academic success was not considered when this list of changemakers was compiled. The impact of their life's work and their popularity or notoriety were the only factors. Yet, we can draw many interesting lessons from studying the people on this list. While a superior intellect is typically credited with the achievements of men and women in scientific and technological fields, it is noteworthy that Pasteur, Edison, and Jobs owe their success more to their passion, grit, and ambition than to their academic record.

This review also spotlights a very interesting aspect of humankind. Most people on this list who pushed boundaries have two or three strong competencies. It is rare to find people with only one competency or with more than three competencies. As is often the case, there are exceptions. The last person on our shortlist embodies six different competencies. Leonardo da Vinci, the Italian polymath whose exceptional accomplishments spanned a broad array of disciplines, had no formal schooling. As the creator of *The Last Supper* and the *Mona Lisa*, he is one of the greatest painters of all time. His immense curiosity led him to make significant contributions to our understanding of human anatomy, flight, paleontology, optics, civil engineering, geology, and more. His feverishly inventive imagination is without a known parallel. Though many of his ideas could not be realized at the time, he is often credited with the designs for a flying machine, parachute, armored fighting vehicle, submarine, adding machine, automated bobbin winder, and even a helicopter. He was also one of the first to understand the circulation of blood in our bodies as well as the fallacy of the heliocentric model. With his paintings and copious notes, he was also a master communicator. His respect for life and living creatures led him, like Pythagoras, to adopt a vegetarian diet and to his habit of buying caged birds and releasing them. It is also believed that he did not publish his design for a submarine out of fear that it would fall into the wrong hands. There is enough in the known life of Leonardo da Vinci that demonstrates his deep curiosity, cognition, empathy, ambition, creativity, and communication skills.

Many of us may have seen some circumstantial evidence that academic success does not correlate well with life outcomes and overall success. The preceding discussion has hopefully illustrated how poor this correlation truly is. A person endowed with some of these competencies may not necessarily be a successful student. However, difficulty in taking risks, empathizing with others, or delaying gratification will most likely result in suboptimal academic as well as life outcomes. A child who is afraid of failure will find it challenging to explore beyond their comfort zone, leading to potential underachievement in school and life. Fostering foundational skills and competencies would often be more effective than simply enrolling academically struggling children in remedial math or language arts classes.

A short thirteen years after the summer at Eton, as far back as in 1962, Gurdon showed that DNA from specialized cells of frogs, like skin and intestinal cells, could be used to generate new tadpoles. The pioneering work of Gurdon has opened new doors as scientists now attempt to create replacement tissues for treating diseases like Parkinson's and diabetes.

It is not unreasonable to assume that Gurdon's teacher's comments represented the expectations of a bygone era. However, it's worth noting that these comments are not inconsistent with the prescription outlined by Bloom's Taxonomy of Educational Objectives,[2] the longstanding gold standard for educators. Benjamin Bloom chaired a committee of educators who identified hierarchical sets of educational objectives in the cognitive, affective, and psychomotor domains. The cognitive domain includes six levels of objectives: remember, understand, apply, analyze, evaluate, and create. The five levels in the affective domain are receiving, responding, valuing, organizing, and characterizing. Gaddum's failure to pass a student who struggles with remembering or understanding cannot be entirely faulted.

Learning is most effective when students are engaged in a problem. In other words, learning begins with recognizing and valuing a problem, which is the third affective skill in Bloom's taxonomy. Gaddum's frustration appears to stem from the expectation that a good student must remember, understand, and engage with lessons even if they are not interested. This highlights a problem with educational systems that rely heavily on students' ability to remember facts. Unfortunately, too many schools tend to focus primarily on cognitive objectives and fail to harness the potential of the affective domain. One could argue that even the affective objectives in Bloom's taxonomy are too complex for everyday use. How can educators intervene effectively if a child does not value, organize, or characterize a set of ideas or experiences? To address this, educators need tools and time to determine the root cause. Is the child lacking curiosity due to a lack of preparation or domain knowledge? Does the topic not resonate with the child's value system? Or perhaps the child lacks mental stamina or grit? Understanding the child's thought processes is crucial in designing effective interventions. Unrealistic expectations, baseless fears, and incorrect association of ideas are some of the common obstacles that hinder a child's progress. Helping a child navigate through this maze requires a deep understanding of their thought processes, as all learning ultimately takes place in the child's mind. Researchers like Howard Gardner, Robert Sternberg, Raymond Cattell, and others have often asserted that intelligence is multidimensional and that noncognitive facets are essential for success in life.[3] Traditional schooling has, historically, focused more on academic results than on the underlying factors that drive these scholastic outcomes. Schools rarely offer programs designed to foster or assess curiosity, ambition, or other developmental precursors. The narrow focus of our schools and their inability to tap into genuine growth opportunities have likely contributed to the frustration experienced by many children.

For instance, William Ned Herrmann, an American researcher in creative thinking, proposed a system in the 1980s that describes thinking preferences and cognitive styles through the "Herrmann Brain Dominance Instrument (HBDI)".[4] In his brain dominance model, Herrmann suggests that learning occurs through four different styles of thinking: analytical thinking, sequential thinking, interpersonal thinking, and imaginative thinking. He also coined the concept of "whole brain thinking" to describe the ability to flexibly employ all four thinking styles depending on the situation and need. The HBDI provides one of the most effective frameworks for the mechanisms that likely contributed to the success of *Homo erectus* in the past and *Homo sapiens* today.

In the following pages, we take a closer look at the six different competencies da Vinci demonstrated: curiosity, cognition, empathy, ambition, creativity, and communication. As our earlier discussion shows, these competencies adequately describe the factors responsible for almost all our key individual and civilizational outcomes. These are also the basic elements that define the human condition. Ideally, we would also need to meet a minimum threshold in all six competencies to function productively in society.

At a high level, the environment provides the experiences that feed our curiosity and open new channels of information for us. Our cognitive abilities process this information and relate it to what we already know. Each of us has our own distinct moral compass, and our value system and empathy enable the valuation of the information we receive from multiple perspectives. While empathy typically refers to our ability to appreciate others' perspectives and circumstances, we cannot be truly empathic unless we also have a good understanding of our own needs. It is this valuation that helps us judge between different possibilities. Ambition is our potential to stretch our abilities and pursue one or more of the possibilities offered by our judgment. Creativity, on the other hand, takes us beyond these known possibilities and entices us to march ahead in new directions even when there is no inkling of a solution or even a well-defined problem for that matter. Since true empowerment requires metacognition and a deep awareness of the learning process, communication skills are essential for building such awareness around our accomplishments, failures, and the opportunities in between.

As discussed in part I, our emergence as the dominant species is largely a result of our restlessness, our ability to imagine different realities, and our urge to connect and share. Our review here shows that while those factors did play a large part, our progress has also benefited tremendously from our empathic abilities, grit, persistence, and ability to defer gratification. These six competencies are independent to the degree that no two competencies are perfectly correlated. In other words, it isn't possible to replace any one of them with some combination of the others. We can't, for example, identify all curious people only by looking at the other attributes. Even though curiosity is essential for creativity, we can't claim that all curious people are creative as well or vice versa.

Also, there are times when strength in one competency could be a hindrance for the development of another. It has been found, for example, that highly creative people are risk-takers who might sometimes run roughshod over others' liberties and feelings. So, creativity and empathy may sometimes be at loggerheads. The right balance between them may depend on the situation and the individual. Similarly, creativity, for instance, is often not compatible with conformity. Neither does it sit well with stifling assignments that are not particularly exciting. Innovation requires risk-taking and some amount of tolerance for boredom and laziness. A pressure-cooker atmosphere that values busywork will not provide enough time for depth and maturation of ideas. Schedules that are cognitively taxing with a short-term focus can frustrate exploratory thinking. It would therefore be very instructive to take a deeper look at these six competencies and understand what opportunities exist for developing these in our children.

Finally, as the bedrock of most learning, environment is often the first rung in an educational experience. In addition to basic needs such as diet and sleep, the environment provides all the sensory input that feeds our body and mind. At a bare minimum, a child's environment should not cause any anxiety or other problems, whether due to physical or emotional threats or a sensory processing disorder. These can limit a child's ability to even function, let alone learn. It is therefore essential for learning experiences to be curated with great care and purpose. They should be designed with the growth opportunities of the learners in mind. Finally, a seeker has to be enchanted by the subject matter. Enchantment feeds off the pleasure that comes from a sense of accomplishment and belonging. Engagement is therefore a useful barometer of this cycle of learning and enchantment and provides valuable insights into the child's purpose.

Fueling Curiosity

> There is frequently more to be learned from the unexpected questions of a child than the discourses of men.
> —JOHN LOCKE

Gregor Mendel was a monk and a teacher with interests in astronomy, meteorology, and plant breeding. He was the son of a poor farmer who struggled to pay for his education. Mendel tried, first in 1850 and again in 1856, to become a certified high school teacher. Having failed the oral part of the examination twice, he settled in as the abbot of St. Thomas's Abbey in Brno, in what is now part of the Czech Republic. The monastic life, in his words, spared him "perpetual anxiety about a means of livelihood."

Mendel had been curious about how traits were transferred from one generation to the next. When our ancestors moved from a hunter-gatherer lifestyle to a more sedentary agricultural society, they soon realized that they could breed plants and animals to promote desirable traits. They were able to turn wild grasses into wheat, for example. Over time, many also noted similarities between parents and children without understanding how these came about. Until the early twentieth century, the prevailing theory was that hereditary influences were a result of blending inheritance. The thinking was that crossing a plant with blue flowers with another from the same species that had yellow flowers would result in a plant with green flowers.

In 1856, Mendel began a series of experiments at the monastery to find out how traits are passed between generations of the common edible pea plants. Between 1856 and 1863, he meticulously studied the inheritance of seven different traits such as flower color, seed shape, and plant height using more than twenty-five thousand plants. Pea plants were wonderful to study since pollen could come from the same flower (self-fertilization), or they could be transferred from another plant's flowers (cross-fertilization) using a small paintbrush. Mendel first observed plants for two years as they self-fertilized to ensure that their traits did not change between generations. He then crossed lines of purebred plants with different traits—for example, crossing plants with purple flowers with those that had white flowers—using artificial pollination. He noticed that the resulting hybrid plants did not have blended traits. He found that all the first-generation hybrids had purple flowers, for example (not pink, as blending would have predicted). However, when he let the hybrid plants self-pollinate, additional traits appeared in the second-generation hybrid plants. After thousands of experiments and careful statistical analysis, Mendel surmised that there must be dominant and recessive variants for the different traits. Dominant traits persevered and recessive traits were suppressed in the first-generation hybrids. He also found that there were three times as many plants with dominant traits as recessive traits in the second-generation hybrid plants.

In addition to detailed correspondence with Carl Nägeli, a leading biologist of his time, Mendel shared his findings with about forty scientists at two separate meetings at the Natural History Society of Brno. Interestingly, the significance of his work still went largely unrecognized. It was only about fifteen years after Mendel passed away that the scientific community was finally able to grasp the implications of his findings, and his insights then began to greatly streamline and accelerate our understanding of genetics and evolution.

Despite his humble pedigree, Mendel was able to obtain outstanding insights that were far ahead of his time by simply honoring his curiosity. Curiosity is one of the most primal human emotions that powers our inquisitive thinking, and the resulting actions are at the root of most human accomplishments. If we must name one human trait that has, above all else, led to our most profound scientific discoveries and our grandest accomplishments, it would be curiosity. Even though there is no known record of Socrates explicitly saying "wisdom begins in wonder," this sentiment aligns well with what we know of Socrates from the records kept by his students and contemporaries. Few would disagree that an important goal of education should be to ensure that the fuel feeding the flames of our curiosity never runs out.

Curiosity is the result of either a thirst to explore or a yearning to close a gap in our understanding. Psychologist Daniel Berlyne classified curiosity along two dimensions: perceptual versus epistemic, and specific versus diversive.[5] Perceptual curiosity is the driving force that motivates us to seek out novel stimuli. A child collects pebbles on a beach, worms from the dirt, or tadpoles from a pond as he or she gets pleasure from the novelty of the find and the excitement of the search. When we experience novelty, our brain produces dopamine. Dopamine is responsible for lifting our mood and giving us a sense of excitement and satisfaction. The child at the pond, for example, continues to explore as long as she draws pleasure from her discoveries. As the novelty fades with continued exposure, so does the curiosity. Berlyne referred to the urge to bridge gaps in our understanding as epistemic curiosity. We see birds fly and we wonder how they do it. Perceptual curiosity is not really an exclusively human emotion. Exploratory behavior is also seen in many animals, including apes, cats, reptiles, fish, and even insects. Epistemic curiosity, on the other hand, is mostly limited to humans.[6]

Along the other dimension, specific curiosity refers to a strong interest in a particular subject or piece of information, while diversive curiosity refers to a general interest across a broad area. The more "diversive" one's curiosity is, the larger the target area and the higher the likelihood of fulfillment. Interestingly, some animals (monkeys, for example) predominantly display specific curiosity, while others such as rats show a more general exploratory behavior.

The human capacity for abstract thinking and curiosity have enabled us to explore further with each succeeding generation. Recent advances have also increased our understanding of how imagination, interpersonal thinking, and a desire for exploration can fuel our growth and development. While it is reasonable to expect that we learn something better if we are curious about it, research has shown that we also learn other incidental material better when we are in a state of curiosity![7]

In fact, Chris Jackson has proposed an interesting learning model that is based on our exploratory behavior.[8] Jackson defined a biological index called sensation seeking to describe the exploratory drive in individuals. According to Jackson, it is mediated by goal orientation, emotional intelligence, conscientiousness, and deep learning and can be used for the prediction of functionally learned behavior such as work performance. And failure to reexpress our exploratory drive using sociocognitive mediation might lead to dysfunctional learning and delinquency. Thus, Jackson claims that sensation seeking provides a common basis for both functional and dysfunctional outcomes. Incidentally, there appears to be considerable empirical evidence supporting his personality-based neuropsychological hybrid model of learning.

Despite the broad recognition of the significance of curiosity, it has been difficult to come up with a quantitative measure for it. Jirout and Klahr define curiosity as "the threshold of desired uncertainty in the environment that leads to exploratory behavior."[9] At the same time, there has been some progress in our understanding of the biology of curiosity. In a landmark publication in the journal *Neuron*, John Roder and Bechara Saab from the Samuel Lunenfeld Research Institute of Mount Sinai Hospital in Toronto presented their findings on the interaction between two proteins in the dentate gyrus, a small region of the brain that is part of the hippocampus.[10] They studied the effect of increasing the content of neuronal calcium sensor-1 (NCS-1) in the dentate gyrus of the test mice population by 50 percent. Roder and Saab noticed that this increase in the protein content gave the mice superior spatial memory on complex tasks. Perhaps more importantly, it also seemed to result in a significant increase in their exploratory behavior. Interestingly, the researchers discovered that blocking the NCS-1 protein from binding to the dopamine receptors in the dentate gyrus hurt both their memory and their exploratory behavior. This is perhaps the most direct evidence to date pointing to the correlation between curiosity and memory. This makes good sense since as Richard Whately, the English logician, said, "Curiosity is as much the parent of attention, as attention is of memory."[11]

It is often assumed, however, that curiosity, as opposed to intelligence, is a magical gift and not really a skill we can easily foster. In fact, it almost seems as if any regimen or structure would be counterproductive. Many great thinkers have, for example, lamented the role of formal schooling in suppressing children's curiosity. As we grow up, many factors conspire to diminish our curiosity. Age and experience appear to foster a sense of expectation and understanding that undercut and stifle the thirst for novelty. For instance, millions upon millions have likely seen fruit fall from a tree and countless witness this every day. Yet how many wonder as deeply as Newton did about why it falls to the ground?

Some of our challenges with supporting curiosity stem from an entrenched social resistance to change. For example, "The State of Curiosity" survey conducted online by the Harris Poll between August 13 and September 3, 2015 is quite revealing.[12] Only 12 percent of the 2,606 US workers who participated in the survey reported that their employers greatly valued workplace curiosity. Also, while only 22 percent described themselves as curious at work, as many as 66 percent reported that they faced barriers when they asked questions at work.

We should therefore try hard to ensure that formal education and childhood experiences do not rob children of their curiosity. While repetition may lead to mastery for the child searching for pebbles on a beach, it can also erode her excitement over time. It is necessary to maintain a steady stream of challenges to fuel children's curiosity. It helps to provide novelty as frequently as possible, since this will also prime their brain to be more open to change and new experiences. In fact, brains appear to retain significant plasticity even into adulthood. Research has shown that new experiences—perhaps as simple as a right hander deciding to eat with the left hand—can promote new brain-cell growth in adults. This process of positive feedback, also called *kindling*, can promote curiosity by increasing our comfort level and thirst for novelty.

Just as wisdom begins with wonder, it also begins with a knowledge of our ignorance. But this is easier said than done. Knowledge of our ignorance is not a pleasant experience, and many may want to avoid new information that contradicts their current understanding and view of the world. Therefore, one of the most effective ways to sustain and fuel students' curiosity is to ensure that educational experiences are always thought-provoking, so they are more comfortable taking risks and keeping an open mind. Education should help individuals develop a more nuanced understanding of complex issues and be better equipped to handle ambiguity and uncertainty. While expanding their brains, education should also leave them with humility and a deeper appreciation of the true gamut of what they don't know so they are not left with a false sense of certainty.

Valuing children's questions more than their answers is another good strategy for promoting their curiosity.[13] Developing an ability to anticipate and visualize potential outcomes can also motivate curiosity. Exposure to a rich set of experiences from an early age can help children more readily envision a broader array of outcomes to a given problem. This freedom to venture requires empowerment, especially since potential outcomes of our curiosity often excite us more when they carry meaningful implications. Empowerment from an early age would lay the foundation for unfettered development of our faculties for curiosity and critical thinking. Often, as social creatures, children would also want to share the joys and discoveries of their exploration. It is therefore important to provide them with suitable platforms.

We should also strive to minimize impediments to a child's curiosity. Fear of the unknown, fear of failure, insecurity, high expectations, entrenched dogmas, and habituation to apathy are some common barriers that diminish curiosity. Children from war zones and broken homes, for instance, are unlikely to feel safe enough to seek novelty. One of the biggest hindrances also comes from excessive emphasis on success and disapproval of failure. Exploration can naturally result in occasional failure and disappointment. When parents and teachers instill fear or otherwise show disapproval, children might retreat to safety, so they should be trained to be resilient against failure. A child who perseveres is therefore someone who likely has a deeper reserve of confidence, resilience, and self-esteem. Finally, a curriculum that introduces excessive terminology, concepts that are not accessible to a child, insufficient development of context, projects that are too mundane, obstacles to seeing the big picture, and excessive guidance can all seriously diminish a child's natural curiosity.

Fortunately, as we exercise our curiosity muscles and make a persistent effort to overcome these barriers, it should get progressively easier to return to childlike wonder and curiosity. Training a child in abstract thinking, in thinking outside the box, in exploring multiple routes to end goals, and in the art of questioning will help build confidence that he or she has the required tools to shepherd their natural curiosity to the best possible outcome. Of course, as Chris Jackson's hybrid model of learning suggests, an excessive urge to explore can sometimes lead to poor social outcomes and dysfunctional learning unless other attributes such as cognitive skills, empathy, and ambition are able to channel it appropriately. As a result, it's also important to have a good understanding of how curiosity plays into the overall competency profile of a child.

Stimulating Cognition

We may be aware of a truth, yet until we have felt its force, it is not ours. To the cognition of the brain must be added the experience of the soul.

—ARNOLD BENNETT

In simple terms, cognition is what most people commonly recognize as intelligence. To be more specific, it refers to our mental capacity for information processing—that is, the problem-solving skills that are at the root of most forms of intelligence. In this book, cognition is synonymous with information gathering through attention and memory as well as analytical skills that contribute to perception, attribution, and knowledge acquisition. In other words, by cognition, I refer to all the processes by which meaning and context are assigned to information. Our IQ and cognitive skills help us harvest the information uncovered by our curiosity. Incidentally, recent research has challenged the traditional belief that there is little we can do to improve our IQ. IQ is now believed to be malleable up to adolescence and become relatively stable thereafter.

Piaget is one of the earliest researchers to trace the development of human intelligence from birth. His research identified four different stages: sensorimotor during the first two years, preoperational before seven years of age, concrete operational between seven and eleven years of age, and finally the formal operational stage. The most important takeaway from his work and that of many other researchers is the criticality of the windows of opportunity that exist for various skills such as language acquisition and musical intelligence. Their work emphasizes the necessity of providing appropriate stimuli in a timely manner. This requires an intimate knowledge of the cognitive development of a child.

Learning is mediated by the cognitive processes of acquisition, storage, and retrieval of information. Attention is our ability to properly attenuate the large amount of information taken in by our senses so that there is greater focus on what we need. In this context, mind wandering and other distractions add to the noise that degrades both information acquisition and storage. Memory consolidation or the stabilization of memory traces is what enables us to recall what we learn at a later time.[14] Sheth et al. have shown that noise signals that compete with the memory trace of interest to us are one of the key factors impacting memory consolidation.[15] It is important to distinguish between the desirable exploratory thinking and the undesirable mind wandering. This is why chaos in the brain is only healthy up to a point.

In a popular book titled *The Invisible Gorilla*, cognitive psychologists Christopher Chabris and Daniel Simons drew attention to "inattentional blindness."[16] In one of their experiments, volunteers were asked to keep track of the number of times certain basketball players tossed a basketball. At some point, someone in a gorilla suit walked across the basketball court—in plain view—yet many of the volunteers failed to notice this. A later study raised the disturbing possibility that such perceptual limitations might even be life threatening.[17] Three psychology researchers at Brigham and Women's Hospital in Boston—Trafton Drew, Melissa Vo, and Jeremy Wolfe—recruited twenty-four experienced and credentialed radiologists and an equivalent number of amateur volunteers for their experiment. The radiologists and volunteers were asked to examine hundreds of ultrathin CT images of a patient's lungs to look for signs of lung cancer. They were also asked to click with a mouse on any tiny white nodules they found, telltale signs of potential cancer. On the final set of images, the researchers inserted a tiny picture of a gorilla into the CT scans. The gorilla was relatively huge, about forty-eight times the size of the nodules, and clearly anomalous. Yet, twenty of the twenty-four radiologists failed to see the gorilla. Eye-tracking data clearly showed that most of those who said that they did not see it had actually stared right at it at least once. This is a good illustration of how not all information we sense is fully registered.

Given how critical our ability to control and focus our mind is for our overall success, assessment and promotion of concentration skills should be a key element of any educational endeavor. It is not super helpful to assess tasks that require concentration without a program to also measure and improve children's attention span. Our ability to pay attention is believed to be mostly governed by the frontal areas of the brain, including the anterior cingulate cortex.[18] Its regulation is an area of active research in cognitive neuroscience. As we have seen earlier, poor development of the frontal lobes has also been blamed for many attention-deficit-related disorders.[19]

There are many short- and long-term strategies for improving our ability to concentrate. Formulation of a clear intent, meaningful organization of information, development of realistic and time-bound goals, adequate rest, ability to handle stress, minimizing multitasking, and seeking a distraction-free environment can all help boost our concentration skills. Research has shown that we are far less effective when we multitask than when we take on one task at a time.[20] We are likely to concentrate well when the prefrontal cortex has the appropriate mix of neurotransmitters, hormones, and other brain-friendly chemicals, particularly dopamine, the so-called pleasure chemical.[21] When we're tired, we're deprived of oxygen, a necessary ingredient for the production of chemicals such as dopamine and adrenaline in the prefrontal cortex. While even one night of tossing and turning can make it difficult to focus and concentrate and give us symptoms that resemble ADHD, researchers are now even wondering if ADHD is sometimes a type of sleep disorder.[22] Also, when we are tense due to bouts of anxiety, anger, or stress, we have a hard time focusing on the task at hand. Our stress hormones rise and our ability to concentrate is impaired. In addition, as we discussed in the previous chapter, healthy diet and aerobic exercise are believed to improve oxygen and nutrient delivery to our brain and thus increase neurogenesis and cognitive awareness. A healthy exercise regimen also helps lower stress and improve memory and concentration skills. Since we cannot completely eliminate stress from our lives, the next best thing is to develop the skills necessary for managing stress well. This can be especially beneficial as we age. There are many studies that show that excessive or chronic stress can increase the risk for dementia.[23]

It is well known that we concentrate best when we are really engaged, like when we watch a good movie. This is why preschool music and art programs at schools such as Waldorf and Reggio Emilia are successful. Young children can pick up a lot of interesting and essential facts through songs, dance, and other fun activities. There is also evidence that increasing the depth or level of processing enhances our attention and engagement and thus our retention success.[24] We can increase the amount of effort we put in to encode information in simple ways such as better organization, distinctive recitation, and conscious elaboration. Tasks that require deliberate concentration such as spelling words backward and playing games such as those that require recalling phrases or answers from an earlier question can all help improve long-term concentration. Klingberg et al. showed, for example, that children with attention deficit disorder were able to improve their attention in just twenty days by regularly playing an attentional training game.[25] In fact, the benefits of such training seem to go far beyond tasks that require attention. There are studies that suggest that this training can also improve our ability to solve problems in novel situations, often referred to as fluid intelligence.[26]

Finally, there is compelling evidence that sustained meditation can significantly improve concentration and attention.[27] Meditation is one of the most explicit strategies for sustaining increasingly larger periods of concentration through daily practice. It is a great vehicle to grow our ability to stretch our attention span. A study by Hölzel et al. shows that mindfulness meditation also produces changes in gray matter concentration in brain regions involved in learning and memory processes.[28]

As Richard Whately said, attention is often seen as the parent of memory. Attention helps us maximize the available mental bandwidth for making new synaptic connections. It primarily helps our short- and long-term memory acquisition. Transient observations made by our senses are referred to as sensory memory. While we can perceive up to twelve or so items, our sensory impressions will not last for more than a second or two. Attention can help sensory memory transfer into short-term memory. Short-term memory allows us to remember only around four or five items, but for up to a minute or so. In addition to attention, rehearsal and chunking have been known to enhance short-term memory.[29] Baddeley and Hitch's working-memory model, for instance, elaborates on the role of attention in memory enhancement.[30] The model has four different components: central executive, phonological loop, visuospatial sketchpad, and multimodal episodic buffer. Attention helps the central executive channel information to the three memory processing units. The episodic buffer is believed to reconcile information across acoustic, visual, and spatial domains and interpret the underlying chronological order. The episodic buffer also provides a pathway to long-term semantic coding. While short-term memory is coded acoustically or visually, longer-term memory is coded semantically and requires competency in encoding, storage, and retrieval. Our ability to pay attention is particularly critical for successful encoding. Incidentally, the working-memory model is quite effective at explaining several empirical observations. For instance, it can explain why it is easier to perform visual and verbal tasks at the same time than two visual tasks or two verbal tasks.

Interestingly, our memory has been shown to improve, even under stress, when information about the learning context is included.[31] For example, when memory retention tests were conducted in the same room and under the same cues (similar sights, sounds, smells, ambience, and so on), the detrimental effects of stress on memory were mitigated. Perhaps even more interesting are studies that show that our memories are not just recorded at the time of an incident. In many cases, our memory is created for the first time when we try to recall an event.[32] As a result, it is quite possible to misremember when we are given misleading or incorrect information. This is another important reason why attention and broader and deeper encoding are so paramount.

In addition, nourishment, a supportive home life, and access to greater opportunities have all been shown to play a significant role in enhancing cognition.[33] These can be in the form of physical exercise, nutrition, sleep, meditation, and stress management. They can all help strengthen long-term memory storage and recollection.[34] The depth of our learning depends on the richness of our experiences and exposure. Exposure to new people, ideas, environments, and subjects can all be a great catalyst for awareness and learning. It is well known, for instance, that greater exposure will enhance recognition of human emotions and development of emergent skills such as facial recognition and language acquisition. The environment provided by parents and caregivers can thus have a large impact on a child's development.

Of course, learning ultimately happens in the mind of the learner. As Khalil Gibran, the Lebanese artist and writer, said eloquently, "The teacher who is indeed wise does not bid you to enter the house of his wisdom but rather leads you to the threshold of your mind."[35] It is often quite difficult to assess the level of understanding, especially in real time, as the child is discovering something new. Our daughter became very agitated one night at dinner when she was about two and a half years old. She was almost on the verge of a tantrum, feverishly pointing toward the kitchen and attempting to vocalize. After listening closely, my wife and I felt that we heard her say twenty-three or something that sounded similar. We looked at the stove, breakfast bar, pantry, and refrigerator and could not quite identify what she might be after, at least something that would sound like twenty-three. We pointed to a few possible items, but she shook her head vigorously. She was, by now, crying inconsolably. It suddenly occurred to us that she was probably referring to the track number of a song on a compact disc near the pantry. We had noticed, a few days prior to this incident, that she was trying to look at the track numbers on the player while we were out driving.

Our daughter stopped crying and was looking at us with anticipation when my wife played track 23 of the CD in the player. The crying resumed as soon as the song came on. Fortunately, my wife flipped through a few discs and picked one that she thought had one of our daughter's favorite songs on track 23. We hit the jackpot as her face suddenly lit up. That was a moment of revelation for us. Her desire and her ability to memorize the track numbers of dozens of songs revealed the depth of her passion for these songs. This incident is a good illustration of the power of internal motivation. It helps to pay close attention to the child as we select experiences and topics for further exploration. Active participation is much more meaningful and empowering than passive consumption of information. It empowers students to freely construct their own learning as they try to understand the world around them. Child-led inquiry-based learning requires students to be both critical (or convergent) and creative (or divergent) thinkers. With judicious scaffolding, students can learn to work through all of the different phases of the learning process: engagement with the objectives, design of experiments, independent inquiry, data analysis, synthesis of new understanding, recognition of opportunities for further investigation, and reflections on the learning process.

Incidentally, shravanam (listening to an educated person or a teacher), mananam (reflecting on the true meaning of what we heard, reconciling with prior information, and seeking clarifications if needed), and nidhidhyasanam (contemplating, analyzing, and meditating even more deeply on the essence so we can internalize its meaning and implications) were the three steps in the learning process used by the ancient gurukuls.

Active engagement can also help children improve sensorial, cultural, and contextual perception, thus making them more alive to possible gaps between their perception and reality and the key drivers behind such gaps. For instance, teachers in Reggio Emilia schools are encouraged to work, as opportunities arise, through mistakes, errors, and confusion in as transparent a manner as possible. Mentoring opportunities and field trips can also help promote engagement. Trips to factories that are not as efficient can be just as valuable as trips to state-of-the-art facilities. For instance, I found errors in my middle school math textbooks to be more valuable than accurately worked-out proofs. We should constantly explore ways we can get our children to engage more.

Figure 5.2. Sankalpa Academy students at an exhibition at the Cockrell School of Engineering.

Just as physical exercises help promote strength, endurance, and neurogenesis, there is growing evidence that working-memory training through brain exercises can improve a wide range of cognitive skills.[36] However, the benefits of brain exercises are not always transferable to domains that are not explicitly trained. Many researchers have suggested that brain training should focus on novelty, discovery, and growth.[37] If brain training does not constantly challenge the child, it may become more of an autonomous, muscle-memory training exercise. It appears that novel activities that exercise our brain in new ways can help create new synaptic connections and facilitate the construction of new learning. Constant exposure to new activities has been shown to prime our brains. Not only do we learn more, such exposure is believed to also elevate motivation and stimulate the creation of new neurons. More research is needed to better understand the activities and exercises that can channel these benefits to multiple aspects of cognition.

Children as young as a year stop what they are doing and look up at you with great interest and a sense of wonder when you show them something new. It's clearly up to us to channel this innate curiosity and to use it to design suitable experiences that can develop their perception and understanding.

Inspiring Empathy

Knowing others is wisdom, knowing yourself is Enlightenment.

—LAO TZU

As the son of a wealthy merchant, Giovanni was somewhat pampered by his parents. He had expensive tastes and well-to-do friends. But he grew increasingly disillusioned by both his father's trade as well as his own traditional education. He eventually dropped out of school at the age of fourteen. With a growing fascination for war heroes and their exploits, he decided to pursue training in archery, horseback riding, and wrestling instead. And when fighting broke out with a neighboring town, it seemed like the opportunity he was waiting for, and he eagerly enlisted. However, significantly outnumbered by the opposing forces, Giovanni's troops did not last long. Many were quickly captured and some brutally murdered. Those with expensive outfits or other possessions were taken as prisoners. It made sense for the enemy to use the more well-to-do prisoners as barter for hefty ransoms. Giovanni was one of them, but his release did not come as briskly as he had hoped. He suffered in a dank underground cell for about a year before negotiations concluded and his captors received payment from his father.

Giovanni was a very different man by the time he was released. The mental and physical scars from his yearlong imprisonment left a lasting impression on him. He was disillusioned by the losses and the vastly different treatments meted out to the various prisoners. He felt a loss of purpose and mooring.

Some months later, when a beggar came to him while he was in the middle of a transaction in the marketplace, Giovanni abandoned his wares and ran after the beggar, giving him everything he had in his pockets. This greatly infuriated his father, and Giovanni was severely reprimanded. Over time, episodes like these became increasingly frequent, and he found himself thinking a lot more about God. On one occasion, he embraced and kissed a leper, who, earlier in his life, would have been considered untouchable.

Over the next few years, inspired by visions of God, he worked tirelessly on restoring several ruined chapels in the countryside around his town.

His extreme poverty and Christlike love of the poor was a radical notion at the time when the Christian church and its leaders were, in general, very wealthy. He felt drawn to restore Jesus Christ's original values to the church. Thousands were drawn by his charisma, compelling message, and ministrations. And Giovanni, later known as Francis of Assisi, soon had a huge following. On April 16, 1210, Pope Innocent III constituted the official founding of the Franciscan Order.

Francis was also known for his tremendous love of animals and nature. Stories abound about how he would talk to animals and preach to all of God's creation. Francis of Assisi died on October 3, 1226, at the age of forty-four, in Assisi, Italy, and was canonized as a saint just two years after his death. On November 29, 1979, Pope John Paul II declared Saint Francis the Patron Saint of Ecology.

St. Francis was neither the first nor the last person to draw new meaning and purpose from the deep scars life presented. About eighteen hundred years before he found his life's calling, Mahavir, Buddha, and Confucius undertook very similar journeys. It is quite likely that there are countless others who have also been deeply moved by their empathy for the less fortunate. Many like Beatrice Webb, Mohandas Gandhi, and George Orwell were inspired by either events in their own lives or their immediate environment.

Empathy is a wonderful quality; it is especially gratifying to witness it in a young child. At a birthday party for the daughter of one of our cousins, my wife and I ran into a two-year-old child who suddenly began crying inconsolably. We then saw an eighteen-month-old boy gather up a few balloons and hand them to the crying child. The boy appeared deeply concerned and in some pain. We were really surprised when the boy stayed around the crying child for some time. His parents told us later that their son often tends to children who are upset.

Many of us witness this kind of compassion in young children from time to time. Often, when a baby cries, other babies in the vicinity begin crying as well. They appear to recognize a baby in distress. Development of empathy clearly has its roots in infancy, even though it often takes many years to mature. In fact, Frans de Waal, a Dutch primatologist and ethnologist, has suggested that such empathy resides in parts of the brain so ancient that we even share them with rats.[38] One problem, however, is that lofty instincts in young children must compete with their other, more self-centered impulses. As toddlers, most children begin to develop an ego and their own distinct identity. They increasingly focus inward. Until they turn seven or so, there is an intense conflict between their own needs and their desire not to see others suffer. It is not easy for them to share their favorite dump truck or their cuddly teddy bear. Their needs and wants come first and often cannot wait. Recognition of this dichotomy is an important first step on the road to greater compassion. The forces that hold a child's world together include both their apparent inconsiderate behavior and their aversion to suffering. Children often try to avoid having to choose between the two.

Many psychologists break empathy down into three components: cognitive, emotional, and compassionate. Cognitive empathy refers to the ability to take another person's perspective by placing ourselves in their shoes. We need emotional empathy to feel the other person's emotions and compassionate empathy to take action.

There is also interesting research on the biology of empathy. As we have seen earlier, mindfulness meditation produces changes in the gray matter concentration in brain regions in the amygdala and elsewhere that are involved in emotion regulation, self-awareness, and empathy.[39] The size of the amygdala also appears to be a good biological index of the spiritual progress of a yogi. Research suggests that there is a direct correlation between the size of the amygdala and the quantity and quality of a person's social network.[40] Long-term potentiation in the amygdala is seen as a mechanism for emotional learning and memory. Bucher et al.'s research shows that monkey mothers with amygdala damage can lose their maternal instinct and can neglect or even physically abuse their infants.[41] The role of the amygdala thus appears to be quite profound and reasonably well understood. Research has also uncovered a physiological stimulus for empathy. It has been shown that affectionate relationships and pleasant social interactions are likely to foster greater emotional awareness by boosting oxytocin levels.[42]

The broader community of religious leaders, thinkers, and scientists has long argued that empathy is indispensable for human survival and success. Einstein compared our inability to connect well with others to a prison. In his words,

> A human being is a part of the whole called by us universe, a part limited in time and space. He experiences himself, his thoughts

> and feeling as something separated from the rest, a kind of optical delusion of his consciousness. This delusion is a kind of prison for us, restricting us to our personal desires and to affection for a few persons nearest to us. Our task must be to free ourselves from this prison by widening our circle of compassion to embrace all living creatures and the whole of nature in its beauty.[43]

While compassion has always been vital, it is especially indispensable today in our heavily interconnected world. As resources become increasingly scarce, our inability to appreciate each other's needs and constraints would make the world ever more volatile. In a meta-analysis that summarized the findings from seventy-two different studies of American college students from 1979 to 2009, University of Michigan researcher Sara Konrath found that there was a 34 percent decrease in perspective-taking and a 48 percent reduction in empathic concern over the thirty-year period.[44] As Goleman said, we can't be successful if we don't have the ability to fluently transcend the cultural, political, social, economic, and behavioral divides in everyday life. Gang-related violence, classroom bullying, school dropout rates, and teen pregnancies are all manifestations of this decline in empathy and self-esteem.

While it is therefore essential to take steps to nurture empathy, it is also important to understand all the forces that can make us less empathetic. Stanley Milgram, a psychology professor at Yale in the 1960s, researched the intersection of human motivations and ethics. He was greatly bothered by the thought that many people were willing to kill based on the orders of the Nazis during the Holocaust. He learned a great deal about how we sometimes outsource control of our behavior to the environment. Milgram's investigations looked at the influence of authority and social pressure. His experiments revealed that normal people can be persuaded to torture others if they are given the right rationale. Participants in his study willingly administered painful shocks to a screaming victim just because they were urged to do so by an authoritative man in a lab coat.[45] Unfortunately, indulgence in inappropriate behavior due to social pressure is all too common. Outsourcing control over our behavior toward others is more widespread than we realize. We should therefore be very mindful that it is not easy for children to become inured against this common human failing.

Research has identified many strategies for promoting empathy. There is rarely a more effective, authentic, or credible role model for children than their parents. So, true lessons in compassion invariably begin at home. Children internalize the valuable cues they obtain from the demeanor, generosity, and tone of their parents, and from their consistency or lack thereof. Research has shown that parental modeling of compassionate behavior toward children, and toward others in their presence, is highly correlated with the development of prosocial attitudes and behavior in children.[46] Discussions of the lives of highly empathic people can help children appreciate the outcomes that are possible through empathy. Our efforts at understanding the cause of someone's hurtful or otherwise inappropriate behavior should be transparent to our children. They should see that we truly care and that we often think about ways to brighten someone else's day. Role-playing with toys or imaginary characters and discussion of real-life incidents or movies and other programs on television can also be used to promote empathy. It has been shown that reasoning with children, even very young ones, about the impact of their behavior on others and the need for compassion and kindness can help promote their empathy.[47] Beyond such self-awareness, they need to be exposed to cultures and environments that provide a rich set of experiences. Without such experiences, it's hard to obtain deeper understanding and compassion. Exposure to the suffering of victims of natural disasters and social inequities can help drive home the practical consequences of indifference. Volunteer work or service learning at a soup kitchen or a homeless shelter can also help older kids improve their sense of purpose and meaning and thus also their own sense of well-being. The support children receive during their formative years is largely responsible for the empathy they eventually carry into their adult life.

We cannot be effective role models without first building up the necessary influence through a strong and healthy relationship with children. Strong relationships also contribute to the sense of safety and security children need. We can build healthy relationships only when we treat children as independent individuals with minds of their own. If they're convinced that we truly believe that their beliefs, desires, and emotions motivate their behavior, they're more likely to think about other people's minds and how they work.

Mary Gordon, an internationally recognized child advocate and parenting expert, created the successful Roots of Empathy program in 1996 and Seeds of Empathy in 2005. These programs focus on expanding children's sense of belonging and connectedness. They introduce new experiences by creating relationships with babies and their young parents. Her organization now offers these programs in every province of Canada and over thirteen other countries.

Also, it is difficult to open our minds to others' concerns without strong self-esteem and self-awareness. Such confidence and self-esteem can only come if a child feels empowered. Children must therefore first understand their own needs and emotions. We can neither fully understand another person nor relate and respond to their experiences if we don't first appreciate our own abilities, hopes, fears, and desires. Lack of self-awareness often leads to difficulty in the management of our emotions. If we struggle to understand ourselves, these difficulties will handicap our ability to empathize with others. In a sense, self-awareness skills provide the foundation for both self-regulation and empathy. As children gain more self-awareness, they will be able to regulate their emotions and resist the urge for gratification. Such self-control will enable them to look beyond themselves and their own needs.

And, as with empathy toward others, children can understand themselves faster if we are able to model self-awareness for them. As they grow older, self-awareness can lead to metacognitive thinking, helping them evaluate their internal thinking processes through reflections on what they know or don't know.[48] As Vygotsky pointed out decades ago, we also need the ability to understand how we reason.[49] In fact, many suggest that we can foster a culture of deep thinking even from a young age and that we can make thinking visible through appropriate questioning, listening, documentation, and facilitative thinking routines.[50] Finally, empathy for others can also help us look inward, and make us more aware of our own strengths and weaknesses.

It is also important to leverage opportunities to identify differences between people since what makes one person happy may not necessarily make someone else happy. For example, if children are in distress, it's necessary to identify and acknowledge the root cause of their emotions and not discount their suffering. This is one of the best ways to help them cope with their feelings. Indifference or inconsistencies in our response to children's emotional needs, for example, have been associated with low levels of empathy in children.[51] Of course, as children grow up, they need to master the ability to handle stress on their own and at their own pace. It's hard for someone to be empathic when they're burdened by emotional pain. Expanding children's vocabulary through a focus on emotional literacy can help them identify and label the emotions they feel. This can also, in turn, help us validate their emotions and experiences. Along similar lines, instead of asking a child to simply apologize when they misbehave, it may be more useful to explore the consequences of their actions with them.[52] Finally, research has long established that threats and punishment are counterproductive most of the time.[53] Threats, rewards, and bribes are often unhelpful as they steer the discussion away from the true implications of undesirable behavior.

We should also help children recognize how our perception is clouded by the "hot-cold empathy gap."[54] Many of us have probably experienced how difficult it is to fully appreciate the suffering caused by illness until we are unwell ourselves, or how hard it is to really feel the pangs of hunger when we are full. Similarly, those who are in the throes of emotional turmoil may not always recognize that their judgment is clouded by their visceral state. When children become sick or are on the receiving end of bad behavior or a snub, we should take the opportunity to talk about the challenges posed by the "hot-cold empathy gap." Thousands of years ago, the *Bhagavad Gita* pointed out that extremes—happiness or despair, for example—are equally harmful to our equanimity (and thus to good judgment). Verses 18 and 19 in chapter 12 of the *Bhagavad Gita* say:

> samaḥ śatrau ca mitre ca tathā mānāpamānayoḥ
> śītoṣṇa-sukha-duḥkheṣu samaḥ saṅga-vivarjitaḥ
> tulya-nindā-stutir maunī santuṣṭo yena kenacit
> aniketaḥ sthira-matir bhaktimān me priyo naraḥ
>
> *I like the one who is balanced between enemies and friends,*
> *is equipoised in honor and dishonor, cold and heat, joy and*
> *anguish, alone or in society, in both praise and criticism,*
> *and remains content in any unfolding situation.*

This is a valuable insight. These and other accompanying verses point out how excessive attachment to our egos is the root cause of our roller-coaster emotions. This is also consistent with research that has shown that gratitude is essential for personal growth since gratitude is incompatible with inflated egos. Further, when we are overly sensitive to criticism, it can be hard to be open to feedback or new learning, as it can result in stress. Clearly, while many of us can recognize the truth in this observation, mastery is a different story.

There is also interesting research that suggests that reading literary fiction, as opposed to popular fiction or serious nonfiction, helps people perform better on tests measuring empathy, social perception, and emotional intelligence.[55] Since literary fiction often leaves more to the imagination, it invites readers to make inferences about characters. This can help prime their sensitivity to emotional nuance and complexity.

Finally, it has also been shown that living through others' experiences can help foster higher levels of empathy.[56] Young and healthy medical students who wore goggles covered with transparent tape to simulate the effects of cataracts and heavy rubber gloves to limit hand movement ended up showing much greater empathy toward older people. We don't always have to design such elaborate role-playing to promote empathy. Advances in virtual reality (VR) have made it possible for us to assume other avatars and thus get much closer than ever before to more easily living others' experiences. Also, studies suggest that we can enhance our capacity for empathy by imitating the facial expressions of people we want to empathize with.[57] Recognizing good deeds and attributing them to the intrinsic nature of the child are also likely to promote desirable behaviors.

From time to time, we come across people with a capacity for extraordinary compassion, from well-known legends like Mother Teresa to unsung heroes such as the eighty-two-year-old scavenger Chen Shangyi and his eighty-one-year-old wife Zhang Lanying from Anding, a small Chinese town on the edge of the Gobi Desert. Shangyi and Lanying provided shelter to dozens of destitute children.[58] Despite their dire economic situation and age, they never hesitated to adopt an abandoned child, even if the child had a serious physical or mental disability. Their reputation was such that local officials always sought them out when they had an unwanted child on their hands.

This generous couple perhaps felt a compelling need to adopt as they were more able than most to feel what it is like to live inside somebody else's skin. Even so, it is necessary to recognize that empathy doesn't necessarily imply or require selfless outreach to everyone who's suffering. Instead, along with cognition, it should inform our judgment so we can decide on the best course of action. In other words, it is also possible that in some circumstances, we may want to temper children's compassion and help them focus more on their own needs.

Activating Ambition

The will to win, the desire to succeed, the urge to reach your full potential... these are the keys that will unlock the door to personal excellence.

—CONFUCIUS

In the words of Walter Cottingham, "A man without ambition is like a bird without wings."[59] Ambition determines the extent to which we are willing to stretch our faculties in the pursuit of a goal. It is the proverbial fire in the belly that propels you in your quest. It should not be difficult to conceive of a curious, talented individual with excellent cognitive abilities who is content with just the low-lying fruit. We encounter such people all the time. Then there are those who are not just resourceful but can also dream big, but unfortunately lack the skills to chart their way to success. It is therefore useful to recognize ambition as the ability to formulate and pursue a challenging goal, distinct from other important traits such as curiosity, cognition, and creativity. It requires good executive functioning, goal-setting, and perseverance. Ambition need not necessarily imply pursuit of a more powerful or more active role; it can also sometimes involve stepping away into a more reflective life.

As we learned in part I, our success is due, in large part, to our urge to imagine and share a new reality. Ambition begins with this restlessness. Historically, it has typically been harder to pursue such ambition and push the envelope if you are not a man. We can only imagine how much harder still it might have been for a woman who was both blind and deaf. This is what makes Helen Keller's life a model of human restlessness. It is of course true that Keller was born into a life of privilege. She was also very fortunate to have found an extraordinary master teacher in Anne Sullivan. Yet Keller had to be truly ambitious to doggedly pursue social reform in the face of fierce opposition. She traveled to over forty countries and fought for people with disabilities, women's rights, and for all forms of equity. She wanted children born into poor families to have similar opportunities to the ones she'd had. She was also a tireless pacifist who waged a relentless campaign for world peace.

Ambition need not be limited to personal accomplishments; people can also be ambitious for those they love and care about. Ambition can motivate us to assist them in their own quest for excellence. There is not a walk of life where people don't benefit from an ambitious outlook. For instance, given our hectic lives, we need some degree of ambition to achieve even a modestly healthy lifestyle; investment in our physical and mental well-being requires a significant degree of prioritization and commitment. Students need determination and drive to both do well in school as well as sustain a healthy discipline for sports, yoga, or other forms of physical exercise. Ambition is more than a driver of individual success; it is also a great foil against the vicissitudes of life. It is the internal compass that picks out goals and helps us navigate to them, so it is vital for this compass to stay well-tuned. At the same time, misplaced, inappropriate, or untamed ambition could be more harmful than a lack of ambition. Ambition is often synonymous with a grueling journey; however, the journey will add little value if the destination is not worthwhile. Ambition therefore serves us best if it is informed by keen perception, a healthy dose of compassion and metacognition, and well-developed judgment skills.

Judgment, the first step toward ambition, is a higher-order skill that relies on our cognitive and affective abilities. While cognition is the recognition of new information and its reconciliation with prior knowledge, valuation of this information is essential for good decision-making. Such valuation is often colored by our experiences and hence true understanding also requires good empathy and emotional awareness. These foundational abilities contribute to the development of good judgment, enabling us to prioritize and discern among competing demands and opportunities. In other words, our executive functioning requires fluency in selection, assessment, and valuation of information. This ability to navigate a range of choices is highly valued. Exceptional perception and judgment are key traits of great leaders who seize opportunities during crises to bring about long-lasting changes. A good understanding of the mental processes involved in a judgment call is therefore essential.

Good judgment first requires that we are adept at recognizing emotional biases. Such biases can creep in in various ways. A study on recollecting details of the Oklahoma City bombing illustrates this risk well.[60] Participants of a survey were asked to recall either two or ten details of this incident, and those who were requested to recall more details perceived the bombing as less personally significant. This study highlights the role of the gulf between perception and reality. Accessing emotions related to the difficulty of recollection can apparently alter the perception of an event's relative importance. Our minds often infer that an event is less important if we struggle to recall sufficient details.

For many, one of the primary goals of education is to get children to take ownership of their own learning. This is possible only if the child is ambitious and desires scaling new heights. Getting a child to recognize processes that help generate and promote an ambitious outlook has to be one of the foremost objectives of education. However, most educational systems are typically two steps removed from this. Few schools even recognize ambition as a curricular objective, let alone design a program to help the child be more ambitious.

Nevertheless, helping a child develop an ambitious outlook is entirely feasible. A curriculum that helps children assess and prioritize can in fact begin even in kindergarten. We can help children overcome barriers and nurture their confidence in their ability to persevere. Often role models can do wonders in helping children overcome mental roadblocks. Access to role models and inspiring narratives of real-world experiences can help build children's confidence. Nothing, however, can build their self-confidence better than the story of their own success. The practices of Reggio Emilia schools, therefore, are worth emulating. These schools often prominently display the projects of their students. Teachers also use a variety of tools to document the daily activities of every child and showcase their growth. This positive feedback loop gives children confidence in their ability to pursue reach-out goals.

Ambition without excellent visualization skills is often not very efficient. As we have discussed in part I of this book, visualization is a uniquely human ability. Clear visualization of what is possible can help boost confidence and bring ambitious goals to within striking distance. Also, learning to thoroughly identify and clarify our "intentions" before embarking on any new project can help us focus our minds on the task at hand. There was an interesting daily ritual that sisters Indra and Chandrika Krishnamurthy's mother had them participate in during dinner when they were eight to eleven years old. Each night, they played the role of a different president or a prime minister. They had to give a speech on what their priorities were, and their mother would pick the most compelling speaker each night. Their mother hadn't attended college or held a professional position, but she surely knew how to help her daughters dream big. Indra Nooyi went on to become the CEO of Pepsico and Chandrika Tandon served as the chairperson of Tandon Capital Associates as well as a member of the board of directors at the Lincoln Center for the Performing Arts.

A methodical delineation of what a particular outcome would entail can be a powerful visualization aid. The more details someone adds to a narrative, the more likely it could seem. VR, for example, can be used to create irresistible immersive experiences. The amazing advances in the quality of VR simulators and the accompanying sensory input and haptic feedback can also play a vital role in helping us imagine our futures. They can be a safe and inexpensive way to experience possible futures. For instance, biometric data collected from VR participants has revealed telltale biological signs of distress such as elevated pulse rates and blood pressure when they were exposed to events that shocked them. As several VR products (in Stanford's Virtual Human Interaction Lab and elsewhere) have shown, reliving artificial machine-generated experiences can trigger emotions and elicit responses that are almost as strong as those caused by real experiences in the brick-and-mortar world. The compelling proposition of VR prompted giants like Meta to jump headlong into the opportunities presented by the virtual world. At some point, however, we need to transition from depending on deliberate activities to a more reflexive ability to fluently imagine our possible futures. This is especially important when we are feeling tired or defeated. In such moments, it can be empowering to hold strongly to our memories of past accomplishments and tether them to the vision of our future success. It's crucial though that any external scaffolding is thoughtfully designed and minimally used so it doesn't inhibit personal growth.

We have learned a lot about how visualization works. For example, behavioral scientists such as Daniel Kahneman have identified "availability bias" as a key factor that affects our ability to correctly gauge future risks.[61] Many people have difficulty envisioning damage to their homes due to natural disasters, as this is not a pleasant or a common occurrence, but are often able to believe that they have reasonable odds of winning a lottery! It was this understanding of the impact of access on risk assessment, for instance, that led insurance underwriters to sell policies for travel insurance at airports in the 1950s. Active imagination and the ability to anticipate potential future outcomes can come either from external sources or from our own past experiences.

Greater control over our thoughts and senses through attention and goal commitment can also lead to increased tolerance of delayed gratification.[62] Interestingly, as we have seen earlier, gaining better control over our mind and senses has been an important theme even from ancient times. For instance, the 67th verse of chapter 2 in the *Bhagavad Gita* says:

> indriyāṇāṁ hi charatāṁ yan mano 'nuvidhīyate
> tadasya harati prajñāṁ vāyur nāvam ivāmbhasi
>
> *Just as a boat on the water can lose control to a strong wind, the senses too can lead a man's intelligence astray if the mind is subservient to them.*

This popular verse in the *Bhagavad Gita* elaborates on gratification deferment, describes the reasons for its significance, and prescribes ways for achieving control over our senses and desire for gratification. As we have seen time and again, insights into human motivation and the need for mind control have been with us for a long time.

The Stanford Marshmallow Experiments conducted by Walter Mischel in the 1960s and 1970s, for example, showed good correlation between the gratification deferment skills of four-year-olds and their success in adult life.[63] Of greater interest, perhaps, are the experiments that showed that it is possible to increase control over our urges for instant gratification with practice.[64] Interestingly, while Bryant and Veroff had demonstrated that savoring can enrich our positive emotions and sense of joy, they have also shown that greater intensity and fulfillment is reached when there are fewer savoring moments overall.[65] In other words, gratification deferment appears to be more beneficial when coupled with a deeper sense of gratitude and enjoyment. This is also in alignment with Daniel Goleman's identification of delayed gratification as an important element of emotional intelligence.[66]

Development of an ambitious outlook also requires periodic reflection and perseverance. These important life skills are indispensable for identification and prioritization of opportunities. They can lend new perspectives to old skills, uncover flaws that we might have been unaware of, and help us reassess short- and long-term goals. These insights create the vision that powers our goals and ensures that we are mindful of the most promising paths and that we don't lose what we worked hard to master. As we discussed earlier, metacognition and judgment skills are essential for these assessments. Some children may be more interested in novelty and exploration, and not have the stomach to pause and reflect. As such, it is helpful to periodically introduce opportunities that encourage such reflection.

Visualization is only one side of the coin. We should also develop the ability to correctly judge roadblocks or challenges during such a visualization exercise. Otherwise, we cannot stretch beyond the obvious goals. As Lao Tzu reportedly said (the exact source of this quote though is uncertain), "Ambition should have one heel nailed in well, though she stretches her fingers to touch the heavens." To venture beyond our comfort zone, we must possess an understanding of the risks and benefits as well as the self-esteem and resilience to endure failure. The ability to focus on a longer-term goal or a higher-level purpose is necessary to be able to stomach the risks. Resilience also depends on our ability to handle stress. As Helen Keller said, "Character cannot be developed in ease and quiet. Only through experience of trial and suffering can the soul be strengthened, ambition inspired, and success achieved."[67] Too little stress would probably produce little in terms of character development. Too much stress, on the other hand, might simply cause irreparable harm. Many missed opportunities and setbacks in life are often the result of our inability or unwillingness to handle stress. Lewis and Linder published an interesting study that looked at the effect of choking under pressure.[68] When the abilities of amateur golfers were assessed with a video camera turned on, their game fell a couple of notches below what they produced during a prior practice round of golf. However, their handicap didn't suffer when they were asked to count backward from one hundred or if the video cameras were turned on during their practice rounds. The distraction of counting backward from one hundred prevented the participants from focusing too much attention on the odds of failure. Thus, these results supported self-focus mediated misregulation as the mechanism for choking and ruled out the distraction hypothesis. Stress is like a tax on working memory. This has also been shown in a study of students solving math problems under the pressures of monetary incentives, peer pressure, or potential social evaluation.[69] As suggested by Lewis and Linder's study, developing fluency in focusing on just the mechanics can help reduce the associated stress. Internalizing intention this way ensures that the focus is more on the mechanics of an activity rather than on nonactionable and unproductive aspects such as consequences of failure.

To summarize, we therefore need to master five high-level skills: the ability to (1) identify the most valuable opportunities, (2) visualize possible paths to these goals, (3) assess the risks and benefits of any barriers that are identified, (4) formulate and internalize the necessary resolve to ensure successful outcomes, and (5) the patience to persevere. It would of course be desirable to be able to measure ambition. While there is some research into this, more investigations are needed to design a reliable gauge for this valuable trait.[70] Once we have an accurate assessment of a child's skills and learning abilities, we should also seek out the child's own assessments of the utility of other reach-out tasks and the barriers to their mastery. Such assessments would be helpful both for child empowerment as well as for the design of exercises that can enhance their visualization and risk-assessment abilities. It is also important to start small and not stretch too far too soon. Even as we pursue success and stay positive, we should also build the necessary resilience and adaptability to deal with setbacks.

Ambitious individuals are often resilient with unrelenting focus, self-control, the ability to resist the urge for gratification, and tolerance for failure. They also have an almost indomitable faith in the odds of their success.

Nurturing Creativity

To See a World in a Grain of Sand
And a Heaven in a Wild Flower,
Hold Infinity in the palm of your hand
And Eternity in an hour.
—WILLIAM BLAKE, "AUGURIES OF INNOCENCE"

Ermal (Ernie) Fraze was the owner of a successful machine tool business. When he was at a picnic one day with his friends and family, he realized that he forgot to bring his can opener for the drinks. Fortunately, he was able to use his car bumper to pry the cans open. However, the need to carry around a separate can opener gnawed at him. A few months later, as he lay in bed one night, he pondered this problem while waiting to fall asleep. He woke up the next morning with the idea of the pull-tab opener, an improved beverage opening method that eliminated the need for a separate tool. With a patent for the invention in 1963, his company made over $500 million in annual revenue by 1980 supplying can-end machinery worldwide.

The creative process and the motivation of a creative mind are both routinely misunderstood. Creative minds are incredibly restless and often see patterns across multiple domains. In fact, creative individuals sometimes hide in plain sight. Hedy Lamarr was a glamorous Hollywood actress who starred alongside legends such as Clark Gable, Judy Garland, and James Stewart. Frustrated by how she was offered only narrowly defined stereotypical roles, she cofounded her own production studio. In 1960, Lamarr, who originally immigrated from Austria, was honored with a star on the Hollywood Walk of Fame. However, many of her coworkers were unaware that she was an actress by day and an inventor by night.

Despite her lack of formal education, Lamarr had acquired a great deal of knowledge of military technologies and communications during her marriage to Friedrich Mandl, an arms merchant based in Vienna. Lamarr had presided over many of their lavish parties, often attended by Hitler and Mussolini, among others. In fact, Lamarr had also been a regular attendee at her husband's business meetings. However, unable to tolerate her husband's controlling and domineering behavior, she fled to Paris disguised as a maid. Eventually she made her way to London first and then to the United States. When Lamarr learned that radio-controlled torpedoes, an emerging technology in naval war, could easily be jammed and set off course, she came up with a frequency-hopping signal that could not be tracked. With the help of composer and pianist George Antheil, she filed a patent for the spread-spectrum communication technology in which a noise-like signal is added to the original signal with a higher bandwidth. Incidentally, spread-spectrum technologies are the backbone of modern wireless communications such as Bluetooth and Wi-Fi.

Later, to help Howard Hughes improve the speed of his airplanes, she convinced him to change their square shape to a more streamlined contour that mimicked the shapes of the fastest birds and fish. Lamarr worked on improving traffic lights, created a tablet that when dissolved could produce carbonated water, discovered the potential for a ski resort at Aspen, and even laid the groundwork for cosmetic surgery by telling her doctors where and how incisions should be made. She received the Electronic Frontier Foundation Award in 1998 and was also posthumously inducted into the National Inventors Hall of Fame.

Creativity is a relatively complex competency.[71] For instance, curiosity motivates our pursuits, and our cognitive abilities process the information we obtain as a result and relate it to what we already know. Empathy gives each of us our own distinct moral compass and this enables valuation of the information we process, often from multiple perspectives. This valuation helps us judge between different possibilities. Ambition then is our potential to stretch our abilities to live up to the possibilities offered by our judgment. An ambitious person can forge ahead even when he or she is faced with very heavy odds. Often, however, the goals are rather well delineated. We don't necessarily venture into unknown territory. Creativity, on the other hand, requires us to march ahead even when there is no inkling of the possibility of a solution to the problem we're faced with, let alone a path to the solution. Creativity has been a significant ingredient in human progress through the ages. It is the quintessential element that extends the limits of our understanding.

While cognition is all about understanding what exists, creativity, put simply, is the ability to create something completely new. For example, a presiding judge would be expected to demonstrate high levels of cognition: really understand the law, its limits and presumptions, the positions and claims of the prosecution and defense, the precedents on record, and the impact of possible judgments. However, we wouldn't expect the judge to be overly creative in interpreting the law. It is quite possible for someone to be wise with a high degree of cognition and yet not be creative. Similarly, it is quite possible for an artist to be less creative than a car dealer or an insurance agent. Creativity is simply the knack for coming up with innovative ideas and out-of-the-box concepts. When the Wright brothers began working on human flight, it was already a well-recognized problem; many other teams were trying to find a solution. The Wright brothers were curious, passionate, and ambitious. But in a creative pursuit, few others even recognize a problem, let alone work toward a solution. This is not to say that the Wright brothers did not have creative breakthroughs along the way. Creativity is often considered a mysterious process that lights a spark and provokes a completely original thought in our heads. If curiosity is all about the range and depth of questions, creativity is more about the answers we come up with to questions that are not even being asked. Curiosity can of course sometimes spark the process that leads to creative breakthroughs.

Incidentally, psychologist Benjamin Baird, in researching daydreaming, has found that there is a trade-off between cognitive tasks that require a heavy focus on the here and now versus imaginative tasks that let the mind roam.[72] He found that while mind wandering can hurt tasks that require intense focus, it is essential for creative exploration. This is one notable example of the likely tension between different competencies and the need to balance them.

There have been many attempts to get at the core of human creativity. Conceptual blending, the Explicit-Implicit interaction theory, and the Honing theory are a few that seek to explain the biological processes of creativity.[73] Researchers such as Gregory Feist have found that creative people tend to be highly ambitious and impulsive and often exhibit high levels of self-confidence and self-esteem as well as an ability to ignore conventions while taking risks. Surprisingly, they have also found that many creative individuals often had lower levels of conscientiousness and few qualms about exhibiting some degree of arrogance, contempt, and hostility.[74]

Research has demonstrated that there are distinct biological signatures to creative thinking. For instance, it has been shown that the prefrontal cortex is used more for insightful thinking.[75] Martindale and Lozanov also showed that there is more alpha-wave activity in the brains of creative individuals.[76] Of course, this does not suggest that creativity can only be inherited, and not acquired. Even though Fink, Marshall, and their colleagues published a groundbreaking study in *Nature* that buried the romantic notion of lateralization of brain functions, it is still true, as a gross generalization, that the right brain provides the wide-angle, big-picture view while the left focuses on the details.[77] Fluency in recognizing the big-picture context is essential for novel and creative out-of-the-box thinking. Most of our education is unfortunately focused more on minutiae. It is largely tailored to stimulate left-hemisphere activities such as logical and systematic thinking, and this only helps to further strengthen the left half, which is already strong in many of us.

The launch of Sputnik 1 in 1957 ushered in a time of great introspection in the US. Fascination with science and engineering reached feverish heights and bold thinking came to be highly valued. Around the same time, the Creative Education Foundation at the University at Buffalo (SUNY Buffalo) launched a formal program to promote critical thinking using the Parnes-Osborn model. It is therefore probably not unfair to credit Sputnik 1 with the spurt in research into human intelligence and creativity in the US.

Graham Wallas was perhaps the first to propose a model for the creative process. In his 1926 work, *The Art of Thought*, he lists (1) preparation, (2) incubation, (3) illumination, and (4) verification as the four stages of this process.[78] There used to be a widespread belief that children with the highest IQ were the ones who were also the most creative. But J. P. Guilford's work established that there is a threshold IQ level above which the correlation between creativity and classical intelligence breaks down.[79]

Williams, Treffinger, Torrance, and Piirto are some of the many researchers who have worked on instruments for the identification and promotion of creativity.[80] Guilford's work inspired two of the common tests used today for the assessment of student creativity, the Torrance Test of Creative Thinking (TTCT) and the Williams Creativity Assessment Packet.[81] While the Torrance test focuses on divergent thinking, the Williams taxonomy calls for eight hierarchical thinking skills; four are cognitive in nature, and the other four focus on affective abilities.

Williams's four cognitive skills—fluency, flexibility, originality, and elaboration—are quite similar to those in the TTCT. *Fluency* looks at the quantity of ideas, responses, and possibilities people can generate in any given situation. This is a very important skill since the best way to generate a good idea is to be able to produce a lot of—likely bad—ideas. *Flexibility* entails the ability to generate variations, alternatives, and adaptations that take initial ideas and thoughts even further. This looks at our ability to keep an open mind or our resistance to premature closure. *Originality* is an even higher-order skill, and as the term suggests, it involves our ability to generate unique or novel responses—that is, solutions that break new ground. Finally, *elaboration* refers to our ability to expand our ideas in greater detail. This is another important skill as it is essential for ensuring that a proposal is thoroughly vetted. Additionally, we sometimes generate or elicit even more ideas or a deeper understanding when we pause to clearly articulate them.

Williams's four emotional skills are risk-taking, complexity, curiosity, and imagination. *Risk-taking* is defined as our ability to experiment and get out of our comfort zone. We can't be too creative without venturing into the unknown. The next higher-order skill, *complexity*, is the ability to not only stay calm in chaotic situations but to envision or create new structures out of such chaos. This skill can be very helpful, because it allows us to create new paradigms and see missing parts, so we can seize the opportunities that crises often present. In fact, it is also often during the chaos resulting from a setback that people are most willing to entertain larger structural changes. Given that Feist has associated high levels of confidence and lower levels of conscientiousness with highly creative people, it appears likely that they would also be most immune to the harmful effects of stress and thus most prepared to benefit from complexity. The third affective skill is *curiosity*, or the ability to wonder or puzzle. As we discussed earlier, curiosity is key to most new learning and exploration and is an important competency in itself. The fourth affective skill that Williams listed as essential for creativity is *imagination*, the ability to visualize or build mental pictures of new possibilities.

According to Williams and Torrance, fluency and originality of ideas are assumed to flow from risk-taking. Incidentally, we noted in part I that the learner profile of the International Baccalaureate (IB) programs requires students to be risk-takers.[82] It characterizes disruptive thinking that reaches beyond someone's comfort zone as risk-taking. While the intent is obvious and the emphasis is essential, this language can be prone to misinterpretation. We have a risk whenever success is not assured. We're believed to be taking obvious risks when we're not diligent in weighing the odds. We can also take risks by not following protocol. This type of behavior can be quite dangerous during emergency events, for instance. Also, if taking a risk surprises those who depend on us, we may be considered less reliable. On the other hand, those who are risk-averse likely cannot tolerate even a small amount of uncertainty. They typically need ironclad guarantees.

Unfortunately, the term *risk-taking* in itself does not suggest any reason to take the risks. When children test boundaries, they're either motivated by curiosity or by a desire to rebel against authority. If they're motivated by curiosity, they're often not consciously aware of the risks. On the other hand, when they decide to rebel, there is often more than necessary motivation to take on the risks. By requiring children to conform to excessive rules, we push them along the path from curiosity to disobedience through a power struggle. In this sense, risk-taking is an unfortunate outcome of an inherently destructive process. We should try to nurture children's curiosity, so they have fewer restrictions and can explore further. Creative children are impulsive and are lured more by the potential for novelty and new frontiers than by the outcome of a risk-benefit analysis.

Creative people also have elevated levels of tolerance for failure. They don't necessarily perceive failure as a negative outcome. They don't forge ahead because they have modulated their judgment to accept more risk. A person with a creative outlook can thus see a completely different set of odds and hence a very different risk-benefit profile. From their perspective, the balance in the risk-benefit analysis is shifted from where the rest of us would have perceived it. Their behavior appears to be risky only to those of us who fear the odds and are not as creative. It may therefore be helpful to focus more on experimentation skills and the definition of failure and tolerance levels than on risk-taking.

Ultimately, everyone should take on risks when the odds are attractive or at least acceptable from their own perspective. This requires a good understanding of the purpose and its value proposition and an emotional engagement with the objectives. An understanding of the purpose comes through empathy and cognition. One needs judgment to assess the risks and benefits and a healthy ambition to pursue the "risky" activity. While it is true that we should not be needlessly risk-averse, it may not be appropriate either to assume that risk-taking is always beneficial for creativity. It may be better to rely on judgment to determine the acceptable levels of risk.

In an article in *Educational and Psychological Measurement*, Kim, Cramond, and Bandalos have shown that the two factors in Kirton's Adaptor-Innovator theory are an excellent model for the latent structure of TTCT.[83] High scores in fluency and originality indicate that the subject is a good innovator, while adaptive skills are reflected in higher scores on elaboration and abstractness of titles. Both the Torrance and Williams creativity tests have been shown to be highly reliable, though they can be a bit tedious to administer. While these tests have greatly advanced our ability to understand and assess creativity, there have also been some concerns about the limitations of these tests. In an article in the *Creativity Research Journal*, Zeng, Proctor, and Salvendy have identified insufficient predictive, construct, and discriminant validities as well as neglect of domain expertise as some of the major weaknesses of these instruments.[84] It is perhaps for these reasons that creativity tests are most often used alongside other corroboratory data such as parent or teacher reporting and project samples.

Mumford and Meusburger summarized the general consensus that creativity is the process of producing something novel, original, and worthwhile.[85] A key point here is that the product of creativity has to be useful; it must have some value. While the affective skills that Williams has cited do help create a fertile ground for creativity, his metrics don't assess the relevance of these novel or creative ideas to a problem at hand. In our list of competencies, we should consider creativity as the ability to search past known paradigms for a solution with a higher-value proposition than those currently available.

In the words of the American psychologist R. J. Sternberg, "Creativity is often obvious in young children, but it may be harder to find in older children and adults because their creative potential has been suppressed by a society that encourages intellectual conformity."[86] This suggests that many of us are actually born more creative than we grow up to be. Researchers have identified the need for conformity, fear of failure, ridicule, embarrassment, and our susceptibility to these fears and expectations as some of the key reasons for the erosion of our creativity. Additionally, it's difficult to be creative when we're under mental stress or conditioning. As we grow up, many of us have to deal with the stress caused by the increasing complexity of our lives. Stress can hamper us from recognizing the opportunities crises present. Also, for most children, the skills to cope with these challenges take several years to develop. All too often, children eager to obey and conform will likely please most parents and educators and thus appear to possess the traits of high achievers. Unfortunately, while conformity is essential for an orderly society and a predictable educational experience, it is often also an impediment to creativity. The conflict between these competing needs leaves many parents and educators in a quandary about the best way to balance them.

Just as there are behaviors and circumstances that can stifle creativity, there are also behaviors that can foster creativity. Given that answers are to creativity what questions are to curiosity, one obvious strategy for promoting creativity is to hold back on providing ready answers to the questions children may have. Since children are often more engaged with questions that arise in their own heads, these questions present excellent opportunities for creative exploration. The ability to question the status quo and to question all explanations is indispensable for the promotion of creativity. Creative processes benefit from a healthy dose of naïveté, an unwavering belief in oneself, and an absolute lack of fear. It is helpful to develop such a thirst for understanding from a young age. Getting children to hypothesize possible answers would be good training in avoiding premature closure. Along the same lines, acknowledging children's expressions of creativity can be very nurturing. It may not always be easy for us to recognize that a seemingly mundane thought or perspective is in fact a novel breakthrough for a child. We should be on the lookout for such insights and experiences. Empowering children so they can own as many decisions in their lives as appropriate should also be beneficial since agency is essential for creativity.

As noted earlier, most creative activities originate in the pursuit of a worthwhile goal. They begin with the search for a solution to a problem, even if many others don't even recognize the problem. As Stephen Estes, an American social entrepreneur, has pointed out, we can motivate children best when they are challenged to solve real-world problems.[87] We can perhaps ask them to think of different conclusions to popular stories, implications of altering known scientific phenomena or mathematical laws, motivations for a friend's behavior, or reasons for any of the rules at home or school.

Figure 5.3. The creative storefront of a proud Sankalpa Academy student.

It is best to get them thinking more about processes and possibilities. Also, as the English proverb goes, necessity is often the mother of invention. Fluency with a problem and its repercussions often greatly helps promote creativity. Creativity is essential to venture past the familiar boundaries of many of our pressing problems and into the uncharted territories that likely host the best solutions. Brainstorming is one well-known strategy for generating a large quantity of ideas and thoughts. Brainstorming involves suspending judgment so we can be fluent in the production of ideas. Suboptimal or nonrelevant ideas are typically weeded out at a later stage.

The breadth of our experiences can help expand our minds to more possibilities. There are many wonderful resources parents and teachers can consult for suggestions on activities that can promote creativity.[88] The world of art, for instance, offers interesting possibilities. Art has often been a safe and accessible medium of expression for channeling hopes and frustrations, and the creativity that artistic freedom can produce can be seen even in very young children. The freedom to play also has similar beneficial effects in children. A study by Sally Grantham-McGregor from the Institute of Child Health at University College London has revealed a significant increase in IQ even in severely malnourished preschool children when they were given opportunities to play.[89] This study, published in *The Lancet*, demonstrates the importance of fantasy play and, in fact, of all activities that seek to boost self-esteem and child empowerment. Researchers have also suggested that, in addition to divergent thinking, training in the reappraisal of emotional events and narrative cognition can also help promote creativity.[90]

Also, even though many inventors are typically remembered for one or two creations, they often leave behind a long trail of inventions since tinkering is a contagion that is caught early and difficult to shed. While Alexander Graham Bell's work with the hearing-impaired likely inspired him to work on creating a telephone, he also has many other inventions under his belt. When he was only eleven, he created a tool that could clean wheat. As a grown-up, he later invented a photophone, a metal detector, and other sonic technologies. Similarly, in addition to the lightbulb, Edison is credited with the carbon telephone transmitter, a phonograph, a movie camera and viewer, an alkaline storage battery, and more. In fact, Edison garnered a total of 1,093 patents—more than one patent for every month of his life. In the later stages of his life, Edison was even rumored to be working on a "spirit phone" for conversing with the dead! A creative mind often doesn't recognize any limits.

As Robert McKim says in his book *Experiences in Visual Thinking*, "No one who dreams can say that they are not creative, and everyone dreams."[91] Reimagining education so it is better able to nurture children's creativity can reap rich dividends for our collective future.

Facilitating Communication

> The single biggest problem in communication
> is the illusion that it has taken place.
> —GEORGE BERNARD SHAW

The 1920s were a relatively disappointing decade for the Indian National Congress (INC) overall and Gandhi in particular. Gandhi had led successful agitations at Champaran and Kheda in 1917 and 1918 to help the peasants. Despite significant reservations, he also helped recruit Indians to fight alongside the British in the First World War. With this act of solidarity with the British, he hoped to hasten India's own independence. However, when the British only offered minor concessions after the war ended, Gandhi was upset and responded with a call for Satyagraha (a civil disobedience movement). The British countered with the Rowlatt Act and threatened indefinite preventive incarceration, without judicial review, of all those who joined his protests. But as support still grew steadily for the noncooperation and Swadeshi (purchase of only items made in India) movements, the British eventually arrested Gandhi in March 1922. With Gandhi locked up, the movement began to splinter and drift in different directions. Even after Gandhi's release in 1924, it took the Congress leadership many years to regroup and reengage the population in the freedom movement.

Hindus and Muslims began to increasingly pursue separate paths, and many were disillusioned by Gandhi's decision to help the British militarily in World War I. Finally, on December 27, 1929, at its plenary session, the INC adopted its Purna Swaraj (complete independence) resolution. Gandhi had been continuing to promote his philosophies of Satyagraha and Swadeshi after his release from prison, but he had also been mulling over a way to both rally his countrymen as well as win more support from the European diplomats and the general British population. The Congress Party began creating plays in various Indian languages that showcased Gandhi's ideals through Indian mythology and legends. This helped elevate Gandhi to the status of a folk hero for most of the population. In the meantime, the British had used the Rowlatt Act to unleash violence against the protestors, and Gandhi was determined that these measures should be countered only through nonviolence.

Gandhi finally decided that an attack on the salt tax was the most effective vehicle for reinvigorating his movement and dismantling British rule. Salt was an essential part of the Indian diet, required by Hindus and Muslims and the rich as well as the poor. It was also available in abundance along India's long coastline. However, its production and distribution in India had long been a lucrative monopoly of the British, and it amounted to about 8.2 percent of its revenue. Indians were forced to buy expensive, heavily taxed salt that was often imported. Gandhi proposed that Congress and millions of its workers defy the British and make their own salt. However, this was initially received with incredulity by the Congress working committee. Many were bemused and felt let down—they were expecting a call for more direct action from Gandhi or at least a revenue boycott of some sort. *The Statesman*, a prominent newspaper, wrote at the time: "It is difficult not to laugh, and we imagine that will be the mood of most thinking Indians."[92]

Gandhi laid out meticulous plans for his Salt Satyagraha. American, European, and Indian news media were informed, and their expectations steadily raised to ensure that he had a wide audience. Gandhi also wrote a letter to the British Viceroy, Lord Irwin, informing him of Congress's demands for a repeal of the salt tax, among others, as well as his intention to launch a Salt Satyagraha if their demands were not met. Lord Irwin and his counselors did not take this as a serious threat, and their initial response was to ignore the matter. As a result, at dawn on March 12, 1930, Gandhi and seventy-eight of his followers from different castes and religions set out on foot on their 240-mile march from his Sabarmati Ashram to the coastal town of Dandi in Gujarat. Gandhi expected to be beaten or at least arrested, but the British were afraid of the backlash and chose not to respond. Thousands joined Gandhi's group along the way, and it turned into about a two-mile-long procession.

Gandhi spoke to hundreds of thousands of people as they traveled through four districts and forty-eight villages at roughly twelve miles a day. They routinely stopped in these villages, eating what was offered, accepting water to wash themselves, and sleeping in the open. The procession reached Dandi on April 5 and was received there by more than fifty thousand people. In addition to the multitudes that greeted them en route, Gandhi also spoke to the press along the way and wrote articles explaining the rationale for their demands, the nature of the agitation, and the behavior of the British. He became a household name around the globe, received daily coverage from the *New York Times*, and ended up as *Time* magazine's Man of the Year. His efforts also helped him draw thousands more of his fellow citizens into this struggle.

After Gandhi and his followers made salt at Dandi, millions of Congress workers as well as common people across India began to make and sell it. The British government could no longer remain a silent spectator and eighty thousand people were arrested by the end of the month, but the peaceful noncooperation eventually spread beyond the salt tax. The government machinery began to come to a standstill. British troops often responded with violence, but this was mostly met with disciplined nonviolence. The one-sided brutality led to a public backlash in the US, Britain, and elsewhere. This event is widely considered the beginning of the end of British control over India.

Gandhi's philosophy of Satyagraha also inspired Martin Luther King's fight for equity and racial justice in the US and countless other movements around the world. Gandhi paved a path that was uplifting for the oppressors as well as for the millions of oppressed in his country and elsewhere. His strategy, campaign, and communication were carefully orchestrated based on an astute understanding of the motivations and desires of all stakeholders, including their tolerance for failure and hardship. This is what makes Gandhi's approach both remarkable and timeless.

Incidentally, a larger upheaval was also brewing elsewhere in the world around the same time. Germany faced significant consequences as a major aggressor of World War I. The Treaty of Versailles imposed territorial losses, financial reparations, disarmament, and war guilt on Germany. The "War Guilt" clause was a source of great resentment in Germany and contributed to a sense of injustice and humiliation. In response, the German government resorted to printing money liberally, initially to fulfill wartime commitments and later for reconstruction and reparations. This led to hyperinflation, and the stock market crash of 1929 only exacerbated Germany's economic woes. American banks, which had lent money to Germany for reparations, grew concerned and began demanding repayment. The resulting financial meltdown pushed the nation into a dire situation and compounded Germany's post-war humiliation.

During this bleak period, the National Socialist German Workers' Party (Nazism) capitalized on the anxieties and fears of the population. Its extreme ultranationalist philosophy quickly spread from the fringe to the mainstream. By 1933, Adolf Hitler became the chancellor, and after the death of President Hindenburg in 1934, he assumed the role of president as well. Germany underwent a major transformation under Hitler's watch. Through persuasive tactics and strategic utilization of existing laws, he curtailed personal liberties and eventually dismantled the democratic system. As his grip tightened, he intensified religious and racial suppression. He first excluded Jews from cultural, social, and political life. He then proceeded to revoke their citizenship rights. Subsequently, their wealth and economic activities were curtailed, and their properties seized. He then deployed the Gestapo to suppress any opposition.

Initially, Hitler's racial theories and persecution of Jews faced staunch opposition from both Catholic and Protestant churches. However, capitalizing on fear and public sentiment, Hitler managed to silence much of the opposition. His domestic success also emboldened him to embark on a foreign campaign. Hitler maintained friendly relations with neighboring countries while he consolidated his political standing internally. While the neighboring countries initially received relatively modest demands from him, these steadily escalated into aggressive ultimatums. Germany eventually withdrew from the League of Nations, renounced the Versailles Treaty, and successfully rebuilt its military with minimal international opposition. In March 1935, Hitler introduced conscription, rapidly expanding the German Air Force, navy, and army. With the acquisition of the Saar Basin, an alliance with Mussolini's Italy, and the annexation of Austria and Czechoslovakia, Hitler's expansion was well underway. He then launched a pogrom to exterminate Jews, occupied Poland and France, and waged war against Britain and the Soviet Union. However, his unbridled fascism, ruthlessness, and brutality only hastened his downfall. The defeat of Germany and Hitler's subsequent suicide in 1945 marked the end of his tyranny.

Both Gandhi and Hitler left a significant impact—one inspirational and uplifting and the other divisive and catastrophic—that belied their humble origins. Neither hailed from wealthy or politically influential families. It is, however, important to note that their ideologies did not develop in a vacuum. Hitler's childhood experiences and the prevailing political environment in Germany shaped his receptiveness to populist figures like Viennese mayor

Karl Lueger. In Gandhi's case, he was influenced in his childhood by poet and Jain philosopher Shrimad Rajchandra and later by thinkers such as Tolstoy, Ruskin, and Thoreau. Hitler rode to power on the coattails of Germany's collective humiliation and sense of hurt. His ability to tailor and evolve his narrative in an opportunistic manner allowed him to manipulate public opinion, consolidate his power, and undermine societal values and conscience over time. Gandhi, on the other hand, faced numerous challenges. He waged a multifaceted struggle against the entrenched caste system, Hindu-Muslim conflicts, and British oppression. Gandhi opted to suspend his protests and go on hunger strikes whenever religious or caste-based strife flared up. Building support for his principles of Satyagraha was a slow and arduous process, one that held greater importance for him than mere independence from British rule. Persuading millions to break free from deeply ingrained habits and traditions, willingly endure physical punishment, and accept imprisonment demanded extraordinary integrity and credibility compared to appeasing the masses with grand visions of the future. The life stories of Gandhi and Hitler illustrate the immense power of communication—from elevating humanity to greatness to unleashing evil by channeling the demons in us. Intimate awareness of this potential is a key educational imperative. Communication is a vital competency for shaping the course of our shared existence for the better.

As discussed in the first part of this book, storytelling has been an important part of the human journey. *Homo sapiens* prevailed due to their ability to envision alternative realities and to convince others to embrace them. With its ability to change the course of history and even the future of our race, communication is a critically important competency. Communication skills are essential at almost every stage of life, even if our goals are modest. A good understanding of the role of communication skills is also essential to ensure that the fabric of our social discourse stays healthy and vibrant. From the influence we wield on our friends and colleagues to success in our careers and relationships, communication is a vital cog that turns the wheel of life. It is not uncommon to get into a misunderstanding that is caused by a misspoken word, an unspoken word, or a change in plans or a change of heart that was not properly disclosed. While the motivation might often be innocent, this may also, on occasion, be the result of taking someone for granted. The impact of a communication breakdown can be disastrous sometimes; countries have gone to war on occasion, as we have seen. Despite their extraordinary significance, communication skills don't always get the attention and prioritization they deserve. We routinely run into children—and even adults—who are compassionate and creative and gifted problem solvers, but not adequately articulate.

Children try to communicate almost from birth. They try to employ every tool at their disposal, pointing to objects, vocalizing incoherently, or throwing a tantrum. When he was a year old, our son used to push my cheek and twist my head toward him if he wanted my attention. Of course, the needs of infants are often met without much communication. For the most part, parents are attentive and on standby to cater to every need of their newborn. When necessary, babies cry to signal that they are hungry, sleepy, or need a diaper change. Fortunately, most parents get to know their babies well enough that they often respond quickly and correctly to their crying baby. Ironically, as children grow up and begin to use language, this communication sometimes breaks down. Graduation from crying to talking does not necessarily imply that children have also mastered the necessary emotional awareness and that they now can correctly identify or efficiently articulate their needs. As babies grow, it is therefore necessary for parents to evolve as well, almost in tandem. Parents should step back and create opportunities for young children to articulate their needs. Children should be encouraged to advocate for themselves and communicate their desires.

Experts also recommend that parents talk often with toddlers. Talking to them helps them recognize both the vocabulary itself and the power of language and communication in general. Often, young children are immensely interested in names of places, people, food, and objects. This stems from their inherent curiosity as well as their recognition that they need these names to communicate their growing needs and wants. Family discussions can help children develop the ability to articulate their thoughts. We should resist the temptation to complete children's sentences or thoughts for them or to cater to all their needs without much discussion. Communicating with as much specificity as possible will help the development of critical thinking and communication skills. As children grow up, it's also necessary to expose them to multiple languages and literary experiences. In a rapidly shrinking world, it's important to ensure that children's perspectives and the range of their vocabulary have both the necessary breadth and depth.

Often, there is adequate focus on reading and writing in most schools. But compelling communication skills demand more. While reading and writing are important tools, we should also ensure that there is an emotional connection between the child and the subject matter. The attention a child pays to a communication task typically depends on their motivation to communicate. It helps to ensure that children have ample real, pressing, and actionable needs. This is yet another reason for children's empowerment—they need to feel able and encouraged to use their voices. For instance, even very young children should be able to choose from a variety of pictures and tell us what they like best about their choice. A periodic "show and tell," for example, can be an excellent vehicle for promoting communication skills.

The more adults instruct or dictate to children, the harder it is for them to feel empowered. They need opportunities for reflection and such opportunities are difficult to come by without empowerment. This does not absolve adults of their responsibility to "teach," inspire, or model. In fact, the expectations are even higher due to the breakdown of extended families. At the same time, parents need to also seize the opportunities for promoting reflection as they arise. Reflection leads to a prioritization of wants and needs. Often, only opportunities that carry actionable consequences would require serious reflection and would in turn promote meaningful communication and growth.

In a similar vein, children should also be asked to review literary samples and provide feedback on attributes such as relevance, clarity, precision, undercommunication, and overcommunication. Such reflection can be an effective learning tool. Similarly, when a child writes, it would be more beneficial for the child to revisit and edit the piece after a period of time before peers or a teacher edit it. Our brains need time to soak in, evolve, and generate ideas with increasing depth and clarity. We cannot expect children to learn this vital life skill if they are not afforded opportunities during their schooling.

To help children blossom into effective communicators, we need to help them master all aspects of communication. Communication is an emergent reality that results from the synthesis of the selections we make for the information, its understanding or misunderstanding, and its presentation.[93] For example, the significance of an emotional connection comes from the fact that the most important aspect of any communication is its authenticity. Regardless of the medium of communication, it is hard to hold someone's attention when the narrative does not hold together. We should help children develop the courage and integrity needed to be as honest as possible and necessary in their communication.

Figure 5.4. The Badgerdog program from the Austin Public Library fosters the writing skills of Sankalpa's budding authors.

The second step in the process of communication requires careful consideration of the audience as well as possible communication strategies. Good communication skills are not possible without good listening skills. Consideration of the audience requires intimate awareness of the currency that the audience values. Empathy is therefore a key prerequisite for good listening skills. Listening helps us accurately perceive emotions from all sources, our own and from others. Understanding others well also improves our chances of being understood. Children also need to be trained in nonverbal communication signals. Body language can make a lot of difference. It can betray a variety of emotions such as confidence, fear, sincerity, and arrogance. In addition to heightened awareness of our own body language, we should try to gain mastery in reading others' body language. Cultural understanding is often necessary to ensure that we don't misread nonverbal cues or send the wrong message. We also need to be intimately aware of how our message is being received. Eye contact is often helpful for emphasizing emotional involvement and sincerity. Of course, even as we are emotionally invested, we should not let the circumstances stress us out. It is difficult to have a rational conversation when we're unduly stressed. It is also essential to frequently check for understanding. This ensures that we don't lose our audience midway through a conversation. Finally, while content is a critical component of any message, its formulation and delivery are also important and should not be underestimated.

Once we accurately identify and understand our audience and hone our message as well as the communication strategy, the final step is to carefully sequence our communication so the flow from the aspirations of our audience to the crux of our message is clear. Also, for clarity, it is important to ensure a logical flow such that only one new idea is introduced at a time. True eloquence requires exceptional precision, both in tailoring a message and in its delivery. In the words of Dorothy Nevill, a nineteenth-century English writer, "The real art of conversation is not only to say the right thing at the right place but to leave unsaid the wrong thing at the tempting moment."[94] This obviously requires a careful evaluation of all communication in terms of its overall utility, with special attention paid to the perspectives of our audience.

The tapestry of communication can often be quite rich. From communication strategy to timing, from the vehicle chosen to the actual content, and from what we say to what our audience hears, the various layers contribute in their own ways to the overall objective. Developing skills in all these aspects should therefore be an important element of any educational program.

CHAPTER SUMMARY

- Almost all notable human accomplishments are fueled by our six foundational competencies: curiosity, cognition, empathy, ambition, creativity, and communication.
- While there are polymaths like Leonardo da Vinci who embody all six competencies, most changemakers' claim to fame only comes from two or three.

- It is remarkable that human accomplishments have a stronger correlation to these competencies than to traditional academic outcomes. More importantly, our proficiencies are not entirely preordained at birth.
- Education therefore needs to pay more attention to these competencies. Also, at times, strength in one competency might be a handicap for another. As such, it is essential to tailor experiences per the unique needs of each learner.
- Environment provides the experiences that feed our curiosity and open new channels of learning. At the same time, we should ensure that our growth through learning and experience doesn't result in certainty that stifles our epistemic curiosity.
- Our cognitive abilities process the information we receive and relate it to what we already know. Active learning through rich experiences and novel activities that exercise our malleable brain in innovative ways can help create new synaptic connections and facilitate the construction of new learning.
- Each of us has our own distinct moral compass. Our value system and empathy enable the valuation of the information we receive, often from multiple perspectives. This valuation helps us judge between different possibilities.
- Fluency in traversing the hot-cold empathy gap can help us develop all three key dimensions of empathy: cognitive, emotional, and compassionate.
- Ambition is our potential to stretch our abilities and pursue one or more of the possibilities offered by our judgment. It often begins with restlessness and is sustained by our ability to delay gratification.
- Creativity, on the other hand, takes us beyond known possibilities and entices us to march ahead in new directions even when there is no inkling of a solution or even a well-defined problem. There is a threshold IQ level above which the correlation between creativity and classical intelligence breaks down.

- Since true empowerment requires metacognition and a deep awareness of our learning process, communication skills are essential for building such awareness around our accomplishments, failures, and the opportunities in between.
- This chapter provides an in-depth analysis of what the six competencies entail. In addition, it also describes many teaching strategies and practices for strengthening these competencies.
- While holistic development and proper diet, sleep, and exercise can promote the brain functions needed to support the growth of these foundational competencies, curricular innovations help us sharpen our focus on the various skills that underlie them.

6

Individualized Programs

Restlessness is discontent and discontent is the first necessity of progress.
—THOMAS EDISON

Andrew had a typical childhood for a weaver family in Scotland. It was not an easy life. Their cottage's only main room was shared with another weaver family. It also served as their dining room, living room, and bedroom. The family, however, fell into even harder times when Andrew was thirteen. His father lost his job, and his mother struggled as the primary breadwinner. Though they were fortunate enough to be able to borrow money from a family friend, they were still unable to make ends meet. Eventually, they decided to try their luck in America. They moved to Allegheny, Pennsylvania, in September 1848. Both father and son were able to quickly find employment at Scottish-owned Anchor Cotton Mills. Andrew joined as a bobbin boy, changing spools of thread in a cotton mill twelve hours a day, six days a week. He was paid $1.20 per week ($42 in 2023 US dollars, when adjusted for inflation). Andrew was a diligent employee who put his heart into his work. His attitude and abilities were quickly recognized, and Andrew was able to soon find better-paying opportunities. This was fortunate, for he was the primary breadwinner after his father left the cotton mill. Within a few months, Andrew moved on to work for a bobbin manufacturer for $2 a week. It was hard work, but he persisted. By 1849, he took a position as a telegraph boy and was making $2.50 a week. But one of the biggest breakthroughs of his life came when Colonel James Anderson invited working boys to use his personal library. The four hundred or so volumes there opened up a whole new world for him, and he made full use of this opportunity.

Meanwhile, his career was an American dream come true. He moved to the Pennsylvania Railroad Company in 1853 and worked for Thomas A. Scott as a telegraph operator at $4.00 a week ($146 in 2023 dollars). By the end of 1859, Andrew became the superintendent of the Western Division at a salary of $1,500 a year ($51,065 in 2023 dollars). Promoted to Superintendent of Military Railways in 1861, Andrew personally supervised the telegraph services and transportation of the Union troops and munitions during the Civil War and played a significant role on the side of the Union forces. He was finally able to also save enough to invest some of his money. His close relationship with Scott and his understanding of market forces helped him place his bets wisely. He began with investments in railroad-related industries such as manufacturing of sleeping cars, bridges, and rails. He was also one of the early investors in the Columbia Oil Company. This turned out to be a very profitable venture, and it became a springboard for his later investments in steel production and steel mills. After the war, he left the railroads and formed Keystone Bridge Works and Union Iron Works. With innovations in manufacturing processes and supply-chain management, Andrew Carnegie's new venture, the Carnegie Steel Company, became the largest steel manufacturer in the US by 1892.

Over this time, he also cultivated friendships with the English philosopher Herbert Spencer, American humorist Mark Twain, and many other statesmen and literary figures. Even as he tasted extraordinary success in his business pursuits, he grew to detest the single-minded pursuit of money. He felt that it had the potential to debase him beyond redemption. He transferred his holdings in 1901 to the United States Steel Corporation for a payout of about $226 million ($8.23 billion in 2023 US dollars). After he officially handed over his business responsibilities, Carnegie spent most of his time and resources supporting projects for the public good, especially those benefiting social, educational, and cultural advancement and world peace. Of all his projects, establishing free public libraries was perhaps the dearest to him, and he ended up funding about three thousand libraries in the US and around the world. In addition to Carnegie Mellon University, he also invested heavily in many other educational institutions. By the time he passed away in 1919, about 90 percent of his wealth had already been given away, and the rest was disbursed shortly thereafter.

Does Success Depend on Formal Education?

We discussed several examples in the previous chapter of folks who tasted great success despite lackluster schooling. We can't alter history to see if Andrew Carnegie would have been just as successful if his father had continued working and Andrew was enrolled in school like most of his peers. We might justifiably argue that real life is a harsher teacher and that even as it might produce a small number of outstanding specimens like Andrew, the overwhelming majority would fare much worse.

It also seems plausible that our educational system is geared more toward serving those with an academic bent. But it turns out that this is not entirely accurate. As the son of a poor blacksmith with little formal education, Michael Faraday did not have the math skills to defend his claim that visible light is a form of electromagnetic radiation. Nevertheless, he forged ahead. Bad experiences in school left Thomas Edison with a distaste for mathematics, from which he never recovered. But his accomplishments don't reflect his difficulties. Alexander Graham Bell, Charles Darwin, and countless others survived similar setbacks at school to become pioneers in their chosen pursuits. In fact, Francis Hooton, an ecology research intern at the University of Glasgow, found that only 54 percent of the more than three hundred experimental scientists who became Fellows of the Royal Society in the UK earned a first-class honors degree in their undergraduate studies. While almost a third received a second-class honors degree or worse, about 10 percent did not even receive a degree.[1] So, it is not just that success is possible without schooling, it is almost as if schooling is barely relevant to professional success!

Some might argue that those without formal education had a greater chance of success in the decades after the First Industrial Revolution than in more recent times. Since most of the Western world was in the throes of a transformation in those years, it is possible that schools and colleges were not yet ready to guide children to the best opportunities. But there are many more recent examples as well. Jack Horner did not enjoy school, as he found reading, writing, and mathematics to be extremely difficult. Horner failed high school algebra and went on to flunk college seven times. While he was interested in science and evolution, finding suitable employment to pursue his passion proved difficult since he never graduated with a formal degree. However, after struggling with odd jobs, Horner eventually found his way. With his discovery of the Western Hemisphere's first-known dinosaur eggs, recognition came quickly. This legendary paleontologist, and consultant to the four *Jurassic Park* films, had a big hand in our collective understanding of these incredible reptiles. Similarly, Richard Branson, worth over $4 billion, dropped out of school at just sixteen! And neither Steve Jobs, the founder of Apple, nor his cofounder Steve Wozniak graduated from college, Jobs having dropped out after just six months. The legendary automaker, Henry Ford, was born into abject poverty and never went to school. The list of successful school dropouts is long!

Can Schooling Erode Our Children's Potential?

In fact, we might have an even bigger problem. It is not widely recognized that schooling could even hurt our overall success. Schooling has been blamed for conditioning and constraining children's minds, stifling their creativity, and even tamping down initiative and agency. In Einstein's words, "It is, in fact, nothing short of a miracle that the modern methods of education have not yet entirely strangled the holy curiosity of inquiry."[2] So, not only is factory education often focused on the wrong objectives, but it can also disincentivize skills and competencies critical for our success. These sentiments have been echoed by Mark Twain, Oscar Wilde, George Bernard Shaw, Thomas Edison, Henry David Thoreau, Bertrand Russell, Ralph Waldo Emerson, Theodore Roosevelt, and Anne Sullivan, among many others.

The culture around testing, for instance, has been a growing concern. Colleges and schools—and consequently students and their families—celebrate those with the highest GPAs. Many teachers, understandably, teach to the tests since results from standardized tests often impact numerous local, state, and national budgetary allocations in addition to college admission decisions. Such standardized testing is perhaps convenient and cost effective, but it can easily lead us down a slippery slope, perpetuating an ecosystem that values test scores over active learning and thirst for deeper understanding. No one should be surprised that many of our classrooms are less than optimal learning environments. Ask any high school teacher who has to prepare students for an AP exam and the seriousness of this issue will hit home. As discussed earlier, AP classes are often highly effective in promoting higher-level thinking skills through a rigorous curriculum. At the same time, the overwhelming majority of AP classes are compelled to focus almost exclusively on the content necessary to answer questions on the AP tests.

This is unavoidable, considering the significance of these exams for college admissions. As a small example, there is extensive use of TI-83 calculators in the AP calculus curriculum. The TI-83 can, of course, graph functions quickly and accurately, allowing students to visualize graphs, and deepen their learning by exploring various mathematical properties and relationships. However, an educator or a student who believes in minimal scaffolding or one who values insights gained through the use of Taylor series expansions more may find it difficult to make time for them.

Separately, while several test providers claim that performance on their tests will measure proficiency and understanding more than processing speed, obtaining data to validate this claim is not easy. In fact, every educator I have interviewed has expressed some concern about the heavy reliance of several AP tests on speed. For instance, the SAT and ACT explicitly instruct test-takers not to move on to a later section if they finish a section ahead of the scheduled time. This raises the question: what is the true value of a test grade when tests blur the line between content testing and speed testing? The pervasive emphasis on speed in our educational system needs to be reconsidered given the harm it can cause to many students, especially since speed is rarely a determining factor in humanity's greatest achievements.

As a result of all the expectations from the testing regimes, while some children keep up, many fall behind over time. The focus of many children turns to tactical skills necessary for success on tests. Ironically, since most of our educational apparatus is designed to promote success on tests, children are quickly assimilated into an ecosystem of tests and grades and thus into a culture of mediocrity. As schools are also required to meet ambitious schedules, children are awarded a grade and advanced even if their preparation hurts their readiness and self-confidence for later grades. This approach can pigeonhole children who are not as prepared and thus leave them with a damaged self-narrative. As every child will advance, the need for targeted intervention and the need to deeply understand a child's learning are lower. Unfortunately, few parents have the motivation and wherewithal to help their children pursue a more fulsome education. Sadly, parents and educators alike often remain powerless spectators as many children gradually lose their thirst for deeper understanding.

Perhaps the most compelling evidence for how much human capital is being wasted comes from a case study in the US, one of the most developed nations on the planet. While most colleges only open their doors to those with compelling résumés and top-notch SAT and ACT scores, the University of Texas (UT) system has been admitting students based on the state-mandated "Top Ten Percent" rule. As of 2022, the top 6 percent of the students from any high school in the state, regardless of their grades or SAT scores, are eligible for a spot in the UT system. The academic success of students with a few hundred points or so lower SAT scores is often not on par with those who had higher SAT and ACT scores. These students typically struggle and many eventually drop out. Yet something remarkable happened within the first few years after this new admissions process was introduced at the University of Texas at Austin. David Laude, a science professor, created a special support group for students who were struggling in his chemistry classes and gave them extra attention and support for the first few semesters. But this was not a remedial program. These students were still given the same challenging material as all other students, same tests, and were graded on the same curve. They were only provided additional academic support. Interestingly, within a year, a large majority of these struggling students were able to integrate seamlessly with their peers who came with higher SAT scores and perform just as well as them. When he became vice provost in 2012, Laude took his learning campuswide and helped launch many more support pathways through peer mentoring, access to counseling, study groups, and more. Laude was perhaps especially motivated, as he was himself from a small farming town, obtained low SAT scores, and had a frustrating college experience. This experiment is clear evidence of how colleges and standardized tests like the SAT and ACT might be filtering many students out of brighter futures.

Even while traditional schools appear to meet the minimum needs of many, the majority continue to be very dissatisfied with the status quo. Differences in aptitude, skill levels, parent participation, and social and financial circumstances can all contribute to suboptimal learning. Some students are too self-conscious or too disengaged or simply not ready to ask for the help they need to manage their classwork, and they can get lost in the system. Unwarranted peer pressure and physical or psychological bullying are other challenges that confront many children. All these problems can greatly damage the self-esteem and harm the engagement and ability of children to thrive. In addition, the pressure-cooker atmosphere induces high levels of anxiety in many children, especially those in middle and high school.

A growing fraction in the US, about two million as of 2011 and 3.1 million as of 2022, according to best estimates, were so dissatisfied that they chose to homeschool their children.[3] This represents a more than 200-fold increase over the numbers from 1975. While most of this dissatisfaction has been traced to religious or moral grounds, lack of personalization and individual focus also contribute significantly to the decision of these parents to pull their children out of traditional schools. Rising interest in homeschooling, the clamor for after-school enrichment programs and admission to the coveted gifted programs, and high dropout rates are all evidence that there are many constituencies that are ill-served by our public schools today.

The potential of each child is too valuable to not honor the promise of each with the respect they deserve. We first need to believe that there is a Gandhi or a Marie Curie in every child waiting to be unwrapped!

The Case for Greater Individualization

The desire for deeper understanding, which is at the heart of all active learning, is indispensable if we want to unleash a child's full potential. We cannot develop the growth mindset required for such lifelong learning without a strong sense of purpose and engagement. Adequate emphasis on purpose is a key ingredient that is often lacking in most educational approaches. Also, divergent actions for meaningful progress often come from strong individualistic thinking that defies the prevailing conventions and culture with contrarian views. A one-size-fits-all approach cannot foster the self-confidence required to develop such a strong belief system. Every child deserves a shot at this promise, and we should not have to lower our expectations as the cost of more affordable education. This is, however, difficult to achieve without a keen enough understanding of where a child is and what the child's motivations are. Creating experiences that foster such purpose and cultivate a growth mindset in every child, therefore, requires significant investments.

Three-year-old Jonathan absolutely adores Curious George. He is quite anxious whenever George gets into trouble. However, he blames the man with the yellow hat for many of the mishaps. Jonathan feels that the man with the yellow hat is often preoccupied with something else and does not pay sufficient attention to George. Jonathan likes the good little monkey so much that he often asks his dad for a playdate with Curious George. After some hesitation, his dad eventually lets Jonathan in on the secret. He explains to Jonathan that Curious George is a fictional character and that someone made up all the adventures. Curious George does not really exist.

Jonathan is initially a bit conflicted. He does not want to believe his dad. Yet, he wants to make sense of this new information. Jonathan tries to reconcile it with his own understanding by considering the possible scenarios. He can assume that his dad is pulling his leg or lying to him and that his dad perhaps either did not want to take the trouble to arrange a playdate or did not really know where Curious George lived. Alternatively, Jonathan can look at what Curious George does in the stories and look for inconsistencies with his understanding of animal behavior and relationships between humans and animals. Jonathan therefore tries to first make sense of this new information using his own internal mental templates. This is what Jean Piaget refers to as assimilation into existing cognitive structures.[4] Jonathan might discover a flaw in his understanding and decide to tweak or update an existing mental structure to improve consistency with available information. He may alternatively need new mental imagery to better accommodate all his observations. Accommodation occurs when existing schemas are modified, or new templates are created to make sense of a new fact or observation. In other words, assimilation of new realities sometimes requires new structures for proper accommodation. At some point, when Jonathan first encountered the proposition that one can depict unreal images and events, he would have had to accommodate his internal mental schemas to accept this new information. From that point on, it would likely be more straightforward to assimilate other experiences that rely on this possibility.

According to Piaget, intellectual development is fueled by this harmonization between assimilation and accommodation. As we assimilate new learning, our brain tries to reconcile it with our prior understanding and, as needed, adjusts by extending its repertoire of mental schemas. Clearly, these processes of assimilation and accommodation are very personal. This is why learning can only come together in the mind of a seeker. There cannot be much progress without the active involvement of the learner. Recitation of new facts or observations without real accommodation is often of little value.

This illustrates why we should pay close attention to the selection of the learning experiences. And even though experience, instruction, and reflection can all challenge and extend our intellect, experience and reflection are often considered the most effective teachers. It is widely accepted that we cannot develop situational awareness and adaptability without cutting our teeth on experiences. In fact, many typically learn best through failures. As Mullah Nasruddin, the thirteenth-century Sufi philosopher has been reported to have said (the exact source of this quote though is uncertain), "Good judgment comes from experience and experience often comes from bad judgment." The wisdom we gain through experience is often etched deeper than what we obtain through observation or instruction. As we've discussed in the previous chapters, the development of the whole child requires a keen understanding of a child's physical and emotional health and value system, among other aspects. In addition, our success also depends on individual competencies and passions. As such, selection of experiences to support each child's potential also requires an individualized approach.

At the same time, the experiential stimulation needed for intellectual growth also depends on a child's readiness. As Edison said, discontent with the status quo and a healthy appetite for understanding are necessary to foster optimal conditions for these opportunities. Of course, contentment with personal circumstances and impatience with ignorance and stagnation need not be mutually exclusive. In other words, meaningful reflection is often only possible when it is actively sought by an individual. It is well known that direct instruction, especially if it is misaligned, can suppress curiosity and thus limit a child's thirst for learning.[5] When parents help a child with homework, for example, they run the risk of tuning the child out of the problem. Excessive assistance can inhibit creativity and ownership and end up promoting mediocrity. On the other hand, accommodation demands intellectual honesty and an ability to take intellectual risks. This is not always easy as it is difficult to discard the comforts of familiarity. However, painful as it may be, true accommodation of new learning can be made even more difficult by external imposition. In other words, both the teachability of a moment and the ensuing learning are largely a personal journey.

Incidentally, most experiences and worthwhile pursuits entail some amount of stress, frustration, and occasional failures. Smooth seas don't make skillful sailors. However, while frustration is not always undesirable, not everyone may have the same ability to manage stress and frustration. And not all children may have the ability to persist until it comes together in their head. In other words, both the optimal vehicles for learning (experiences) and the tools to operate these vehicles (competencies and biology) vary greatly from individual to individual.

In this context, Benjamin Bloom's findings in 1984 that the average individually tutored student performed better than 98 percent of the students in a traditional class should not come as a surprise.[6] It is nevertheless remarkable that 90 percent of the individually tutored students in his study achieved results that only the top 20 percent of a traditional class could accomplish. There can't be clearer evidence than this of the need for greater individualization. Instead of training every child to meet the requirements of state testing, educational experiences should be tailored to optimize each child's pursuit of meaning and success. It behooves us to study the lives of people like Andrew Carnegie to understand how education can help more of our children reach their full potential without breaking the bank.

What Does Individualization Entail?

The need to keep all students engaged has led to the creation of differentiated access to advanced material in some schools. While this is a step in the right direction, such differentiation can be most beneficial when there is more of a continuum. Students would then be able to make more meaningful progress with learning that works best for them. A child can theoretically be at grade level 5 in math and only grade 3 in reading, for example. While many educators distinguish between differentiated, personalized, and individualized education, the difference is really in the degree of customization and associated costs. It should be possible to balance the level of customization based on an intimate understanding of the needs of a child and the nature of the learning goal.

Additionally, not all pursuits benefit equally from individualization. In subjects like math, conceptual understanding is critical, but the puzzle can only come together in the mind of each child. And if children have difficulty with a concept, they're likely to fall further behind as they move on to more advanced topics since knowledge acquisition is typically very cumulative. The net effect of this on the children's self-confidence is especially worrisome, so individualization is much more important for these subjects than for those that primarily involve acquisition of discrete facts or information. Also, there are subjects where the zone of proximal development can provide a significant benefit. Children can be inspired by peers in activities that involve risk-taking, for example. Team sports and activities that inspire empathy or help build character can benefit from the participation of role models. Individualization can have a limited role in these pursuits. In other words, collaborative skills remain extremely important and the emphasis on individualization should not be construed as downplaying the significance of collaboration. Collaboration is of course a higher order competency that relies on abilities such as empathy, cognition, and communication. A careful understanding of the role and benefits of both individualization and collaboration is therefore indispensable.

Recognizing that learning is a journey and not a process to pigeonhole students, some schools have embraced the philosophy of a "not-yet" grade and others have gone further and embraced a mastery-based learning protocol.[7] The focus in these approaches is on mastering a set of predetermined grade-level skills like creating an experimental design, finding the area of a circle, or identifying the main thesis in a story. Unlike a conventional classroom that allocates only a fixed amount of time for understanding a concept, mastery-based learning allows learners the time needed for mastery before they move to the next set of skills. Various metrics can be used to determine if a student has minimal familiarity or true mastery of a skill and where the child's learning edge is for each of the concepts. Mastery-based learning has started taking hold in many states in the US, including Vermont, Maine, New Hampshire, New York, Idaho, and Illinois. While mastery-based learning has the potential to replace standardized testing in the not-too-distant future, its success requires a stronger pivot to individualized learning.

At its heart, education is largely a labor of love. Most parents and educators, especially at the lower grade levels, embody this love and devotion. It is difficult to not get your children engaged when your care and passion for their welfare and development are transparent. We need to build further on these relationships. For instance, even if we can't afford fully personalized education, schools can try to ensure that there is something unique and interesting at school for every child every day of the week. Education can be transformative if every child can go to bed excited about what the school has to offer them the next day. School should be a playground for children to proudly develop and share their shtick. Educators need to understand their children well enough to be able to create this compelling proposition. Schools should not be anything short of an exciting adventure for every child. This will go a long way since active learning demands such fascination and engagement. In this context, we should recognize that individualized learning also entails individualized parent education. Each home and family presents a unique set of circumstances, and so individualization of parent education is likely to bear rich dividends in the overall customization of a child's education.

No discussion of optimal education is complete without a careful consideration of the role of homework. The history of homework in the US is particularly fascinating. American society had traditionally disapproved of homework as many abhorred its intrusion into the sanctity of family time. In fact, California passed legislation in 1901 to abolish homework for children in kindergarten through the eighth grade.[8] However, the Cold War with Russia changed all that. Along with a resurgence of science education and space research, homework began to be broadly embraced after the 1950s. In recent decades, however, there has been a growing debate again about the effectiveness of homework. In 1989, Harris Cooper, a leading researcher in social psychology, used a large metastudy to show that elementary schoolchildren received almost no benefit from homework and that middle and high school students received only a modest boost.[9] However, more interestingly, he noticed that increasing homework from about ten minutes per day per grade level to about fifteen minutes per day per grade level actually hurt the standardized test scores of the middle school and high school students. Of course, Cooper merely looked at the preparation of students for tests and not necessarily their true learning. All in all, while there was some immediate benefit for the middle and high school students, these studies were not able to establish that there were enduring long-term benefits from homework.

The desire for homework is often based more on philosophical considerations than on scientific research. It stems from the expectation that success requires application, diligence, and careful time management and that these skills can be strengthened through homework. Advocates also believe that homework gives students, especially those that learn at a slower pace, an opportunity to consolidate their basics and thus improve their engagement at school. In addition, they believe that the additional practice at home helps children's long-term retention. Some also argue that homework promotes independent thinking and creativity as the home environment provides a welcome contrast to the restrictive confines of most classrooms. Of course, it is often possible to achieve these objectives only if homework is carefully customized for each student. There is broad consensus that children need to be convinced that teachers and parents truly value the homework assigned. In his book *The Homework Myth: Why Our Kids Get Too Much of a Bad Thing*, Alfie Kohn, a leading voice in progressive education, makes a compelling case against homework, arguing that it often ends up denting a child's love of learning.[10] Kohn urges teachers to be more thoughtful about homework—to only assign work as needed and to not passively "standardize" homework assignments. Sara Bennett and Nancy Kalish also call attention to the damage caused by poorly conceived homework in their thought-provoking book, *The Case against Homework: How Homework Is Hurting Our Children and What We Can Do about It*.[11] Many opponents point out that homework often comes with huge opportunity costs, as children could otherwise be spending their time pursuing other, higher value passions.

To be fair, many advocates of homework also agree that homework should be designed to serve a specific and well-thought-out purpose. In fact, many researchers have found that successful teachers often involve students in the design of their homework. It can be a chore to get children motivated if they're not interested in the assignments. Such aggravation can steer them away from the joys of learning and exploration. Often, there can also be unfortunate economic implications to homework designed as a supplement to schoolwork. Donna Shalala, former US Secretary of Health and Human Services and president of the University of Miami, recalled an interesting incident: "The economic dimension is very clear. I was at a dinner party, a mother got up, who's a very distinguished scientist, and said she had to get home and help her daughter with her homework. The two waiters, their faces changed. They were working their second jobs; they couldn't get home to help their kids with homework."[12]

Most importantly, schools should not look at homes as an extension of their classrooms, homework should never be a tool for getting through the syllabus at home. Else, public schools can end up perpetuating the significant learning gaps that exist today across the economic divide. Laura Hillenbrand, an American author, once said, "For me, being a writer was never a choice. I was born one. All through my childhood I wrote short stories and stuffed them in drawers. I wrote on everything. I didn't do my homework so I could write."[13] Hillenbrand's comments reveal the essence of the problem with most homework assignments. As we all probably know from personal experience, it is not that children detest working at home. Far from it. It is just that they want to work on what they desire. To summarize, the problem with homework is intricately linked to widespread problems with child empowerment and individualization. Much of the frustration with homework will likely dissipate if children own more of their own learning and homework is appropriately customized.

The Benefits of Child-Centered Education

Educators such as Maria Montessori reimagined classrooms as they recognized the need for more personalization and active, child-initiated learning. Many innovations such as smaller classroom sizes, lower student-teacher ratios, increased reliance on formative assessments, and division of classes into ability groups moved us toward individualized education with manageable increases in cost.

There has also been broad interest in quantifying the benefits of personalized education. The conclusions from a three-phase study in Tennessee are particularly illustrative.[14] The first phase, project STAR (Student-Teacher Achievement Ratio), was launched in 1985. It randomly assigned teachers and students to three groups, "small" classes (with thirteen to seventeen children per class) and "regular" classes (with twenty-two to twenty-five children per class) with and without a paid aide. About 6,500 students from approximately 80 schools and 330 or so classrooms participated in this phase. This study concluded that small classes produced "substantial improvement in early learning and cognitive metrics" with about twice the benefit for minority students. The second phase of this study found that children who were originally enrolled in smaller classes continued to outperform their peers even when they later joined regular-sized classrooms. The third phase of this study showed that it is possible to significantly improve the academic performance of even the most economically disadvantaged school districts with small class sizes. Additional analysis of the data produced by these studies also showed that children in smaller classes were more than six months ahead of their peers in regular classes by the time they got to the third grade. It is remarkable that even this small step toward increased individualization has yielded such pronounced benefits.

It is relatively obvious that children can get more attention in smaller classes. In addition to receiving a tailored curriculum that is more relevant, such attention helps children improve their focus on the tasks at hand and thus adapt better to school. There is also research that shows that smaller schools fare better than larger schools.[15] Smaller learning communities appear to generally produce superior educational outcomes. Smaller classes and schools can also foster richer emotional development by enabling closer relationships among children and between children and teachers.

Figure 6.1. Typical small-group instruction at Sankalpa Academy.

Finally, the costs of excessive scaffolding and spoon-feeding ready-made lesson plans are likely to be far higher than the costs of skillful empowerment, especially if we also factor in the longer-term benefits of such an investment. There is significant evidence, for instance, that early childhood intervention for disadvantaged young children is much more effective than interventions that come later in life.[16] A study of the Perry Preschool Project, an active participatory learning program for three- and four-year-old at-risk children from poor neighborhoods, found that children who received the program ended up with significantly superior educational accomplishments and life outcomes.[17] The resounding success of HighScope, the early childhood education approach developed in Ypsilanti, Michigan, in the 1960s, is a great example of an active learning curriculum. It employs a variety of materials and sensitive use of adult scaffolding through nurturing interactions to expand children's thinking.[18] Interestingly, one popular study found that this HighScope-based project returned more than eight dollars to the participants and society for every tax dollar invested in it. This amounted to a 12 percent rate of return to society and a 4 percent rate of return to the participants.[19] Similar results were found for the Carolina Abecedarian Project.[20]

While most of these studies were focused on children from economically disadvantaged families, there is no reason to believe that similar benefits would not accrue for other socioeconomic groups as well. Though these investments make enough financial sense to justify them as good public policy, the overall benefit to society is much more profound and often extremely challenging to quantify. It is difficult, for instance, to estimate all the benefits that future generations would receive solely due to the higher educational attainment of the current generation.

Challenges of Individualizing Education

There are many schools—such as the highly selective private Sidwell Friends schools in Bethesda, Maryland, and Washington, DC—that have a teacher for every ten or so students in primary classes. But most school districts and taxpayers are reluctant to pay for the high costs that smaller classrooms entail. Our hopes for personalization do face stiff odds. This is likely due to our inability to fully grasp the enormity of the potential that personalized education can unleash and its potential benefits to society. But some of it could also be due to our inability to accurately estimate its costs. Initially, individualized programming and testing can be quite expensive. However, these costs are likely to come down as children are able to take more ownership of their education. We should expect greater engagement from them if their pursuits align better with their abilities and passions. A lot more research is needed to better quantify the true costs of individualized education.

Additionally, not enough teachers are trained to optimally respond to the developmental cues of children. There are studies that show that many teachers are not adequately prepared to teach in small classes and that training teachers to teach in smaller classes can further amplify the benefits of small class sizes.[21] Individualization places a heavier burden on educators as they should be able to recognize windows of opportunity and design the most promising interventions. Intimate familiarity with the current understanding of a child (mental schema), their developmental roadblocks (dogmas, fears, misconceptions, etc.), and their tolerance levels for frustration and stress is essential to ensure that the learning experiences are commensurate with a child's competencies. Incidentally, Data-Based Individualization (DBI) has recently codified and streamlined what skilled teachers have been practicing for a long time.[22] DBI is a research-based adaptive process for individualizing intervention based on the results and learning from these tailored lesson plans. This kind of intensive intervention is offered through the Tier 3 program in some schools.

It's not possible to define the contour of best learning opportunities without such intimacy. Plowing ahead by only focusing on higher-level academic outcomes such as numeracy skills or reading ability can be inefficient and even counterproductive. Children might feel overwhelmed, and their frustration can be debilitating. A child coming from a household where English is either a second language or not spoken at all might find the expectations for reading proficiency quite onerous compared to a child who is a native English speaker. Any progress reviews, for instance, should focus more on these developmental roadblocks and competencies than on traditional academic outcomes. Curriculums should embrace the learning edge for the child and not simply the outcomes mandated by the grade level. In short, education is essentially a process of intelligent evolution, evolution to increasingly complex skill sets guided by the intelligence of the child's current competencies and roadblocks.

This kind of individualized guidance—especially in early grades—using highly qualified master teachers can be immensely valuable. However, as an increasing number of teachers are deserting their profession, offering this will likely be an especially difficult challenge. Highly qualified teachers are already a rare breed. They also typically gravitate toward the higher grades due to prevailing teacher certification standards, social expectations, job requirements, and financial realities. In many countries, teachers in the higher grades are often paid more and expected to be more experienced. I witnessed this at close range in the school I attended in India. Many of my classmates and I were very impressed by Ms. Girija, our new seventh-grade English teacher. She had just joined our school that year. Her classes were very engaging and innovative. She had no compunctions about deviating from prescribed lesson plans. We had impromptu discussions, extemporaneous précis writing, and much more. In short, Ms. Girija had most of the class engaged in the true business of learning. Her accomplishments did not go unnoticed for long. Sister Philomena, the principal of our school at the time, was well known for her hands-on approach and her talent-development skills.

She promoted Ms. Girija the very next year to teach the tenth-grade classes. And, the year after that, she went on to teach literature for the undergraduate classes at a sister institution. She eventually became the assistant principal of that college. We need to essentially invert this pyramid if we are serious about child empowerment. We need the best minds interacting with our youngest children. The ability to connect with young minds is a rare gift and cultivating this talent pool would pay rich dividends. It is not unreasonable to also expect that better-prepared children will need less scaffolding in the higher grades.

Figure 6.2. A Sankalpa Academy learner sharing his passion for music through a piano recital.

Unfortunately, there have been a few red herrings in discussions about individualization. For example, a lot has been written about the variation in learning styles between children. There is a school of thought that some students are better visual learners, some understand better by listening, and yet others learn through conceptual thinking. Yet, as appealing as this sounds, there is little evidence for the significance of such a difference in children's learning styles.[23] In fact, by restricting their exposure to a few modes, we might be doing the children a great disservice.[24] Education needs to help children develop a flexible repertoire to choose from so their learning is more fluid. They need to thrive in various contexts.

The Future of Individualization

While there are many challenges, there is also light at the end of the tunnel. Several technological innovations appear to bode well for individualized learning. With over 118 million users as of 2020 and 12.4 billion learning minutes in just 2020, the resounding success of Khan Academy speaks volumes about the appeal of "on-demand" availability of lessons for the YouTube generation.[25] While about 45,000 K–12 students took a course online in 2000, more than three million K–12 students did so nine years later in 2009.[26] "Is K–12 Blended Learning Disruptive?" profiles some emerging schools that leverage online content in classroom environments at least some of the time.[27] An analysis by the Department of Education shows that online learning is as effective as traditional classroom learning, and that blended learning that combines both is considerably more effective than either of them.[28] This makes good sense since mentoring, access to a culture of high expectations, and holistic development that includes social skills and more are often indispensable for excellence.

The 2020–2022 COVID-19 crisis has highlighted the significance of face time for dispensing timely feedback. The large-scale shift to remote learning during the coronavirus pandemic was a stress test of our ability to further innovate in the area of online education. While the reach and potential of distance learning exceeded our expectations, its limitations were also unambiguous. The digital divide exacerbated all manner of inequities: racial, economic, social, and more. Additionally, while some children adapted well, others were far less engaged. It was also clear that almost all students need well-designed interventions along the way to sustain their motivation to continue to make progress. We have to hope that policymakers and schools will act on the valuable lessons from this experience.

Incidentally, there are other key limitations with a resource like Khan Academy. It is not easy to ensure that children can stretch themselves as they seek new understanding and not get too used to readymade solutions. Carpe Diem Collegiate High School in Arizona and Rocketship Education in

California provide a glimpse of what is possible in blended environments. Given that 60 percent of its students take advantage of free or reduced-price lunch, and that 48 percent of its students are minorities, it is very impressive that Carpe Diem came in first in its county in student performance in math and reading and was ranked among the top 10 percent of all Arizona charter schools in 2010.[29] Carpe Diem blends online content with real-time support such that every student can progress at his or her own pace, a pace set by feedback through formative assessments. In 2010, Rocketship's two schools ranked in the top fifteen among all California schools where at least 70 percent of the students were from low-income families. In 2018-19, socioeconomically disadvantaged students at Rocketship outperformed similar students at other schools in California by 10 points or more in language arts and 24 points or more in math. It stands to reason that personalized attention in elementary schools can prepare students to extract the most value out of the hybrid or blended curriculum in middle and high schools. While online content delivery has been around for many years, programs that leverage online content in a blended environment based on individual needs are still in their infancy. Growing budgetary pressures, parent demand, advances in technology, increased investment and competition, and the outcry for better educational outcomes are all likely to continue to drive additional innovations in these programs.

Also, a lot of offline content is increasingly appearing in the form of video games. Advanced VR–based video games can be self-correcting and take the role of an intelligent, personalized coach. They can break down complex tasks into manageable chunks, track interests and progress, assess gaps in learning, and provide real-time feedback. Unlike human tutors, they can also let users control the navigation of the game so they can explore and experiment in many more ways. It stands to reason that investing in authentic representations in virtual environments can further enhance their benefits. While VR can be especially useful for conveying complex spatial representations, research shows that collaborative problem-solving and experimentation can help alleviate some of the cognitive overload associated with VR environments.[30] The ability to formulate a hypothesis, design an experiment, record the observations, and draw conclusions in the virtual world has enormous potential for cost control and quality, especially in science education where investments tend to be large.

Even while much of the potential of video games is yet to be fully unearthed, various independent studies have already established the positive impact of these interactive games on student behavior, problem-solving skills, and overall learning.[31] At the same time, we also need to ensure that the benefits of this new technology are accessible to all demographics.[32] It is very encouraging that broad recognition of the potential of these technologies is rapidly translating into increased investment in their research and development. The US Department of Education announced some years ago that it would provide initial funding for the nonprofit National Center for Research in Advanced Information and Digital Technologies.[33] This center offers grants to organizations or corporations that seek to bring new educational technologies to market. Also, the National Education Association has been serving as a consultant, advising teachers on the incorporation of video games into their curriculum.

There have been many specific products on the market that have received rave reviews. *SimCity* from Electronic Arts has been a hugely popular electronic game for designing a metropolis.[34] *Immune Attack*, developed by Escape Hatch Entertainment in collaboration with the Federation of American Scientists, challenges its players to save a patient from bacterial infection.[35] In the process, students pick up a lot of cellular biology and molecular science knowledge. Similarly, *VirtualSpeech*, *HoloLens*, and *Google Expeditions* are some of the many virtual and augmented reality products that have offered immersive learning experiences at low cost. Instead of suffering through an actual dissection, for example, students can explore the internal organs of a frog using *Froggipedia*. While there are many popular apps such as *Bedtime Math*, *Me: A Kid's Diary*, and *The Human Body*, it is widely expected that the sophistication and benefit of apps, video games, and virtual reality experiences will only accelerate in the coming years.

Beyond VR and video games, the availability of a "wise" personal mentor for every child is the holy grail of individualization. Since we have established that an education based on a holistic curriculum and foundational competencies would result in the best life outcomes, we should expect that the mentor has the necessary skillset to attend to these needs of the learner. He or she should also be able to read the child's emotions and tailor the growth opportunities accordingly, in an age- and personality-appropriate manner. For example, the personalized coach should be able to strengthen the child's risk-taking ability if needed. He or she should be able to get the child to understand when to ask for help if that is an area of growth. Alternatively, the mentor should be able to coach the child in developing persistence and delayed-gratification skills if those are the vital growth opportunities for the child. Similarly, he or she should be able to interest the child in self-care, including exercises to support physical and mental health.

Readers who view these expectations as a tall order or an impossibility cannot be faulted. These expectations are too far removed from the reality most of us experience. At the same time, we are on the cusp of a major upheaval that is likely only comparable to the Agricultural and Industrial Revolutions. The release of ChatGPT-3, a multitalented, AI-trained chatbot launched by OpenAI in November 2022 and GPT-4 in March 2023, for example, have taken us by storm. This chatbot can do a lot more than engage humans in conversations. ChatGPT can write and edit essays; write and debug computer programs; and compose music, plays, limericks, and even fairy tales. New versions are expected to be even more revolutionary: significantly smarter and a lot more disruptive. It is believed that GPT-3 has 175 billion parameters and was trained on 570 gigabytes of text!

As generative AI systems are trained on increasingly larger volumes of data using ever more powerful optimality and compute farms, they will surely benefit from massive amounts of human insight and ingenuity. ChatGPT has led to many conversations in college hallways about the future of college essays and the impact on the employment prospects of English majors and more. Blaine Greteman, an associate professor of English at the University of Iowa, is among many who feel that ChatGPT already writes better essays than many undergraduate students.[36] The uncertain future is certainly arriving fast. It is up to us to decide how to use this technology, whether for good or ill, and as an aid or as a crutch. If we so choose, AI can add great value to our zone of proximal development, serving as a personal coach by helping us pursue the best growth opportunities in the most optimal manner.

When all is said and done, education is a personal journey that rests on the bedrock of human relationships and culture. In part III of the book, we look at how the best practices identified so far can be employed to deliver an individualized growth experience.

CHAPTER SUMMARY

- Success in life has a stronger correlation with foundational competencies than with academic credentials. Significantly, the competency profile varies greatly between individuals.
- In addition, for various reasons, the biology, experiences, and preparation of students in a classroom also often vary greatly. As a result, the processes of assimilation and accommodation are very individualized as well.
- This is why most kids don't fare equally well in all subjects. For instance, some are far ahead in math while struggling in language arts.
- Further, meaningful progress often comes from strong individualistic thinking that defies prevailing conventions and culture with contrarian views. A one-size-fits-all approach cannot foster the self-confidence required to develop such a strong belief system.
- There are activities—such as those that involve some amount of risk-taking—where most progress can be made through participation in a team (i.e., where the zone of proximal development can play a big role). Then there are other kinds of activities—such as those where persistence or mental accommodation is more vital—where individual effort provides the largest return on investment.
- For all these reasons, it is essential to tailor educational experiences to the unique needs of every learner. Thoughtful and minimalist scaffolding requires individualized attention. It also more fully comes to life through active learning, involving strong, purposeful engagement and a desire for deeper understanding.
- At the same time, promoting children to higher grades without adequate understanding and mastery might safeguard their emotional well-being but undermine self-efficacy, an important precursor to all learning and growth.

- The benefits of greater individual attention are well established. Small classes, for instance, have been shown to produce substantial improvement in early learning and cognition, with about twice the benefit for minority students. These benefits have been shown to persist even if children are later moved to larger classrooms. Training educators to teach effectively in small classes has been shown to further amplify the benefits of small class sizes.
- Mastery-based learning and the award of "not-yet" grades are other approaches that move us closer toward individualized education.
- Research has shown that online learning is as effective as traditional classroom learning and that blended education that combines both is considerably more effective than either of them. While this is promising for individualized education, we should be mindful of the "digital divide" that can exacerbate existing racial, social, and economic inequities.
- Individualized learning can be even more effective when it also entails individualization of parent education and homework assignments.

III

Raising Stakeholders

The Rubber Hits the Road

The great aim of education is not knowledge but action.
—HERBERT SPENCER

We can shoot for the stars and formulate expansive and aspirational curricular objectives. However, any such goals are of little use unless we can also identify practical ways to achieve these objectives. Thoughtful, well-delineated experiences are essential for building vitality, knowledge, positive mindframes, and foundational competencies. Part III explores some of the key structural elements necessary for realizing the educational objectives detailed in part II. We look into the design of growth experiences and learning communities that can meet these curricular goals.

Transformative education is always built on the foundations of a strong culture and meaningful relationships. Therefore, all educational programs need to first ensure that they have an optimal environment for emotional engagement. It is important to account for the impact of the climate on all learners while assessing our ability to cultivate a desirable culture. This is the focus of chapter 7.

The effectiveness of the environment can only be measured by its success in promoting the right values, attitudes, and behaviors. Transformation is a result of the interplay between the environment and the learner. In chapter 8, we focus on the learner side of this equation: the internal climate of the learners that helps them get ready for and stay engaged in the educational journey. Specifically, we explore how relationships, purposeful goals, and biases and beliefs can be used to form the bedrock of a strong growth mindset culture.

While we have discussed the three pillars of holistic curriculum, foundational competencies, and individualization at great length in part II, they are only useful if we integrate them into a coherent curriculum. We look at some strategies for doing this in chapters 9 and 10. We investigate how the three pillars can support the growth of all learners across the age spectrum. In chapter 9, we begin by leveraging the best aspects of leading childhood philosophies to design a comprehensive program for our youngest learners. The objective is to nurture the competencies of individual learners while instilling sound ideas and habits that can help foster a healthy, lifelong love of learning, discovery, and curiosity. Higher-order thinking skills, planning, and metacognition are introduced gradually for older children. Assessments of their competencies will help us craft meaningful programs that leverage their individual strengths and shore up their key opportunities. A broad assortment of curricular focus areas is used to ensure children's holistic development. The templates provided in chapters 9 and 10 show us how we can seamlessly leverage existing approaches and lesson plans to meet the aspirations of the three pillars.

7

A Labor of Love

The child must know that he is a miracle, that since the beginning of the world there hasn't been, and until the end of the world there will not be, another child like him.

—PABLO CASALS

Given our breathtaking progress and domination of the planet, we are sometimes not as aware as we should be of all that we share with other species. Nurturing our young, for example, is not an exclusively human trait; many animals also are exceptional parents. Elephant mothers deliver 250-pound babies after a 22-month pregnancy, nurse their babies until they are about five years old, babysit for other elephants, and even help groom others' young into socially adjusted members of the herd. And then there are the heroics of the emperor penguin. These have now become legendary, thanks to the documentary *The March of the Penguins*. The father penguins assume responsibility for the egg and withstand months of harsh Antarctic winters while mothers go out to sea to feed. During this time, fathers mostly stand in one location, covering the eggs with a feathered flap. Emperor penguin fathers typically lose about 25 pounds or so in the process as they cannot really eat anything during this time. While just as remarkable, the devotion of the sand grouse is probably not as well known. One must marvel at the father Namaqua sand grouse. He flies as far as 50 miles a day to soak his feathers in water so his chicks back at the nest can quench their thirst! These are only a few examples of the extraordinary parents in the animal kingdom. Clearly, there are many species that sacrifice a great deal to simply get their young ones to stand on their own feet.

The evolution of the limbic system is responsible for the survival instincts related to fight-or-flight responses as well as hunger, reproduction, and nurture in many species. But the parental responsibilities of our own race have steadily increased over the centuries; they now far exceed what we have genetically inherited with the limbic system. The skills children have to acquire before they can thrive on their own and the number of years they remain in the care of a guardian are a clear testament to this. It pays to delve into the significance of human nurture as its complexity has led to large inequities in the care children receive.

British ornithologist and police officer E. C. Stuart Baker reported an interesting case of a leopard child in the *Journal of the Bombay Natural History Society* in July 1920.[1] He described a boy taken by a female leopard from his home in the North Cachar Hills near Assam, India, in 1912 and recovered three years later:

> When visiting Dihungi I interviewed the head man and also the man who actually caught the child and they both corroborated the father's tale in every detail. It appeared that at the time the child ran on all fours almost as fast as an adult man could run, whilst in dodging in and out of bushes and other obstacles he was much cleverer and quicker. His knees had hard callosities on them, and his toes were retained upright almost at right angles to his instep. The palms of his hands and pads of his toes and thumbs were also covered with very tough horny skin. When first caught, he was found with the leopardess's cubs. He bit and fought with everyone and any wretched village fowl which came within his reach was seized, torn to pieces and eaten with extraordinary rapidity.

There are many stories throughout history of such feral children who grew up with little or no human contact or nurture.[2] In fact, there have been more than a hundred documented examples of feral children in just the last twenty years. In many of these cases, animals were reported to have played a part in raising the children. Two common themes among such children were their lack of social skills and difficulty mastering spoken language. Many of the children recovered from the wild went around on all fours and had trouble picking up a language, even though they seemed to have exceptional hearing skills.

An incident that occurred in the late 1980s in South Africa received a great deal of attention.[3] Residents of Sundumbili found an unkempt five-year-old boy in a forest area near the Tugela River in KwaZulu-Natal in 1987. His behavior was strange—he was roaming with monkeys and scavenging fruit discarded by passersby. He was also moving around using both his arms and legs. While he seemed to like all kinds of fruit, bananas were his favorite. He was also adept at climbing trees and rooftops. After the boy was caught, the police placed him in the care of the Ethel Mthiyane Special School for the disabled. The school named the boy Saturday Mthiyane, after the day of the week he was found and the school founder's last name. When he first arrived at the center, he used to roam around naked, as he hated clothes. He also tossed food into his mouth and dug holes in the ground with his bare hands. He didn't like playing with other kids and was quite a handful. His behavior continued to be challenging despite staying at the center for over a decade. The school was not able to secure a speech therapist, and the teachers could not help Saturday learn to speak. While Mthiyane felt that Saturday understood what she told him, it was hard to be sure since he rarely responded.

There have also been other cases of feral children in more recent decades. In 2008, Russian social workers rescued a seven-year-old boy who had been confined by his thirty-one-year-old mother to a small aviary in a tiny two-room apartment all his life.[4] He was surrounded by cages with dozens of birds. They found that this "bird boy" did not speak or understand any human language and only communicated by "chirping" and flapping his arms like birds. He was never physically harmed but had also not received any stimulation from human interactions. He was treated just like another pet by his mother.

A girl named Madina, found in Russia in 2013, had spent the first three years of her life among dogs and learned to move on all fours and eat and growl like a dog.[5] A boy around twelve years old was found in the Andes mountains in Peru in 1990. He had apparently lived with goats in the wild for eight years, drinking their milk and eating roots and berries. A team from the University of Kansas and Kansas State University investigated the goat boy and named him Daniel.

Since the discovery of many feral children in the 1600s, philosophers have wondered about the process of enculturation and whether human children straddle a natural boundary between humans and animals. Carolus

Linnaeus, the highly influential natural historian, even defined *Homo ferens* as a new feral human species! Jean-Marc-Gaspard Itard, a French physician and educator, spent a considerable amount of time trying unsuccessfully to educate Victor of Aveyron, a wild boy caught in 1800 in the forests near Lacaune, France. These interactions and studies have fueled intense debates on the relative roles of nature and nurture. Maria Montessori was intrigued and inspired by Itard's work, and this drew her to investigate the education of children with disabilities. Her success as the director of Scuola Ortofrenica, where she worked with children from the asylum who had learning disabilities, is well known. Several eight-year-olds in the program had even obtained higher-than-average results on the Italian state examinations. While the examples of the various feral children and their development show that language acquisition is a highly social process, Montessori's work is further powerful evidence of the potential of nurture.

While one may be skeptical about the veracity of the anecdotal observations relating to feral children, the long-term, controlled study of institutionalized children in Romania is unequivocal in highlighting the need for social interactions and sensory stimulation for children's social, emotional, and cognitive development.[6] By the fall of Romania's Ceausescu regime in 1989, there were approximately 170,000 children in 700 overcrowded, impoverished institutions across the country. This was a great opportunity for researchers to investigate the benefits of foster care versus institutionalization. Over a twelve-year period, children in foster care and institutions were separately assessed for physical and emotional development and cognitive growth. The study found that children who remained institutionalized had a significantly lower average IQ and suffered from various social and emotional disorders. The sooner an institutionalized child was moved into foster care, the better their chances of improvement. In another landmark study, Shonkoff et al. showed that early childhood experiences and environmental influences can be causally linked to emerging brain architecture and thus to long-term health.[7] Their work presented extensive evidence that toxic stress in the early years can lead to a wide variety of adverse life outcomes related to learning, behavior, and physical as well as mental well-being.

While the nature-nurture debate persists, there is enough evidence to conclude that the role of the environment is too large to ignore. Researchers have also begun looking into epigenetics, the field that examines how environmental factors even control and modulate gene expression. In other words, epigenetics claims that our life outcomes are not independently due to our inherited genes and our environment but also biologically mediated by their interaction.

Michael Meaney, a brain researcher at McGill University, and his colleagues observed the grooming behavior of mother rats and divided them into high-licking and low-licking groups.[8] They found that pups reared by low-licking mothers carried a methyl mark on their genes that normally inhibits stress responses. As adults, these animals showed a greater stress response than animals reared by high-licking mothers. This was an interesting finding as it suggests that biological pathways exist for us to predict health outcomes such as depression or cardiovascular problems based on childhood experiences like neglect or abuse. Meaney and his team also found that these traits were passed on to the next generation: high-licking rat mothers had daughters who went on to lick their own litters more frequently than the daughters of low-licking moms. One might surmise that the amount of licking was perhaps an inherited trait. However, the researchers found that when an offspring of a low-licking mother was fostered by a high-licking rat, this child of a low-licking mother adopted the high-licking behavior of the foster mother with its own babies later. This suggests that the amount of licking was not genetically determined. Instead, the researchers found that the methyl markers that silence the genes responsible for handling stress had been removed or erased in rats that received a lot of maternal love even if they were not raised by their biological mothers!

It is an extraordinary finding that our environment can influence the expression of our genes and turn them on and off. However, researchers were also curious about the possible inheritance of these changes in gene expression. Susan Strome and her team at the University of California, Santa Cruz, have shown that epigenetic information carried by paternal sperm chromosomes in the nematode worm *Caenorhabditis elegans* results in changes in gene expression in the offspring.[9] Lead researcher Kiyomi Kaneshiro selectively removed a specific histone mark from the sperm chromosomes and fertilized eggs with the modified sperm. The histone marks chosen by Kaneshiro et al. were intended to suppress the genes that turn germline cells into neurons. Such suppression was required to ensure that the reproductive germline cells only end up as a sperm or an egg. The researchers used sperm from a British strain and eggs from a Hawaiian strain of *C. elegans*. Since these two worm strains had evolved independently over a long period, it was easier to distinguish between the chromosomes inherited from the sperm versus those inherited from the egg. Also, *C. elegans* was a good model for their study since histone packaging is fully retained in its sperm chromosomes. The researchers found to their surprise that the histone marks were removed whenever the sperm chromosome made it to the offspring. And, consequently, the offspring's germline cells began developing into neurons! It is remarkable that changes in gene expression patterns can also be inherited. In other words, the impact of childhood experiences can also persist in subsequent generations and is not limited to the life outcomes of the individual alone.

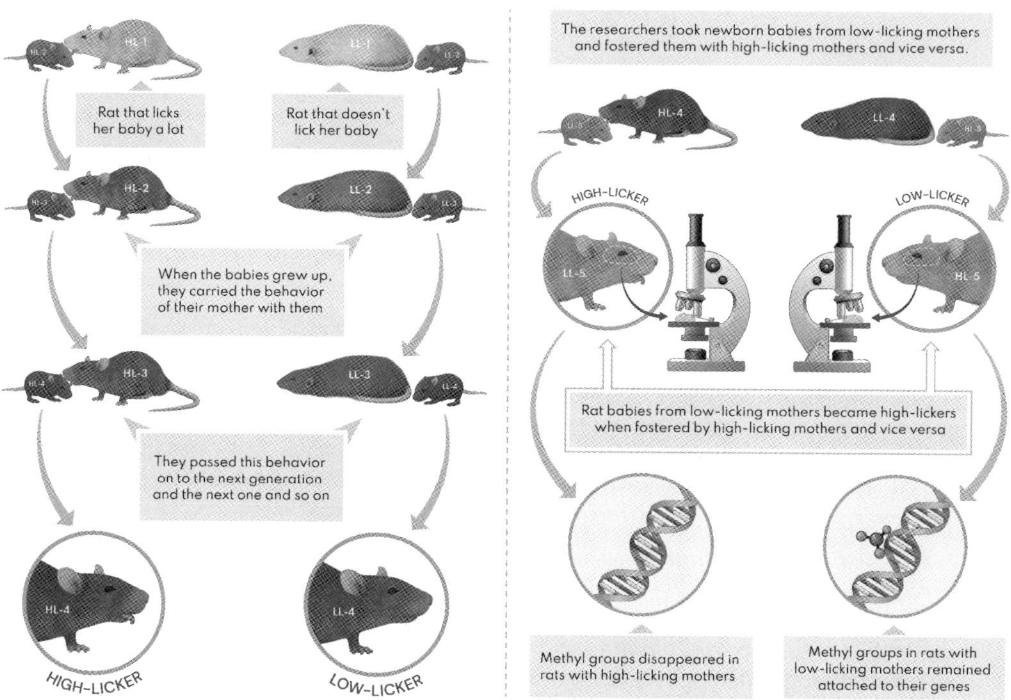

Figure 7.1. Maternal love has been shown to bestow some resilience against stress in mice offspring.

While genes play a vital role in shaping our future, researchers now believe that there is more to this story. Correlation is sometimes confused with causation, and some people attribute more significance to genetic determinism than is warranted, while the reality is often closer to genetic predisposition. For instance, it is now believed that individual genes, acting alone, only account for about 2 percent of our diseases. This is often referred to as the "missing heritability" problem.[10]

In this context, it is encouraging that we also have preliminary research identifying genetic markers that result from exposure to family training, in addition to research demonstrating the positive role of family training in improving the attention of children from underserved socioeconomic backgrounds.[11] We need additional studies to understand the role of the environment and the various windows of opportunity more quantitatively. This insight needs to inform and guide the educational objectives and methods of the future, including the most optimum investments for individualization. The biological reality of epigenetics reinforces the significance of childhood environment and parenting. Most parents want to instill in their children the values and skills needed for positive life outcomes. Even as we seek a deeper understanding of how best to help our kids, it is not easy for this learning to keep pace with intergenerational cultural evolution. While financial constraints and education limit parental investment for many families, transcending biases and cultural constraints is a challenge for almost everyone. Yet, what biology seems to be suggesting is that our limitations can have an outsized impact on how future generations will turn out. This was likely true in the past, it is true in the age of robots and artificial intelligence, and it will be true far into the future.

We must not lose sight of the fact that, above all else, our care for the young is and will always be a labor of love. Such unconditional love is the foundation on which children's self-esteem and ingenuity are built. It is the foundation for their empowerment, and it is at the core of the human experience. We need to take to heart Lebanese poet Khalil Gibran's refrain: "Your children are not your children. They are the sons and daughters of Life's longing for itself."[12] Regardless of how well we think we understand our children, we need to approach every child with a completely open mind to give the child the best opportunities we can for growth and development. Abiding love and devotion require nothing less. However, it can be quite challenging to truly consider our child a stranger since we all typically have our own values, customs, aspirations, and desire that our children walk in our footsteps. Therefore, a deep and abiding conviction in the limitless possibilities of a child is required for us, in turn, to instill such conviction and the confidence that this engenders in our children. They need to grow up truly believing in their multifaceted potential.

In the context of a classroom, emotional engagement between teachers and students has long been recognized as the bedrock of a good education. Most educators know that children need to feel seen and heard. Every child should feel loved, valued, and cherished in his or her learning community. Unfortunately, too many educators are not adequately equipped to avoid some common traps that can be very damaging for children. Susceptibility to stereotypes or implicit bias, for example, can lead to pigeonholing children and greatly limiting their potential. In this context, culturally responsive teaching (CRT) is a good example of a useful framework that can provide concrete training and help teachers relate better to the cultural sensitivities of students.[13] By requiring teachers to be intimately aware of their own cultural frames of reference, CRT can allow them to reflect meaningfully on diverse cultures and thereby tap into the cultural capital of their students. Showing up this way will promote a deeper rapport with students, reduce overall anxiety and stress levels, and make learning more relevant and meaningful. This is only the first step in helping students feel heard in a classroom. We should also guard against overgeneralization and be responsive to the unique needs of each learner. These are essential aspects of responsive teaching that are informed by culture but not limited by it. However, without true self-assurance, it would be difficult to look past ourselves. Independent seekers who are naturally curious and genuinely believe that the possibilities are endless need to be comfortable in their own skin. It is not difficult to see why epigenetics suggests that positive emotional engagement is a force multiplier.

Shinichi Suzuki—a world-renowned teacher and violinist—narrated a remarkable story about how he once taught a blind child to play the violin.[14] Very young children typically didn't receive formal training in playing musical instruments in the past, but Suzuki successfully pioneered a revolutionary teaching method for developing their innate musical ability. This method, called Talent Education, is based on the premise that all children are born with the ability to learn. He maintained that difficulties in teaching, in an overwhelming number of cases, are due to deficiencies in the teaching methods and not due to children's limitations. He was a big believer in creating the right environment for child development and did not accept heredity as a significant limitation.

Suzuki's reputation naturally led to solicitations from numerous parents for assistance in the education of their children. One such request was from Mr. Tanaka. He brought with him his blind son, a letter of introduction, and a rather ambitious request. He wanted Suzuki to accept Teiichi, his blind five-year-old son, as his student. Despite his remarkable accomplishments, teaching a blind child was still a rather far cry for Suzuki. However, he was not one to turn down a challenge. He requested a week's time to think through the possibilities. That evening, after reflecting on possible approaches, he turned off the lights and closed his eyes. He tried to envision and experience the challenges that Teiichi would face. He quickly realized that vision did not make a big difference to him as he was intimately familiar with his violin.

Armed with this insight, he then embarked on a yearlong enterprise, in partnership with Teiichi's parents. He came up with an arduous but meticulous program of exercises for familiarizing Teiichi with his violin, the bow, and the graceful movements of the bow to make music. This training program took a tremendous amount of dedication, persistence, and resolution from Suzuki, Teiichi, and his parents. After steady progress over a period of about a year, Teiichi was able to join some of Suzuki's other young students on stage at Hibiya Hall in Tokyo playing the Seitz concerto. The depth of Suzuki's ability and dedication can also be seen from how he was able to help Hiroko Chan, a developmentally delayed child, become the first woman member of the Berlin Radio Symphony. These are great testaments to what love, conviction, and dedication can accomplish.

Suzuki's experiences and observations, remarkable as they are, are by no means an exception. From Maria Montessori's work with mentally disabled children to the National Network of Youth and Children's Orchestras in Venezuela and the silent struggles of countless parents the world over, we have numerous compelling narratives that speak to the possibilities of love and dedication.[15] In fact, we can argue that the dedication that motivated parents and teachers bring to the table is key to the development of child-centric curriculum and teaching methods.

I am often reminded of an incident one of my cousins shared with me. She used to drive her two-wheeler about ten miles each way to teach at a small rural school in the state of Andhra Pradesh in India. The children mostly came from very poor families, and it was a great accomplishment for them to even attend school. Many of them did not pay enough attention to basic hygiene. They often wore clothes that were not washed for a week or two and several did not even comb their hair. Despite numerous entreaties, my cousin was unable to get the children to tidy up. She finally brought a couple of combs with her to class one day and announced that if any of her students came with unkempt hair the next day, she would comb their hair. She also told them that she would visit their homes to show them how to wash their clothes. That did the trick. Social hierarchy continues to be etched deeply in the psyche of folks in India, especially in rural India. Her students were shocked that my cousin, who happens to be an upper-class Brahmin, would even visit their homes, let alone actually wash their clothes. The seriousness of her care and interest in their well-being struck a deep chord. It is difficult to not get your students engaged when they feel your empathy and believe in your passion for their welfare and development.

There are many reasons why it is essential to earn such trust and credibility from the children. Welcoming guidance and feedback can be difficult for most of us, especially since authentic feedback is not always pleasant. This process can be especially difficult if there isn't much trust. Even while there is broad recognition and acknowledgment that children need to be encouraged and valued, there isn't, unfortunately, sufficient appreciation of the importance of authentic feedback. Hollow or insincere accolades are sometimes doled out to keep children from losing faith in themselves. This can be counterproductive since it can keep them from realizing their true potential. Children can also, at some point, see through this hollowness and stop valuing all feedback. Real confidence and empowerment can only come from within and through genuine accomplishment. Adults therefore need to strive to provide encouragement without losing sight of authenticity.

Additionally, while children relish some amount of control and ownership, they also seek conformity and validation. Good role models are therefore indispensable. Parents who want their children to learn the violin or the piano typically look for a good music school. What if, in addition, as Suzuki suggested, they also learn it themselves and play it when feasible? Instead of compartmentalizing our schools and classrooms, we should instead consider fostering a divergence of interests. Perhaps the math teacher would want to play the violin during recess or at a school event. What if the physical education teacher and the science teacher recited poetry or held a friendly art contest? And could the art teacher and history teacher discuss different ways to estimate the area of a polygon? Our teachers should embody the excitement of learning and discovery. It needs to be an obvious and palpable aspect of school culture and should be self-evident to students. This is what true role modeling and immersion need to look like. Immersion and empowerment are often much more effective than instruction and overscheduling. Additionally, learning does not only happen between school bells and within four walls. Similar growth opportunities are therefore needed outside school as well.

At the same time, support for children does not always manifest itself in joyful ways. I still vividly recall a life lesson I received when I was about eleven years old. One evening, on my way out to play cricket with my friends, I noticed a five-rupee (about 64 cents in 2023 terms) note on a shelf. I couldn't resist the temptation to pick it up. I went straight to a corner store that one of my friends' mothers ran next to our small cricket field. I bought all the candy I could with my five rupees and shared it with my friends who showed up that day. Five rupees was a lot of money then and we ended up with a lot of candy. Once I got home, I realized that I had greatly underestimated my mother. She ran a very tight ship, and it did not take her long to realize that a five-rupee note was missing. And it took her another fifteen minutes or so to extract a confession from me. As expected, I was then given a lecture on the importance of honesty and integrity.

What happened the next day will stay with me forever. My mother came with me to the cricket field and took me directly to the corner store. My friends were curious about my mother's visit to the field, and they gathered around us. My mother then proceeded to berate both the lady who gave me candy and my friends. She asked them why they were not surprised that an eleven-year-old who had never had any money with him before spent five rupees buying a whole bunch of candy. She asked them to reflect on what this incident says about their own integrity and friendship. There was no mistaking the tough love. It took me years to fully appreciate how difficult this episode must have been for her.

Parents obviously have a large role to play in the proper upbringing and education of their children. As we have discussed, their limitations, biases, and worldview can unfortunately limit their children's potential. They should therefore be very mindful of subtle subtexts that could be projected onto children by their words and actions. At the same time, it is not easy to walk the fine line between empathetic understanding and tough love. This is why extensive investments in parent education are often made at many schools.

For example, as key members of a community of learners, parents at Sankalpa Academy were encouraged to attend at least two parent education events every year. At these events, we shared each other's experiences and reviewed programs such as Conscious Discipline and Collaborative Problem

Solving. In addition to learning from experts, we tried to promote openness to new ideas and viewpoints. We were also humbled by the number of parents who volunteered their time. Some helped in the classrooms, some on the playground, and some others shared their training and expertise through our parent education events. Yet others helped with marketing and community outreach. It was truly a village. Incidentally, one of the key lessons from our parent education program was the recognition of the benefit that these support systems can offer to even prospective parents.

Figure 7.2. Sankalpa Academy parents and teachers help construct a playground fence.

In this context, I need to specifically commend the contributions from Swetha Balasubramanian. Balasubramanian had worked at Microsoft in Seattle and Facebook in Menlo Park before moving to Austin. To make a long story short, her son was enrolled in our Pre-K program and Balasubramanian volunteered full time at Sankalpa Academy in various capacities. She helped in the garden and in the classrooms and was always present when there was a need. She eventually also joined our leadership team and helped with the development of a framework for our curriculum.

Even though we find many examples of nurturing across various species, the art of tough love and the developmental scaffolding that comes with it are likely most developed in humans. We can overcome significant odds if our lives are securely anchored. As Socrates is reported to have said, one of the primary goals of education should be to produce children who are aware of what they know and what they don't know. Children should be able to develop an unshakable confidence in their ability to master or accomplish anything that they set their minds to. High self-esteem enables children to courageously seek a fuller understanding of the world around them. For children to reach their full potential, we need to look at them as the gift they are and ensure that they feel fully empowered. Wrapping our minds around this notion and recognizing that children often have to operate in a world of expectations with limited skill sets and capacities does take patience and the work of a community.

Figure 7.3. A Sankalpa Academy parent volunteering in a classroom.

CHAPTER SUMMARY

- Nurturing the young is not an exclusively human trait; many animals also are exceptional parents. However, given the skills children must now acquire before they can thrive on their own, the duration and complexity of human childrearing are in a league of their own.
- Discovery of feral children in the last few centuries has led to deeper insights into the potential of nurture, specifically the processes of enculturation and language acquisition.
- Early childhood experiences and environmental influences have been causally linked to emerging brain architecture and our long-term physical, mental, emotional, and intellectual development.
- Epigenetics has shown that our life outcomes are not solely due to our inherited genes or our environment but mediated by both. Biological pathways exist for us to predict even outcomes such as depression or cardiovascular problems based on childhood experiences such as neglect and abuse. Our environment can influence the expression of our genes and turn them on and off.
- It has been shown that changes in gene expression patterns can also be inherited. In other words, the impact of childhood experiences is far more consequential than previously believed; it is not limited to an individual's life outcomes, it can also carry forward into subsequent generations.
- Approaching every child with a completely open mind and a resolute faith in his or her aspirations and potential gives the child the best opportunities for growth and development.
- Culturally responsive teaching and Shinichi Suzuki's Talent Education are good examples of frameworks that can provide concrete training and help teachers relate better to the cultural sensitivities and individual aptitudes and competencies of learners.
- Positive role models, thoughtful design of immersive experiences and environments, and empowerment can help set children up for the best outcomes in life.

8

Cultivating Growth Mindset

The key to growth is the introduction of
higher dimensions of consciousness into our awareness.
—LAO TZU

While many undoubtedly dreamed of human flight for centuries and some like Leonardo da Vinci even came up with very early designs, it was not until the early 1900s that we had enough technological prowess that it became a matter of serious pursuit. Of the many who were trying to crack this puzzle, Samuel Pierpont Langley, the secretary of the Smithsonian Institution, was probably the one with the best education, credentials, and resources.

At age fifty, Langley was already well known. He was a respected astronomer, a tenured professor at the University of Pittsburgh, and previously a director of the Allegheny Observatory at the US Naval Academy. He was fascinated by the problem of human flight, and he spent the 1880s and 1890s perfecting the "aerodrome," his vision of the flying machine. He was eager to be in the same league as Alexander Graham Bell and Thomas Edison, and the human flight problem presented a great opportunity. His efforts were supported by the Smithsonian and funded by the War Department. It helped that he knew many of the most innovative thinkers of his time through his association with Harvard; this allowed him to recruit some of the best minds for his project. His stature made him a darling of the establishment and the public, and thus also of the press.

There were also many second-tier teams pursuing this dream. In addition to the Wright brothers, Clément Ader, Gustave Whitehead, Richard Pearse, Karl Jatho, Traian Vuia, and Alberto Santos-Dumont had been attempting to solve the flight problem. Several had succeeded in making powered hops and lifts. While lift and power are essential for human flight, they are not sufficient. Controlled human flight also requires balance. Mastery of control and balance is what differentiated the Wright brothers from others. They were more persistent and passionate about studying and experimenting than most, and this is likely why they were the first to solve the problem of controlled human flight.

Compared to Langley, the Wright brothers were amateurs with limited resources. It was a case of David versus Goliath. In fact, they had not even attended college. They dropped out of high school in 1889 and started a printing business. They later used the income from their print shop to start a weekly newspaper called *West Side News*. After about three years, they jumped onto the bandwagon of safety bicycles and started a bicycle shop, doing repairs first and then manufacturing their own brand by 1896. News reports around that time of Langley's efforts and setbacks fueled the Wright brothers' interest in aviation. They did not have any financial backers, nor did they know anyone who could help them with the technical aspects. Their bike shop provided the only—meager—source of funding for their research. Few paid them much attention.

They wrote to the Smithsonian to gather details about Langley's efforts and devoured information on what was attempted, what worked, and what did not work. This research convinced them that it was only a matter of time before controlled human flight was possible. Once they were sold on the viability, they persisted in their design process: experimenting and tweaking to overcome the numerous hurdles that came their way.

There was a key difference between the Wright brothers and Langley. The Wright brothers were enamored with the prospect of human flight and had a strong belief that success was only a matter of time. Their passion, belief, and determination gave them a greater sense of purpose, and this is what enabled them to put their own money into the project. Langley, on the other hand, was driven more by the lure of fame that would come from this kind of an accomplishment. He badly wanted his name associated with an invention that was on par with Alexander Graham Bell's telephone and Thomas Edison's lightbulb. A mind focused and fueled by the challenges of a problem will often engage more with it than one enamored of the results that would follow. On December 17, 1903, in the Kill Devil Hills of North Carolina, Wilbur and Orville Wright made the first successful controlled manned flight in history. The brothers made four flights that day, with the longest lasting 59 seconds and traveling 852 feet.

People need faith, purpose, and passion to be able to draw the difficult lessons from each failure. The process of discovery unfolds in very different ways when someone is focused more on the problem than on personal success. It also helped that Wilbur and Orville Wright had a very productive relationship. While their success in aviation has received a lot of attention, this is only the pinnacle of a long history of partnerships. As discussed earlier, they successfully collaborated on many innovative businesses. A key element of their partnership was their ability to invite and relish task conflicts without letting them escalate into personal conflicts. Their arguments were sometimes so loud and prolonged that their sister threatened to leave the house. The brothers called this process "scrapping," and they apparently enjoyed this intellectual back and forth. Many don't have the chops for this. On the other hand, when results and spotlight drive your hunger, it is difficult to persevere when someone else gets to the goal first. This is likely why Langley was ready to fold after just two attempts. It is amazing that the power of flight was unleashed by two brothers who were uneducated and virtually unknown to most of the world.

The plasticity of the heritable measures of intelligence is an active area of research. For example, Carol S. Dweck (1946–), an American psychologist, had interesting, practical, and actionable insights into the benefits and dangers of perceptions of intelligence. In her landmark 2006 book *Mindset*, she investigated the interplay between motivation, personality, and development. The book proposed entity and incremental theories of intelligence, coining and popularizing the concept of a "growth mindset."[1] According to her, those who view intelligence as an unchangeable entity are risk-averse and often underachieving. Dweck defined a fixed mindset as one that believes more in innate capabilities, strengths, and weaknesses—that is, abilities that are fixed and likely inherited at birth. Growth mindset, on the other hand, implies a willingness to struggle and take risks. Paradoxically, Dweck claimed that praising students' intelligence can potentially stunt the growth of their intelligence. It is far more beneficial to applaud someone's efforts than their innate abilities or results. Of course, there is a continuum between fixed and growth mindsets. While Langley could not have been interested in the problem of human flight without a growth mindset, the degree of passion and commitment and the level of tolerance for failure were likely lower than what the Wright brothers brought to the table.

We can see another great example of the focus on struggle and tolerance for failure in James Stigler's account of an incident in Japan. Stigler, a professor of psychology at UCLA, was interested in the differences between the cultures and attitudes in the East and West. He recounts an incident that happened in a fourth-grade Japanese math classroom in 1979.[2] He was in Japan studying the teaching methods there as part of his graduate work at the University of Michigan. On one occasion, he had an opportunity to sit in the back row of a math class for nine- and ten-year-olds. The class was asked to draw a three-dimensional cube on paper. The teacher then walked around the room inspecting the students' work. He eventually picked out the student who was having the most difficulty and asked him to come up and draw the cube on the board. His cube looked cockeyed.

Stigler was surprised since usually the best kid in the class is invited to take part in such show-and-tell in American classrooms. He watched with interest at first and then with increasing trepidation as many minutes rolled by and the child continued to struggle. To make matters worse, the rest of the classroom was watching him and periodically commenting on his progress. Stigler saw many of them shaking their heads, and he expected the struggling kid to burst into tears at any moment. But the student kept working on the problem until he finally got it right. Stigler was surprised but very relieved. The child had a huge smile, and the rest of the class broke into applause.

The fact that the kid managed to keep his head down for that long—and not start crying—was an epiphany for Stigler. He had a newfound appreciation for the role of struggle and grit in intellectual and emotional development. While many parents in the West may look at the need to struggle as a sign of weakness, those in the East are more likely to look at the willingness to struggle and persist until they prevail as an indication of emotional maturity. His observations and Dweck's subsequent research have firmly established the significance of growth mindset in child development.

Interestingly, growth mindset also has been an important theme since ancient times. For instance, the 47th verse of chapter 2 in the *Bhagavad Gita* says:

> karmaṇy-evādhikāras te mā phaleṣhu kadāchana
> mā karma-phala-hetur bhūr mā te saṅgo 'stvakarmaṇi
>
> *We have a right and a duty to perform actions but are not entitled to the fruits of our actions. We should also accept that the causes of the ensuing results are not solely our actions. At the same time, this should not be taken as an excuse not to perform the actions needed to meet our obligations.*

While a growth mindset is superior to a fixed mindset as it liberates more of us to pursue growth, not even requiring attribution of success to our efforts and developing the ability to focus more exclusively on the journey can be even more empowering. How can we instill such courage of conviction, purpose, and passion in our children? Are this focus and passion solely genetic, or can we cultivate and nurture them? Passion and a growth mindset largely flow from a sense of purpose. Passion and purpose stem from meaningful experiences. In yogic parlance, *dharma* is an apt term for this sense of purpose, for our calling. This is what some personality tests also try to ascertain, for example. One person may see social work as his *dharma*, another may be drawn to environmental stewardship, and yet another may be drawn to building her own niche business. We sometimes see people who enthusiastically pursue material gain or professional success and yet lack contentment. Then there are some who are full of energy and passion even though they are not successful in the traditional sense. And finally, there are those who somehow manage to straddle both worlds successfully.

If we feel pressured or coerced into a life that does not comport well with who we are, then that life of *adharma* can be disempowering. It gets projected as boredom, frustration, excessive self-criticism, or even depression. Of course, the purpose that gives us joy and contentment often changes over the years, usually the result of a process that moves between introspection, inertia, and evolution of our values. By reflecting on the gaps between our perception and reality, we can identify and minimize self-limiting beliefs. Only through such reflection can we embrace purposeful goals and actions and foster growth through an empowering intention (*sankalpa*). This is one way people can get onto the path of a growth mindset. Similarly, it is vital that children are also trained to identify and exit unproductive thinking as quickly as possible before it builds on itself and damages their mindset.

Also, as discussed in chapter four, developing the ability to savor enriching experiences can help children get more joy out of their lives and help build a reserve against future setbacks.

At Sankalpa Academy, for instance, we sought to cultivate a love of learning and problem-solving in our students through an intentional focus on awareness, growth mindset, and a sense of purpose using individualized learning plans, yoga, and reflection practices. Such engagement is what sets students on the path to becoming the changemakers of the future. As we have seen in earlier chapters, academic skills have rarely been adequate for empowering changemakers to tackle the pressing challenges of their times. They have also needed the ability to think beyond conventional norms, an abiding hunger to reach ambitious goals, a willingness to reflect on their strengths, biases, and shortcomings, and the readiness to collaborate and communicate productively with others. A strong belief system and trust in their ability to persevere toward increasingly higher expectations are worthy objectives and essential elements of such a mindset. But, as we have seen in the case of the Wright brothers, people cannot easily achieve this in the absence of hunger that comes from a sense of purpose. If they have meaningful goals that they have bought into, they're more likely to jump through hoops to make progress. Providing access to inspirational role models and exciting opportunities is therefore essential for building a growth mindset.

While documenting their accomplishments can be helpful, documenting their journey and perseverance is just as valuable, if not more so. We should of course celebrate both accomplishments and failures. Fear of failure can often discourage us from attempting something new. Talking about Edison's resilience, for example, Walter S. Mallory once said:

> I then learned that he had thus made over nine thousand experiments in trying to devise this new type of storage battery, but had not produced a single thing that promised to solve the question. In view of this immense amount of thought and labor, my sympathy got the better of my judgment, and I said: "Isn't it a shame that with the tremendous amount of work you have done you haven't been able to get any results?" Edison turned on me like a flash, and with a smile replied: "Results! Why, man, I have gotten a lot of results! I know several thousand things that won't work."[3]

An emphasis on perseverance and tolerance for failure is most effective when it permeates the culture at both school and home. This should be another key component of the parent education programs in schools.

Many studies show that self-awareness of cognitive processes is as much an element of general intelligence as processing speed, working memory, and reasoning. Canadian American psychologist Albert Bandura proposed the concept of self-efficacy as self-awareness-driven judgment of an individual on how prepared they are to deal with whatever comes their way.[4] This belief in their ability to succeed often has a large domino effect on how they feel and behave. A strong sense of self-efficacy is therefore essential for a growth mindset. Awareness of our flaws and strengths will likely prevent us from getting easily discouraged by setbacks.

However, we also need to be cautious about strong feelings of certainty. Fabienne Picard, a researcher at the Medical School of Geneva, proposed a neurological explanation for these feelings of certainty based on her research on epilepsy.[5] Picard suggests these feelings can be caused by a dysfunction of the anterior insula. The insula, as we have discussed earlier, is a part of the brain that is involved in empathetic, interoceptive, and self-reflective functions. Its purpose seems to be to avoid uncertainty about our understanding of the world by comparing predicted states of reality to actual states. This comparison can create estimates of risk and uncertainty, sometimes signaling that we do not understand and that there is ambiguity. When we are unable to compare predicted states and actual states, potential mismatches between predicted and actual states are no longer processed and we are thus spared any discomfort or unease from a sense of uncertainty. This false sense of emotional confidence and certainty about our view of the world can of course be very detrimental to our growth.

This does not necessarily imply that the potential for self-awareness and self-efficacy is fully determined at birth. Also, as we have discussed earlier, many studies using magnetic resonance imaging have shown that meditation practices can result in a significant increase in gray matter in the insular cortex and other areas of the brain. This dependence on the anterior insula and its amenability to modulation certainly warrant more research.

The untold cost we all pay in our everyday lives due to our biases, overconfidence, and subscription to echo chambers is difficult to overestimate. They can severely limit our ability to grow. With its advanced encryption scheme, cameras, and multimedia, the BlackBerry was once one of the most secure, versatile, and capable smartphones around. It was an undisputed leader. From celebrities to corporate executives to teenagers, it seemed like the whole world loved the BlackBerry. President Barack Obama, Katy Perry, Justin Timberlake, and countless others were among its devout followers. Eric Schmidt, Executive Chairman of Google from 2001 to 2011, was a longtime BlackBerry user even though BlackBerry was a competitor of the smartphones using Google's Android operating system. It was a shocking decline for BlackBerry to rapidly lose ground to the iPhone and the other Android smartphones after its peak in 2012, when it sold about fifty million devices a year. Yes, the BlackBerry continued to be modestly successful for many years, even after the introduction of the iPhone in 2007. While BlackBerry focused on the QWERTY keyboard, security, and apps that met its efficiency criteria for size, battery life, and bandwidth, Apple challenged this mindset. Apple eyed the billions of potential new users while BlackBerry remained fixated on its loyal base of millions. BlackBerry's operating system was too restrictive for app developers, and the company also dragged its feet about switching to Android or iOS.

Similar biases affect the way children often approach and interact with the world. We have all likely seen many examples of how peers hold a great deal of influence over young children. My sister once described an interesting incident that occurred during one of my fifteen-month-old niece's visits to her pediatrician. Until then, my sister and brother-in-law hadn't really seen my niece ever getting scared. However, for some inexplicable reason, my niece appeared terrified by a large ridable animal at the doctor's office. Their attempts to convince her that it was friendly and cuddly were not successful. A little while later, a slightly older child walked in with her parents. The older child almost immediately started riding the large stuffed animal. As soon as my niece saw this, she apparently dropped whatever she was playing with and wanted to get onto the animal as well. Clearly, the actions of the older child spoke much louder than the assurances of my sister and brother-in-law. Of course, this should not really come as a surprise. The depth of influence peers have on young children is not really a groundbreaking discovery.

The fact that children learn much more readily from the actions and examples set by their peers is, for instance, at the root of Lev Semyonovich Vygotsky's zone of proximal development.[6] While Darwin explored the role of our genetic makeup, Vygotsky (1896–1934), a well-known Russian psychologist, studied intelligences that feed off social activity. He was one of the leading voices in exploring the impact of the environment on behavior. He was especially interested in the role of collaborative skills in defining and augmenting human intelligence. In his view, intelligence is not really a state or a trait but more a process shaped by social activity. He proposed the term *zone of proximal development* (ZPD) to describe the capacity for collaborative problem-solving skills over and above the abilities people have when working independently. He claimed that the impact of a child's cultural background on the nature of his or her social interactions and thus on the ZPD was quite significant. While most animals can develop habits as a reaction to the environment, they cannot really alter their environment or receive much developmental scaffolding from it. On the other hand, through the support of mentors, children can learn skills or aspects of a skill that go well beyond their actual developmental level. In fact, studies show that in addition to enhancing children's cognitive development, the quantity and quality of verbal scaffolding can also be important for their overall learning and development.[7]

Many children—as well as adults—also experience cultural forces in social encounters. We find it quite difficult to not conform to an established culture. Most young children, for instance, behave much better at a daycare facility or school than at home. They even seem to sleep and eat better there. They quickly perceive expected norms and order. Maria Montessori spoke extensively about the absorbent, spongelike minds of children. In fact, our environment continues to exert a large influence on our behavior even as we grow older. It is not uncommon to find the very same person behaving very differently in different social contexts. Many wear different hats to adjust to the different cultures and traditions in foreign lands, for example.

The examples of Stigler and my niece and the theories of Dr. Dweck are enlightening. But are these childhood experiences truly consequential for life? Our conscious mind gives us our sense of identity. It makes plans and holds our dreams and aspirations. It can review our past, draw lessons, and project into the future. It is the mind that disconnects us the most from the present moment unless we are task-focused. The subconscious, on the other hand, is primarily a repository of learned habits and behaviors. It provides the default behavior that comes from years of environmental cues or training, especially in our early years. These automated responses to stimuli often seem instinctual. We can write journals and make New Year's resolutions, but unless the subconscious program is rewritten, it is difficult to consistently provide a different response to a stimulus. Some even claim that these autopilot programs in our subconscious mind shape more than 95 percent of our life experiences![8] This is why early life experiences are very critical.

Dr. Rima Laibow has described the development of different stages in brain activity in quantitative EEG and neurofeedback.[9] For the first two or so years, the brains of babies operate at their lowest EEG frequency, from 0.5 to 4 Hz. These high-amplitude neural oscillations are referred to as delta waves. And between about two and six years of age, our brains spend more time at a higher frequency of about 4 to 8 Hz. This frequency range, called theta waves, has been found to put us in a more suggestible state. This explains how the biology of young children helps them easily and quickly internalize a lot of what they observe into strongly held beliefs, behaviors, and attitudes. The observations get programmed into the subconscious mind as synaptic pathways that are harder to change. As we grow older, our brain activity can reach higher and higher frequencies: 9–14 Hz alpha waves associated with calmness, 15–40 Hz beta waves associated with deep focus, or even higher-frequency gamma waves during high-attention states that process and make sense of multiple stimuli. It becomes harder and harder to override the programming that took place when we were younger.

Early childhood learning adds to the inherited capabilities of the limbic system. This system, for example, plays a vital role in managing our basic behavioral and emotional responses. It is responsible for our fight-or-flight responses, hunger, reproduction, and nurture. It is in the part of the brain that includes the hippocampus, amygdala, cingulate gyrus, and thalamus. It is vital that children's early life experiences help create a constructive belief system within their subconscious and contribute to a growth mindset.

While the conscious mind can plan the future or reminisce about the past, the subconscious mind is always engaged with the present. If we acquired great confidence or patience as a child or if we internalized a growth mindset, that can be a big asset for achieving lofty goals. However, at the same time, subconscious programs can also be liabilities. If we grow up believing in our intelligence or lack thereof, it is not difficult to slip into a fixed mindset. We develop strong impressions at a young age on the relative importance of innate ability versus effort and perseverance. In these early years, our mind is primed to be more receptive to certain kinds of inputs, be it as simple as trusting people in a suit more than those with hoodies.

Our childhood experiences therefore play an extremely critical role. The process of enculturation that takes place in the first six to ten years of life determines our subconscious programs as well as most of our epigenetic makeup. This is why children told they can achieve anything they set their minds on end up with a more positive outlook and more confidence than children told they will never amount to much. Many of the limitations programmed into our subconscious behaviors are often acquired through our perceptions based on the unconscious observations of our parents and teachers. In 1975, Robert Ader and Nicholas Cohen pioneered psychoneuroimmunology and showed how beliefs can even impact immunity through conditioning.[10] Neuropsychology and the role of beliefs continue to be active areas of research. A great example of the strong hold that belief systems can have on our collective psyche can also be seen in the Harry Potter series. In this fictional world, we can only empathize with the unwavering belief of the house elves that they only exist to serve their masters. Hermione Granger tries unsuccessfully to break the grip of this collective conditioning with her Society for the Promotion of Elfish Welfare (SPEW).

One of the first influences on children's development is the culture they experience. Social expectations and the environment affect our behavior in a variety of ways, some of which we understand and some that we don't readily recognize. It appears that the environment can have a key role to play even in the case of adults. When President Nixon was informed that more than 15 percent of the American forces in Vietnam were addicted to heroin, he created an office for drug abuse prevention and rehabilitation and tasked Jerome Jaffe with running this program. Nixon wanted to understand what happened to the addicted service members after they returned home.

Jaffe recruited a well-respected psychiatric researcher, Lee Robins, to study this issue. Robins found that while about 20 percent of the service members were actively addicted in Vietnam, only 5 percent of those who became addicted in Vietnam relapsed within ten months after their return, and only 12 percent relapsed, even briefly, within three years. Robins also found that the returning veterans had access to heroin after their return and could therefore have easily relapsed if they were so inclined.[11] At the time, this finding flew in the face of conventional wisdom and made little sense. Up until then, scientists believed that people changed behavior by changing goals and attitudes. They also believed that heroin addiction was virtually irreversible.

It literally took decades for the research community to fully appreciate the lessons of this Vietnam study. Many now believe that environmental cues become deeply ingrained, and we outsource control of our behavior to the environment when we repeat it enough times. The environment back home was so different from the environment in Vietnam that the returning soldiers lost most of the cues that would have encouraged a relapse. This is one of the earliest studies documenting the significant role environment can play in reinforcing acquired behavior.

Understanding this is important since peer pressure and environment can be either an asset or a significant impediment. Most of us have been programmed to start our lives off on a positive note. Our progress slows down as social referencing and peer approval begin to be valued. While our interactions with peers can provide valuable developmental scaffolding, our need for conformity and validation can imperil our sense of direction and progress. The experiments with capuchin monkeys by Frans de Waal, the Dutch primatologist and ethnologist, clearly demonstrate the sense of entitlement that we extract from social referencing.[12] While a capuchin monkey was initially happy with a piece of cucumber as a reward for handing a small rock to a lab worker, it was very upset when another monkey received a grape for the same task. This suggests that our notions of fairness are more relative than absolute. Our senses of accomplishment and frustration can depend more than they probably should on the emotional influence we grant to our peer network. As the Swiss psychologist Jean Piaget pointed out, as children evolve from egocentrism to sociocentrism, their answers change from being intuitive to being factual to being socially acceptable since social acceptance becomes a key concern.

Given the significance of these dynamics, the culture of a classroom is often a critical element in the growth mindset of a child. A classroom is a virtual melting pot, with children bringing in their own unique personalities and behaviors that they pick up at home and elsewhere. The promotion of beliefs and behaviors needed for a growth mindset can sometimes be quite frustrating to teachers and classroom guides. It is essential, though not trivial, to come up with programs to manage a classroom culture by disrupting or suitably channeling these disparate classroom dynamics. Doing this without projecting excessive expectations of conformity is not easy. Imposition of a rigid structure can of course be detrimental to a learner's independence.

We need to seek empowering environments that stretch children's ingenuity and bring out the best in them. The bottom line is that we must try to recognize and strengthen the culture experienced by each and every child, at home as well as in a classroom. If a child experiences a culture of achievable but high expectations, it adds to the child's growth mindset. At the same time, if the expectations are too high and the child faces failure and disappointment too often or if a parent routinely compares a child unfavorably to another child, it can leave an indelible scar. Pursuing a lot of activities and not having enough time to explore or to fail can result in a similar sense of frustration. This can also happen when helicopter parenting results in too little independence for a child. As we discussed in the context of the Wright brothers, the biggest achievements invariably come with many setbacks. Children's ability to strike out on their own path and get up every time they fall cannot be fostered by anxious parents who want to minimize the chances of failure. The individualized learning plans at Sankalpa Academy, for instance, were designed to allow children to take more ownership of their goals and worry less about comparisons to an external standard.

To build learning communities where a growth mindset is valued, we also need to focus on the growth mindset of parents, teachers, and other key stakeholders in this journey. The prefrontal cortex in humans and other advanced mammals is known to enable reflection, decision-making, and planning. Evolution has given us the ability to observe our instincts and no-brainer reactions and develop more nuanced responses. As such, in principle, our subconscious mind can be rewired by our decision-making self-conscious mind. But, as most of us can vouch for, this is easier said than done. It takes a strong will and considerable effort. There is some evidence that we can alter our mindset and build deeper awareness through mindfulness and other forms of meditation. A brain imaging investigation published in *Psychiatry Research: Neuroimaging* by researchers at Massachusetts General Hospital in Boston and the University of Massachusetts Medical School in Worcester, for example, found that mindfulness meditation alters regions of the brain associated with memory, self-awareness, and compassion.[13]

Also, the widespread use of life coaches suggests that we can utilize the help of experts to guide us on our journey of transformation. We might also soon see a role for virtual reality in this journey. Even though the practice is not as widespread, clinical hypnosis may be another viable intervention for personal growth.[14] So, even though early investment gives us the biggest returns, self-awareness and openness to change and intervention are also possible for an older cohort. In short, instilling a growth mindset in our children is most effective when the learning community models and lives by such a mindset. And, as Robins's findings suggest, cultivating an environment favorable to a growth mindset can be a force multiplier that accelerates the adoption of healthier habits and beliefs in even adults.

Figure 8.1. Nurturing the individual needs of a learner often requires small learning communities.

CHAPTER SUMMARY

- Those who view ability as an unchangeable entity are likely to be risk-averse and often underachieving. A fixed mindset believes that outcomes are mostly a result of innate capabilities, strengths, and weaknesses.
- A growth mindset, on the other hand, represents a willingness to struggle and take risks. Praising students' intelligence, for example, can potentially stunt their growth. It is far more beneficial to applaud someone's efforts than their innate abilities or results.

- While some may look at the need to struggle as a sign of weakness, the willingness to struggle and persist until we prevail is an indication of grit and a key marker of emotional maturity.
- Purpose and passion are the best fuel for a growth mindset. They stem from meaningful experiences.
- A culture of achievable but high expectations adds to a child's growth mindset. Additionally, Vygotsky's zone of proximal development suggests that skillful scaffolding can greatly aid the development of a growth mindset.
- Thoughtful pursuit of empowering goals and actions that are aligned with our values and purpose is more likely to lead to joy and contentment and a life of passion and *dharma*.
- A strong belief system and trust in our ability to persevere toward increasingly high expectations are essential elements of a mindset that fosters high levels of tolerance for failure. This internal belief system is fueled by self-efficacy or self-awareness mediated observational learning.
- Early life experiences are very critical since they feed the autopilot programs in our subconscious mind that shape more than 95 percent of our life experiences. These can therefore either promote confidence and a growth mindset or pose a liability through self-limiting beliefs and unfounded anxieties.
- While it is not easy to override our subconscious-driven response systems, it is not impossible. Reflection on the gaps between our perception and reality, for example, can help identify and minimize our self-limiting beliefs. However, we also need a high level of self-awareness since our biology (dysfunction of the anterior insula) can also sometimes lead to a false sense of emotional confidence and certainty about our view of the world.

9

The Early Years

The child builds his inmost self out of
the deeply held impressions he receives.
—MARIA MONTESSORI

As discussed in the preceding chapters, children's experiences in their early years have a significant impact on shaping their habits and belief systems. These form the core of the subconscious programs that get etched into their personalities. They inform the nature of the person that a child will likely grow into. The early influences are so consequential that American author Robert Fulghum even claims that we learn almost all we need to know in kindergarten itself.[1]

To harness and nurture children's competencies, we need to start when they're very young. Early education begins with the design of an intentional environment conducive to the cultivation of healthy routines, habits, and beliefs. The curriculum should facilitate the holistic development of each child. Intellectual stimulation may not be of as much use if access to good nutrition, sleep, emotional security, and hygiene cannot be assured. In other words, schools should also prioritize children's physical health and emotional well-being.

A key objective of most preschool programs is to ensure that children develop healthy habits and have all the tools they need to hit the ground running in kindergarten. Young children are naturally curious and creative. Most well-designed preschool programs seek to support this curiosity and foster independence, emotional awareness, and respect for self, community, and the environment. As children's confidence grows, teachers can focus on promoting both their sense of agency for exploration and their ability to work through longer blocks of time. These will aid in the development of fine and gross motor skills as well as math and language readiness. It may seem like a tall order, but in Maria Montessori's words, young children soak up environmental cues like sponges.

The strong bonds teachers form with the students help them feel secure and empowered to forge ahead. Well-designed programs include the development of students' self-care skills, a willingness to share and wait their turn, and an ability to use their voice and speak up. Teachers often pursue these objectives through both careful modeling and direct instruction. As a result of this investment, as students advance in a preschool program, they are typically able to focus for longer periods. They also build a deeper understanding of the community around them.

Figure 9.1. A typical yoga class at Sankalpa Academy.

Our preschool program at Sankalpa Academy was also designed to give each child the necessary foundation so they could blossom into independent learners. To meet all these curricular goals as well as those discussed in the last chapter, we took time after the end of the first year to begin the design of a formal curricular framework that borrowed extensively from four leading early childhood education philosophies: Montessori, Reggio Emilia, Waldorf, and Krishnamurti. These four approaches grew out of a strong desire in the mid-twentieth century to move education away from the factory model that churned out obedient workers to a system that promotes active learning, self-reliance, an ability to think and reason independently, and compassion and respect for peers, community, and nature. These approaches were built on the belief that the unique gifts of each child can be best developed through nurturing the child's inner senses, faculties, and latent capacities. In other words, teachers need to wear multiple hats as guides, coaches, cheerleaders, mentors, and more as they keenly observe the different "senses" of the children. Beyond the five physical senses, we all experience a sense of acceptance, warmth, balance, equilibrium, time, distance, and more. Knowing how each child perceives their environment helps unlock a deeper understanding of the child. Such understanding is invaluable in tailoring a child-specific curriculum.

All four approaches also view teachers as scientists and artists who guide and facilitate the development of the whole child with warmth, kindness, and respect. Beyond the high-level alignment, there are also several key differences between these approaches. While we have reviewed some of these philosophies in great detail in part I of this book, a quick summary may be useful to appreciate how they align as well as differ.

A hallmark of the Montessori approach is its belief that children have absorbent minds and that they learn more deeply through both observations and interactions with environment and materials. Well-prepared classrooms are believed to inspire a love of exploration and learning and help children work through uninterrupted blocks of time on practical life, sensorial, math, science, and language projects. And, to build independence and autonomy, Montessori guides are very mindful about providing only the right level of scaffolding.

The popularity of the Montessori method attracted significant research into this approach and also some unfavorable press. First, there are a small number of studies do not support the claim that Montessori education is always correlated with superior academic achievement, especially as compared to outcomes from a traditional school system.[2] On a more practical note, the absence of a trademark or a certification program for the Montessori method has frustrated countless parents. As any school can claim to adhere to Montessori principles, it is an arduous task to assess the authenticity of the Montessori character of a given school. This is partly because there are often many differences in teacher training, emphasis, and adherence to Montessori principles. Internal differences between AMS (American Montessori Society) and AMI (Association Montessori Internationale) programs create further ambiguity, as both are official Montessori methods. Lack of homework and relative assessment through a grading system have also contributed to some parental agony. Even though these run counter to the Montessori philosophy, some schools do hand out homework and others have jumped onto the grading bandwagon. There has also been criticism of the close association between Maria Montessori, the person, and her method. This has been blamed for stifling meaningful research into her teaching methods and materials and hence preventing their potential development and evolution.

Incidentally, criticism of the Montessori method by William Heard Kilpatrick and his mentor, John Dewey, is believed to be largely responsible for the relatively lukewarm reception of this method in the US.[3] The issues they raised reflected legitimate differences between their pedagogical beliefs and Montessori's. First and foremost, Dewey and Kilpatrick believed that children should be allowed to do whatever they want with whatever material they have. For instance, they could build houses, towers, or castles with math blocks, if they so chose. Montessori, on the other hand, was adamant that her materials should only be used for the purposes for which they were designed and also only when the guide determined that the child was ready. Dewey and Kilpatrick argued that this rigidity can stifle the creativity of a child.

Another common criticism of Montessori teachers is that they do not see value in pretend play and other such activities that do not entail immediate or tangible academic benefits. Montessori herself once said, "If I were persuaded that children needed to play, I would provide the proper apparatus; but I am not so persuaded."[4] Montessori lessons are widely perceived as serious business. But this should not be concerning, as all children's activities should be taken seriously, since respect and independence are important end goals.

Dewey and Kilpatrick also felt that the Montessori system did not pay adequate attention to group work and the development of social skills. There has been criticism that, as a result, emotional intelligence and growth do not figure prominently in the Montessori method. There are also differences between Dewey and Montessori on reading. While Dewey, like Waldorf, felt that children should not read until they are seven or eight, Montessori believed that children as young as four or five could be ready. Also, while Montessori promoted phonics, Dewey believed in the "look-say" type of sight-based approach to reading.

Another approach that has been growing in popularity is the Reggio Emilia method. It recognizes that children are innately curious and that they thrive in an environment where they have agency. Topics that engender a significant amount of interest and uncertainty are therefore taken up as short- or long-term projects. A key Reggio Emilia precept is to recognize the environment as the third teacher. To make learning visible, classrooms are decorated with student work and the growth of both the children and teachers is meticulously documented. This method also subscribes to the view that children speak with a hundred languages (art, music, drama, etc.). The guides therefore work closely with parents to understand the interests and needs of each child. Given the high degree of customization and individualization, teacher expertise is a lot more critical for a Reggio Emilia classroom than for other modalities. A Reggio Emilia teacher has to be willing to take risks and navigate uncomfortable places if that is where the child heads. The relatively open-ended nature of this philosophy—viz., the hundred languages—also makes it difficult to compare the impact of this pedagogy vis-à-vis the other approaches.

The Waldorf method—the third pedagogical approach we looked at—has been around for a long time. Unlike the Montessori method, it does not subscribe to the view that all of a child's work has to be rooted in reality or structure. In fact, artistic endeavors such as music, drama, and fantasy, as well as unstructured creative play, are important elements of a Waldorf education. The guides are therefore trained to identify, encourage, and showcase a child's expressions of imagination and creativity. Art and foreign language programs are also used to encourage creativity and ingenuity.

While, as we discussed earlier, early education at Waldorf schools emphasizes oral listening and speaking skills to foster a child's imagination through the visual and performing arts, it delays the introduction of reading and writing skills until a child turns seven. Whereas students in traditional schools are typically able to read by the time they are in kindergarten or the first grade, Waldorf students would normally get there only when they are in the third grade. Even though this has led to considerable anxiety for many parents, Waldorf students do seem to be able to catch up with students in regular schools within a couple of years.[5] This delay might, however, be an issue for students who have learning disabilities that can then go undetected for a longer period.

Educating the educator and developing sensory and emotional awareness to nourish the inner lives of children and teachers are quintessential values of the fourth approach we considered, the Krishnamurti method. Yoga, meditation, and reflection exercises are great vehicles for fostering mindfulness and strengthening the vital skills of listening, observing, and internalizing. Krishnamurti was also very passionate about helping children identify biases and conditioning. Relating well to peers, extended community, and nature is a key value shared by the Reggio Emilia and Krishnamurti philosophies. The Krishnamurti approach also treats outdoor exploration as an important focus area for promoting respect for nature and the sense of interconnectedness of living things.

Figure 9.2. Hatched butterflies are released in the Sankalpa Academy garden.

In addition, all four approaches recognize the significance of extensive parental involvement in children's education. Minimizing differences between school and home environments, culture, and expectations can go a long way in strengthening a child's moral compass. While our curriculum drew from these four proven approaches, we made them our own by allowing room for exploration.

Table 9.1 summarizes the key aspects of our curriculum and how they were inspired by the Montessori, Reggio Emilia, Waldorf, and Krishnamurti approaches. We chose the best features of these philosophies to curate this list of fourteen different focus areas for our preschool program. We found that a blended curriculum is better able to meet the needs outlined in the previous chapters. Giving children agency and access to master educators, for example, is a shared characteristic of all four approaches. Explicit programming to build emotional and social skills and outdoor activities that are focused on exploration of nature and imaginative play are, on the other hand, inspired by the Reggio Emilia, Waldorf, and Krishnamurti philosophies. It should be emphasized that this table is a gross simplification to represent key priorities of these four approaches. It is not intended to suggest that the priorities of all Montessori schools (or any of the other philosophies) exactly match the list of features in the table. Many other schools might promote mindfulness for sensory and emotional awareness, for instance, even though it is the stated objective of only the Krishnamurti approach.

While some children are fortunate enough to experience a rich preschool program, for many, their first experience of gathering in a learning community outside of home occurs in kindergarten. And, while it has long been known that children's early years are very consequential, most parents receive little education or training to prepare for this significant undertaking. For all these reasons, programs that prepare and educate prospective parents can be very valuable.

Outside the home, it is in preschool and kindergarten that many of the key life skills are first introduced. While children do pick up useful academic skills, as discussed earlier, these years are valued more for the lifelong habits and beliefs they instill. Experienced educators help build routines that promote sharing, impulse control, independence, self-advocacy, and peaceful conflict resolution skills. This is why there was so much concern about the steep drop in kindergarten enrollment during the COVID-19 pandemic. A national study from the University of Oregon, for instance, found that 17 percent of

Sankalpa Education	Reggio Emilia	Montessori	Waldorf	Krishnamurti
Children are very curious and thrive in an environment where they have agency	X	X	X	X
Projects inspired by children's interests	X			
Off-the-shelf programming to develop sensory appreciation, fine and gross motor skills		X	X	
Off-the-shelf programming to develop imagination and creativity			X	
Mindfulness for sensory and emotional awareness				X
Programming for building emotional and social intelligence	X		X	X
Explicit programming for intellectual, physical, and psychological development			X	X
Implicit learning through prepared classroom materials		X		
Large uninterrupted blocks of time to foster purposeful learning		X		
Developing a reflective mind that cares about itself, the environment, and community	X			X
School serves as a community where everyone is a learner				X
Outdoor exploration for fostering respect for nature and imaginative play	X		X	X
Documentation of student achievements	X			
Experienced mentors who have a keen sense of a child's learning edges	X	X	X	X

Table 9.1. Features of the Sankalpa Academy's blended curriculum.

American families chose not to send their kindergarten-age children to a physical school in the fall of 2020.[6] Many more who started kindergarten in fall 2019 would have likely seen a shorter academic year. While there has been mounting evidence for the adverse emotional impact of virtual schooling on children of almost all ages, there is a lot more worry about the longer-term impact of the loss of foundational years for the younger ones, especially since many were unlikely to have received adequate support at home from work-from-home parents. The increase in awareness of the emotional needs of young children and the significant role teachers play in meeting these needs are perhaps an unexpected silver lining of this tragedy.

CHAPTER SUMMARY

- Well-designed preschool programs seek to instill healthy habits, support a child's curiosity, and foster independence and agency, emotional awareness, and respect for self, community, and the environment.
- The strong relationships teachers build with their students help young children feel secure, empowered to forge ahead, and socially comfortable.
- The preschool program at Sankalpa Academy borrowed extensively from four leading early childhood education philosophies: Montessori, Reggio Emilia, Waldorf, and Krishnamurti.
- These four approaches grew out of a strong desire in the mid-twentieth century to move education away from the factory model that churned out obedient workers to a system that promotes active learning, self-reliance, an ability to think and reason independently, and compassion and respect for peers, community, and nature.
- A hallmark of the Montessori approach is its belief that children have absorbent minds and that they learn more deeply through both observations and interactions with the environment and other materials. Maria Montessori was a pioneer whose insights left a lasting legacy in child development.

- The resounding popularity of the Montessori method also attracted more than a fair share of critics. There has been criticism that the insistence that Montessori materials only be used for the purposes for which they were designed and further only when the guide determines that the children are ready would stifle children's creativity and agency even though some claim that this would promote gratification deferment skills. Another common criticism is that the Montessori approach does not see value in pretend play and other such activities that do not entail immediate or tangible academic benefits.
- The Reggio Emilia philosophy grew from the belief that children construct new knowledge and understanding through experiences and relationships. The emphasis is therefore more on producing the right learning conditions than on measuring learning. Agency, exploration, play, and community interactions are key features of this innovative approach. The Reggio Emilia model views the environment as the third teacher.
- Given the high degree of customization and individualization, teacher expertise is a lot more critical for a Reggio Emilia classroom than for other modalities. A Reggio Emilia teacher must be willing to take risks and navigate uncomfortable places if that is where the child heads with his or her hundred languages.
- Cultivation of imagination and creative thinking abilities is an important component of the Waldorf education, not simply through its curriculum but also through its governance structures. The Waldorf curriculum employs oral speaking skills and various arts and crafts to foster the emotional development of the child.
- Educating the educator and developing sensory and emotional awareness to nourish the inner lives of children and teachers are quintessential values of the Krishnamurti method. It views education as the primary vehicle for fighting the dual threats of conformity and conditioning.
- Finally, all four approaches also recognize the significance of parent education and close parental involvement in the education of their children.

10

Embracing the Three Pillars

There are only two lasting bequests we can hope to give our children. One of these is roots, the other, wings.
—JOHANN WOLFGANG VON GOETHE

"Your beliefs become your thoughts. Your thoughts become your words. Your words become your actions. Your actions become your habits. Your habits become your values. Your values become your destiny." This inspirational quote is traditionally attributed to Gandhi, though similar sentiments have been credited to many other thinkers as well down through the centuries. In fact, the process described is cyclical. We are creatures of habit, so our habits can feed backward and help reinforce our beliefs as well.

Therefore, while we embarked on the design of a K–12 curriculum at Sankalpa Academy to meet the objectives of a holistic, foundational, and individualized approach (Figure 10.1), we were also mindful that school life is only part of a child's ecosystem.

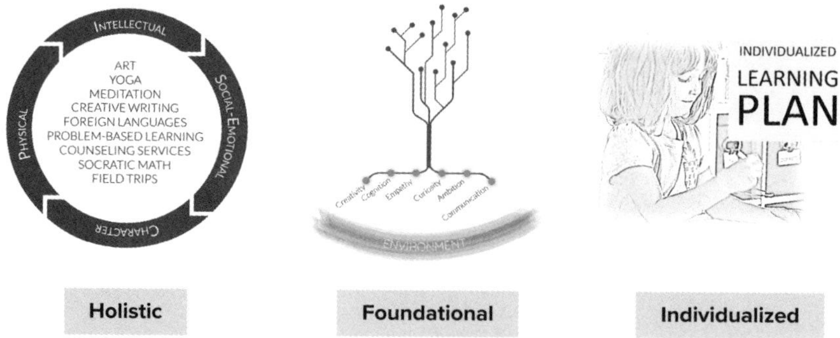

Figure 10.1. An illustration of the Holistic, Foundational, and Individualized pillars.

The values that nurture and promote holistic and foundational growth should ideally permeate all aspects of children's lives. The culture and upbringing at home should be imbued with the same values and practices. Ideally, these values would also be reflected in social norms and interactions. Such seamless, organic experiences that support and reinforce each other are likely to lend the curricular efforts in a classroom the authenticity they need to help children build stronger roots and a deeper belief system. This is why Montessori and Waldorf schools, among many others, go the extra mile to help families recreate similar ethos and expectations at home to what children experience at school.[1] I revisit this aspect later in the chapter, but for now it suffices to note that several features of the curricular development discussed below would also apply outside the school environment.

Sankalpa Academy brought together many curious kids, eager parents, and passionate educators. Our teachers loved the flexibility to pursue their mission. Many parents were pleased by the emphasis we were able to place on yoga and counseling. The small classes and individualized attention helped foster close relationships between students and teachers.

We focused on hiring staff who had a broad educational background. Our master teachers collectively had decades of experience in multiple modalities, from public schools to small and large private and charter schools as well as homeschools. Some had experience with the Montessori and Reggio Emilia methods, while there were others with experience in KIPP (Knowledge is Power Program) and yet others with IB. While some had taught exclusively in the US, others had experience from around the world, including from countries such as Venezuela, Hong Kong, and India. We felt that this breadth of experience was essential to support the ambitious vision of Sankalpa

Academy. Almost all the teachers had a master's degree with specialization in subjects like literature, math, special education, and educational psychology. Most importantly, they came with the conviction that every child would thrive if they were given access to skilled teachers who understood and believed in the strengths of the learners. Our teachers and parents worked closely with our specialist in school psychology to come up with an individualized learning plan (ILP) for each of the kids to meet their academic and socioemotional needs. In addition to addressing basic academic outcomes, our program focused on several overarching projects and themes the children helped select. They then had multiple opportunities to delve deeply into those topics. As the children learned more about their specific interests, they were also encouraged to share their learning with others. This was about Africa in some cases and outer space in others. During the latter part of our first year, we also began using a "sankalpa" journal to guide children through intention setting. The teachers were also huge believers in documentation. It could be a piece of writing, a new skill achieved, a piece of art or design, or some other such accomplishment. Each child had a digital portfolio as well as a "hard" portfolio. These helped to chronicle students' educational journeys and served as a wonderful reminder of all their accomplishments.

Figure 10.2. Use of a visual aid in a math lesson at Sankalpa Academy.

Almost always, the first question on the table is not how something should be taught, but what should be taught. The aspirations of a holistic education can only be realized through a thoughtful selection of curricular experiences and subject areas. Table 10.1 shows the domains or topical areas and a list of associated subdomains that we shortlisted at Sankalpa Academy.

This is by no means the gold standard or a comprehensive list that covers all key domains for all children or all cultures. Instead, it was our first attempt to help prepare children so they will be able to function well as adults. We added several new focus areas or subdomains to traditional subjects (such as Bad Science and Social Acceptance in the domain of Science or Economics and Logic under Math or Culture under Foreign Languages). For instance, many schools often strip valuable historical insights and riveting stories of personal adventure and triumph from math and science lessons. This is a missed opportunity for promoting student interest and engagement. The focus on STEM education should also not come at the expense of investments in social studies.

Our highest-value contribution was the addition of entirely new domains. For example, our focus on developing and cultivating a positive and intentional culture is reflected in the addition of a new domain called Culture. In addition to community engagement and parent education, this domain supports the development of a curriculum that prepares children to take on leadership roles in the sustenance, embodiment, growth, and outreach of their school culture and values. As a lifelong journey, education is most productive when there is good cultural alignment between the different aspects of our lives. Many cultures traditionally place a significant emphasis on the promotion of values such as integrity and kindness. The cultivation of a moral compass that supports civic mindedness and ethics of the highest order is a shared responsibility between educational institutions and families. This is a key curricular goal under the domain of Culture.

In addition, we see references to culture in the domains of Social Studies and Foreign Languages as well. Similarly, yoga shows up under both Socioemotional well-being and Physical Health. A holistic practice of yoga has other benefits as well. For instance, Patanjali's Ashtanga yoga system[2] from the second century BCE—one of the oldest disciplines that pursues a truly holistic development of individuals—can help strengthen the partnership between schools and families in many ways.

When people speak about yoga, they're often referring to only one of the elements in Patanjali's Ashtanga (eight-limbed) yogic system: the Asanas

Culture	Language Arts	Science	Math	Social Studies	Socio-emotional	Physical Health	Foreign Languages	Projects
Community Expectations	Listening	Bad Science	Number Skills	Geography	Yoga	Nutrition	Comprehension	Self
School Expectations	Comprehension	Social Acceptance	Measurement	History	Meditation	Yoga	Reading	Family
Classroom Expectations	Reading	Eureka	Addition & Subtraction	Civics	Play	Motor Skills	Writing	Friends
Classroom Administration	Writing	Life Science	Place Value	Culture	Fine Arts	Strength	Speaking	Community
School Administration	Speaking	Earth & Space	Multiplication & Division	Human Condition	Visual Arts	Cardio	Culture	Planet
Community Liaison		Physics	Fractions & Decimals	Opportunities	Psychology			Future
Parent Education		Chemistry	Geometry		Social Structures			Career
		Technology	Probability					
			Data Analysis					
			Economics					
			Logic & Algebra					
			Calculus					

Table 10.1. A Sankalpa Academy proposal for key learning domains.

(or the Poses). Patanjali developed his yogic framework as a blueprint for comprehensive wellness of the body and mind. The Ashtanga system is a set of practices designed to anchor and center us as we pursue various responsibilities and opportunities in life. The eight limbs of this system are Yamas (restraints), Niyamas (rules for personal observances), Asanas (physical poses), Pranayama (breath control), Pratyahara (control of the senses to increase internal awareness), Dharana (mind control), Dhyana (meditation), and Samadhi (disengaging through stillness). While most yoga studios focus on Asanas and perhaps on Pranayama and Dhyana, Patanjali recommends a series of sequential steps, so we are ready and prepared for each of these stages and thus for our life's journey.

The word *Yama* is often loosely translated as the set of behaviors to avoid and *Niyamas* as a set of habits or rules to adopt for healthy living. Yamas are typically associated with specific restraints such as avoidance of violence in thought, word, or deed, falsehood, excessive consumption, etc., and their relevance is largely believed to be timeless and enduring. In other words, the recognition that there will always be certain behaviors that we should avoid is what is paramount. While Yamas typically focus on our interactions with others, Niyamas take us inward and focus us more on personal rules and habits such as cleanliness, contentment, discipline, humility, and self-awareness.

According to Patanjali, our success on the mat comes from our attitude and observances off the mat. For example, Asanas, or the practice of yogic poses such as the Downward Dog or the Tree, require mastery of restraint and reflection to be truly beneficial. Similarly, we can more efficiently harness and direct breath and sensory control when the practice of Asanas precedes them. While our hectic lives often limit our practice to Asanas and Pranayama, optimum use of all eight foundational elements can be valuable for our long-term success in life. Also, while many schools of thought tell us that there is no wrong way to meditate and urge us to plunge right in, Patanjali urges preparation through Pratyahara and Dharana. These refer to our ability to control and temper our senses and the mind. The essence of yoga therefore lies in the cultivation of unity of purpose, awareness, and daily living through this hierarchy of practices.

The domain of Projects is the second interesting addition to our list. We all pursue several "projects" in life. This is a hallmark of the human condition. One distinguishing feature between the various kinds of projects is the nature of the customer. We take up many projects for our personal benefit where we are the intended customer. There are other projects that we embark on to help a family member. These can be long projects such as the years we spend in childrearing or a short project such as when we pitch in to help an ailing family member or help them relocate. Similarly, we take on projects to help our friends or pitch in for a food drive or a Habitat for Humanity project to help our community. Many lives are defined by the types of projects people invest in and are enriched by the networks of people they touch. Some also take up projects simply for the well-being of the planet or perhaps the flora and fauna that contribute to ecological balance. People may also invest in educational projects or other undertakings that only produce benefits for future generations. Yet others pursue careers that are projects with a distant and abstract customer or set of customers.

Projects represents a great domain that lends meaning to the process of enculturation and education itself. It brings awareness to how, while we enjoy the fruits of liberty and pursue our unique interests and passions, we also invest in our communities and our future. This domain brings the much-needed purpose to our life's work. This domain, however, should not be confused with Project Based Learning (PBL).[3] While PBL typically has associated curricular objectives in STEM or languages, our emphasis in Projects is more on developing the ability to judiciously apply and leverage the skills and knowledge that children already possess.

The lesson plans for the different continuums in each of the subdomains need to meet the specific curricular objectives of the relevant unit as well as the associated foundational competencies. These objectives range from the more traditional run-of-the-mill curricular goals to those that are very novel. For example, we may want children to understand the multiplication of fractions, the concept of energy conservation, or Newton's laws of motion. Then there are those that challenge the learners to uncover potential falsehoods in a historical narrative or resolve ethical conflicts in situations where there is no clear right answer.

There are also creativity exercises that impose an increasing number of constraints commensurate with the learner's proficiency. An excellent illustration of a practice that combines exceptional intellectual prowess and creativity is the ancient art form from south India called Avadhaanam.[4] Avadhaanam showcases an artist's extraordinary abilities to multitask using skills of both memory and creativity. The performer, referred to as the "avadhaani," is presented by a panel with various simultaneous tasks and constraints: from composing *ex tempore* poetry that uses specific themes, meters, or words; to answering philosophical questions in multiple languages; to solving complex mathematical problems. The avadhaani is also expected to engage with the audience in a continuous dialogue at the same time. It requires great mental agility and decades of practice to excel in this exhibition of knowledge and improvisation. Avadhaanam would be an excellent pursuit for promoting students' neural development.

The foundational pillar requires that we add competencies as additional goals of these units. In many cases, this modification also ends up strengthening the mastery of the traditional objectives. However, in some cases (depending both on the child and the objectives), we may have to prioritize between the development of competencies and the mastery of the traditional skills.

We prioritize traditional objectives (and likely also the direct-teach approach) when the objectives are relatively fundamental in nature and their mastery relies on muscle memory. Some examples of cases where traditional objectives should be pursued through a direct-teach approach are handwriting skills, understanding basic conventions and definitions (such as what numbers represent), the ability to play a musical instrument, basic ethics and behavior (especially for younger children), and new skills such as those required for sports, yoga, or meditation.

There are many situations in which exploration and experimentation are more valuable. These include acquiring an understanding of how something works, experimentation to rule out hypotheses, and so on. Exploration of mathematical concepts, scientific understanding, evaluation of social structures, and artistic endeavors are examples of areas that are more amenable to use as vehicles for the development of competencies. In these cases, the competencies should be at least as important as the academic goals. With this in mind, we can target specific competencies and associated teaching strategies either directly through dedicated new units or through modifications to traditional lesson plans.

Identification of the different phases in the learning process is another important dimension of the foundational pillar. We considered the phases of nourishment (physical, emotional, and mental readiness of a child), domain selection, problem selection, purpose clarification, sankalpa setting, exploration, validation, reflection, and feedback for each of the units. Table 10.2 features a simple illustration of some of the teaching and learning models and strategies we identified for these different phases. While all strategies will likely have some individualization, some will have a higher degree of individualization (highlighted in gray) than others.

Phase	#	Strategy	Examples/ Comments	Curiosity	Cognition	Empathy	Ambition	Creativity	Communication
Nourishment	TSN1	Pursue the objectives in the physical and socioemotional health domains	Such as exercise, meditation, yoga, sleep, nutrition, stress, wellness, downtime, etc.	X	X	X	X	X	X
Domain	TSD1	Pick one or more of the domains		X	X	X	X	X	X
	TSD2	Pick problems from current learning edges, recently discovered concepts and objectives that were mastered a long time ago, with most of the focus on the learning edges	Don't always stay only at learning edges; periodically and randomly go back to both prior topics and intersections of prior topics and multiple domains so children are constantly challenged	X	X	X	X	X	X
	TSD3	Periodically provide multidomain problems		X	X	X	X	X	X
	TSD4	Only offer a unit to learners who have met prerequisites	Learner should have enough mastery of the prerequisites of any curriculum presented	X	X	X	X	X	X
Problem	TSPr1	Begin every lesson with a question, problem, or activity that promotes curiosity or cognition		X	X		X		
	TSPr2	Reinforce general school- and classroom-level expectations (as needed) in addition to any lesson-specific expectations		X	X	X	X	X	X
	TSPr4	Content of each continuum should meet the goals and aspirations of equity (i.e., reflective of diversity, especially of the minority or majority groups that are not receiving their due representation)		X	X	X	X	X	X
	TSPr6	Expose learners to a diverse set of new experiences	Handlooms, hypnotism, welding, lasers, origami, martial arts, ...	X	X	X	X	X	
	TSPr8	Create opportunities for unstructured downtime with access to books, tinkering materials, art supplies, etc.		X	X			X	
	TSPr11	Ensure that learning goal is sufficiently tedious per the resilience of the learner					X		
	TSPr12	Ensure that learning goal is sufficiently complex per the resilience of the learner			X		X		
	TSPr14	Ask learners to meet a list of constraints as they choose from multiple solutions to a problem	Use only eight lines to draw, etc.					X	
	TSPr17	Ask learners to identify the pattern(s) or rule(s) in scenarios or examples			X	X			
	TSPr19	Ask learners to anticipate or forecast the evolution of a state (a scenario, a chemical reaction, etc.)		X	X	X		X	
	TSPr21	Provide a problem with missing information	The info should be inferred, estimated, or assumed (assumptions, estimates, etc., should be listed)	X	X			X	
	TSPr22	Ask learners to find errors and/or inconsistencies in a body of work or experience		X	X	X	X		
	TSPr26	Provide opportunities for a learner to delay their gratification	Identify what each child craves and develop individualized plans for how they can develop delayed gratification				X		

Phase	#	Strategy	Examples/ Comments	Curiosity	Cognition	Empathy	Ambition	Creativity	Communication
Purpose	TSPu1	Survey student interests and justifications		X	X	X			X
	TSPu3	Test learners' interest and potential for engagement after the introductory problem	The right time to introduce a topic: will the child(ren) be able to generate at least 70% of the possible questions on the topic	X	X				X
	TSPu4	Ask learners to create or identify experiences that contain a given pattern	Describe an example of privilege and challenge learners to find more examples			X			
	TSPu5	Ask learners to generate a list of all possible questions they can think of		X				X	X
	TSPu8	Ask learners to explore and explain why, when, and how the problem is not realistic or important		X	X				X
Sankalpa	TSS1	Ask learners to reflect on related past learning			X	X			
	TSS2	Ask learners to prioritize past learning based on relevance			X		X		
	TSS3	Ask learners to create a sankalpa (intentions with heart and mind)	So the reflections are more actionable			X	X		X
Exploration	TSE2	Ask learners to generate a comprehensive list of all items that have a first-order relationship to a specified item	List everything related to a "learner" (sources: where we learn from; content: what we may learn; time: when might we learn; methods: how might we learn, etc.)					X	
	TSE5	Ask learners to identify the elements of a problem that have the least impact on a desired solution	Superfluous information in a math problem; science experiments with misleading cause and effect; superfluous or conflicting statements in a persuasive article	X	X	X			X
	TSE6	Ask learners to make the least number of changes to a problem so they can change an unknown problem into a known problem			X		X		
	TSE9	Ask learners to estimate using relevant, justifiable criteria		X	X	X			X
	TSE10	Ask learners to rank-order items based on their likelihood (of occurrence, acceptance, survival, etc.)	The problem or activity should have items that vary in their likelihood of occurrence, acceptance, survival, etc.		X	X			
	TSE12	Ask learners to make an initial guess and then evaluate changes so it matches more of the specified constraints					X	X	
	TSE13	Use Socratic questions and avoid directly answering questions	The teacher should not be the answer key				X		
	TSE17	Ask learner to create or identify experiences that contain a given pattern	Describe what a sense is and ask them to identify more senses			X		X	
	TSE19	Make as much time as possible so the learners can struggle on their own	Make sure that children are not frustrated		X		X		

Phase	#	Strategy	Examples/ Comments	Curiosity	Cognition	Empathy	Ambition	Creativity	Communication
Validation	TSV1	Ask learners to identify possible reasons why their solution is incomplete or inaccurate			X		X		
	TSV2	Ask learners to design a test or an exercise to validate their solution			X		X		
	TSV4	Ask learners to identify elements of the problem that are least understood			X				x
Reflection	TSR1	Ask learners to identify the strategies that helped in solving the problem			X		X		
	TSR5	Ask learners to create a reflection at a later time			X		X		
	TSR8	Review learners' reflections			X				X
	TSR13	Devise memory aid for storage of basic information	Mnemonics		X		X		
	TSR14	Identify opportunities for deliberate practice			X		X		
Feedback	TSF3	Identify factors that are most motivational for the learner					X		
	TSF4	Recognize/validate every learner for something new/original at least once a quarter				X	X		
	TSF5	Create clear, relevant, and actionable modules for parental support in their child's education		X	X	X	X	X	X
	TSF13	Provide learner-specific feedback and follow-through such as opportunities for practice or research		X	X				X
	TSF14	Present opportunities to learn from failures	Build pathways from successes as well as failures		X	X	X	X	
	TSF16	Ask learners to identify others' achievements including their behavior and/or lesson-specific contributions			X	X			
	TSF18	Ask learners to share their learning with others			X				X

Table 10.2. Key Sankalpa Academy teaching and learning strategies.

While this list is a result of learning from numerous studies and field experiences, it would be immensely valuable to also obtain a more direct validation of these strategies through deployment in brick-and-mortar schools. John Hattie's work over the last few decades and his summary through *Visible Learning: The Sequel* is a particularly relevant reference for assessment of these strategies.[5] His learning was powered by a multitude of researchers, who, between them, published 2,100 meta-analyses based on over 130,000 studies and 400 million children. As a statistician, I find this to be a powerful resource for understanding the various drivers of achievement. Of course, we always need to be careful while interpreting results from statistical experiments. There may be interactions between different factors (learning strategies in our context). In other words, sensitivity to one factor may only be appreciable when other factors take on certain ranges of values. The sensitivity to individual factors may also depend on their nominal values—for example, lowering class size may perhaps not show a benefit until the class size is smaller than twelve.

The implementation of a learning strategy in a particular study may also be less than ideal. While interpreting the results of a single study can already be challenging, pooling results from multiple studies can be fraught with even more danger since it is difficult to ensure that conditions are consistent between different studies. Of course, despite these caveats, any measured impact is still valid under the circumstances of the experimental design. The limitations only imply that the sensitivity can be more or less under different conditions.

Hattie has carefully explained, for instance, the possible reasons why his metasynthesis has discounted the significance of factors such as small class sizes, subject-matter knowledge of teachers, grit, and growth mindset. As an example, Hattie suspects that teacher expertise might only matter when deeper thinking is essential in a curriculum. Of course, there could even be questions about the validity of teachers' subject-knowledge assessments in the various studies. It is also possible that subject-matter experts were hired more often by lowering the qualifications for teaching skills.

Hattie has also repeatedly emphasized the larger significance of the big story conveyed by the data rather than the details of individual strategies: the impact of the passion that teachers and students bring to the learning process, the positivity of their mind frames, teachers' understanding of their students' learning, and intentional alignment between teaching and learning pathways. The need to focus on the impact of the teaching strategies and respect for teachers are two very unmistakable takeaways from his work.

While several of the high-level lessons from Hattie's data are not necessarily a revelation, they are unfortunately not as widely appreciated or implemented as they should be. So, his book and his efforts serve a very vital need and have undoubtedly helped countless children. His work has also been instrumental in showcasing the significant impact of some underutilized strategies such as the jigsaw method, teachers' video reviews of lessons, and analysis of cognitive complexity of tasks.

Personally, the exceptional alignment between the high-impact factors in *Visible Learning* and some of the techniques I have identified in this book is gratifying, especially the role of *sankalpa* or intention in building alignment between teaching and learning strategies. Other key elements include passion, big-picture learning, and individualization. Table 10.3 highlights some of them for reference. Incidentally, we should also recognize that the goal of *Visible Learning* is to identify parameters that maximize scholastic achievement, while the goal of this book is to improve long-term individual and group outcomes. This is likely why sleep and exercise have not been identified by Hattie as significant factors, ethics does not feature as a learning goal, and also why emotional intelligence only has an impact factor of 0.5.

#	Visible Learning	Sankalpa Education
1	Collective teacher efficacy	Focus on culture, teacher training, and purpose (e.g., TSPr3, TSPr7)
2	Cognitive complexity and cognitive task analysis	Several (e.g., TSPr12, focus on individualization)
3	Field-independent learners	Emphasis on big-picture learning (e.g., TSD3, TSPr6)
4	Response to intervention	Focus on individualization (e.g., TSF9, TSF12, TSF13)
5	Jigsaw method, reciprocal teaching	TSF18: ask learner to share their learning with others
6	Mnemonics	TSR13: devise memory aid for storage of basic information
7	Conceptual change programs (science)	Strategies such as TSV1, TSV4, TSF14
8	Elaboration and organization	Focus on creativity (e.g., TSE2, TSE12, TSE17, TSR13)

Table 10.3. A high-level comparison between leading Visible Learning impact factors and equivalent strategies from this book.

At the end of the first year of Sankalpa Academy, we created several model lesson plans to illustrate the use of various strategies for the different phases. While a detailed discussion of lesson plans is beyond the scope of this book, illustration of some of the key concepts promoted by the three pillars can be very useful, so this is taken up here through an overview of parts of a few lesson plans.

Our first example was created for prekindergarten children. In this exercise, the children are asked to sound out a resulting word with different possibilities for a missing letter. The purpose is to promote learner participation and engagement. The children also get an opportunity to exercise their phonics.

1. m__t
2. c__t
3. ba__
4. __at

In the second step, they will get to choose from among the popular answers in step 1 to associate with a given picture.

1. m__t 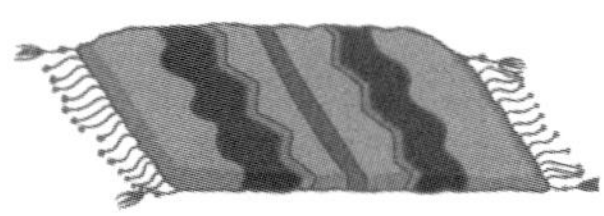
2. c__t 
3. ba__ 
4. __at 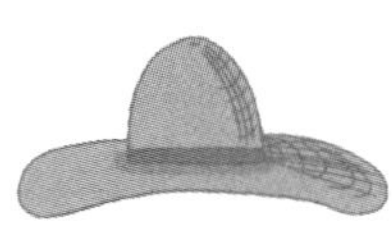

In the third step, the children will get to think about which of the following scenarios are most likely and which of them are least likely and rank-order them based on likelihood. Of course, the purpose is not as much about the right answer as it is to engage their creative thinking skills and sharpen their ability to justify their choice.

1. cat had a bat

2. cat wore a hat

3. cat sat on a mat

We finally provide some images and see if anyone wants to change their answer. We also give the children an opportunity to justify their decisions.

1. cat had a bat

2. cat wore a hat

3. cat sat on a mat

This relatively simple lesson plan embodies the key lessons from the research-based science of reading.[6] It promotes phonemic awareness, develops phonic skills, grows vocabulary and comprehension, and can thus help build comfort and fluency over time. In some scenarios, teachers may also consider adding facial expressions to promote emotional intelligence skills. As you can see, this lesson plan engages a child in problem-solving through the use of multiple skills and domains. The exercise of rank-ordering scenarios can take on subtler aspects over time and also involve many more domains and dimensions. In addition, this example involves the use of the phases of exploration, validation, and reflection. As the tasks become more complex, a planning phase through the sankalpa stage can also be added. This format lends itself to various explorations of implicit biases and hurtful stereotypes as well, thus helping children build richer emotional awareness.

Another interesting lesson plan came from Leanne Paulin, our art and math teacher. This project was offered to children of varying ages at a farmers market near Sankalpa Academy. Paulin is a homeschooling parent, a teacher with the Austin Area Homeschooler's Math Team, a private tutor, and our dear family friend. She was a very gracious collaborator and a key pillar of the community at Sankalpa Academy, as well as a constant source of inspiration and support.

Paulin's art project involved the creation of a suncatcher using translucent paper, scissors, and glue. This exercise involved experiential learning through passion, enthusiasm, and grit on the one hand and motor skills, mirroring, and pride on the other. Paulin shared her reflections with the broader Sankalpa Academy community through a detailed blog. In making origami stars with translucent paper, mirroring manifests first through the reflectional and rotational symmetry of the stars. As the suncatcher takes shape, one piece at a time, joy, surprise, and pride are reflected by the child and mirrored by the teacher and parents. There will likely be additional reflection and pride as the suncatcher is displayed in a special place in the child's home, hopefully in a way that captures its full glory.

Reflection on how the lesson went, including any unanticipated extensions and special interactions, will undoubtedly be of interest to the teacher. At the end of our very first lesson, we learned several things.

First, three-year-olds really love to use paper, glue, and scissors! The activity and result don't matter as much as the tools and the opportunity to exercise their nascent motor skills. And that is itself a lot of joy.

Figure 10.3. The Sankalpa Academy suncatcher lesson at the Mueller Farmers Market.

Second, though precision can enhance the appearance of an origami product, perfection is not the goal, especially for this age group. Mistakes might often be irritating to adults but are indispensable for growth. While it might be tempting to help, it is essential to allow children to own the process. It's more beneficial to offer questions that pave the way to deeper understanding: "What's different and what's the same between the pieces you've just made?," "Which two pieces are the most similar or dissimilar?," "How can you complete your symmetry when you attach that final piece?," or "Do you even prefer to achieve symmetry, or do you like it as it is?"

This brings us to the third point: allowing a child to let their creativity drive the process is far more useful than requiring the child to closely adhere to a given shape. For one girl, her star was a beautiful Christmas flower. She was eager to attach leaves and stems at home. It doesn't matter that Christmas arrived early in July! A boy was inspired to style his suncatcher after the Texas flag. He planned to build extensions on which his flag would be hoisted. His pride was clear, and his work had immediate and immense value to him. And yet another student attached her suncatcher to a string and flew it around as a kite. The pride and joy of these children was unmistakable.

Fourth, like most activities, building a suncatcher facilitates learning in multiple disciplines. Discussions of shapes, patterns, symmetry, and fractions can all contribute to mathematical thinking. Design creativity, problem-solving, communication, and the desire to share are always valuable extensions.

Finally, building multiple pieces and assembling them—and restarting from scratch sometimes—is not easy. Working outdoors in the hot Texas summer in the middle of a busy farmers market is a separate challenge on its own. It takes a lot of time for little hands, but the students' passion for this work was clear from their focus and perseverance. Overall, this lesson was a huge success as it enabled the children to feel empowered, successful, and independent. This experience offered a lot of learning and growth for many of the three-year-olds as well as some of the parents!

Our next two sample lesson plans explore concepts in math. To promote wider engagement, these were designed to minimize reliance on prior knowledge. Interestingly, we found that some of these problems occasionally confused those who were widely perceived to be skilled in math more than those who believed that math was a struggle for them! It seemed like those who were trained more in a set of known methods had a harder time tackling novel out-of-the-box scenarios. The challenges that the filling of a pail can pose for keeping an open mind was an eye-opener for us!

The first of these two multiweek lesson plans explored the concept of spatial measurements, and this was introduced to a group of kindergartners and other young elementary school children in an afterschool club.

Problem 1: Understand how short and long can convey very little meaning by themselves. Explain why shorter and longer are more meaningful.

Activity 1

MY BAMBOO STICK: 

Is my bamboo stick (shown above) SHORT or LONG?

Activity 2

MY BAMBOO STICK: 

THE OTHER BAMBOO STICK: 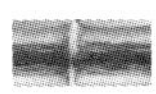

How about now?
Is my bamboo stick SHORT or LONG?

Activity 3

MY BAMBOO STICK: 

THE OTHER BAMBOO STICK: 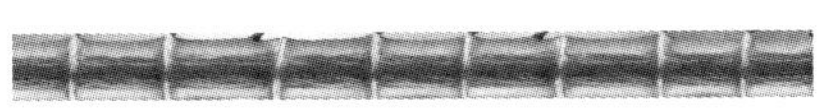

How about now?
Is my bamboo stick SHORT or LONG?

Figure 10.4. Sankalpa Academy children playing in the school's bamboo forest.

Activity 4

When we were clearing the bamboo forest at Sankalpa Academy, we had cut down a large number of bamboo trees. All these bamboo trees were about the same height, but they were too tall to transport. So, we randomly cut them into two pieces each.

ORIGINAL TREE:

Every child received three of these cut bamboo tree parts as shown on the next page. The children were asked to figure out who among their peers had the missing counterparts for each of the three pieces they received.

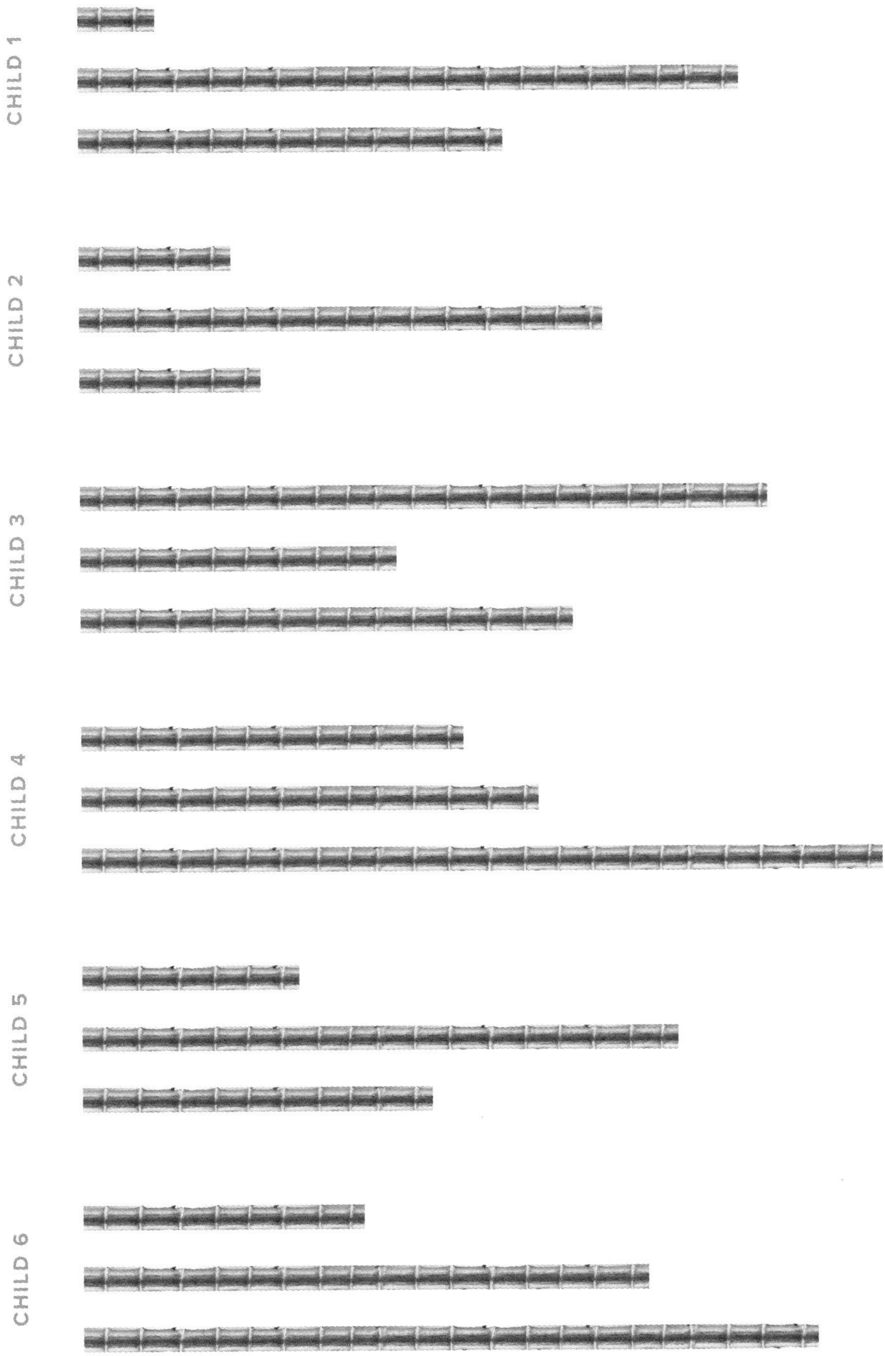
CHILD 1
CHILD 2
CHILD 3
CHILD 4
CHILD 5
CHILD 6

This led to many interesting discussions. Some children began pairing up with every other child to see if any combination of their pieces would result in a length that matched the original bamboo tree length. A few then realized that they could measure the lengths they had using a ruler, subtract them from the original bamboo tree length, and look for classmates who had pieces with the required lengths. One child noticed that the notches were spaced relatively uniformly and that the number of notches could be used as a rough measure for length before more exact measurements were made.

In addition to math skills, this exercise was also designed to promote engagement and collaboration. It helped the children become familiar with the concept of measurement and why measurements are sometimes needed. Based on this understanding, we then graduated to measuring areas.

Activity 5

Areas: We considered several questions: which figure has the larger area? how do we measure area? ... how do we estimate areas of a square, rectangle, triangle, polygon, and circle?

Which has the larger area, the one on the left or the right?

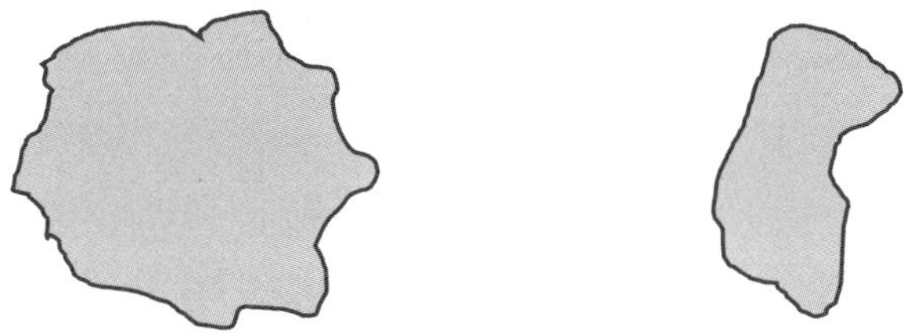

Which has the larger area, the long rectangle or the square?

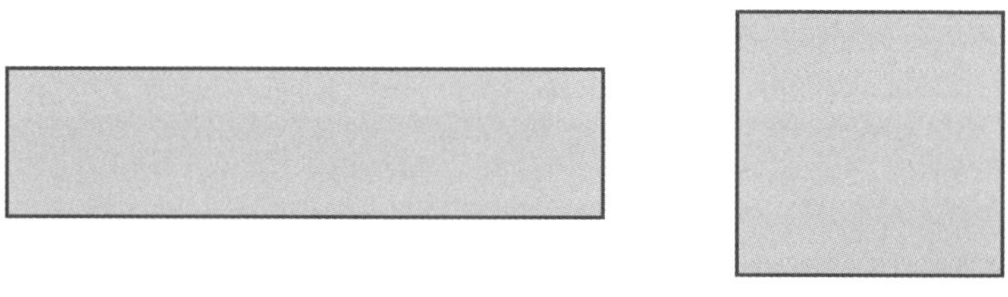

This led to interesting discussions of the concept of area and different ways to measure an area. We then explored the scalability of the area of a rectangle with changes to its length and width. For older students, we explored breaking up a rectangle into different shapes of equal and unequal areas. This naturally led to the topic of finding the area of a triangle, and they were challenged to use their understanding of the areas of rectangles to estimate the areas of triangles.

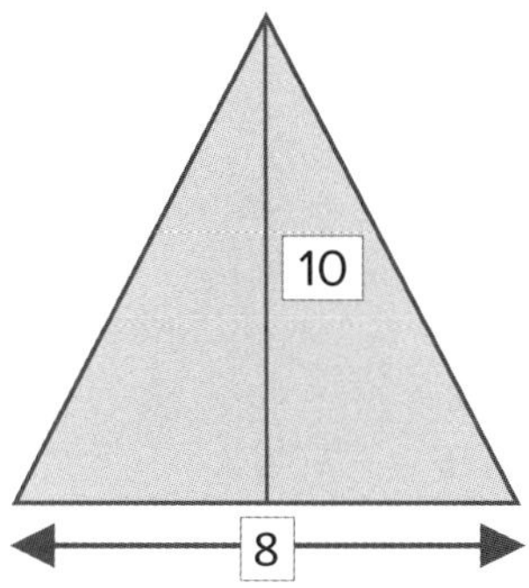

For even older children, this led to a discussion of the areas of polygons that eventually morphed into a discussion of the area of a circle. When infused with enough real-world examples of the areas of different-size pizzas and pizza slices, exploration of the area of a circle can get very interesting. A bit of experimentation will show us that a circle roughly splits the areas between the squares inscribed in it and circumscribed around it. Since these areas are $2 \cdot r2$ and $4 \cdot r2$ respectively, where r is the radius of the circle, we can get an approximate value of ∏ as 3! All of this discussion and experimentation can motivate many children to pursue estimating a more precise value for ∏.

Given that it is impractical to provide representative lesson plans for all the domains and subdomains on our list, two sample lesson plans in math alone may seem excessive. However, there is a particular attraction to math lesson plans. As math and science are two of the most concrete subjects, it should be easier to ensure that they convey immediate meaning and relevance to the learners. Yet, while mathematical discoveries can be a source of great joy and excitement for children, math lesson plans in many schools often don't allow enough time for exploration. In many cases, the rich connections to the real world are also missing.

In this context, it might be interesting to note that the following sample math lesson plan also offers useful extensions into social organization and human progress. This lesson begins with an exploration of the meaning and purpose of symbols.

Activity 1: List three unique symbols.

Activity 2: How many symbols make up the letters in the English alphabet?

Activity 3: Circle the symbol that occurs the most in the list below:

Ƨ 5 Ɛ ¥ o © Ƨ Ɛ © Ɛ 5 Ƨ Ψ Ɛ Ƨ ξ 5 Ψ Ƨ

Activity 4: How many times did that symbol show up?

TWO THREE FOUR FIVE SIX SEVEN

Activity 5: Count how many apples you see below

Activity 6: If you only have ONE symbol ("2"), can you find a way to represent SIXTEEN apples using this symbol? Can you use it to show FIVE apples? In this question and in subsequent questions, we will use English words to indicate the count of an object. We will not use symbols to indicate the count.

Activity 7: Are there any more ways you can use the symbol "2" to show that you have SIXTEEN apples?

Activity 8: Can you use this ONE symbol to show that you have ZERO apples?

Activity 9: Okay, let's now use 0 and 1 to represent ZERO apples and ONE apple. How can we represent ONE HUNDRED apples using these symbols?

Activity 10: If you now have THREE symbols—0, 1, and 2—can you come up with any more ways to show that you have SIXTEEN apples?

Activity 11: How will you show ONE HUNDRED apples using your method?

Activity 12: How will you show SIXTEEN + SIXTEEN = THIRTY TWO using your method?

Activity 13: How will you show THIRTY TWO – FIFTEEN = SEVENTEEN using your method?

Activity 14: What are the advantages and challenges of your method?

Activity 15: If you have TEN symbols—0, 1, 2, 3, 4, 5, 6, 7, 8, 9—what are all the different ways you can show that you have SIXTEEN apples?

Activity 16: Is this method any different from the method you proposed when you had only THREE symbols? How?

Activity 17: How can you now show SIXTEEN using only FOUR symbols: 0, 1, 2, and 3?

Activity 18: How many unique counts can be represented by FOUR symbols if you are only allowed to use up to THREE of them at a time? What if the same symbol can be used more than once? What if no symbol can be used more than once?

This is an interesting discussion that can lead to the role of binary and ternary numbers, their use in computing, the role of fuzzy logic, and their physical realization using semiconductors. This understanding also provides the building blocks for pattern recognition and audio and video definition, transmission, and reception.

Our last model lesson is focused on emotional development, and it can target many objectives. Lessons on emotional development can help us explore the gap between perception and reality, develop the ability to recognize when an apology is needed, and build deeper awareness of our needs and the needs and expectations of others. We also need vigilance to ensure that we don't close our minds and get into a fixed mindset as we take in new information and build new skills. For instance, we designed a field trip planner to balance and diversify the goals for our field experiences and thus help with broadening students' minds. In a similar vein, the following lesson plan can help children build greater awareness by developing their ability to relate to those from other cultures.

In this lesson, we first get an estimate of the populations of the ten most populous countries. We then write down the names of the different countries on slips of paper and create copies of them such that the number of copies is proportional to their respective population sizes. These slips of paper are then folded and randomly mixed in a jar. Each child will get to pick one of the folded paper slips. The children will try to experience aspects of the culture of this randomly selected country on a chosen day the following week. With the guidance of a mentor, they will embrace the clothing, food, and any other belief systems or cultural elements they are comfortable with. This lesson can also be repeated a few times during the academic year, especially for older kids. In addition to broadening awareness and understanding, this exercise will help promote tolerance, humility, and delayed gratification. Teachers can also create extensions by replacing, for example, the different cultures with different professions for older children. With the help of guides, children can use this project to get an immersive experience in a variety of careers.

While programs and curriculum can be updated to provide a more holistic and individualized experience, the changes needed to truly provide foundational growth also require changes to curricular assessments. This is perhaps the hardest part of the transformation. Many schools do pursue programs that hope to foster emotional intelligence and some even provide a curriculum. There are also schools that claim to promote resilience in their students. However, unfortunately, most of these provide general education of the concepts and not context-based training of their growth muscles. As Hattie has observed, "Programs to enhance growth mindset have very low effects partly because the programs fail to appreciate the importance of the optimal conditions to observe and enhance growth thinking; too often, these programs involved generalized training in 'I can' or 'not yet' catch-cries, which have limited effects in situations of not knowing, and they are not specific to the conditions when growth mindsets are most needed."[7] We have also seen this earlier in Lee Robins's study showing how context was a bigger teacher than education on goals and attitudes.

In most cases, if there are any assessments at all, the assessments focus only on the students' grasp of the concepts and not on their personal development, growth, and embodiment. There is very limited utility in a curriculum that cannot document the growth of a child's competencies. Toward this end, we started preliminary work at Sankalpa Academy on the creation of a framework called Blossoms. Its intent was to use relative measurements of the six competencies to arrive at balanced recommendations for a child's individualized learning plan (ILP). While these assessments have the look and feel of IQ tests, there are some singular differences. For the most part, the assessments are initially based on self-reports and inputs from parents and educators. The inputs from educators are collected in real time during everyday observations in the classroom and outside. We envisioned that the development of a database of age-referenced information over time would help provide a larger pool of normative data. This age-referenced information should ideally be as culture blind as possible. Preliminary observations can be used to identify the best-developed competencies, growth opportunities, and program recommendations.

Also, as discussed in parts I and II, one of the key ongoing issues with education is its disengagement from big-picture understanding and its preoccupation with minutiae. One of the most effective ways of countering this would be through the addition of separate assessments for big-picture understanding. For instance, in addition to demonstrating some degree of proficiency in a set of subjects, all students graduating from high school could also be required to be exceptionally fluent in a minimum set of big-picture concepts in a broader set of subjects. In fact, we should also assess the growth in students' passion, curiosity, and engagement in every class, and this should be a significant part of a teacher's performance record. This will go a long way toward improving overall social engagement and life outcomes.

This review of aspects of sample lesson plans as well as our discussion of their framework illustrate how we have reimagined and, in some cases, repurposed curricular objectives and teaching strategies. The goal has been to better support the development of foundational competencies for all-round development of the whole child. This is of course only a start; a lot more investment is needed to flesh out these concepts in greater detail.

CHAPTER SUMMARY

- Curricular content should be carefully curated to maximize the holistic and foundational growth of the learners. For example, new learning domains such as Culture and Projects were added to the Sankalpa Academy curriculum to promote a more seamless integration of academic learning with real-world experiences and deepen the engagement of the children through purpose and passion for their life's work.
- Patanjali's Ashtanga yoga system is a useful model to consider for building physical and mental health. It is one of the oldest disciplines that facilitates the holistic development of individuals. It promotes unity of purpose, awareness, and daily living through a hierarchy of eight practices.

- In most cases, we can integrate specific competencies and associated teaching strategies alongside traditional academic skills through modifications of existing lesson plans. Many of these strategies can also be tailored to individual learner needs.
- The values and practices that nurture and promote holistic and foundational growth should ideally permeate all aspects of our children's lives. This will lend more authenticity to the curricular efforts in a classroom and help build stronger roots and a deeper belief system.
- Further, breaking down the learning process into phases can promote awareness and metacognition. For example, we would need to separately design and evaluate nourishment (physical, emotional, and mental readiness of a child), domain selection, problem selection, purpose clarification, sankalpa (intention) setting, exploration, validation, and reflection for most of the units.
- Finally, there is a great need for the development of assessments to identify the best-developed competencies, growth opportunities, and program recommendations.

IV

Keeping the Faith

Strength Requires Numbers

Education is the point at which we decide whether
we love the world enough to assume responsibility for it.
—HANNAH ARENDT

Mpu Tantular, a renowned fourteenth-century poet of the old Javanese literature, says in his poem "Kakawin Sutasoma" that the truths of Buddha and Shiva are different and yet they are one in their essence if we look deeply.[1] *Bhinneka Tunggal Ika* (unity in diversity) has been co-opted as the official motto of Indonesia, and for good reason. With the large variety in its races, ethnicities, cultures, religions, and languages, Indonesia was wise to seek unity in its diversity. *E pluribus unum* ("Out of many, one"), the motto of the United States, rose out of similar considerations. Leaders of many nations and cultures have long recognized the strength that we can achieve through unity of purpose. We face enough daunting crises that we can scarcely afford to not leverage all the human ingenuity we can summon. In fact, many of the problems confronting us are a result of a lack of consensus on big-picture issues and challenges. The odds of achieving lasting progress improve greatly when we build a broader coalition around a deeper understanding of our time and place in the world.

There are also practical issues. Lack of equity is very likely to lead to significant political instability and social unrest. In our increasingly connected world, even pockets of local unrest can, under the right conditions, rapidly lead to unanticipated global ramifications. Separately, a lack of empowerment, as we have discussed, can lead to a growing sense of despondency and hopelessness and a rise in depression and suicide rates. The impact of these problems on social well-being and healthcare costs can be profound. There is often a vested interest from those benefiting from positions of power to expand their leverage or to at least perpetuate the status quo. This is typically why societies tend to exacerbate inequities over time. A groundbreaking report based on a thirty-year study found that the more unequal a society is, the more likely it is to face grave challenges such as poor health outcomes, obesity, mental illness, depression, loss of empathy, violence, drugs, and large prison populations.[2]

We therefore address concerns related to equity and scale, arguably the most consequential among all the challenges facing K-12 education, in the final part of this book. Educational inequity has been one of the most intractable problems plaguing human society. Therefore, none of us should be under the illusion that this problem has a simple solution. It is also not unreasonable to be skeptical about the prospects of ensuring that an optimal education is available to all children regardless of their circumstances. At the same time, we cannot afford to ignore this elephant in the room. We can't achieve lasting progress until we can secure significantly greater access to a meaningful education. To succeed in this critical mission, we must confront several longstanding challenges and find innovative solutions.

For meaningful progress, more of us need to first acknowledge the significance of early childhood education. Unfortunately, even in the twenty-first century, there isn't widespread recognition of this need. It is also tragic that a great number of people cannot prioritize their children's education without substantial financial assistance. Unfortunately, not enough of us are aware of the true magnitude of this crisis. For this reason, chapter 11 provides a short overview of the various ways that access to basic education is restricted. It explores the scale of this problem, some root causes, and a few possible solutions. Chapter 12 looks at the large disparity in the quality of education children receive. While access to education is a big part of the battle, we cannot claim any sort of victory until education is meaningful enough to truly develop children's individual gifts and add to our collective strength. This chapter considers some strategies for providing the best education we can within available—often meager—financial constraints. Finally, lasting progress is only possible when there is broad community buy-in. The book's concluding chapter—chapter 13—therefore looks at the role communities can play in prioritizing equity in educational quality and access. We can move the needle forward significantly only if many more of us pitch in and commit to being a part of the solution.

11

Opportunity Costs

All that is valuable in human society depends upon the opportunity for development accorded the individual.

—ALBERT EINSTEIN

The second United Nations Millennium Development Goal sought to achieve universal primary education by 2015. The hope was that by 2015 "children everywhere, boys and girls alike will be able to complete a full course of primary schooling."[1] As of 2010, there were more than 60 million primary school–age children around the world, most of them in sub-Saharan Africa and Asia, who were not in school.[2] In 2019, this number still remained stubbornly high at 58 million.[3]

To be clear, we cannot assume that we will achieve universal primary education if we get all primary-age children to a school. The World Bank, in coordination with the UNESCO Institute for Statistics, has determined, for instance, that, as of 2019, 53 percent of all children in low- and middle-income countries could not even read by age ten.[4] Therefore, in addition to enrollment, we also need to ensure that children are able to meet basic literacy and numeracy goals.

There are many reasons for this unfortunate state of affairs. While financial hardship is one of the most pervasive barriers to quality education, many children must also contend with numerous other cultural, geographic, religious, and political hurdles. Ensuring that basic K–12 education is accessible to all families is a steep challenge for many nations. This is truly tragic since education is the cheapest ticket out of poverty and hardship for many low-income families. In fact, studies have demonstrated time and again the strong correlation between an individual's wages and his or her highest level of education.[5] There are of course numerous other tangible and intangible benefits related to empowerment and equity beyond wages that come with higher education. Primary education is therefore only a beginning; it is essential that we also redouble ongoing efforts to improve access to higher education for low-income families.

Grants from national governments, international bodies, and philanthropic individuals and organizations continue to fund or heavily subsidize primary education in many parts of the developing world. It is inconceivable that there can be a solution to this crisis without significant financial assistance from developed nations. Sadly, one estimate suggests that available grants and other pledged donor support only address 15 percent of the need.[6] According to this estimate, there is a $16.2 billion gap between available domestic resources and the amount needed to reach the goals for basic education in the low-income countries. By working with over ninety countries, Global Partnership for Education has raised over $11.2 billion as of 2022 to help address this shortfall.[7] But given the large benefit that an educated population offers to society and the severity of the need, educational investments should, in principle, be financially attractive to philanthropists as well as individual investors and other financial entities. Microloans from small investors and cooperative banks, for instance, can potentially play a large role in meeting this need. If we can come together to address the risks posed by corruption and social and political uncertainty, it is not unreasonable to expect that investments in education would greatly increase.

Given that education can transform lives and communities across multiple generations, it is quite unfortunate that paying for it is such a challenge. A large part of the difficulty stems from the fact that benefits are only realized decades after services are rendered. To arrive at an enduring solution to this problem, we need to address this structural issue. As we discussed in earlier chapters, education should give children a clearer purpose and a stronger emotional engagement. Education is essentially a bequest that every generation receives from prior generations. Acknowledging this gift and paying it forward should be recognized as a key curricular objective. At the same time, we should also redouble our efforts to control costs without sacrificing the quality of education.

Sadly, funding alone will not address this issue since a disproportionately large share of all funds find their way to the wealthiest families as they make up the largest fraction of those at the highest educational levels.[8] It is tragic that as of 2019, 44 percent of girls and 34 percent of boys from the poorest quintile never attended school or dropped out during primary education.[9]

Separately, there is an entrenched urban-rural divide in many countries that is fueled by disparities in economic opportunities and access. In China, for example, due to financial costs and low awareness, while over 70 percent of the urban students are admitted to a college, less than 5 percent of rural students are able to enroll.[10] Similarly, according to the PSLM (Pakistan Social and Living Standards Measurement) Survey in 2019–2020, only 53 percent of the students between ages five and sixteen attend primary school in rural Balochistan in Pakistan.[11]

Educational inequity is not limited to low-income or developing countries. While budgetary constraints have led to many tough choices and limitations on the overall quality of K–12 education even in developed countries, they have had a more punishing impact on the prospects of children from low-income families. Postal zip codes, for example, overwhelmingly determine the quality of local public schools and thus the outcomes for most US children. Schools in areas with higher median incomes typically recruit higher-quality teachers, boast better facilities, provide a richer variety of extracurricular activities, and thus offer more vibrant and enriching environments. This lack of access to high-quality educational opportunities in underserved communities perpetuates longstanding inequities and thus feeds the vicious cycle of poverty, especially in families with lower levels of parent education and income and a dearth of role models.

In addition to financial constraints, a variety of other challenges continue to limit access to high-quality K–12 education. Exposure to cultural diversity is a key educational imperative, especially for social cohesion. Yet, as a 2010 dispute reminds us, meeting this imperative can be challenging. Tens of thousands of people took to the streets in Israel in June 2010 to protest their Supreme Court decision that required integration of its girls' religious school.[12] Parents of European descent, or Ashkenazi, at the girls' school in the West Bank settlement of Emmanuel did not want their children forced to study with Sephardic girls or those of Middle Eastern and North African descent. They argued that the Sephardic girls were not religious enough.

It is true that significant progress has been made in China, India, and some of the other Asian countries over the last few decades on the issue of gender parity. However, globally, too many girls still don't have access to a decent education. Around the world, 32.3 million primary school–age girls have not been able to attend a school as of 2018; this is 20 percent more than the corresponding number for boys.[13] Shockingly, 25 million of them live in South Asia or sub-Saharan Africa. According to the 2019–2020 PSLM Survey, while 69 percent of the men are literate in Balochistan, the literacy rate is only 40 percent for women.[14] Additionally, while two in three countries have achieved gender parity in primary education, only one in two countries have been able to reach parity in lower secondary school enrollment, and one in four in upper secondary enrollment.[15] Social, cultural, and religious traditions continue to impose restrictions on girls' education in many countries. There continues to be widespread reliance on young girls for domestic help, especially in rural areas. Too many girls are still married off at a young age and deemed to have moved "into" the families of their in-laws after marriage. They are also often expected to stay home to raise a family, while boys venture out as they are considered the family's breadwinners.

These cultural norms stack the deck heavily against girls. This is largely why only less than half of the girls who complete primary school can also complete secondary school and why the gender gap worsens with increasing poverty. Even in those cases where families want to educate their girls and where finances are not an impediment, the safety of girls on the ride to school and at school is a significant concern in many communities. Low literacy rates among women and the resulting dearth of role models in general and female teachers in particular have also contributed to this vicious cycle. As of 2022, worldwide, two-thirds of the adults without basic literacy skills are women.

Access to female role models is undoubtedly one of the most effective catalysts for increasing the enrollment of girls. In addition, the involvement of women in the education of their children—boys and girls—can be used to help boost women's and girls' awareness, literacy, and self-esteem. There is a lot that we can learn from the many thoughtful programs worldwide. For instance, in Bangladesh, as of 2019, the Bangladesh Rural Advancement Committee or BRAC has established over 35,957 primary schools and enrolled about 14 million children.[16] Interestingly, 55 percent of the children in BRAC schools are girls. Most of their teachers are women and the attendance of women is considered mandatory at their monthly parent-teacher conferences. The pre-primary schools that BRAC operates also help relieve some of the domestic responsibilities of these women and girls.

Employment of women in local community schools in rural Egypt and Baluchistan became possible due to the focus on cutting down travel times for girls.[17] In partnership with the NWFP Directorate of Schools and Literacy and local teachers and parents, UNICEF has created a similar, immensely successful program in the North-Western Frontier Province (NWFP) in Pakistan.[18] The Mobility Support Scheme that they created in 2003 enabled women to travel safely to their schools in this ultraconservative region. This has not only greatly boosted enrollment of female teachers, but it has also led to an increase in girls' enrollment from about 800 to about 14,000. Even though there is a long road ahead to gender equality, customization of educational programs through careful consideration of prevalent social and cultural concerns and contexts has been paying rich dividends in many countries.

While literacy is an important metric for closing the gender gap, progress can be stymied without women empowerment. Empowerment is an important precursor to true independence and self-esteem. And self-esteem should be the primary objective of all education. It should be no surprise then that programs that focus on empowerment and agency often reap immediate and lasting benefits.

There are many opportunities for education to take on a more active role in nurturing our children's self-esteem. For example, it is important to recognize that cultural dissociation greatly dilutes the educational experience for too many children and damages their self-perception. It is difficult for a child to believe that he or she can accomplish anything they set their mind to if the protagonists in an overwhelming majority of the books they read or the movies they watch are not from their culture, race, ethnicity, or sex. In fact, this also places children who are exposed only to protagonists they can identify with at a disadvantage. It can be difficult for them to recognize ways children from other cultures are similar to them, or to accept that children from other backgrounds can also succeed like the leading characters in the books they read. Kathleen Horning at the Cooperative Children's Book Center at the University of Wisconsin–Madison, for instance, found that only 3 percent of children's books in the US are by or about Latinos, even though nearly a quarter of all public school children today are Latino.[19] In fact, Nancy Larrick from the *Saturday Review* had highlighted this very problem as far back as in 1965.[20] Yet very little has changed in all these years, ostensibly due to a lack of adequate market incentive.

Implicit bias is another widespread, pernicious social ill that is afflicting many communities and nations. One study found that African American students in the US are nearly four times as likely to be suspended from school as their Caucasian classmates.[21] More importantly, the study presents evidence of racial bias even among school principals and assistant principals. The researchers found that African American middle school and high school boys were perceived as troublemakers who engaged in more severe transgressions than their white counterparts for exactly the same behavior. This is just the latest in a long string of studies that arrived at similar conclusions. The damage to the self-esteem and long-term life outcomes of the impacted African American, Hispanic, and other minority children is incalculable. This avoidable tragedy is a blot on the conscience of our society.

Children in many societies also face political barriers. We typically associate political barriers to education with totalitarian and closed societies, but there are grave and ominous dangers even in some of the more open and free societies. While we can come across patently biased information in the context of a totalitarian society, the demands of due process in a free society ensure that any such misinformation is far more subtle and consequently more difficult to recognize. As a result, educators and the general population in a free society need to be extra vigilant and better prepared to guard against the misappropriation of education. We should draw a careful distinction between a free and open discussion based on established or known facts and deliberate or unintentional obfuscation of facts based on spurious information. When cultural biases, political views, and religious beliefs manifest themselves through curricular focus and design—whether through recommended texts, required discussions, or test questions—it is not always easy for students to tease out the unfounded parts of the syllabus that masquerade as legitimate education. While we should be vigilant and strive against subversion of our children's education, the best defense against both subtle and gross indoctrination should ultimately come from the inquisitiveness of the students. This is another reason why education should rely less on memorization of facts and focus more on fostering empowerment through competencies such as curiosity.

Geographic distance is yet another common obstacle to quality education, especially in many developing countries. Daniela Vuri found, for example, that school attendance in Ghana and Guatemala correlated inversely with the distance to school, as one might expect, and that children who did not attend school were more often than not either helping out with household chores, or gainfully employed as child labor, or perhaps both.[22] While poor access due to low population density or due to hostile environmental conditions, as in some high-altitude regions, is an understandable and perhaps even an insurmountable challenge, poor proximity to a more suitable school is unfortunately a much more pervasive concern. Given that many countries have large population densities and too few schools with the necessary resources, long travel times prevent many children from receiving high-quality education. Safety is another important consideration for some communities. While the structural safety of the school building is worrisome in some cases, physical safety due to its location in a high-crime neighborhood is a more frequent concern for too many parents. In a more general sense, access to a top-notch school—because of the tuition and/or the cost of living in the neighborhood of such schools—is often impossible for low-income households.

The medium of instruction has also been shown through studies championed by UNESCO and others to be a significant barrier to student enrollment.[23] Children who received instruction in their mother tongue in their primary years were shown to do better at school and, perhaps as a consequence, were less likely to drop out of school. At the same time, transitioning children in a timely manner to a multilingual context would be needed in some cases to ensure that their prospects for higher education are not impaired. Unfortunately, this is often challenging.

Access to materials for homeschooling and distance or online education can help households that have to deal with issues related to safety or location. However, given the typical demographics of families in these circumstances and especially their financial constraints, options such as homeschooling are often not viable. It is therefore necessary to provide additional financial incentives to facilitate education for children in these circumstances. Also, mobile education has been shown to be successful in some communities under similar situations. For example, the Mobile Female Teacher Training Program in Baluchistan[24] and mobile teachers targeting laborers in the Philippines[25] have yielded exceptional outcomes. We have seen time and again that trusting local teachers and children to help themselves can yield more sustainable results. Therefore, organizations should devise outreach programs that can empower these at-risk communities to design their own local solutions.

Finally, the relative immaturity of children and classroom diversity occasionally join forces to create overwhelming obstacles for some students. We hear all too often about classroom hostilities stemming from income disparity, cultural or behavioral distinctions, sexual orientation, or even physical attributes or handicaps. An unwelcome environment is arguably one of the most pervasive challenges confronting many children today. The severity of these obstacles can range from mild inconvenience to physical or psychological bullying or abuse. These issues cannot be downplayed as real-world learning opportunities. Many children are not mature enough to handle these disruptions without some kind of trauma. Classroom hostility can be too distressing for affected children and significantly harm their learning and growth. These issues should be addressed with sensitivity and care. Unfortunately, however, classroom hostility is often hard to prevent or even detect. Some of these threats can be pretty serious, as evidenced by the significant uptick in the number of students committing suicide due to bullying on social media. To foster a sense of belonging, some schools require uniforms. Many have instituted reporting procedures and other intervention mechanisms to minimize or eliminate these incidents. A smaller fraction have put in place successful proactive programs that seek to promote respect and camaraderie. Preemptive, age-appropriate emotional intelligence education is often the best antidote.

Great primary education that can help address many of these issues is often possible even on a shoestring budget. Access to basic materials and a motivated and empowered teaching force can do wonders for the well-being of a community. Given that it is often a great challenge to even get children to the classroom in some cases, it is critical that we don't lose them at school. Classroom experiences should excite learners' imaginations and secure their engagement. For example, the efforts of the 2020 Global Teacher Prize winner, Ranjitsinh Disale—a teacher at a rural school in the western Indian state of Maharashtra—to expand education for girls from tribal communities are a tale of inspiration.[26] Disale is a passionate educator who personified dedication and innovation. He taught himself the local dialect, translated textbooks into this language, and crafted customized lessons and assignments for his students, sharing them using individualized QR codes. Through his earnestness and outreach, he greatly improved the attendance at his school. He tirelessly strived to engage the largely illiterate parents in the education of their children by spending time with them on their farms and in their homes. Disale even chose to share half of his $1 million prize money with the runners-up so the benefit of the award could collectively reach more children.

While lack of access to primary and secondary schooling is worrisome, it is essential to also address the inequities in access to college education, given the strong correlation between an individual's income and his or her highest level of education. Since median incomes have barely kept up with inflation, it is very worrying that between 1963 and 2020, the cost of tuition increased 355 percent after adjusting for inflation.[27] According to the College Board, the average annual tuition and fees at a private nonprofit four-year college in the US were around $39,400 in 2021–2022.[28] Compare this to the average of about $15,621 that most states in the US spent per year for each of their K–12 students.[29] Unfortunately, this is a universal problem. While there are some exceptions such as the private York College in Pennsylvania that charged as little as $11,664 in annual tuition and fees, college costs are typically too high in most countries as college admissions are highly coveted. This demand is driven by the strong positive correlation between employment prospects and college credentials.[30] It is an understatement to say that these costs have had a devastating financial impact on many young graduates and their parents. Many have no option but to enter the labor force right after high school due to the financial constraints of their families.

College costs have been a growing concern over several decades, and many governments have attempted to provide relief. While some have bemoaned the excesses in the fee structure of many colleges,[31] others have appealed for more generous scholarships, student loans, and tax credits.[32] Colleges are also being asked to provide many more health- and counseling-related services than were offered just a decade or two ago, while many states, at the same time, have been cutting public spending.[33] To manage costs and rising administrative responsibilities, faculty, who once typically taught at least three classes per semester, now teach only about three or four per year.[34] Moreover, since demand far exceeds supply, most colleges don't see any incentive to redesign their programs to lower costs or to attract an even larger number of students. Probably no other industry can contemplate turning away as many customers as our universities. Given this economic reality, many colleges naturally focus more on their ranking and on building and consolidating their brand value. They achieve this by attracting and retaining the best faculty they can with generous tenure, salary, and workloads.[35] Some colleges even extend lavish perks to their alumni and trustees. Authors like Archibald and Feldman argue that since good-quality higher education is delivered by highly educated professionals, a large fraction of these high costs is unavoidable in these labor-intensive service industries.[36]

Most discussions of university budgets and faculty scholarship don't delve enough into one critical aspect of the college experience. Despite the magnitude of this investment, there is often little visibility into the composition of most college budgets, and even less so into how college tuition, faculty scholarship, and productivity add value to student competency. This issue has, however, been well investigated. Jeffrey Selingo claims that interpersonal skills, problem-solving ability, effective written and oral communication skills, the ability to work in teams, and critical and analytical thinking are much more important for success in the workplace than the college major itself and that, sadly, many college graduates lack these critical skills.[37] In fact, based on survey responses, transcript data, and results from the Collegiate Learning Assessment of 2,300 undergraduate students at 29 anonymous universities, Richard Arum and Josipa Roksa concluded that 36 percent of college graduates learned next to nothing after four years of college and that a significant percentage of undergraduates had failed to develop the broad-based skills and knowledge they should have mastered.[38] Even though Arum, Roksa, and Selingo note that students are often more interested in their social life and in the employment opportunities secured by their college credentials than in true scholarship, they do blame the universities for much of this crisis.

The sad reality is that colleges also face many obstacles. There are estimates that more than 40 percent of those entering college in the US need at least one remedial course in reading, writing, or math.[39] While remediation rates have come down slightly over the last decade, they are still too high. More importantly, over half of the students enrolled in remediation classes fail to graduate. Despite such poor preparation of incoming students, there is an overwhelming clamor for college degrees and not as much demand for programs offered by trade and vocational schools.[40] Clearly, there is a large mismatch between student preparation, college offerings, and associated costs. If we can secure more visibility into college budgets and the actual return on student investment, we should have enough of the puzzle pieces to make meaningful progress. Parents and employers need tools to better evaluate the true value proposition of a college. This would go a long way in helping stakeholders make more informed decisions and in controlling the runaway costs of higher education. Additionally, it would help shine the spotlight on institutions that add to students' scholarship at an affordable budget. Predictably, the broad availability of student loans and other sources of funding has helped perpetuate some of these institutional weaknesses.[41]

The irony of the predicament facing many college-bound students is clearly brought home by the success of the Barefoot College, an audacious experiment that Professor Sanjit "Bunker" Roy launched in 1972 in the village of Tilonia in Rajasthan, one of the most arid and impoverished states in India.[42] Roy received his formal education from some of the most elite institutions in Delhi, India's capital. He was also the Indian National Squash Champion in 1965, 1967, and 1971. He was well on his way to a lucrative and highly prestigious career in civil or diplomatic service when fate intervened in the form of a profound experience during his first-ever trip to an Indian village in 1965. The widespread suffering that he witnessed left him in great turmoil. He came face to face with extreme starvation, debt, and despair caused by famine in the Indian state of Bihar. Roy decided to abandon his career plans. Instead, he spent his first five years after graduation digging drinking-water wells in villages around the Ajmer district in the state of Rajasthan.

After he was done constructing over five hundred wells, he embarked on a study tour that took him to over one hundred villages. This tour is a great testament to his values, perseverance, and compassion. He was amazed by the wisdom, skills, and resilience of the villagers. He also began to appreciate more deeply the nature of the problems confronting them. He saw that the illiteracy of the village folk shut them out of most of the opportunities for civic engagement. The caste system also stacked the deck heavily against them. These villagers were often easy targets for exploitation. Their illiteracy disqualified them from enrolling in colleges offering vocational training for some of the higher-paying jobs. The few who managed to get some formal education typically left their villages for greener pastures in towns and cities. Many of these villages were therefore dependent on imports and outside experts. Not only was this a great blow to the confidence and self-reliance of the villagers, but many of the imported solutions were also a poor fit for their local needs.

Roy was convinced that someone who could not read and write was not necessarily uneducated. His experiences had given him great faith in the competence and grit of many of these villagers. Determined to empower them for self-sufficiency and sustainability, Roy and his team of cofounders at Barefoot College devised a thoughtful and ambitious program to tackle these entrenched issues. To begin with, Barefoot College emphasized equality, decentralization, and self-reliance. Everyone received only a living wage, with many choosing to work for far less than the prevailing market wage. No one there was paid more than $150 a month, and no one was paid less than half of the highest salary paid by the college. Barefoot College took a unique approach by not recognizing or issuing paper certificates. This helped it overcome one of the most visible barriers to true learning. No one needed a certificate to learn or to teach, but they did need meaningful skills to succeed. Also, their initial experiences suggested that men were much more likely to migrate out to towns and cities after acquiring the necessary skills at the college. The college therefore turned to enrolling more women and grandmothers. These policies ensured that only those who were truly committed to the college's core mission came on board and that the targeted villages were able to truly benefit.[43]

Barefoot College now trains some of the most illiterate and semiliterate villagers from the lowest rung on the social ladder to take on important jobs as solar engineers, water testers, IT workers, masons, artisans, teachers, pathologists, dentists, midwives, accountants, social workers, and more. About a hundred grandmothers from India and about eighty grandmothers from some of the other underdeveloped countries are trained every year so they can help provide solar electricity to their villages. Over 2.5 million people had benefited from the work of more than 3,500 Barefoot solar mamas in 93 countries as of 2022.[44] Barefoot engineers have also built 1,600 rainwater-harvesting structures with a capacity for collecting over 50 billion liters of rainwater per year. This college has clearly exemplified empowerment. In an article for *Time*, Greg Mortenson wrote that the Barefoot philosophy has trained more than three million people for jobs in the modern world, "in buildings so rudimentary they have dirt floors and no chairs" so that poor students feel at home.[45]

Roy's work has been recognized by numerous organizations the world over, including the Schwab Foundation, the Skoll Foundation, and the Sierra Club. He was also identified as one of the fifty environmentalists who could save the planet by *The Guardian* and as one of the hundred most influential people in the world by *Time*.

Figure 11.1. An artist's rendering of a Barefoot College class for solar cell assembly.

The accomplishments of Barefoot College are no doubt remarkable. The college has torn down some of the most deep-rooted barriers in rural India. By stripping education down to its essentials and focusing on access to a few select skills, it offers many valuable lessons to more mainstream institutions. While Roy's strategy for disruption is not easy to scale, it reveals the possibilities of a minimalist education. This should help us assess the true value of some of the discretionary spending in our colleges. It also offers a shining example of what the dedication of an individual and an institution to students' success can achieve. It showcases the many untapped opportunities for a volunteer corps motivated to contribute to purposeful action. Finally, it also illustrates the innate competencies and capabilities of a committed student population. These accomplishments of Barefoot College help us better appreciate what Ray Bradbury meant when he reportedly said, "I spent three days a week for 10 years educating myself in the public library, and it's better than college. People should educate themselves—you can get a complete education for no money. At the end of 10 years, I had read every book in the library, and I'd written a thousand stories."

Beyond issues related to educational access, most obstacles that stand in the way of a child achieving his or her potential stem from a lack of understanding, poor self-esteem, and a sense of insecurity, or a combination thereof. Empowering all sections of society so that many more people can pursue meaningful objectives in life should be a key social priority. As Plato is widely (and incorrectly) reported to have said, "We can easily forgive a child who is afraid of the dark; the real tragedy of life is when men are afraid of the light."[46] We likely have a long road ahead before the lamp of opportunity can be lit for every child in every country.

CHAPTER SUMMARY

- The second United Nations Millennium Development Goal sought to achieve universal primary education by 2015. Unfortunately, as of 2024, we are still a long way from reaching this ambitious goal.

- In 2010, there were more than 60 million primary school–age children around the world who were not in school. This number remained stubbornly high at 58 million in 2019, with 20 percent more unenrolled girls than boys.
- In fact, given the problems with infrastructure, teacher quality, and more, there are grave challenges that cannot be resolved by simply getting all kids to a school. For example, as of 2019, 53 percent of all children in low- and middle-income countries could not even read by age ten.
- Financial hardship is one of the most pervasive barriers to quality education. According to one estimate, there is a $16.2 billion gap between available domestic resources and the amount needed to reach the goals for basic education in low-income countries.
- Educational inequity related to financial challenges is not limited to developing countries. Postal zip codes in the United States overwhelmingly determine the quality of local public schools and thus children's prospects and outcomes.
- In addition, concerns about neighborhood safety, zoning to failing schools, challenges with geographic access, and undercurrents of implicit bias, stereotyping, and bullying have all led to poor educational outcomes for many.
- Given the entrenched issues with educational inequity, all children should be made aware of the magnitude of this problem. Addressing inequity should be a key curricular goal. In fact, those benefiting from high-quality education should also be reminded of their ethical obligation to pay it forward.
- Empowerment of local communities and the broader society, access to role models from underserved communities and underrepresented demographics, and access to books and other media in which a fair number of the protagonists look like the learners are some of the ways we can help create the climate for more equitable learning outcomes.

- There is a great need for periodic dissemination of high-quality data on educational access so that the magnitude of this problem is widely known. It is difficult to marshal meaningful intervention by governments and international organizations without widespread awareness.
- Despite poor student readiness, the demand for college education remains high. College costs continue to skyrocket due to this unabated demand. This has tragic generational implications for those with limited means.
- Greater visibility to the true benefits of the various four-year college programs will likely lower the unreasonable inflation of the value of college education and hopefully also some of the sticker prices.

12

Excellence for Everyone

The mediocre teacher tells. The good teacher explains.
The superior teacher demonstrates. The great teacher inspires.
—WILLIAM ARTHUR WARD

As discussed earlier, alarm bells about the state of education in the US have been ringing for a long time. Reports such as those from the National Assessment of Educational Progress repeatedly find that more than a quarter of US students lack basic math and reading skills and that the performance and engagement of students in low-income urban communities is even worse. On the other hand, we see time and again that profound learning and growth also require that children have agency, are invested in their work, and are inspired by the challenges. The lack of funding and investment in the high-quality educators required for this kind of work is distressing. Empowerment of students is the underlying story behind Maria Montessori's work, the Waldorf movement, and, for that matter, most child-centered schools. Yet, how many of us would go as far as offering gifted education and high expectations to all students, and especially to struggling students in failing schools? Henry (Hank) Levin was just such a pioneer.

Levin, an education economist, first came to prominence in 1966 when he challenged the findings of the *Coleman Report* and the statistical analyses on which they were based.[1] The *Coleman Report*, commissioned by the US Office of Education, sought to identify the determinants of academic achievement.

Levin's passion for improving the educational outcomes of disadvantaged children led to decades of research in the areas of education reform, equity, and efficiency and eventually to the launch of the Accelerated Schools Project for at-risk children in 1986. The idea was that treating at-risk children as gifted and talented students was the best way to engage them and to accelerate their learning. His program was built on students' own strengths and creativity. By immersing them in relevant and meaningful real-world projects, he gave them purpose and agency.

Contrast this with the remedial approaches prevalent in 1986 that focused on tedious repetition and rote memorization, with very little attention paid to imagination and relevance. In fact, even today, many schools offer drills, worksheets, and other "chew and pour" approaches to disadvantaged children, driving them further away from a love of learning. An independent evaluation of the Accelerated Schools found that they produced strong academic results on test scores at relatively low cost.[2] Levin's approach makes great sense when you consider what Maria Montessori achieved with children with "learning disabilities" or what Dr. Laude accomplished at the University of Texas at Austin with incoming college students with low standardized test scores. In 1992, the *New York Times* named Levin one of "nine national leaders in education innovation," and in 2017, the American Educational Research Association presented him with the Distinguished Contributions to Research in Education Award.

As discussed in chapter 3, through a very different path, Joseph Renzulli, educational psychologist and distinguished professor at the University of Connecticut's Neag School of Education, arrived at very similar conclusions to Levin's. While many look at IQ and mental processing speed to determine giftedness, Renzulli proposed a three-ring model that looked at ability, creativity, and task commitment. Based on his model for giftedness and his understanding of child development, Renzulli advocated that schools provide all students with opportunities to develop higher-order thinking skills. He felt that all children can and should pursue more rigorous content. His Schoolwide Enrichment Model, which supports child-led exploration through enrichment clusters, has gained significant popularity over the years.[3]

As might be expected, similar improvements have also been taking place in schools outside the United States. Levin's Accelerated Schools, for instance, have also been established in Hong Kong. It is noteworthy that in Ghana's capital city of Accra, about 80 percent of the children are now enrolled in preschool by age three. Many preschools in Accra are also moving away from rote memorization to a curriculum that values open-ended questions, reasoning, and reflection. Similar fundamental changes are taking place in elementary classrooms across China, only on a much grander scale. For example, the Adream Foundation has built over 2,700 dream centers across China to foster curiosity and creativity in young children. To promote risk-taking, the foundation has explicitly prohibited judgment and criticism at these centers.

In this context, it is crucial to also pay attention to school governance models. Ultimately, any school oversight needs to ensure that educators are empowered and that children's thinking is not conditioned or limited by prevailing political winds. While governments have an obligation to fund at least the K–12 education, it is not in any nation's self-interest to fully control the levers of education. As discussed earlier, freedom of thought in education was a key passion for Jiddu Krishnamurti. Incidentally, frustration with the paranoia and oversight of school administrations in the US reached such a boiling point that forty-six respected educators and policymakers signed onto a declaration some years ago, claiming that the US educational system has too many standards, tests, and budget reductions, resulting in "uncreative, joyless institutions."[4] Enabling teachers to focus more on children's long-term needs than on short-term societal expectations and metrics is, unfortunately, not easy.

Limiting government control should not be understood to imply the end of public schools. Quite the contrary. Privatization of all education is not a desirable solution. High-quality private schools are neither accessible nor affordable for a large majority of the population. Even if good private schools are a viable option, they typically seek students who are either academically ahead or financially well-off. Private schools are often not motivated to seek out those who need their help the most. Imagine the crisis we would be in if health clinics and hospitals only sought the healthiest patients.

Also, as discussed in earlier chapters, it might be more useful if all schools—public as well as private—were able to identify and strengthen individual areas of mastery (with particular focus on big-picture learning) rather than simply rank students in predefined achievement clusters. For instance, University of Florida researcher Jaime Torre-Halscott sought to identify the traits of those most likely to succeed in the International Baccalaureate (IB) program.[5] He looked at intelligence, sex, GPA, teacher prediction of success, parental background, and home environment. Among these variables, only teacher prediction of student success was found to correlate well with actual student performance.

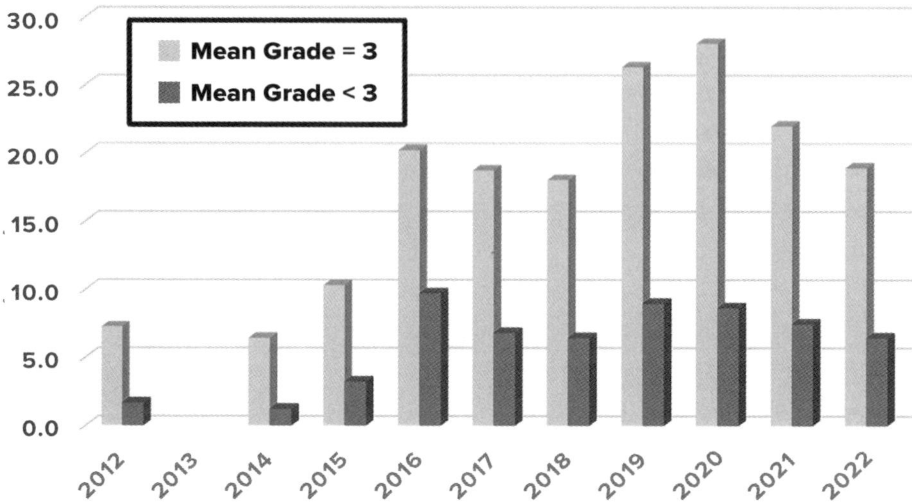

Figure 12.1. Percentage of MYP students in the IB program who achieved a low grade (out of a maximum of 7).

This is an interesting finding that lends credence to the belief that the IB program—like many others—helps those who come in the most prepared the most. Given the stress and anxiety associated with its heavy workload and the emphasis on testing,[6] it is possible that not everyone is able to measure up to the expectations of the program. The statistical bulletins for the Middle Years Programme (MYP) suggest, for example, that about 8 percent of its students have not met the learning requirements to receive the MYP certificate in recent years and that about 22 percent were graded as merely satisfactory.[7]

Also, at the same time, the large body of research on human abilities bolsters the claim that the strategies employed in gifted and talented education are essential for general education as well.[8] Given the decades of research, and a lengthy federal report on improving education for the gifted and talented,[9] it is worth taking a closer look at what gifted education entails.

Most traditional gifted and talented (GT) programs primarily offer enrichment and acceleration to students who do well on a standardized test of cognitive abilities of some kind (IQ scores obtained using a Wechsler test, for example). A small number of schools also offer specialized programs to promote creativity (the QUEST program in the Leander Independent School District in Texas, for instance). These programs use parent or teacher questionnaires, samples of a child's creativity, or normative tests such as the Torrance Test of Creative Thinking to admit students.[10]

While there isn't a universally accepted definition of a gifted student, the *Marland Report* from 1972 offers perhaps the broadest and most complete definition of giftedness.[11] Interestingly, much before Howard Gardner proposed his theory of multiple intelligences,[12] Marland's report recognized students with a high level of functioning in many talents and skills not measurable by an intelligence test also as gifted. According to this report, "Children capable of high performance include those with demonstrated achievement and/or potential ability in any of the following areas, singly or in combination: general intellectual ability, specific academic aptitude, creative or productive thinking, leadership ability, visual and performing arts, or psychomotor ability." And even though the federal report on improving education for the gifted and talented[13] had also recommended that schools broaden the definition of giftedness, there hasn't been the funding necessary to turn these recommendations into a reality. Matthew Mugo Fields, a Harvard-trained educator and entrepreneur and founder of GiftedandTalented.com, goes so far as to assert that the traditional "gifted and talented programs dumb down our students."[14] He wants true gifted education to be the goal for every child and not a gate through which a small percentage enter.

While the *Marland Report* is a significant step forward, it still does not include several of the soft skills and foundational competencies (grit, gratification deferment, and emotional intelligence, for example) that have a significant bearing on life outcomes. These competencies are also typically not the direct or indirect objectives of most school curricula. However, as Jim Stigler had discovered, grit and emotional fortitude are sometimes indirect curricular goals in some cultural contexts (see chapter 8). Gifted education therefore would be most valuable when it is able to also develop the dominant competencies of every child. The benefit would be invaluable to the hundreds of thousands of kids left behind today.

We had previously identified curiosity, cognition, empathy, ambition, creativity, and communication as key competencies. The environment feeds our curiosity and provides the raw material for nurturing the body and mind. Educators therefore often strive to provide a rich set of real-world experiences. Progress also requires an authentic, caring, and empowering relationship between learners and educators. And while exploration and discovery are powerful vehicles for learning, there is also a role for deliberate and thoughtful external scaffolding. It is therefore important to find the right balance between the two. For example, environment can help if it provides optimum scaffolding, as suggested by Vygotsky's model for the "zone of proximal development,"[15] or hurt when it overloads children with a sensory processing disorder.

In earlier chapters, we identified many curricular domains, teaching strategies, and exercises and experiences for developing these competencies. Without this kind of investment, it is difficult to envision how tomorrow's changemakers can be authentic seekers who pursue purposeful and fulfilling lives. Parental input, a child's self-report, and classroom observations can be used, for instance, for understanding the strengths and opportunities presented by a child's environment. The environmental experiences fuel the curiosity a child expresses. This is important since we typically cherish only what we love, we love only what we understand, and we understand only what we experience.

While this vision for a gifted education is rather broad and all encompassing, the reality is that many public schools are struggling to fund even the traditional acceleration-based gifted education that serves no more than 10 percent of the population. We should wonder if it isn't too ambitious then to expect schools to offer a curriculum that includes individualized learning plans (ILPs) for every child and a curriculum that is conversant with the environment and the core competencies of all children. Can we afford to offer all children such a foundational education? Is this only an aspiration or can schools truly deliver on this promise?

We have explored this question in some detail in part III of the book. However, it may be useful to also look briefly at the financials. According to the National Education Association, K–12 education spending averaged $15,621 per child in the 2018–2019 academic year.[16] In other words, with an average class size of twenty-five, we spent about $390,525 per classroom. The average public school teacher's salary for the same period was $61,730 or slightly less than 16 percent of this cost. In other words, a significant fraction of the budget appears to be allocated for auxiliary instructional and support staff, infrastructure, and other fixed costs. While a detailed financial analysis of K–12 spending is beyond the scope of our current discussion, this data does raise hope about the prospects for prioritizing investments in a richer educational offering. Within current or increased budgets, it is critical that we find a way to add additional qualified master educators and to increase allocations to all teachers.

It is not just that most gifted education programs traditionally focus only on children's cognitive skills; it is more that they have been limited to content acceleration and perhaps occasional enrichment. However, while simple content acceleration is cost-effective and may be a good first step in some cases, it does not seek to develop children's full potential. Children gain more foundational skills when presented with gaps in learning that they then must bridge through exploration and risk-taking. Many tools, such as carefully crafted project-based learning and one-on-one Socratic discussions, can be used to gently guide a child, as needed, while the child builds resilience and risk-taking skills. As we have seen from earlier discussions, exploration-based education is not just an aspirational goal; many schools around the world do pursue this with great zeal. The devil is, however, in the details. To support and not frustrate a child, we need to understand each child's needs on an individual basis.

While some schools have been using adaptive software tools to provide an individualized academic experience, these tools, by themselves, often help more with content mastery than with competency development. They are typically unable to focus on a child's curiosity, creativity, empathy, or exploration skills, for instance. A truly gifted education therefore requires significant individualization and access to more innovative technologies and/or qualified master educators. It also requires instruments for competency assessment. It will likely be somewhat expensive to attract the kind of master teachers who can design and deliver these advanced learning experiences. But this is a long-overdue imperative. The good news is that individualization will very likely be cost-effective in the long run as it builds agency and enhances a child's engagement, understanding, and independence.

Authentic and meaningful education entails much more than resilience and risk-taking. With small classrooms, master teachers, and staff such as school psychologists and yoga instructors, it is possible to understand and accelerate the development of a fuller repertoire of children's gifts and core competencies. The ultimate validation of any educational process, however, is in the engagement of the child. We can lead a horse to water, but we cannot force it to drink. Has the child developed the right mindset and love of learning? Is the curriculum too challenging for the child, or is it not challenging enough? Is the child being given enough opportunities for independent investigation, or is he or she being too coddled? Is the child risk-averse or resilient? We have seen from Hattie's work in chapter 10 how these factors have a large impact on a child's achievement.

A curriculum that is empowering, an approach that leverages intentional individualized learning plans, and an environment that is purpose-driven and focused on a growth mindset should provide the best conditions for promoting such engagement. Purposeful achievement and belonging give children a strong sense of joy and pride and strengthen the cycle of further engagement and learning. Finally, understanding each child's engagement through classroom observations and parental input is essential, as it is an important indicator of his or her passion and growth potential.

While these are great aspirations, the reality is that there is an unacceptably large distribution in the quality of instruction at various schools and occasionally even between different classes within a school.[17] It is telling that few educational institutions publish meaningful information on the evolution of their programs or staff, student growth, or parent education. This kind of insight is very hard to come by. The unacceptably large range in the quality of different schools has been an intractable problem. While many agencies offer accreditation services for private schools in the US and elsewhere, participation is often optional. So, the onus is on parents to steer clear of fraudulent fly-by-night educational providers. While pockets of excellence like the International Baccalaureate program, the Advanced Placement program from the College Board, and the accrediting organizations for the Montessori program do exist, these are more of an exception than the rule. Unfortunately, many of the private K–12 schools are not subjected to a rigorous accreditation process. In fact, public schools would also benefit from third-party nonstate accreditation.

In addition to protecting us from schools that peddle low-quality instruction, accreditation has the potential to assist in the professional development of both the teachers and the institutions. A stamp of approval from a reputable accrediting agency can be a significant badge of honor for any school and thus a valuable asset for enrollment and growth. At the same time, the recommendations of an accrediting agency can often intrude on the administrative aspects of a school and potentially impact its financial viability. As a result, it is not unreasonable that there is occasionally some tension between accrediting agencies and the institutions being assessed. Also, some schools, especially smaller ones, can find the cost of accreditation prohibitive. This is a key reason that many schools that claim to adhere to the Montessori principles don't pursue official certification.

It is also worth noting that accrediting agencies often rely on gross metrics such as graduation rates, standardized scores, faculty experience, teacher-student ratios, technology resources, and other student amenities in the assessment of an institution. While these metrics do provide valuable insights, they are often a poor substitute for an in-depth analysis of a school's curricular programs, the teaching ability of the faculty, and their impact on student progress and engagement. It would be valuable for accreditation to focus more on opportunities for improving individual student learning outcomes and institutional strengths and weaknesses. As Will Durant noted, "Quality is not an act, it is a habit."[18]

Accreditation should be more than a simple third-party audit; it ideally should serve as a true force multiplier. There is some legitimate concern, however, as to how accrediting agencies that are supposed to be enforcers of standards can also serve as agents of change. It is therefore quite important to fully understand the metrics being employed by an accrediting agency and their relevance. It is often not easy for any institution to evolve with changing social contexts, especially when its adherence to a specific educational philosophy is being assessed.

Potentially, the mission of accreditation agencies can be quite broad. They should help assess a school's curriculum in light of the latest research on child development, learning, and pedagogy and provide third-party certification of the educational program at a school. They also need to assist schools in their internal assessments and in identification of opportunities for development. This is far more nuanced than approval or rejection of an accreditation application based on cookie-cutter checklists. Adjustments to curricular focus or plans for personnel or resource redeployment, as needed, should obviously be formulated in conjunction with the teaching and administrative staff of a school. It is critical that teachers and schools ultimately maintain complete ownership of a developmental plan since teacher engagement and empowerment are key to student achievement.

There may also be a professional development opportunity here for aspiring teachers and graduates of local universities. In most undergraduate programs today, candidates are assigned to a real classroom for a few weeks so they can gain some practical field experience. While these eight- to twelve-week assignments do help budding teachers gain valuable hands-on experience, they also often end up shaping the outlook of new graduates. These classroom experiences are typically designed to prepare prospective students for real-world challenges. The objective of these internships is usually to learn the ropes and to understand the ground realities in classrooms. It would be more useful if the zeal and passion that the new teachers bring to the table could be tapped to assess and improve the learning environments instead. These experiences should lift the children and teachers to new possibilities and not be viewed as opportunities for the interns to master old ways.

We need to also ponder why many of us have fond recollections of only a few teachers, teachers who may have either ignited our passion for a subject or have simply given us the inspiration to show up at school. If only we had many more such teachers! We clearly cannot achieve universal access to quality education without addressing the questions of teacher quality and school certification. The severe shortage of qualified math and science teachers in the US and across the world, for example, is well known.[19] It is therefore not surprising that a large percentage of elementary and even too many middle school teachers in the US don't have a major or even a minor certification in science.

Additionally, as we discussed, compensation and empowerment have often come up as key impediments to job satisfaction, professional development, and retention of competent teachers. Low standards for teacher certification and inadequate teacher proficiency and engagement on the one hand, and financial hardship, apathy, and ignorance on the part of parents on the other often end up as the leading reasons for some schools' disappointing performance.

While the study of pedagogy and grade-relevant domain knowledge is indispensable, it is much more important to seek out candidates who also have a passion for teaching and its promise. Kane et al. have shown, at least in the limited context of New York City, that teacher performance during their first two years is a more reliable indicator of their long-term effectiveness than their certifications.[20] Rivkin et al. had also found that teachers had a significant impact on student reading and mathematics achievement even though little of the variation in teacher effectiveness was explained by characteristics such as their education or experience.[21] This is of course more an indictment of the certification standards and processes than the necessity of certification. Not everyone who takes up a teaching career may have the necessary disposition and aptitude. Teachers would be more effective in inspiring students if they were themselves burning with passion!

We therefore need to pay attention to teacher compensation, work environment, job satisfaction, and societal attitudes. As long as teaching is not one of the most esteemed professions, it is unlikely that we will attract the necessary number of highly qualified teachers. Teachers and administrators already grapple with numerous challenges. We expect a lot from our teachers—subject-matter proficiency, an understanding of childhood pedagogies, and most importantly, an ability to cater to the emotional needs of two or three dozen kids simultaneously. Further, there can be additional challenges due to low parental involvement and student engagement in schools. Sadly, even when we find some exceptionally qualified teachers, their hands are often tied. They have to contend with large classes, extensive syllabi, a demanding schedule, and numerous administrative responsibilities. To add insult to injury, teachers are often not granted the discretion necessary for their empowerment. Their pace is frequently dictated by their school district!

And the rub is that we also don't want to pay teachers a decent salary. The average annual salary of a US childcare worker was $29,570 in May 2022, which is 5 percent less than that of a parking lot attendant and 13 percent less than that of a janitor.[22] We should count our blessings that we are able to attract as many exceptional teachers as we do, despite this. Studies have found that mathematics and science teachers who either left their profession or moved to other schools often did so for financial reasons.[23] According to the National Center for Education Statistics, the average public teacher salary in 2021 was about 14 percent lower than the average pay of all full-time, year-round workers.[24] Low teacher pay has not been a secret, so it is all the more shocking that the average inflation-adjusted starting teacher salary declined 4 percent between 2012 and 2021.[25] This is the wrong direction. In fact, this is a universal problem that plagues many countries. According to one report, teacher salaries in 2022 were lower than in 2000 in a third of the countries that OECD surveyed.[26]

In most countries, the best students in a graduating class typically flock to business, engineering, or medicine. We need to attract the top third of a graduating class to the teaching profession if we are serious about student achievement.[27] Increasing the qualification criteria and standards is the first step toward this. We need to use salary increases and financial incentives such as bonuses to recognize and reward teacher initiatives and student outcomes. As John F. Kennedy pointed out over half a century ago, “Modern cynics and skeptics ... see no harm in paying those to whom they entrust the minds of their children a smaller wage than is paid to those to whom they entrust the care of their plumbing.”[28] Sadly, so little has changed in all these years.

Often, we hear that teacher pay is higher than what is reported since they can take up other employment over the three summer months. While this is true, teachers will have to spend some of this time pursuing certification for career advancement and preparing for the upcoming academic year. They will also need some downtime, as almost every educator can attest to the stress and burnout teachers experience every day. Further, as in any other profession, job satisfaction and working conditions are also very important factors that affect retention. Positive school environment, parental involvement, strong administrative leadership, and good student engagement can be very helpful in sustaining the enthusiasm and commitment of our teachers. In fact, it is quite likely that passion for teaching and administrative leadership are some of the reasons why teacher retention is not even lower than what it is today. Of course, in the same vein, schools should also have the freedom to let go of teachers who may not be cut out for teaching. It is important that the contracts of the various teachers’ unions encourage such flexibility.

In addition to pay, respect for the teaching profession is a critical ingredient for attracting more of our youth to this honorable profession. Traditionally, teachers were held in great esteem—almost bordering on veneration—in many Eastern societies. In many Indian schools, we often hear the chanting of the following verse:

> Gururbrahmā Gururviṣṇuḥ Gururdevo Maheśvaraḥ.
> Guruḥ Sakṣat Parabr̥ahma Tasmaē Śrī Guruve Namaḥ.[29]
>
> *This poem compares the teacher to the supreme power in the Hindu tradition. In steering us toward wisdom and away from ignorance and misplaced fears, this verse claims that the teacher takes on the roles of a creator, sustainer, or destroyer as necessary.*

There is an urgent need to recreate the glory of this profession and reverse the slide in our expectations.

As we briefly discussed, empowerment is another critical element of job satisfaction. We can't ask more of our teachers and not reward and empower them appropriately.[30] It's unrealistic to expect great results when teachers are expected to comply with an endless litany of rules and regulations. They clearly need to own much more of the curriculum they teach. Remuneration for teachers would likely go up automatically if there were greater empowerment and accountability as well as higher standards for teacher certification. One big reason wages are low though there is a shortage of teachers is that there isn't a uniform, meaningful, and rigorous process for teacher certification.[31] To meet the growing demand for teachers, many school districts in the US have repeatedly chosen to attract more candidates by lowering certification standards.[32]

Wendy Kopp, the founder, and president of Teach for America, has offered an interesting retrospective on how her organization helped close some of the achievement gaps across income levels in *A Chance to Make History: What Works and What Doesn't in Providing an Excellent Education for All.*[33] She showcases inspiring accounts of some of the visionary leaders in its ranks. The passion and faith of these transformational leaders helped create and nurture organizations that pursued educational excellence for all children. Unfortunately, we don't have enough of these leaders who are committed to such an ambitious vision. Not surprisingly, many undergraduate and graduate education programs offer little relief. We need to understand why alternative teacher certification programs often produce many more highly successful teachers than traditional programs.[34]

If we are willing to listen, there are many lessons that we can learn from the experiences of other nations. We can, for instance, look at the systems in countries that have consistently done well on PISA. While the US came in 13th, 38th, and 19th in reading, math, and science respectively in 2018, the top honors have typically gone to Asian countries such as China, Singapore, Hong Kong, Korea, and Japan. There is, however, one Western country that has consistently bucked this trend of Eastern dominance: Finland. In 2018, Finland came in 6th, 16th, and 7th in reading, math, and science respectively and also placed in the top ten in all three subjects some years earlier. So, even if we choose to attribute Asian success to a cultural difference, it's hard to ignore Finland's accomplishments.

It's not difficult to see that Finland's success is not due to the size of the country or its homogeneity. For one thing, Finland's schools weren't always this successful. They were quite mediocre until the early 1970s.[35] Recognizing the significance of education for the modernization of its economy, the Finnish government decided to reduce class sizes, boost teacher pay, and require all teachers to complete a rigorous master's program. As a contrast, we have the example of Norway, their next-door neighbor.[36] Norway has about 4.8 million people as compared to 5.5 million in Finland. Norway has about 10 percent foreign-born residents, while Finland has about 5 percent. So, the demographics of Norway are not much different from those of Finland. Its educational approach, on the other hand, is more like that of the United States. Teachers don't need a master's degree. There is a national system of standardized testing. Classes are large, and access to science laboratories is scarce. Perhaps more interestingly, while decision-making is in the hands of researchers in the fields of education and pedagogy in Finland, politicians are in charge in Norway. Not surprisingly, Norway's placement on the PISA is also very comparable to that of the US. It came in 20th, 28th, and 19th in reading, math, and science in 2018.

It is therefore worth taking a closer look at the investments Finland has made in its children and teachers.[37] Célestin Freinet's recommendations on emotional engagement of the learners have been so influential in Finland that they are still followed religiously today in many schools across the country. Freinet (1896–1966) was a noted French pedagogue and educational reformer and a contemporary of the Swiss psychologist Jean Piaget. He emphasized the importance of authentic, child-driven, and inquiry-based learning.[38] Children in Finland don't start school until they turn seven. Finnish schools don't track or group children by ability. And children are rarely assigned any homework. To ensure that students have a rewarding experience with lab work, science classes in grades seven through nine cannot enroll more than sixteen students. And unlike in other parts of the world, STEM education does not receive exclusive focus in Finland. Students spend a lot of time taking classes in music, painting, cooking, carpentry, metalwork, and textiles. In addition to fostering creativity and collaboration skills, this exposure helps children acquire skills across a broad range of disciplines. Perhaps what is most striking is that there is no standardized testing before the age of sixteen. To get the pulse of the system, only a small, but statistically significant, group of randomly selected students is tested. At age sixteen, some go on to universities to pursue a college education while others seek vocational training.

These policies clearly illustrate the trust that Finland places in its teachers. This should not come as a surprise given its selection process, climate, rewards, and societal esteem for teachers. Teacher education programs in Finland are very selective. Teaching is typically the most admired profession among its high school graduates. It is more difficult to get into a teaching program than it is to get into law or medicine. In one year alone, 2,400 people competed for 120 slots in the fully subsidized master's program for teachers at the University of Helsinki.[39] This stringent admission process naturally confers great prestige on successful applicants. Besides, it is important to note that applicants are assessed not only based on their academic record but also on the basis of their teaching skills and aptitude. Teaching is clearly taken very seriously in Finland. Graduate education for aspiring candidates places a strong emphasis on pedagogical content and is heavily informed by new learning from research.[40] Students must also spend a full year teaching in one of the model schools associated with their university before they can graduate. These model schools are often incubators for research on new teaching methods.[41]

Teachers are compensated well relative to other professions in Finland, but they don't make much more than what teachers in other nations make.[42] While Finnish high school teachers with fifteen years of experience made 2 percent more than what their other fellow university graduates made, they made 35 percent less than their fellow graduates in the United States with comparable experience. It is important to pay careful attention to these statistics. Raw salary data does not fully reflect standard-of-living differences. So, it is more important that teacher pay is high enough relative to other professions within a country. Beyond that, it does not seem to matter.

The more important attraction in Finland appears to be the respect, autonomy, and empowerment that teachers enjoy.[43] Teachers in Finland have complete ownership of their classrooms. They design their own courses and are used to a culture of constant innovation, research, and development. As a result, Finnish teachers are often at the frontiers of curriculum design. Since few other professions can match the joys of teaching, it should not come as a surprise that Finland has an extremely high retention rate for teachers. About 85–90 percent of trained teachers stay in their profession for the duration of their careers.[44] If nations around the world can study the Finnish success story closely and learn the right lessons, there is no reason children everywhere cannot benefit as well.

In other words, there are enough lessons from around the world that show us how excellence in education can easily be within our reach. First and foremost, learning from gifted education needs to be expanded to include more of our competencies beyond cognition and creativity. This makes it ever more essential to invest in a highly qualified and empowered teaching force. Teachers deserve our support and esteem, the necessary tools for growth, and respectable pay. The solutions are not hard to find if we have the courage to seek them.

CHAPTER SUMMARY

- Hank Levin believed that immersing at-risk students in meaningful real-world projects that leverage their creativity and other strengths gives them purpose and agency and accelerates their learning. He considered this a significantly better approach than the joyless monotony of the "chew and pour" remedial programs.
- Similarly, Joseph Renzulli advocated that schools give all students the opportunities needed to develop higher-order thinking skills through enrichment and rigorous content.
- The discussion from earlier in the book shows that gifted education would be most valuable when it is able to nurture the six foundational competencies—curiosity, cognition, empathy, ambition, creativity, and communication—while paying close attention to the strengths and needs of every child.
- We typically cherish only what we love, we love only what we understand, and we understand only what we experience. The learning adventure therefore begins with the experiences we offer a child, as they fuel the curiosity that the child expresses.
- This kind of expert guidance and support is not possible without highly qualified educators. It is therefore distressing that frustration with the paranoia and oversight of school administrations has reached such a boiling point that forty-six respected educators and policymakers signed onto a declaration some years ago that claimed that the large numbers of standards, tests, and budget reductions in the US were resulting in "uncreative, joyless institutions."

- Falling standards for teacher certification, low wages, and poor teacher ability on the one hand and financial hardship, apathy, or poor engagement of our families on the other often end up as the leading reasons for the disappointing performance of some schools even in developed nations such as the United States.
- In most countries, there is also a huge unmet need for transformational leaders who can help create and nurture schools that pursue educational excellence for all children.
- Additionally, many more of our schools can greatly benefit from the services of a competent accreditation agency. There is a strong need for evidence-based, in-depth analyses of schools' curricular programs, teaching ability of faculty, and opportunities for student progress and engagement. While it will no doubt be challenging, accrediting agencies need to simultaneously engage as both enforcers of standards and agents of change.
- We can learn a great deal from countries like Finland, where autonomy, high social regard for the teaching profession, and a culture of constant innovation and research have enabled children to thrive.

13

Gathering the Village

Alone we can do so little; together we can do so much.

—HELEN KELLER

A couple of weeks after the 2020–2021 school year began, Melissa Statz heard children in her fourth-grade class talk about Kenosha.[1] Statz, who was white, had just begun her first year of teaching in Burlington, Wisconsin, her hometown. Violent protests filled the streets after a police officer shot Jacob Blake, a black man, in the back on August 23, 2020, in Kenosha. Burlington, a town of 11,000, is about 89 percent white and around a half-hour drive from Kenosha. The young students in her class seemed to know that something was going on and were very curious.

Statz, the consummate teacher that she was, saw a teachable moment. She decided to lead a discussion on racism using a children's book, an educational video, and a worksheet. Like most kids that age, the children were naturally curious about their place in society and their environment and engaged with a lot of interest. However, as word spread about this lesson, several parents expressed outrage and called her lesson an attempt at indoctrinating the kids. Statz's use of the Black Lives Matter movement in her lesson led people to conclude that she was a liberal who was associated with the Democratic Party. Many on Facebook and other social media sites demanded that the school district discipline Statz. There were heated arguments at a school board meeting in September of that year. Her attempt at introducing a human rights issue to her class led to threats against her, and the school district had a huge controversy on its hands.

This was not an isolated incident. Similar stories played out in multiple communities when schools tried to introduce discussions on racial justice into their curricula after the death of George Floyd at the hands of a white police officer. While a large majority of Americans oppose racism and discrimination, they have also been wary of classroom discussions on equity and justice. An Education Week Research Center survey in June 2020 found that 81 percent of educators support Black Lives Matter and are in favor of including references to it in their antiracism curriculum.[2] At the same time, polls also show that only around 45 to 49 percent of Americans support the Black Lives Matter movement. Discord between school boards and the local communities is not limited to issues surrounding racial justice. Similar fights keep breaking out on issues related to evolution, natural history, mask mandates, books on library shelves, the transgender movement, and more.

Most educational systems are accountable to their local communities. And the majority view in these communities typically dictates the curriculum and tone in many cases. While we may not notice much divergence of thought in homogeneous societies where minority communities are not present in significant numbers, the imbalance in equitable representation in curricular matters is more glaring in majority-minority communities. It can be challenging sometimes to foster the necessary empathy and understanding across this divide in these cases. Education is never really limited to the four walls of a classroom. In fact, the philosopher George Santayana went as far as to say that "A child educated only at school is an uneducated child."[3] It is therefore necessary for classroom discussions to relate to the experiences of children outside the classroom. How can we accomplish this when large segments of our population interpret the same set of facts very differently?

Many African cultures recognize the collective responsibility of a community for its children. Those in the Nigerian Igbo culture are known to name their children "Nwa ora" or children of the village. "Omwana takulila nju emoi" in Lunyoro, "Omwana taba womoi" in Kihaya, and "Enikan lo nbi omo, gbogbo eniyan lonto" in Yoruba are some examples of the popular sentiment in Africa that communities have a significant role in children's upbringing. Incidentally, this sentiment is also seen in many animal groups. Even if communities had no role in defining the curriculum at their local schools, a society that cannot walk together will have a hard time coming together to build a better tomorrow for their children.

In fact, given the realities of the twenty-first century, whether we like it or not, many voices across the global village compete for the attention of children and youth. The internet and the entertainment industry have shrunk the world. Music, video games, popular television shows and other media, and sports leagues have all come to play a large role in children's lives. Overemphasizing parochial content can significantly handicap the next generation of changemakers. In fact, recognition of the influence of the extended community on children's development is at the root of a lot of government regulations governing our social media companies, entertainment options, and more.

On the other hand, even with the best information at hand, it is often not easy to provide an optimum environment for our learners. What children experience is determined by parental education, financial means, and the various barriers discussed in the last two chapters. Not everyone, for instance, can choose to live in an area of the town that provides access to the best schools or community. Unfortunately, too many vulnerable families, even in the US, are compelled to live in neighborhoods with unsafe water or polluted air. Not everyone can afford to pay for the best childcare or the most sought-after enrichment activities. Many may not even understand all the developmental needs of their children. This is why a collective social compact that prioritizes children's well-being is essential. As Nelson Mandela said, "There can be no keener revelation of a society's soul than the way in which it treats its children."[4] While the public school system in the US is based on such a sentiment, unfortunately too many schools are not able to offer an optimal experience.

El Sistema, a publicly financed music education program founded in Venezuela in 1975 as "Social Action for Music" by educator, musician, and social activist José Antonio Abreu, is a good example of a collective effort toward educational equity.[5] In addition to rigorous classical music education and the experience of playing for orchestras, it also provides access to a free instrument. Over many decades, El Sistema has offered real hope, rescuing countless impoverished children from the vicious cycle of drugs and violence. Abreu has literally presided over a revolution in Venezuela. By 2015, El Sistema had enrolled more than 700,000 young musicians at hundreds of centers.[6] International recognition for its orchestras and the success of musicians such as Gustavo Dudamel and Edicson Ruiz have generated worldwide publicity for El Sistema's programs. I would be remiss if I did not point out that El Sistema has also faced more than a fair share of serious controversies.[7] At the same time, the vision and accomplishments of this unique experiment are compelling. Its consistent enrollment of over 100,000 at-risk children in classical music year after year for more than forty years is a remarkable accomplishment by any metric. The fact that El Sistema has had the backing and material support of seven consecutive Venezuelan governments over four long decades, ranging across the political spectrum from center right to far left, speaks volumes.

The resounding success of El Sistema, or the National Network of Youth and Children's Orchestras of Venezuela, should be a wake-up call to all educators, parents, and policymakers. The number of children that this organization has touched over the years is literally in the millions. Each child it has touched is likely a life it has saved. This success could not have been possible if children did not feel empowered by the aesthetics of their music, especially when contrasted with the dangers on their streets.

While Barefoot College and El Sistema are both unique and bold experiments that have empowered thousands of stakeholders, government support has enabled El Sistema to expand its reach much more rapidly. Given the enormity of the challenges, governments around the world need to take similar steps and make universal access to high-quality education a clear priority. While supply and demand can provide one of the most equitable means available to value goods and services, the educational needs of our next generation cannot be constrained by the limitations of the economics of supply and demand. Market forces excel at regulating current commerce but may not always be adept at building capacity for the next decade. It is hard to value a service if its impact is not immediate. This is why governments, on behalf of their people, often seek to influence some kinds of public conduct. Tax regimes, budgetary allocations, and business regulations are all routinely used as instruments for promoting a desirable social outcome.

For instance, governments often choose to create social welfare nets for those below the poverty line or provide tax incentives to seed and jump-start key research priorities. In a similar vein, it is perhaps appropriate to at least waive the tax obligations of our teachers. This is not a big ask to reward those who do so much for the next generation. There are many other ways governments can bring to bear the economies of scale and accelerate the common good. Estate tax or inheritance tax, for example, has been used in the US to minimize the concentration of wealth in a few hands. With the passage of the American Taxpayer Relief Act in 2012, the US Congress has set the individual estate and gift tax exemptions at $5 million (with annual adjustments for inflation) and a maximum tax rate of 40 percent.[8] Estate tax can be an excellent instrument for funding educational opportunities for low-income children. We need to identify more such opportunities so high-quality basic education is accessible to all, not just a fortunate few. For instance, revenue raised through penalties levied for regulatory violations and taxes on industries deemed harmful to society (such as the tobacco industry) can be fully allocated to initiatives that support universal education or those that promote civic engagement.

While government intervention can help us reap the biggest benefits, large foundations and endowments can also play a significant role through both advocacy and financial investments. Foundations such as the Bill and Melinda Gates Foundation, the Ford Foundation, the William and Flora Hewlett Foundation, the Robert Bosch Foundation, the Azim Premji Foundation, and others have a long history of promoting equity in educational access. The United Nations, for instance, has several programs for children living in extreme poverty in many developing parts of the world. There are also many smaller foundations and organizations that are making a huge difference. Dorothy Day Apartments and other low-income housing and childcare provided by Broadway Housing Communities around New York represent one such shining example of an outreach program.[9] There is the Ed Snider Youth Hockey Foundation that uses field hockey as an instrument for improving the educational prospects and communal engagement of at-risk children in select underserved communities in Philadelphia.[10] Similarly, several districts across Illinois are making effective use of antitruancy programs and other tools to help children in difficult circumstances not miss school.[11]

Citizen Schools, an initiative by Eric Schwarz, is a great example of an exceptional role model for poorly performing public schools.[12] Citizen Schools goes to great lengths to level the playing field for students who grow up in low-income households. In addition to helping these students with their academic needs, Citizen Schools ignites their imagination with exciting hands-on projects and exposure to experts and mentors from a wide variety of professions—bike repair experts, filmmakers, journalists, lawyers, engineers, and experts from other STEM professions. It is no wonder then that, with its program of active intervention, Citizen Schools has managed to interest

80 percent of its students in its STEM program for science and engineering careers. For reference, nationally, only about 33 percent of eighth graders across the US say that they are interested in STEM careers.

Regardless of the significance of the external environmental influences, the foremost source of influence on a child is often the home. In the words of Stephen Covey, the American educator and author, "When it comes to developing character strength, inner security, and unique personal and interpersonal talents and skills in a child, no institution can or ever will compare with, or effectively substitute for, the home's potential for positive influence."[13] Home life has been central to the human experience for much of our recorded history. No amount of instruction can compete with the lessons that children internalize from the powerful role models they see at home. They know that their home is as real as it gets. Their acceptance of its authenticity lends their experiences at home an exceptional amount of credibility.

Parental income and education are two of the most referenced indicators for the success and well-being of a child.[14] A healthy and consistent home environment is just as important for children to thrive. Children need caregivers who pay attention to their nutritional needs, are alert to their physical and emotional cues, and stay on top of their cognitive and emotional development. Given the variety of possible developmental challenges, parents need a keen understanding of all the competing needs of their children. While it is true that children are resilient, adverse childhood experiences stemming from strife in a dysfunctional home can indeed produce a profoundly negative impact many years down the road.[15] Finally, as good role models, parents also need an intimate understanding of the aspirations of their children. Even though many of us may have little or no preparation for the challenges of parenting, the responsibility is nevertheless quite onerous. As George Bernard Shaw said, "Parentage is a very important profession, but no test of fitness for it is ever imposed in the interest of the children."[16] Parent education and training are a critical need. It is well known that parents already begin to shape the destiny of their children during pregnancy and, in fact, even well before conception. The importance of maternal nutrition on the health of a pregnancy and the well-being of the child, for example, has been thoroughly studied by many researchers.

The village outside the home, for most children, first begins to form at the local elementary school. As children leave home for the first time in their lives, parents worry about their emotional well-being and ability to cope. As children get older, many parents, as discussed extensively in earlier chapters, find themselves worrying about their grades, work habits, friendships, and more. And educators around the world continue to investigate ways to better support and nourish the villages that form within the schools.

At the same time, results from a large, nationwide survey that looked at educational attainment and parental influence and a more recent yearlong study are very revealing.[17] Laurence Steinberg makes a compelling case that we need to look beyond schools for the problems afflicting children's commitment to educational achievement in the US. His analysis of 20,000 high school students in the US suggests that educational reform will not succeed since many of the problems originate outside school. He found a widespread peer culture that looked down on adolescents who are serious about education and a shocking indifference on the part of many parents to their children's academic growth. While cultural intervention is not a simple undertaking, the calling is unmistakable. There is a need to foster the mindset needed for stepping up and securing the well-being of the upcoming generations.

In this context, it may be instructive to reflect on Esther Wojcicki's insights in *How to Raise Successful People: Simple Lessons for Radical Results*.[18] She is the founder of the Media Arts programs at Palo Alto High School, a vice chair of Creative Commons, and instrumental in launching the Google Teacher Academy. By almost any measure, her three daughters have each found remarkable success in their careers by rising to the top in male-dominated professions. Susan was a CEO of YouTube, Janet is a professor of pediatrics at the University of California in San Francisco, and Anne is the cofounder and CEO of 23andMe. While any mother would be proud of such accomplished children, Wojcicki is prouder of the fact that they are caring, passionate, and purpose-driven individuals who value integrity. Through her decades of experience as a parent and educator, Wojcicki has identified five basic values that she feels parents need to prioritize in raising their children: trust, respect, independence, collaboration, and kindness. These, according to her, will help children the most in their pursuit of meaning and fulfillment.

Whether you are getting on a bicycle for the first time or jumping into the water for your first swim lesson, progress is predicated on your willingness to take some risks. Trust involves a certain amount of risk-taking and a leap of faith. For children to push against injustices or pursue an ambitious project beyond their comfort zone, they need to feel empowered and unfettered. Helicopter parenting might ensure that children meet minimum expectations.

However, it does not leave enough room for them to spread their wings or develop the resilience needed to thrive in the real world. Due to our fears, we are in a crisis of trust the world over.

Respect and independence build on the trust we place in children. We all want the best for them, and our urge to step in and guide them is understandable. Yet, each child brings a set of gifts that are unique, and these might often be different from what the adults cherish or desire. Respecting children's autonomy and individuality is a key responsibility, and this is a vital investment in nurturing their gifts, passions, and sense of purpose.

A culture of trust and respect allows children both to make mistakes and to learn from their mistakes. This is how they internalize self-control and responsibility early in life. They become independent faster and develop the ability to think for themselves and to innovate. They are also likely to be more capable of coping with adversity, disappointment, and boredom.

Collaboration is another valuable skill, especially in the twenty-first century, according to Wojcicki. Role modeling collaboration is easier when we are open-minded and ready to hear children's voices. Collaboration is a key skill, especially when we attempt to solve complex problems since they likely require outreach to large groups. This sense of service and community spirit requires awareness, selflessness, compassion, and kindness. This is why Wojcicki feels that it is important for parents to model kindness and gratitude and help children embody these attitudes from a very young age.

There are key parallels between Wojcicki's values and the Yamas and Niyamas we discussed in chapter 10. Trust, respect, and independence are key ingredients that help cultivate the Yamas of overcoming fear and arrogance, for example. Similarly, kindness and collaboration are easier when one follows the Niyamas of austerity, humility, and contentment.

Wojcicki also sees the decline of purpose and community-mindedness as the root cause of depression and disillusionment in our society. She feels that the widespread focus on personal success—from accumulating wealth to having the fanciest houses and cars to taking the coolest vacations—is producing many unhappy millionaires and billionaires. Incidentally, this was also the lesson Ted Turner learned from his father's suicide. He realized that we should set goals beyond our reach so there is always something to live for. Given the discussion in earlier chapters about the spiraling rise in disillusionment and depression, there is a huge need for all of us to invest more in building a larger sense of purpose in children.

Incidentally, there is interesting research from the University of Toronto's Rotman School of Management and the University of California at Berkeley that sheds some light on who is more likely to be compassionate enough to be their brother's keeper.[19] Results from a battery of seven separate studies involving over a thousand people suggested that, on average, the wealthy are more likely to pursue unethical and even illegal behavior for personal benefit and are less likely to be philanthropic or considerate of the needs of others. The authors suggest that the rich are more statistically likely to value greed highly, often at the cost of ethical considerations such as honesty, integrity, and compassion. Even while poorer people have relatively more to gain through fraud, their dependence on the rest of society makes them more sensitive to the needs of others. It is not difficult to see that pursuits that are shallow and with little meaning and purpose could produce narcissists and thrill addicts who carry the burden of a sense of emptiness. This is probably why teenagers who volunteer with younger children were found to experience both decreased negative moods and cardiovascular risk.[20]

In some situations, aggressive pursuit of self-interest might not stem from greed. It may be fueled by the trauma of an immigrant experience or the need to secure financial independence. Talk of excessive self-interest may not therefore resonate well with those who can barely make ends meet or those who are already quite responsive to the needs of their community. Additionally, it is important to recognize that while pursuing investments that promote equity may appear to be an altruistic endeavor, they also have the potential to uplift us and provide meaning and purpose to those making such investments. In other words, they are essential for our well-being.

There are, of course, numerous social entrepreneurs who have dedicated their lives to building stronger communities. Deacon Jones Foundation, for example, funds all college expenses of students who were willing, in exchange, to invest some of their time after graduation in improving the living conditions in their communities.[21] While Deacon Jones and Ed Snider had the resources to invest in their inner-city intervention programs, the accomplishments of Rajesh Kumar Sharma, a man of meager means and a college dropout himself, are in a league of their own.[22] Sharma first began teaching poor laborers' children in New Delhi by following them around. Eventually, he set up a school for children from neighborhood slums under a highway bridge. The children were eager to attend his school, but convincing the local laborers and farmers to let their children study—and forgo their contribution to the family income—was no small feat.

Then there is Daniel Moss, whose father grew up poor during the Great Depression.[23] By the time of his passing in 2020 during the COVID-19 pandemic, he owned sizable liquid assets and a large home in East Hampton, New York. Moss and his wife originally planned to use their wealth for their children's education and for down payments on future homes, the sort of thing most parents do if they can. Their children, however, had other ideas. They felt responsible for remedying the grievous injuries caused by longstanding racial injustices. They insisted on giving away all their inheritance.

For the moment, these stories are still few and far between. Yet there is hope. A shining example is the large, silent majority of passionate teachers who stay committed to their profession despite unbelievable odds. They are a source of endless pride and inspiration. Our history is replete with many courageous pursuits of the greater good. Purposeful and persistent advocacy from communities around the world would go a long way toward ensuring that future generations have the wherewithal to manage their increasingly complex opportunities.

This book shows us what high-quality education and universal access look like and how they can get us past the crises that engulf us and pave the way forward toward a more tolerant world through the pursuit of common ground and higher purpose. We should not passively accept events as they unfold. We must actively forge a future that is genuinely worthy of how far we have come since our arrival tens of thousands of years ago. There is no shortcut. We cannot afford to look to someone else to lead us forward. There is no other way to secure our future than for each and every one of us to commit to doing our part to help promote universal access to high-quality education—education that would promote awareness and facilitate the opportunities required for each of us to take our lives into a higher orbit.

CHAPTER SUMMARY

- Productive collaboration between educators and parents can be challenging when there are serious conflicts between their values and beliefs. This can greatly harm the well-being of children, especially in majority-minority communities.
- Since it takes a village to raise a child, a society that cannot walk together will have a hard time coming together to build a better tomorrow for their children, especially since children must increasingly contend with many global as well as local influences.
- While individual initiatives such as the Barefoot College can help thousands, programs such as El Sistema can, through government support, reach millions. Consistent enrollment of over 100,000 at-risk children in classical music year after year for more than forty years is a remarkable accomplishment for El Sistema.
- Even while governments need to exercise restraint in their oversight, there is still a significant role for them in the promotion of educational equity. From regulations that support higher standards for teacher certification to reform of tax regimes and other financial support, the sky is the limit.
- In addition to governments, large organizations such as the United Nations and the Global Partnership for Education and foundations such as the Bill and Melinda Gates Foundation, the Ford Foundation, the William and Flora Hewlett Foundation, the Robert Bosch Foundation, and the Azim Premji Foundation have also had a long history of investments in pursuit of educational equity.
- While there is a significant role for governments and schools in the education of the young, external influences can never compete with the lessons that children can internalize from the powerful role models at home. It is very noteworthy that a large study concluded that educational reform will not suffice since many of the problems with engagement originate at home and in the communities outside school.

- The decline of purpose and community-mindedness has been widely blamed for the rise of depression and disillusionment in our society. At the same time, there are also many who have selflessly stepped up and invested heavily in improving the outcomes for underprivileged kids.
- Universal access to high-quality education is an existential imperative. More of us need to embrace the transformational reimagination of education. We can only forge the destiny we aspire to for our children through an intentional pursuit of common ground and a higher purpose.

Acknowledgments

As is often the case, the inspiration for this book came from countless experiences over many decades. Of these, the valuable lessons I received from my paternal grandfather as a young child have been the most impactful. They shaped my mindset and approach to life, and I am convinced that without those formative experiences, I would not have made the journeys that led to this book. I continue to be in awe of his life, but that is a story for another time.

I am also forever grateful for the ethical clarity that my mother tried to model for me. She trusted me implicitly but has also never failed to summon tough love when a situation warranted it. I have been blessed, too, with a father who left no stone unturned in constantly lifting his family up to a better future. I am endlessly thankful to my sisters, whose love and support I could always count on. Finally, I would be remiss if I didn't acknowledge the enriching influence of the many educators in my extended family—Parthasarathi Rao Pasumarthy (maternal grandfather), Narasinga Rao Pasumarthy (maternal uncle), and Lakshmi Nagavarapu (cousin)—through their passion and inspiring work ethic.

Writing a book is an inherently labor-intensive undertaking. Doing so when one has a demanding career and young kids will result in untold hardship and frustration for a spouse. I am, therefore, truly indebted to my wife for her patience, support, and encouragement; this book would not have seen the light of the day without her forbearance. You will quickly realize, as you read through the chapters, that my wife and I learned a lot from our children. Don't we all? Raising them has given us the clarity that could not be obtained solely from poring over surveys and research findings. I am grateful for these gifts.

While I have also been blessed by the support of numerous friends, the steadfast encouragement I have received from Leanne Paulin has been extraordinary. There are numerous demands on Leanne's time: she homeschools her four kids, volunteers at a local homeschool community, and fosters dogs in need. I am in awe of her patience and her selfless contributions of time to this project and, in fact, to all my ventures in education. Words cannot adequately express my gratitude for her friendship and support. Among the many other well-wishers and supporters of my various projects, Samir Patel and Swetha Balasubramanian are in a league of their own. Their passion and zeal for reforming our curricular practices always warm my heart. They have volunteered countless hours to curriculum building, classroom teaching, and community outreach activities. I fondly cherish their friendship and contributions to my humble efforts.

At its core, this book rests on centuries of scholarly investigations by some of the best specimens among us. The book would have been far less valuable without their labors and the benefit of their wisdom. Also, it is no exaggeration to say that artwork by Manjari Roy Chowdhury, Viktor Karazhov, and Anusha Mudigonda breathed life into this all-important story and made it so much more accessible. I am grateful for their patience and attention to detail.

Finally, without Meg Oliveira's guidance, this work would have remained a collection of loosely strung ideas. I am thankful that Meg corralled my writing with a steady hand. I'd especially like to acknowledge the contributions of the talented Reedsy editors whose diligence, passion for perfection, and mastery of wordcraft lifted the book up to a completely different realm. The insights and intellectual rigor of the editors have clarified the narrative in a way that I did not think possible. I am forever indebted to these consummate professionals.

Notes

Preface

1 C. C. Bryant, "Israeli Archaeologist Finds Common Ground Underneath Sinai's Shifting Sands," *Christian Science Monitor*, April 17, 2013, https://www.csmonitor.com/World/Middle-East/Olive-Press/2013/0417/Israeli-archaeologist-finds-common-ground-underneath-Sinai-s-shifting-sands.

2 Centers for Disease Control and Prevention, *Mental Health among Adolescents*, Youth Risk Behavior Survey Data Summary & Trends Report: 2009–2019 (Washington, DC: Centers for Disease Control and Prevention, 2020).

3 L. Steinberg, *Beyond the Classroom: Why School Reform Has Failed and What Parents Need to Do* (New York: Simon and Schuster, 1997).

4 A. Robbins, *The Teachers: A Year Inside America's Most Vulnerable, Important Profession* (New York: Dutton, 2023).

5 FAO, IFAD, UNICEF, WFP, and WHO, *The State of Food Security and Nutrition in the World 2021: Transforming Food Systems for Food Security, Improved Nutrition and Affordable Healthy Diets for All* (Rome: FAO, 2021), https://doi.org/10.4060/cb4474en.

6 S. A. Marcott et al., "A Reconstruction of Regional and Global Temperature for the Past 11,300 Years," *Science* 339 (2013): 1198–1201.

7 T. Templin et al., "The Overweight and Obesity Transition from the Wealthy to the Poor in Low- and Middle-Income Countries: A Survey of Household Data from 103 Countries," *PLOS Medicine* 16, no. 11 (2019): e1002968, https://doi.org/10.1371/journal.pmed.1002968.

8 Centers for Disease Control and Prevention, *Mental Health among Adolescents, Youth Risk Behavior Survey Data Summary & Trends Report: 2009–2019* (Washington, DC: Centers for Disease Control and Prevention, 2020), https://www.cdc.gov/nchhstp/newsroom/docs/factsheets/dash-mental-health.pdf.

1. Unpacking Our Roots

1 H. Päs, *The One: How an Ancient Idea Holds the Future of Physics* (New York: Basic Books, 2023).

2 I. Roffman et al., "Stone Tool Production and Utilization by Bonobo-Chimpanzees (*Pan paniscus*)," *Proceedings of the National Academy of Sciences (PNAS)* 109 (2012): 14500–14503, PMID: 22912400.

3 J. Neufuss et al., "Nut-Cracking Behaviour in Wild-Born, Rehabilitated Bonobos (*Pan paniscus*): A Comprehensive Study of Hand-Preference, Hand Grips and Efficiency," *American Journal of Primatology* 79 (2017): e22589, DOI: 10.1002/ajp.22589.

4 K. Tylén et al., "The Evolution of Early Symbolic Behavior in *Homo sapiens*," *Proceedings of the National Academy of Sciences (PNAS)* 117, no. 9 (2020): 4578–4584, DOI: 10.1073/pnas.1910880117.

5 Y. Prat, M. Taub, and Y. Yovel, "Everyday Bat Vocalizations Contain Information about Emitter, Addressee, Context, and Behavior," *Scientific Reports* 6 (2016): 39419, DOI: 10.1038/srep39419.

6 C. C. Croney and S. T. Boysen, "Acquisition of a Joystick-Operated Video Task by Pigs (*Sus scrofa*)," *Frontiers in Psychology* 12 (2021): 631755, DOI: 10.3389/fpsyg.2021.631755, PMID: 33679560, PMCID: PMC7928376.

7 R. M. Church, "Emotional Reactions of Rats to the Pain of Others," *Journal of Comparative and Physiological Psychology* 52, no. 2 (1959): 132–134, DOI: 10.1037/h0043531, PMID: 13654562.

8 I. Ben-Ami Bartal, J. Decety, and P. Mason, "Empathy and Pro-Social Behavior in Rats," *Science* 334, no. 6061 (December 9, 2011): 1427–1430, DOI: 10.1126/science.1210789. Erratum in: *Science*. 2012 Jan 27; 335 (6067):401. PMID: 22158823, PMCID: PMC3760221.

9 F. de Waal, *Are We Smart Enough to Know How Smart Animals Are?* (New York: Norton, 2017).

10 E. van de Waal, C. Borgeaud, and A. Whiten, "Potent Social Learning and Conformity Shape a Wild Primate's Foraging Decisions," *Science* 340, no. 6131 (April 2013): 483–485, DOI: 10.1126/science.1232769, PMID: 23620053.

11 S. R. James, "Hominid Use of Fire in the Lower and Middle Pleistocene: A Review of the Evidence," *Current Anthropology* 30, no. 1 (February 1989): 1–26. DOI: 10.1086/203705.

12 R. Wrangham, *Catching Fire: How Cooking Made Us Human* (New York: Basic Books, 2009).

13 A. B. Wittman and L. L. Wall, "The Evolutionary Origins of Obstructed Labor: Bipedalism, Encephalization, and the Human Obstetric Dilemma," *Obstetrical & Gynecological Survey* 62, no. 11 (2007): 739–748, DOI: 10.1097/01.ogx.0000286584.04310.5c, PMID: 17925047, S2CID: 9543264.

14 H. M. Dunsworth et al., "Metabolic Hypothesis for Human Altriciality," *Proceedings of the National Academy of Sciences (PNAS)* 109, no. 38 (2012): 15212–15216, DOI: 10.1073/pnas.1205282109.

15 S. T. Piantadosi and C. Kidd, "Extraordinary Intelligence and the Care of Infants," *Proceedings of the National Academy of Sciences (PNAS)* 113, no. 25 (2016): 6874–6879, DOI: 10.1073/pnas.1506752113.

16 H. Coqueugniot et al., "Early Brain Growth in *Homo erectus* and Implications for Cognitive Ability," *Nature* 431, no. 7006 (2004): 299–302.

17 P. D. MacLean, *The Triune Brain in Evolution: Role in Paleocerebral Functions* (New York: Plenum Press, 1990).

18 F.-X. Neubert et al., "Comparison of Human Ventral Frontal Cortex Areas for Cognitive Control and Language with Areas in Monkey Frontal Cortex," *Neuron* 81, no. 3 (2014): 700–713, https://doi.org/10.1016/j.neuron.2013.11.012.

19 C. Butti and P. R. Hof, "The Insular Cortex: A Comparative Perspective," *Brain Structure & Function* 214, no. 5–6 (2010): 477–493.

20 T. Suddendorf, *The Gap: The Science of What Separates Us from Other Animals* (New York: Basic Books, 2013).

21 L. Margulis, *Symbiosis in Cell Evolution* (San Francisco: Freeman, 1981).

22 E. Schrödinger, *What Is Life? The Physical Aspect of the Living Cell* (Cambridge: Cambridge University Press, 1944).

23 Y. N. Harari, *Sapiens: A Brief History of Humankind* (New York: HarperCollins, 2015).

24 J. C. A. Joordens et al., "*Homo erectus* at Trinil on Java Used Shells for Tool Production and Engraving," *Nature* 518 (2015): 228–231, https://doi.org/10.1038/nature13962.

25 D. Nadel et al., "Stone Age Hut in Israel Yields World's Oldest Evidence of Bedding," *Proceedings of the National Academy of Sciences (PNAS)* 101, no. 17 (2004): 6821–6826, DOI: 10.1073/pnas.0308557101.

26 T. F. Strasser et al., "Stone Age Seafaring in the Mediterranean: Evidence from the Plakias Region for Lower Palaeolithic and Mesolithic Habitation of Crete," *Hesperia: The Journal of the American School of Classical Studies at Athens* 79, no. 2 (2010): 145–190, https://www.jstor.org/stable/40835484.

27 I. Martínez et al., "Human Hyoid Bones from the Middle Pleistocene Site of the Sima de los Huesos (Sierra de Atapuerca, Spain)," *Journal of Human Evolution* 54, no. 1 (2008): 118–124.

28 D. L. Everett, *How Language Began: The Story of Humanity's Greatest Invention* (New York: Norton, 2017).

2. Back to the Future

1 R. J. Davenport, "Urbanization and Mortality in Britain, c. 1800–50," *Economic History Review* 73, no. 2 (2020): 455–485, DOI: 10.1111/ehr.12964, EPUB 2020 Feb 21, PMID: 32355360, PMCID: PMC7186836.

2 M. Scully, *Dominion: The Power of Man, the Suffering of Animals, and the Call to Mercy* (New York: St. Martin's Press, 2002).

3 Gartner, "Forecast: PCs, Ultramobiles and Mobile Phones, Worldwide, 2010–2017, 4Q13 Update," Gartner Research (Stamford, CT: Gartner, 2013), https://www.gartner.com/doc/2639615.

4 F. Laricchia, "Connected Wearable Devices Worldwide 2016–2022," Statista, February 14, 2022, https://www.statista.com/statistics/487291/global-connected-wearable-devices/#:~:text=The%20number%20of%20connected%20wearable,than%20one%20billion%20by%202022; L. Wood, "Global Connected Wearable Device Market in Healthcare, Wellness, and Fitness 2023: Sector to Reach $10.5 Billion by 2028," *Business Wire*, January 24, 2023, https://www.businesswire.com/news/home/20230124005738/en/Global-Connected-Wearable-Device-Market-in-Healthcare-Wellness-and-Fitness-2023-Sector-to-Reach-10.5-Billion-by-2028---ResearchAndMarkets.com.

5 Committee on America's Climate Choices, *America's Climate Choices* (Washington, DC: National Academies Press, 2011).

6 S. A. Marcott et al., "A Reconstruction of Regional and Global Temperature for the Past 11,300 Years," *Science* 339 (2013): 1198–1201.

7 S. Manabe and R. T. Wetherald, "Thermal Equilibrium of the Atmosphere with a Given Distribution of Relative Humidity," *Journal of Atmospheric Sciences* 24, no. 3 (1967): 241–259; C. Parmesan and G. Yohe, "A Globally Coherent Fingerprint of Climate Change Impacts across Natural Systems," *Nature* 421 (2003): 37–42.

8 United Nations University, "5 Facts on Climate Migrants," 2015, https://ehs.unu.edu/news/news/5-facts-on-climate-migrants.html.

9 D. Rye, "My Life at X10," *AVSystemsMag*, Home Toys, October 1999, https://web.archive.org/web/20140930080338/http://hometoys.com/emagazine.php?url=%2Fhtinews%2Foct99%2Farticles%2Frye%2Frye.htm.

10 M. R. Frank et al., "Toward Understanding the Impact of Artificial Intelligence on Labor," *Proceedings of the National Academy of Sciences* 116, no. 4 (2019): 6531–6539; M. Muro, R. Maxim, and J. Whiton, "Automation and Artificial Intelligence: How Machines Are Affecting People and Places," January 2019, https://hdl.handle.net/11540/9686; C. B. Frey and M. A. Osborne, "The Future of Employment: How Susceptible Are Jobs to Computerisation?," *Technological Forecasting and Social Change* 114 (2017): 254–280, ISSN 0040-1625.

11 A. G. Haldane, "Labour's Share," speech by Andrew G. Haldane, Executive Director and Chief Economist of the Bank of England, at the Trades Union Congress, London, November 12, 2015, https://www.bis.org/review/r151203a.pdf.

12 L. Nedelkoska and G. Quintini, "Automation, Skills Use and Training," *OECD Social, Employment and Migration Working Papers*, no. 202 (Paris: OECD Publishing, 2018).

13 D. Thompson, "Your Creativity Won't Save Your Job from AI," *The Atlantic*, December 1, 2022, https://www.theatlantic.com/newsletters/archive/2022/12/why-the-rise-of-ai-is-the-most-important-story-of-the-year/672308/.

14 T. Adams, "David Cope: 'You Pushed the Button and Out Came Hundreds and Thousands of Sonatas,'" *The Guardian*, July 10, 2010, https://www.theguardian.com/technology/2010/jul/11/david-cope-computer-composer.

15 Adams, "David Cope."

16 T. Lappalainen et al., "Genomic Analysis in the Age of Human Genome Sequencing," *Cell* 177 (2019): 70–84.

17 R. Chen et al., "Personal Omics Profiling Reveals Dynamic Molecular and Medical Phenotypes," *Cell* 148, no. 6 (2012): 1293–1307.

18 J. Muenzer et al., "CHAMPIONS: A Phase 1/2 Clinical Trial with Dose Escalation of SB-913 ZFN-Mediated in Vivo Human Genome Editing for Treatment of MPS II (Hunter Syndrome)," *Molecular Genetics and Metabolism* 126, no. 2 (2019): S104.

19 G. Pandey, "India's First 'Saviour Sibling' Cures Brother of Fatal Illness," BBC, October 27, 2020, https://www.bbc.com/news/world-asia-india-54658007.

20 T. M. S. Chang and M. Poznanski, "Semipermeable Microcapsules Containing Catalase for Enzyme Replacement in Acatalsaemic Mice," *Nature* 218, no. 5138 (1968): 242–245; R. Haldar et al., "Artificial Blood: A Futuristic Dimension of Modern Day Transfusion Sciences," *Cardiovascular & Hematological Agents in Medicinal Chemistry* 17, no. 1 (2019): 11–16.

21 Y. Hachmo et al., "Hyperbaric Oxygen Therapy Increases Telomere Length and Decreases Immunosenescence in Isolated Blood Cells: A Prospective Trial," *Aging* (Albany, NY) 12, no. 22 (2020): 22445–22456, DOI: 10.18632/aging.202188, EPUB 2020 Nov 18, PMID: 33206062, PMCID: PMC7746357.

22 S. Ogawa et al., "Brain Magnetic Resonance Imaging with Contrast Dependent on Blood Oxygenation," *Proceedings of the National Academy of Sciences (PNAS)* 87, no. 24 (1990): 9868–9872.

23 M. A. Nitsche and W. Paulus, "Excitability Changes Induced in the Human Motor Cortex by Weak Transcranial Direct Current Stimulation," *Journal of Physiology* 527, pt. 3, no. 3 (2000): 633–639.

24 S. J. Matar et al., "Transcranial Direct-Current Stimulation May Improve Discourse Production in Healthy Older Adults," *Frontiers in Neurology* 11 (2020): n.p.; H. Arciniega et al., "Frontoparietal tDCS Benefits Visual Working Memory in Older Adults with Low Working Memory Capacity," *Frontiers in Aging Neuroscience* 10 (2018): n.p.; V. Axelrod et al., "Increasing Propensity to Mind-Wander with Transcranial Direct Current Stimulation," *Proceedings of the National Academy of Sciences* 112 (2015): 3314–3319.

25 V. P. Clark et al., "TDCS Guided Using fMRI Significantly Accelerates Learning to Identify Concealed Objects," *NeuroImage* 59, no. 1 (2012): 117–128.

26 S. Adee, "Zap Your Brain into the Zone: Fast Track to Pure Focus," *New Scientist*, February 1, 2012, https://www.newscientist.com/article/mg21328501-600-zap-your-brain-into-the-zone-fast-track-to-pure-focus/.

27 Y. Wu, M. Kosinski, and D. Stillwell, "Computers Judge Personalities Better Than Humans," *Proceedings of the National Academy of Sciences (PNAS)* 112, no. 4 (2015): 1036–1040, DOI: 10.1073/pnas.1418680112.

28 J. M. Digman, "Personality Structure: Emergence of the Five-Factor Model," *Annual Review of Psychology* 41 (1990): 417–440; L. R. Goldberg, "The Structure of Phenotypic Personality Traits," *American Psychologist* 48, no. 1 (1993): 26–34, DOI: 10.1037/0003-066x.48.1.26, PMID: 8427480.

29 D. Mook, *Classic Experiments in Psychology* (Westport, CT: Greenwood Press, 2004).

3. Our Enduring Aspirations

1 P. Peterson et al., eds., *International Encyclopedia of Education*, 3rd ed., 8 vols. (Amsterdam: Elsevier Science, 2010).

2 J. Bowen, *A History of Western Education*, 3 vols. (London: Routledge, 2003).

3 S. B. Lynch, "Marking Time, Making Community in Medieval Schools," *History of Education Quarterly* 61, no. 2 (May 2021): 158–180.

4 J. Lin, *Education in Post-Mao China* (Westport, CT: Praeger, 1993).

5 A. Gupta, *Going to School in South Asia* (Westport, CT: Greenwood, 2007).

6 J. Locke, *An Essay Concerning Human Understanding*, ed. R. Woolhouse (New York: Penguin Books, 1997).

7 F. M. Asher, *Nalanda: Situating the Great Monastery* (Mumbai: published by Radhika Sabavala for the Marg Foundation, 2015), ISBN 978-93-83243-07-5.

8 R. L. Wollons, ed., *Kindergartens and Cultures: The Global Diffusion of an Idea* (New Haven, CT: Yale University Press, 2000).

9 L. Cadwell, *Bringing Reggio Emilia Home: An Innovative Approach to Early Childhood Education* (New York: Teachers College Press, 1997); V. Hewitt, "Examining the Reggio Emilia Approach to Early Childhood Education," *Early Childhood Education Journal* 29, no. 2 (2001): 95–100.

10 P. Wingert, "The Best Schools in the World," *Newsweek*, December 1, 1991, https://www.newsweek.com/best-schools-world-200968.

11 J. S. Renzulli and S. M. Reis, *The Schoolwide Enrichment Model: A Comprehensive Plan for Educational Excellence* (Mansfield Center, CT: Creative Learning Press, 1985).

12 J. Chattin-McNichols, "What Does Research Say about Montessori?," in M. H. Loeffler, ed., *Montessori in Contemporary American Culture*, 69–100 (Portsmouth, NH: Heinemann Educational Books, 1992); A. S. Lillard, *Montessori: The Science behind the Genius*, 3rd ed. (Oxford: Oxford University Press, 2016).

13 S. M. Reis and P. M. Peters, "Research on the Schoolwide Enrichment Model: Four Decades of Insights, Innovation, and Evolution," *Gifted Education International* 37, no. 2 (2021): 109–141.

14 D. S. Mitchell, "Social-Emotional Education and Waldorf Education," *The Online Waldorf Library* 14, no. 2 (September 18, 2009), https://www.waldorflibrary.org/images/stories/Journal_Articles/RB142mitchell.pdf.

15 A. Kumar, "Creating an enabling learning environment at 12,000 Feet: SECMOL Alternate Institute," *The Educationist*, January 17, 2014, https://www.theeducationist.info/creating-an-enabling-learning-environment-at-12000-feet; S. Wangchuk, "Education in India: Are Students Failing or the System?!," *TEDxGateway*, April 5, 2016, https://youtu.be/qH1HCYy1NTc.

16 H. Gardner, *Frames of Mind: The Theory of Multiple Intelligences*, 2nd ed. (New York: Basic Books, 2011).

17 B. A. Visser, M. C. Ashton, and P. A. Vernon, "Beyond g: Putting Multiple Intelligences Theory to the Test," *Intelligence* 34, no. 5 (2006): 487–502, https://doi.org/10.1016/j.intell.2006.02.004.

18 M. P. Driscoll and K. J. Burner, *Psychology of Learning for Instruction*, 4th ed. (Hoboken, NJ: Pearson, 2021).

19 L. S. Siegel, "Amazing New Discovery: Piaget Was Wrong!," *Canadian Psychology* 34, no. 3 (1993): 234–249.

20 P. M. Sadler et al., *AP: A Critical Examination of the Advanced Placement Program* (Cambridge, MA: Harvard Education Press, 2010); A. D. C. Peterson, *Schools across Frontiers: The Story of the International Baccalaureate and the United World Colleges*, 2nd ed. (Chicago: Open Court, 2003); R. Alexander, ed., *Children, Their World, Their Education: Final Report and Recommendations of the Cambridge Primary Review* (London: Routledge, 2010).

21 Peterson, *Schools across Frontiers*.

22 J. Krishnamurti, *Relationships: To Oneself, to Others, to the World* (Ojai, CA: Krishnamurti Foundation of America, 2010).

23 D. E. Moody, *The Unconditioned Mind: J. Krishnamurti and the Oak Grove School* (Wheaton, IL: Quest Books, 2011).

24 R. S. Moore and D. N. Moore, *Better Late Than Early: A New Approach to Your Child's Education* (New York: Readers Digest Press, 1975).

25 R. S. Moore and D. N. Moore, *Better Late Than Early*; R. S. Moore and D. N. Moore, *Home Grown Kids: A Practical Handbook for Teaching Your Children at Home* (Waco, TX: W Pub, 1981); R. S. Moore and D. N. Moore, *Home School Burnout: What It Is. What Causes It. And How to Overcome It* (Brentwood, TN: Wolgemuth & Hyatt, 1988).

26 J. Holt, *How Children Fail*, rev. ed. (Boston: Da Capo Press, 1995); J. Holt, *How Children Learn*, 50th anniv. ed. (Boston: Da Capo Press, 2017).

27 J. Holt and P. Farenga, *Teach Your Own* (Boston: Da Capo Press, 2003).

28 L. Lyons and G. Gordon, "Homeschooling: Expanding Its Ranks and Reputation," Gallup, 2002, https://www.gallup.com/poll/5941/homeschooling-expanding-its-ranks-reputation.aspx.

29 M. F. Cogan, "Exploring Academic Outcomes of Homeschooled Students," *Journal of College Admission*, no. 208 (2010): 18–25.

30 J. W. Taylor, *Self-Concept in Home-Schooling Children*, doctoral dissertation, School of Education, Andrews University, 1986, Dissertation Abstracts International, 47, 2809A, ERIC Digest 372460.

31 B. D. Ray, "Homeschooling Grows Up," NHERI, 2003, https://www.hslda.org/research/ray2003/.

32 J. Catsoulis, "The Overscheduled Child," *New York Times*, September 9, 2010, https://www.nytimes.com/2010/09/10/movies/10race.html.

33 National Commission on Excellence in Education, *A Nation at Risk: The Imperative for Educational Reform* (Washington, DC: National Commission on Excellence in Education, 1983), http://edreform.com/wp-content/uploads/2013/02/A_Nation_At_Risk_1983.pdf.

34 D. Desilver, "U.S. Students' Academic Achievement Still Lags That of Their Peers in Many Other Countries," *Pew Research Center*, February 15, 2017, https://www.pewresearch.org/fact-tank/2017/02/15/u-s-students-internationally-math-science/.

35 W. Deresiewicz, *Excellent Sheep: The Miseducation of the American Elite and the Way to a Meaningful Life* (New York: Free Press, 2015).

II. Paving the Way

1 D. Khanna and A. Peterson, "State-Led Education Reform in Delhi, India: A Case Study of the Happiness Curriculum," Brookings Institution, February 10, 2023, https://www.brookings.edu/research/state-led-education-reform-in-delhi-india/.

4. Holistic Curriculum

1 R. M. Church, "Emotional Reactions of Rats to the Pain of Others," *Journal of Comparative and Physiological Psychology* 52, no. 2 (1959): 132–134, DOI: 10.1037/h0043531, PMID: 13654562.

2 H. F. Harlow and R. R. Zimmermann, "Affectional Responses in the Infant Monkey," *Science* 130 (1959): 421–432, https://doi.org/10.1126/science.130.3373.421; H. F. Harlow, R. O. Dodsworth, and M. K. Harlow, "Total Social Isolation in Monkeys," *Proceedings of the National Academy of Sciences of the United States of America* 54, no. 1 (1965): 90.

3 C. L. Ogden and M. D. Carroll, "Prevalence of Obesity among Children and Adolescents: United States, Trends 1963–1965 through 2007–2008," National Health and Nutrition Examination Survey, 2010, https://www.cdc.gov/nchs/data/hestat/obesity_child_07_08/obesity_child_07_08.pdf.

4 C. M. Hales et al., "Prevalence of Obesity and Severe Obesity among Adults: United States, 2017–2018," *NCHS Data Brief*, no. 360 (Hyattsville, MD: National Center for Health Statistics, 2020), https://www.cdc.gov/nchs/data/databriefs/db360-h.pdf.

5 T. Templin et al., "The Overweight and Obesity Transition from the Wealthy to the Poor in Low- and Middle-Income Countries: A Survey of Household Data from 103 Countries," *PLOS Medicine* 16, no. 11 (2019): e1002968, https://doi.org/10.1371/journal.pmed.1002968.

6 WHO, "Obesity and Overweight," World Health Organization, 2003, https://web.archive.org/web/20170713190601/https://www.who.int/dietphysicalactivity/media/en/gsfs_obesity.pdf.

7 X.-F. Pan, L. Wang, and A. Pan, "Epidemiology and Determinants of Obesity in China," *The Lancet* 9, no. 6 (2021): 373–392.

8 G. L. Blackburn and W. A. Walker, "Science-Based Solutions to Obesity: What Are the Roles of Academia, Government, Industry, and Health Care?," *American Journal of Clinical Nutrition (American Society for Clinical Nutrition)* 82, no. 1 (2005): 207S–210S; D. Behan et al., *Obesity and Its Relation to Mortality and Morbidity Costs* (Schaumburg, IL: Society of Actuaries, 2010).

9 F. Lifshitz and J. Z. Lifshitz, "Globesity: The Root Causes of the Obesity Epidemic in the USA and Now Worldwide," *Pediatric Endocrinology Reviews* 12, no. 1 (2014): 17–34; X. Lin and H. Li, "Obesity: Epidemiology, Pathophysiology, and Therapeutics," *Frontiers in Endocrinology (Lausanne)* 12 (2021): 706978; R. Wilkinson and K. Pickett, *The Spirit Level: Why Greater Equality Makes Societies* Stronger (New York: Bloomsbury Press, 2009).

10 J. E. Donnelly et al., "Nutrition and Physical Activity Program to Attenuate Obesity and Promote Physical and Metabolic Fitness in Elementary School Children," *Obesity Research* 4 (1996): 229–243; R. Kersh and B. Elbel, "Childhood Obesity: Can Public Policy Make a Difference?," in D. Bagchi, ed., *Global Perspectives on Childhood Obesity: Current Status, Consequences and Prevention*, 2nd ed. (London: Academic Press/Elsevier, 2019); R. Khera, "Mid-Day Meals in Primary Schools: Achievements and Challenges," *Economic and Political Weekly* 41, no. 46 (2006): 4742–4750; V. Walt, "School Lunches in France: Nursery-School Gourmets," *Time*, February 23, 2010, https://www.time.com/time/magazine/article/0,9171,1969729,00.html.

11 J. D. Watson and F. H. C. Crick, "A Structure for Deoxyribose Nucleic Acid," *Nature* 171, no. 4356 (1953): 737–738.

12 P. V. Sharma, *Charaka Samhita* (English translation) (Varanasi, India: Chaukhamba Orientalia, 1981); V. Lad, *Textbook of Ayurveda*, Vol. 1: *Fundamental Principles* (Albuquerque, NM: Ayurvedic Press, 2001).

13 S. Narayanan, "The Thermal Qualities of Substance: A Cross-Cultural Account," *Proceedings of the 30th Annual Conference of the Cognitive Science Society*, 2290–2295 (Austin, TX: Cognitive Science Society, 2008).

14 A. Ramzy, "China's Tainted Milk Scandal of 2008," *Wikipedia*, January 28, 2023, https://en.wikipedia.org/wiki/2008_Chinese_milk_scandal#:~:text=The%20 2008%20Chinese%20milk%20scandal,other%20kidney%20damage%20in%20 infants.

15 L. Buder, "Beech-Nut Is Fined $2 Million for Sale of Fake Apple Juice," *New York Times*, November 14, 1987, https://www.nytimes.com/1987/11/14/business/ beech-nut-is-fined-2-million-for-sale-of-fake-apple-juice.html.

16 D. McCann et al., "Food Additives and Hyperactive Behaviour in 3-Year-Old and 8/9-Year-Old Children in the Community: A Randomised, Double-Blinded, Placebo-Controlled Trial," *The Lancet* 370, no. 9598 (2007): 1560–1567; C. H. Farlow, *Food Additives: A Shopper's Guide to What's Safe & What's Not*, 7th ed. (Escondido, CA: KISS For Health Publishing, 2013).

17 T. Andreyeva et al., "Availability and Prices of Foods across Stores and Neighborhoods: The Case of New Haven, Connecticut," *Health Affairs* 27, no. 5 (2008): 1381–1388.

18 D. Ornish, *Dr. Dean Ornish's Program for Reversing Heart Disease: The Only System Scientifically Proven to Reverse Heart Disease without Drugs or Surgery* (New York: Ivy Books, 1995); N. D. Barnard, *Dr. Neal Barnard's Program for Reversing Diabetes: The Scientifically Proven System for Reversing Diabetes without Drugs* (Emmaus, PA: Rodale Books, 2017); N. D. Barnard, J. K. Reilly, and S. M. Levin, *The Cancer Survivor's Guide: Foods That Help You Fight Back* (Summertown, TN: Healthy Living Publications, 2017); C. B. Esselstyn, *Prevent and Reverse Heart Disease: The Revolutionary, Scientifically Proven, Nutrition-Based Cure* (New York: Avery, 2008).

19 F. L. Crowe et al., "Risk of Hospitalization or Death from Ischemic Heart Disease among British Vegetarians and Nonvegetarians: Results from the EPIC-Oxford Cohort Study," *American Journal of Clinical Nutrition* 97, no. 3 (2013): 597–603.

20 J. L. Lusk and F. B. Norwood, "Some Economic Benefits and Costs of Vegetarianism," *Agricultural and Resource Economics Review* 38 (2009): 109–124.

21 F. M. Lappé, *Diet for a Small Planet*, 50th anniv. ed. (New York: Ballantine Books, 2021).

22 M. P. Walker, "The Role of Sleep in Cognition and Emotion," *Annals of the New York Academy of Sciences* 1156, no. 1 (2009): 168–197, DOI: 10.1111/j.1749-6632.2009.04416.x.

23 K. Bonuck, K. Freeman, R. D. Chervin, and L. Xu, "Sleep-Disordered Breathing in a Population-Based Cohort: Behavioral Outcomes at 4 and 7 Years," *Pediatrics* 129, no. 4 (2012): e857-65. doi: 10.1542/peds.2011-1402.

24 G. B. Feld and S. Diekelmann, "Sleep Smart—Optimizing Sleep for Declarative Learning and Memory," *Frontiers in Psychology* 6 (2015): 622, DOI: 10.3389/fpsyg.2015.00622.

25 R. Glosemeyer et al., "Selective Suppression of Rapid Eye Movement Sleep Increases Next-Day Negative Affect and Amygdala Responses to Social Exclusion," *Scientific Reports* 10, no. 1 (2020): 17325, DOI: 10.1038/s41598-020-74169-8.

26 M. P. Walker, "Cognitive Flexibility across the Sleep–Wake Cycle: REM-Sleep Enhancement of Anagram Problem Solving," *Cognitive Brain Research* 14, no. 3 (2002): 317–324, DOI: 10.1016/s0926-6410(02)00134-9.

27 B. A. Mander et al., "Wake Deterioration and Sleep Restoration of Human Learning," *Current Biology* 21, no. 5 (2011): R183–R184, DOI: 10.1016/j.cub.2011.01.019.

28 C. Cotman and N. C. Berchtold, "Exercise: A Behavioral Intervention to Enhance Brain Health and Plasticity," *Trends in Neurosciences* 25 (2002): 295–301.

29 C. H. Hillman, K. I. Erickson, and A. F. Kramer, "Be Smart, Exercise Your Heart: Exercise Effects on Brain and Cognition," *Nature Reviews Neuroscience* 9, no. 1 (2008): 58–65; C. N. Rasberry et al., "The Association between School-Based Physical Activity, Including Physical Education, and Academic Performance: A Systematic Review of the Literature," *Preventive Medicine* 52, suppl. 1 (2011): S10–S20.

30 B. Winter et al., "High Impact Running Improves Learning," *Neurobiology of Learning and Memory* 87 (2007): 597–609, https://dx.doi.org/10.1016/j.nlm.2006.11.003.

31 S. Bathina and U. N. Das, "Brain-Derived Neurotrophic Factor and Its Clinical Implications," *Archives of Medical Science (AMS)* 11, no. 6 (2015): 1164–1178, https://doi.org/10.5114/aoms.2015.56342.

32 Blue Cross Blue Shield, *Major Depression: The Impact on Overall Health*, The Health of America Report, May 10, 2018, https://www.bcbs.com/sites/default/files/file-attachments/health-of-america-report/HoA_Major_Depression_Report.pdf.

33 H. Hedegaard, S. C. Curtin, and M. Warner, "Increase in Suicide Mortality in the United States, 1999–2018," NCHS Data Brief, no. 362 (Hyattsville, MD: National Center for Health Statistics, 2020).

34 Centers for Disease Control and Prevention, *Mental Health among Adolescents*, Youth Risk Behavior Survey Data Summary & Trends Report: 2009–2019 (Washington, DC: Centers for Disease Control and Prevention, 2020).

35 L. A. Lebrun-Harris et al., "Five-Year Trends in US Children's Health and Well-Being, 2016–2020," *JAMA Pediatrics* 176, no. 7 (2022): e220056.

36 S. H. Konrath, E. H. O'Brien, and C. Hsing, "Changes in Dispositional Empathy in American College Students Over Time: A Meta-Analysis," *Personality and Social Psychology Review* 15, no. 2 (2010): 180–198, DOI: 10.1177/1088868310377395.

37 N. R. Carlson and M. A. Birkett, *Physiology of Behavior*, 13th ed. (New York: Pearson, 2021).

38 T. Sagvolden et al., "A Dynamic Developmental Theory of Attention-Deficit/Hyperactivity Disorder (ADHD) Predominantly Hyperactive/Impulsive and Combined Subtypes," *Behavioral and Brain Sciences* 28, no. 3 (2005): 397–468.

39 P. Jessiman et al., "School Culture and Student Mental Health: A Qualitative Study in UK Secondary Schools," *BMC Public Health* 22, no. 619 (2022), https://bmcpublichealth.biomedcentral.com/articles/10.1186/s12889-022-13034-x.

40 A. Schwarz, "A.D.H.D. Seen in 11% of U.S. Children as Diagnoses Rise," *New York Times*, March 31, 2013, https://www.nytimes.com/2013/04/01/health/more-diagnoses-of-hyperactivity-causing-concern.html?pagewanted=all.

41 S. V. Faraone et al., "The Worldwide Prevalence of ADHD: Is It an American Condition?," *World Psychiatry* 2, no. 2 (2003): 104–113.

42 D. Demontis et al., "Genome-Wide Analyses of ADHD Identify 27 Risk Loci, Refine the Genetic Architecture and Implicate Several Cognitive Domains," *Nature Genetics* 55 (2023): 198–208; G. Sudre et al., "Mapping the Cortico-Striatal Transcriptome in Attention Deficit Hyperactivity Disorder," *Molecular Psychiatry* 28, no. 2 (2023): 792–800.

43 A. Charach et al., "Interventions for Preschool Children at High Risk for ADHD: A Comparative Effectiveness Review," *Pediatrics* 131, no. 5 (2013): e1584–e1604, peds.2012-0974; DOI: 10.1542/peds.2012-0974.

44 N. D. Volkow, "Therapeutic Doses of Oral Methylphenidate Significantly Increase Extracellular Dopamine in the Human Brain," *Journal of Neuroscience* 21, no. 2 (January 15, 2001): RC121 (pp. 1–5); N. Del Campo et al., "The Roles of Dopamine and Noradrenaline in the Pathophysiology and Treatment of Attention-Deficit/Hyperactivity Disorder," *Biological Psychiatry* 69, no. 12 (2011): e145–e157.

45 M. Lerner and T. Wigal, "Long-Term Safety of Stimulant Medications Used to Treat Children with ADHD," *Journal of Psychosocial Nursing and Mental Health Services* 46, no. 8 (2008): 38–48.

46 B. S. Molina et al., "The MTA at 8 Years: Prospective Follow-Up of Children Treated for Combined-Type ADHD in a Multisite Study," *Journal of the American Academy of Child & Adolescent Psychiatry* 48, no. 5 (2009): 484–500.

47 W. Sears and L. Thompson, *The A.D.D. Book: New Understandings, New Approaches to Parenting Your Child* (New York: Little, Brown, 1998); S. Enriquez-Geppert et al., "Neurofeedback as a Treatment Intervention in ADHD: Current Evidence and Practice," *Current Psychiatry Reports* 21, no. 6 (2019): 46; M. Arns et al., "Neurofeedback and Attention-Deficit/Hyperactivity-Disorder (ADHD) in Children: Rating the Evidence and Proposed Guidelines," *Applied Psychophysiology and Biofeedback*, 45 (2020): 39–48.

48 H. Marzbani, H. R. Marateb, and M. Mansourian, "Neurofeedback: A Comprehensive Review on System Design, Methodology and Clinical Applications," *Basic Clinical Neuroscience* 7, no. 2 (2016): 143–158.

49 M. Bonhauser et al., "Improving Physical Fitness and Emotional Well-Being in Adolescents of Low Socioeconomic Status in Chile: Results of a School-Based Controlled Trial," *Health Promotion International* 20, no. 2 (2005): 113–122, DOI: 10.1093/heapro/dah603.

50 A. L. Dunn et al., "Exercise Treatment for Depression: Efficacy and Dose Response," *American Journal of Preventive Medicine* 28, no. 1 (2005): 1–8, PubMed: 15626549; R. V. Milani and C. J. Lavie, "Impact of Cardiac Rehabilitation on Depression and Its Associated Mortality," *American Journal of Medicine* 120, no. 9 (2007): 799–806, PubMed: 17765050.

51 M. Babyak et al., "Exercise Treatment for Major Depression: Maintenance of Therapeutic Benefit at 10 Months," *Psychosomatic Medicine* 62, no. 5 (2000): 633–638.

52 F. B. Bryant and J. Veroff, *Savoring: A New Model of Positive Experience* (London: Psychology Press, 2006).

53 I. Qureshi, "Maharashtra: India Village Goes Offline Daily to Help People Talk," *BBC*, October 11, 2022, https://www.bbc.com/news/world-asia-india-63169149.

54 B. K. S. Iyengar, *Light on Pranayama: The Definitive Guide to the Art of Breathing* (London: HarperCollins, 2013).

55 G. K. Pal, S. Velkumary, and M. Trakroo, "Effect of Short-Term Practice of Breathing Exercises on Autonomic Functions in Normal Human Volunteers," *Indian Journal of Medical Research* 120, no. 2 (2004): 115–121; R. P. Brown and P. L. Gerbarg, "Sudarshan Kriya Yogic Breathing in the Treatment of Stress, Anxiety, and Depression. Part II—Clinical Applications and Guidelines," *Journal of Alternative and Complementary Medicine* 11, no. 4 (2005): 711–717.

56 S. P. Slovacek, S. A. Tucker, and L. Pantoja, *A Study of the Yoga Ed Program at the Accelerated School* (Los Angeles: Program Evaluation and Research Collaborative, Charter College of Education, 2003).

57 M. F. Mason et al., "Wandering Minds: The Default Network and Stimulus-Independent Thought," *Science* 315 (2007): 393–395.

58 L. Q. Uddin et al., "Network Homogeneity Reveals Decreased Integrity of Default-Mode Network in ADHD," *Journal of Neuroscience Methods* 169, no. 1 (2008): 249–254.

59 J. A. Brewer et al., "Meditation Experience Is Associated with Differences in Default Mode Network Activity and Connectivity," *Proceedings of the National Academy of Sciences* 108, no. 50 (2011): 20254–20259, DOI: 10.1073/pnas.1112029108.

60 T. C. Clarke et al., "Use of Yoga, Meditation, and Chiropractors among U.S. Adults Aged 18 and Over," *NCHS Data Brief*, no. 325 (Hyattsville, MD: National Center for Health Statistics, 2018), https://www.cdc.gov/nchs/data/databriefs/db325-h.pdf.

61 D. Oman et al., "Meditation Lowers Stress and Supports Forgiveness among College Students: A Randomized Controlled Trial," *Journal of American College Health* 56, no. 5 (2008): 569–578.

62 Oman et al., "Meditation Lowers Stress and Supports Forgiveness among College Students," 570.

63 L.-C. Chu, "The Benefits of Meditation vis-à-vis Emotional Intelligence, Perceived Stress and Negative Mental Health," *Stress & Health* 26, no. 2 (2010): 169–180.

64 M. Kyriazis, "Clinical Anti-Aging Hormetic Strategies," *Rejuvenation Research* 8, no. 2 (2005): 96–100; S. I. S. Rattan, "Hormesis in Aging," *Ageing Research Reviews* 7, no. 1 (2008): 63–78.

65 B. Roy, C. Riley, and R. Sinha, "Emotion Regulation Moderates the Association between Chronic Stress and Cardiovascular Disease Risk in Humans: A Cross-Sectional Study," *Stress* 21, no. 6. (2018): 548–555; Y. V. Shcherbatykh, "Self-Regulation of Autonomic Homeostasis in Emotional Stress," *Human Physiology* 26, no. 5 (2000): 641–642.

66 S. Cote and C. T. H. Miners, "Emotional Intelligence, Cognitive Intelligence and Job Performance," *Administrative Science Quarterly* 51, no. 1 (2006): 1–28.

67 J. R. Snarey and G. E. Vaillant, "How Lower- and Working-Class Youth Become Middle-Class Adults: The Association between Ego Defense Mechanisms and Upward Social Mobility," *Child Development* 56, no. 4 (1985): 899–910; G. J. Feist and F. Barron, "Emotional Intelligence and Academic Intelligence in Career and Life Success," paper presented at the Annual Convention of the American Psychological Society, San Francisco, June 1996.

68 S. G. Barsade, "The Ripple Effect: Emotional Contagion and Its Influence on Group Behavior," *Administrative Science Quarterly* 47 (2002): 644–675.

69 Aristotle, *The Art of Rhetoric*, ed. and trans. H. C. Lawson-Tancred (London: Penguin Books, 1991).

70 M. Beldoch, "Sensitivity to Expression of Emotional Meaning in Three Modes of Communication," in J. R. Davitz, ed., *The Communication of Emotional Meaning*, 31–42. (New York: McGraw-Hill, 1964); W. L. Payne, *A Study of Emotion: Developing Emotional Intelligence; Self Integration; Relating to Fear, Pain and Desire*, doctoral dissertation, Union for Experimenting Colleges and Universities, 1986, Dissertation Abstracts International 47, p. 203A (University Microfilms No. AAC 8605928).

71 S. I. Greenspan, "Emotional Intelligence," in K. Field, B. J. Cohler, and G. Wool, eds., *Learning and Education: Psychoanalytic Perspectives*, 209–243 (Madison, CT: International Universities Press, 1989); P. Salovey and J. D. Mayer, "Emotional Intelligence," *Imagination, Cognition, and Personality* 9 (1990): 185–211.

72 D. Goleman, *Emotional Intelligence: Why It Can Matter More Than IQ* (New York: Bantam, 1997).

73 J. O. Dozier, *The Weeping, the Window, the Way* (London: Tate, 2010), 130.

74 G. Matthews, M. Zeidner, and R. D. Roberts, *Emotional Intelligence: Science and Myth* (Cambridge, MA: MIT Press/Bradford, 2004); J. Ciarrochi, J. P. Forgas, and J. D. Mayer, eds., *Emotional Intelligence in Everyday Life*, 2nd ed. (New York: Psychology Press, 2006).

75 J. N. Giedd, "The Teen Brain: Insights from Neuroimaging," *Journal of Adolescent Health* 42, no. 4 (2008): 335–343; B. J. Casey and R. M. Jones, "Neurobiology of the Adolescent Brain and Behavior," *Journal of the American Academy of Child & Adolescent Psychiatry* 49, no. 12 (2010): 1189–1285.

76 S. F. Brosnan and F. B. M. de Waal, "Monkeys Reject Unequal Pay," *Nature* 425, no. 6955 (2003): 297–299.

77 K. Amunts et al., "Cytoarchitectonic Mapping of the Human Amygdala, Hippocampal Region and Entorhinal Cortex: Intersubject Variability and Probability Maps," *Anatomy and Embryology* 210, no. 5–6 (2005): 343–352.

78 K. C. Bickart et al., "Amygdala Volume and Social Network Size in Humans," *Nature Neuroscience* 14, no. 2 (2011): 163–164.

79 B. K. Hölzel et al., "Mindfulness Practice Leads to Increases in Regional Brain Gray Matter Density," *Psychiatry Research* 191, no. 1 (2011): 36–43.

80 H. Y. Weng et al., "Compassion Training Alters Altruism and Neural Responses to Suffering," *Psychological Science* 24, no. 7 (2013): 1171–1180.

81 C. A. Hutcherson, E. M. Seppala, and J. J. Gross, "Loving-Kindness Meditation Increases Social Connectedness," *Emotion* 8, no. 5 (2008): 720–724.

82 R. Bar-On et al., "Exploring the Neurological Substrate of Emotional and Social Intelligence," *Brain* 126, no. 8 (2003): 1790–1800; G. Šimić et al., "Understanding Emotions: Origins and Roles of the Amygdala," *Biomolecules* 11, no. 6 (2021): 823.

83 J. Hogeveen, C. Salvi, and J. Grafman, "'Emotional Intelligence': Lessons from Lesions," *Trends in Neuroscience* 39, no. 10 (2016): 694–705; S. Bajaj and W. D. S. Killgore, "Association between Emotional Intelligence and Effective Brain Connectome: A Large-Scale Spectral DCM Study," *NeuroImage* 229 (2021): 117750, ISSN 1053–8119.

84 T. Merton, *No Man Is an Island* (New York: HarperOne, 2002).

85 F. M. Logan, "Kindergarten and Bauhaus," *College Art Journal* 10, no. 1 (1950): 36–43; N. Janni, *Bringing the Steiner Waldorf Approach to Your Early Years Practice*, 3rd ed. (New York: Routledge, 2016).

86 S. Brown with C. Vaughan, *Play: How It Shapes the Brain, Opens the Imagination, and Invigorates the Soul* (New York: Avery, 2010).

87 S. Hoberman, "'Poor' Woman Leaves Close to $2 Million to Salvation Army," ABC News, January 25, 2012, https://abcnews.go.com/blogs/headlines/2012/01/poor-woman-leaves-close-to-2-million-to-salvation-army/.

88 M. K. Gandhi, *Autobiography: The Story of My Experiments with Truth* (New York: Dover, 1983), 6.

89 Josephson Institute, *The Ethics of American Youth: 2002*, CHARACTER COUNTS!, 2002, https://charactercounts.org/programs/reportcard/2002/.

90 Josephson Institute, *The Ethics of American Youth: 2012*, CHARACTER COUNTS!, 2012, https://charactercounts.org/programs/reportcard/2012/.

91 C. Siemaszko and E. Kaplan, "College Admissions Scheme Mastermind William Rick Singer Wore Wire to Expose Scam," NBC News, March 12, 2019, https://www.nbcnews.com/news/us-news/alleged-mastermind-cheating-scandal-involving-lori-laughlin-wore-wire-expose-n982421.

92 L. K. Treviño and M. E. Brown, "Managing to Be Ethical: Debunking Five Business Ethics Myths," *Academy of Management Executive* 18, no. 2 (2004): 69–83; C. K. Gunsalus, *The Young Professional's Survival Guide: From Cab Fares to Moral Snares* (Cambridge, MA: Harvard University Press, 2012).

93 J. L. E. Dreyer, *A History of Astronomy from Thales to Kepler*, 2nd ed. (New York: Dover, 2011); B. L. Van der Waerden, "The Heliocentric System in Greek, Persian and Hindu Astronomy," *Annals of the New York Academy of Sciences* 500, no. 1 (1987): 525–545; H. Thurston, *Early Astronomy* (New York: Springer-Verlag, 1994).

94 Dreyer, *A History of Astronomy from Thales to Kepler*; O. Gingerich and J. H. MacLachlan, *Nicolaus Copernicus: Making the Earth a Planet*, Oxford Portraits in Science (New York: Oxford University Press, 2005).

95 K. C. D. Tan and M. Kim, eds., *Issues and Challenges in Science Education Research: Moving Forward* (Dordrecht, The Netherlands: Springer, 2012), back cover.

96 J. P. Gaskell, "Science, Technology and Society: Issues for Science Teachers," *Studies in Science Education* 9 (1982): 33–36; P. J. Fensham, "Familiar but Different: Some Dilemmas and New Directions in Science Education," in P. J. Fensham, ed., *Developments and Dilemmas in Science Education*, 1–26 (London: Falmer Press, 1988).

97 C. Peoples, "Sputnik and 'Skill Thinking' Revisited: Technological Determinism in American Responses to the Soviet Missile Threat," *Cold War History* 8, no. 1 (2008): 55–75.

98 T. Jarvis and A. Pell, "Changes in Primary Boys' and Girls' Attitudes to School and Science during a Two-Year Science In-Service Programme," *Curriculum Journal* 13, no. 1 (2002): 43–69; Y. Xie and A. Achen, *Science on the Decline? Educational Outcomes of Three Cohorts of Young Americans*, PSC Research Report no. 09-684 (Philadelphia: University of Pennsylvania, Population Studies Center, 2009); Royal Society Science and Mathematics Education, *A "State of the Nation" Report on the Participation and Attainment of 14–19 Year Olds in Science and Mathematics in the UK, 1996–2007* (London: Royal Society, 2008), https://royalsociety.org/-/media/Royal_Society_Content/Education/policy/state-of-nation/SNR2-full-report.pdf.

99 NCES, *The Nation's Report Card: Science 2019*, NCES 2021045 (Washington, DC: National Center for Education Statistics, Institute of Education Sciences, US Department of Education, 2021), https://www.nationsreportcard.gov/highlights/science/2019/.

100 B. Alberts, "Redefining Science Education," *Science* 323, no. 5913 (2009): 437.

101 D. D. Thornburg, "Five Challenges in Science Education," 2009, https://tcse-k12.com/pages/science.pdf.

102 C. Sagan, *Broca's Brain: Reflections on the Romance of Science*, 2nd ed. (New York: Ballantine Books, 1986).

103 National Research Council, *Taking Science to School: Learning and Teaching Science in Grades K–8*, eds. R. A. Duschl, H. A. Schweingruber, and A. W. Shouse (Washington, DC: National Academies Press, 2007).

104 National Research Council, *Ready, Set, Science! Putting Research to Work in K–8 Science Classrooms*, eds. S. Michaels, A. W. Shouse, and H. A. Schweingruber (Washington, DC: National Academies Press, 2007).

105 B. France and V. Compton, eds., *Bringing Communities Together: Connecting Learners with Scientists or Technologists* (Rotterdam, The Netherlands: Sense Publishers, 2012); D. C. Wilson, *The Paradoxes of Transparency: Science and the Ecosystem Approach to Fisheries Management in Europe* (Amsterdam: Amsterdam University Press, 2010).

106 J. Solomon and G. Aikenhead, eds., *STS Education: International Perspectives in Reform* (New York: Teacher's College Press, 1994).

107 G. Charpak, *La main à la pâte: Histoire des sciences à l'école primaire* (Paris: Flammarion, 1996).

108 C. Adelman, "The Toolbox Revisited: Paths to Degree Completion from High School through College," 2006, https://www2.ed.gov/rschstat/research/pubs/toolboxrevisit/index.html.

109 Mathematical Sciences Education Board, *Everybody Counts: A Report to the Nation on the Future of Mathematics Education* (Washington, DC: National Academies Press, 1989).

110 N. Li, I. A. C. Mok, and Y. Cao, "The Evolution of Mathematical Thinking in Chinese Mathematics Education," *Mathematics* 7, no. 3 (2019): 297, https://doi.org/10.3390/math7030297.

111 L. Ma, *Knowing and Teaching Elementary Mathematics: Teachers' Understanding of Fundamental Mathematics in China and the United States*, Studies in Mathematical Thinking and Learning Series, 2nd ed. (Abingdon, Oxfordshire, UK: Routledge, 2010).

112 J. Harper, "Some Thoughts on Why Japanese Students Are Better Than U.S. Students on International Mathematics Assessments," NCTM, 2001, https://www.nctm.org/resources/content.aspx?id=1560.

113 J. W. Stigler and J. Hiebert, *The Teaching Gap: Best Ideas from the World's Teachers for Improving Education in the Classroom* (New York: Free Press, 2009).

114 W. Schmidt, "At the Precipice: The Story of Mathematics Education in the United States," *Peabody Journal of Education* 87, no. 1 (2012): 133–156, https://www.jstor.org/stable/23120559.

115 E. P. Torrance, "A Longitudinal Examination of the Fourth Grade Slump in Creativity," *Gifted Child Quarterly* 12 (1968): 195–199.

116 Mathematical Sciences Education Board, *Everybody Counts.*

117 W. Schmidt et al., *The Preparation Gap: Teacher Education for Middle School Mathematics in Six Countries*, MT21 Report (East Lansing: Michigan State University, 2007), https://www.educ.msu.edu/content/downloads/sites/usteds/MT21Report.pdf.

118 NCES, *The Nation's Report Card: Mathematics 2015*, NCES 2015–136 (Washington, DC: National Center for Education Statistics, Institute of Education Sciences, US Department of Education, 2015), https://www.nationsreportcard.gov/reading_math_2015/; G. J. Duncan and R. J. Murnane, *Whither Opportunity? Rising Inequality, Schools, and Children's Life Chances*, copublished with the Spencer Foundation (New York: Russell Sage Foundation, 2011).

119 J. Block, "Assimilation, Accommodation, and the Dynamics of Personality Development," *Child Development* 53, no. 2 (1982): 281–295; J. E. Ormrod and B. D. Jones, *Essentials of Educational Psychology: Big Ideas to Guide Effective Teaching*, 5th ed. (Boston: Pearson Education, 2018).

120 P. Black and D. Wiliam, "Assessment and Classroom Learning," *Assessment in Education: Principles, Policy & Practice* 5, no. 1 (1998): 7–74.

121 T. P. Carpenter, E. Fennema, and M. L. Franke, "Cognitively Guided Instruction: A Knowledge Base for Reform in Primary Mathematics Instruction," *Elementary School Journal* 97, no. 1 (1996): 3–20; T. P. Carpenter et al., *Children's Mathematics: Cognitively Guided Instruction*, 2nd ed. (Portsmouth, NH: Heinemann, 2014).

122 AMTE, *Standards for Elementary Mathematics Specialists: A Reference for Teacher Credentialing and Degree Programs* (San Diego: AMTE, 2010).

123 P. Black and D. Wiliam, "Assessment and Classroom Learning"; T. P. Scot, C. M. Callahan, and J. Urquhart, "Paint-by-Number Teachers and Cookie-Cutter Students: The Unintended Effects of High-Stakes Testing on the Education of Gifted Students," *Roeper Review: A Journal on Gifted Education* 31, no. 1 (2009): 40–52.

124 D. W. Shwalb, S. Sugie, and C. M. Yang, "Motivation for Abacus Studies and School Mathematics: A Longitudinal Study of Japanese 3rd–6th Graders," in D. Shwalb, J. Nakazawa, and B. Shwalb, eds., *Applied Developmental Psychology: Theory, Practice, and Research from Japan*, 109–135 (Greenwich, CT: Information Age Publishing, 2005).

125 Y. Ku et al., "Sequential Neural Processes in Abacus Mental Addition: An EEG and fMRI Case Study," *PLOS ONE* 7, no. 5 (2012): e36410; T. Hanakawa et al., "Neural Correlates Underlying Mental Calculation in Abacus Experts: A Functional Magnetic Resonance Imaging Study," *NeuroImage* 19 (2003): 296–307.

5. Foundational Competencies

1 F. Gaddum, "School Report for John Gurdon for Biology," *Eton College* (Berkshire: Eton, 1949).

2 B. S. Bloom, M. D. Engelhart, E. J. Furst, W. H. Hill, and D. R. Krathwohl, *Taxonomy of Educational Objectives: The Classification of Educational Goals*, Vol. Handbook I: *Cognitive Domain*. (New York: Longmans, Green, 1956); D. R. Krathwohl, B. S. Bloom, and B. B. Masia, *Taxonomy of Educational Objectives: The Classification of Educational Goals*. Handbook II: *Affective Domain*. (Philadelphia: David McKay Co., 1956); E. J. Simpson, *The Classification of Educational Objectives in the Psychomotor Domain* (Washington, DC: Gryphon House, 1972).

3 H. Gardner, *Frames of Mind: The Theory of Multiple Intelligences*, 2nd ed. (New York: Basic Books, 2011); R. J. Sternberg, *Beyond IQ: A Triarchic Theory of Human Intelligence* (New York: Cambridge University Press, 1985); R. B. Cattell, *Abilities: Their Structure, Growth, and Action* (Boston: Houghton Mifflin, 1971).

4 N. Herrmann, *The Whole Brain Business Book* (New York: McGraw-Hill, 1996).

5 D. E. Berlyne, "A Theory of Human Curiosity," *Journal of Psychology* 45, no. 3 (1954): 180–191.

6 Berlyne, "A Theory of Human Curiosity."

7 M. J. Gruber, B. D. Gelman, and C. Ranganath, "States of Curiosity Modulate Hippocampus-Dependent Learning via the Dopaminergic Circuit," *Neuron* 84, no. 2 (2014): 486–496, ISSN 0896-6273.

8 P. C. O'Connor and C. J. Jackson, "Learning to Be Saints or Sinners: The Indirect Pathway from Sensation Seeking to Behavior through Mastery Orientation," *Journal of Personality* 76 (2008): 1–20; C. J. Jackson, P. Baguma, and A. Furnham, "Predicting Grade Point Average from the Hybrid Model of Learning in Personality: Consistent Findings from Ugandan and Australian Students," *Educational Psychology* 29, no. 7 (2009): 747–759; C. J. Jackson, *An Applied Neuropsychological Model of Functional and Dysfunctional Learning: Applications for Business, Education, Training and Clinical Psychology* (Sydney, Australia: Cymeon, 2005).

9 J. Jirout and D. Klahr, "Children's Scientific Curiosity: In Search of an Operational Definition of an Elusive Concept," *Developmental Review* 32, no. 2 (2012): 125–160 (quote on 125).

10 B. J. Saab et al., "NCS-1 in the Dentate Gyrus Promotes Exploration, Synaptic Plasticity, and Rapid Acquisition of Spatial Memory," *Neuron* 63, no. 5 (2009): 643–656.

11 R. Whately, *Bacon's Essays, with Annotations*. Vol. 3, no. 22. (London: Parker, 1856), 491.

12 Merck, "State of Curiosity," Harris Poll, 2015, https://www.multivu.com/players/English/7648551-merck-kgaa-smarter-together/document/f639a5f0-5583-41d8-9784-8f407d3010cf.pdf.

13 M. E. Hill and J. McGinnis, "The Curiosity in Marketing Thinking," *Journal of Marketing Education* 29, no. 1 (2007): 52–62.

14 Y. Dudai, "The Neurobiology of Consolidations, Or, How Stable Is the Engram?," *Annual Review of Psychology* 55 (2004): 51–86.

15 B. R. Sheth, N. Nguyen, and D. Janvelyan, "Does Sleep Really Influence Face Recognition Memory?," *PLOS ONE* 4, no. 5 (2009): e5496.

16 C. Chabris and D. Simons, *The Invisible Gorilla: How Our Intuitions Deceive Us* (New York: HarperCollins, 2011).

17 T. Drew, M. L. H. Vo, and J. M. Wolfe, "The Invisible Gorilla Strikes Again: Sustained Inattentional Blindness in Expert Observers," *Psychological Science* 24, no. 9 (2013): 1848–1853.

18 D. H. Weissman et al., "Dorsal Anterior Cingulate Cortex Resolves Conflict from Distracting Stimuli by Boosting Attention toward Relevant Events," *Cerebral Cortex* 15, no. 2 (2004): 229–237.

19 R. A. Barkley, G. Grodzinsky, and G. J. DuPaul, "Frontal Lobe Functions in Attention Deficit Disorder with and without Hyperactivity: A Review and Research Report," *Journal of Abnormal Child Psychology* 20, no. 2 (1992): 163–188; J. Castaño, "The Contribution of Neuropsychology to the Diagnosis and Treatment of Learning Disorders," *Revista de Neurologia* 34, suppl. 1 (2002): S1–S7; H. Madera-Carrillo et al., "Quantitative Electroencephalogram Analysis Confirms the Presence of Frontal Lobe Deficit among Attention Deficit Disorder with Hyperactivity Children," *Gaceta medica de Mexico* 143, no. 5 (2007): 391–400.

20 K. P. Madore and A. D. Wagner, "Multicosts of Multitasking," *Cerebrum: The Dana Forum on Brain Science*, March-April 2019, cer-04-19.

21 L. J. Palladino, *Find Your Focus Zone: An Effective New Plan to Defeat Distraction and Overload* (New York: Atria Books, 2011).

22 European College of Neuropsychopharmacology, "Is ADHD Really a Sleep Problem?," *ScienceDaily*, September 4, 2017, www.sciencedaily.com/releases/2017/09/170904093443.htm; R. D. Chervin et al., "Sleep-Disordered Breathing, Behavior, and Cognition in Children Before and After Adenotonsillectomy," *Pediatrics* 117, no. 4 (2006): e769-78, DOI: 10.1542/peds.2005-1837.

23 L. Schwabe and O. T. Wolf, "Learning under Stress Impairs Memory Formation," *Neurobiology of Learning and Memory* 93, no. 2 (2010): 183–188.

24 F. I. M. Craik and R. S. Lockhart, "Levels of Processing: A Framework for Memory Research," *Journal of Verbal Learning and Verbal Behavior* 11 (1972): 671–684.

25 T. Klingberg et al., "Computerized Training of Working Memory in Children with ADHD: A Randomized, Controlled Trial," *Journal of the American Academy of Child and Adolescent Psychiatry* 44, no. 2 (2005): 177–186.

26 R. E. Nisbett et al., "Intelligence: New Findings and Theoretical Developments," *American Psychologist* 67, no. 2 (2012): 130–159.

27 K. A. MacLean et al., "Intensive Meditation Training Improves Perceptual Discrimination and Sustained Attention," *Psychological Science* 21, no. 6 (2010): 829–839; C. J. Norris et al., "Brief Mindfulness Meditation Improves Attention in Novices: Evidence from ERPs and Moderation by Neuroticism," *Frontiers in Human Neuroscience* 12 (2018): 315.

28 B. K. Hölzel et al., "Mindfulness Practice Leads to Increases in Regional Brain Gray Matter Density," *Psychiatry Research* 191, no. 1 (2011): 36–43.

29 G. A. Miller, "The Magical Number Seven Plus or Minus Two: Some Limits on Our Capacity for Processing Information," *Psychological Review* 63, no. 2 (1956): 81–97.

30 A. D. Baddeley, "The Episodic Buffer: A New Component of Working Memory?," *Trends in Cognitive Science* 4, no. 11 (2000): 417–423.

31 L. Schwabe and O. T. Wolf, "The Context Counts: Congruent Learning and Testing Environments Prevent Memory Retrieval Impairment Following Stress," *Cognitive, Affective & Behavioral Neuroscience* 9, no. 3 (2009): 229–236.

32 G. R. Loftus, "When a Lie Becomes Memory's Truth: Memory Distortion After Exposure to Misinformation," *Current Directions in Psychological Science* 1 (1992): 121–123.

33 A. Diamond, "Biological and Social Influences on Cognitive Control Processes Dependent on Prefrontal Cortex," *Progress in Brain Research* 189 (2011): 319–339.

34 G. W. Small et al., "Effects of a 14-Day Healthy Longevity Lifestyle Program on Cognition and Brain Function," *American Journal of Geriatric Psychiatry* 14, no. 6 (2006): 538–545.

35 K. Gibran, *The Prophet* (New York: Knopf, 1923).

36 S. M. Jaeggi et al., "Improving Fluid Intelligence with Training on Working Memory," *Proceedings of the National Academy of Sciences* (*PNAS*) 105 (2008): 6829–6833; S. L. Tennstedt and F. W. Unverzagt, "The ACTIVE Study: Study Overview and Major Findings," *Journal of Aging and Health* 25, 8 suppl. (2014): 3S–20S.

37 P. Fissler et al., "Novelty Interventions to Enhance Broad Cognitive Abilities and Prevent Dementia: Synergistic Approaches for the Facilitation of Positive Plastic Change," *Progress in Brain Research*, 207 (2013): 403–434; S. Gupta, *Keep Sharp: Build a Better Brain at Any Age* (New York: Simon & Schuster, 2021).

38 F. de Waal, "Do Humans Alone 'Feel Your Pain'?," *Chronicle of Higher Education*, October 26, 2001, https://chronicle.com/article/Do-Humans-Alone-Feel-Your/26238.

39 B. K. Hölzel et al., "Mindfulness Practice Leads to Increases in Regional Brain Gray Matter Density"; H. Y. Weng et al., "Compassion Training Alters Altruism and Neural Responses to Suffering," *Psychological Science* 24, no. 7 (2013): 1171–1180.

40 C. A. Hutcherson, E. M. Seppala, and J. J. Gross, "Loving-Kindness Meditation Increases Social Connectedness," *Emotion* 8, no. 5 (2008): 720–724; K. C. Bickart et al., "Amygdala Volume and Social Network Size in Humans," *Nature Neuroscience* 14, no. 2 (2011): 163–164.

41 K. Bucher, R. Myers, and C. Southwick, "Anterior Temporal Cortex and Maternal Behavior in Monkey," *Neurology* 20, no. 4 (1970): 415.

42 K. Uvnäs-Moberg and M. Petersson, "Oxytocin, ein Vermittler von Antistress, Wohlbefinden, sozialer Interaktion, Wachstum und Heilung [Oxytocin, a Mediator of Anti-Stress, Well-Being, Social Interaction, Growth and Healing]," *Zeitschrift für Psychosomatische Medizin und Psychotherapie* 51, no. 1 (2005): 57–80, DOI: 10.13109/zptm.2005.51.1.57, PMID: 15834840; G. Domes et al., "Oxytocin Improves 'Mind-Reading' in Humans," *Biological Psychiatry* 61, no. 6 (2007): 731–733.

43 W. Sullivan, "The Einstein Papers. A Man of Many Parts," *New York Times*, March 29, 1972, https://www.nytimes.com/1972/03/29/archives/the-einstein-papers-a-man-of-many-parts-the-einstein-papers-man-of.html.

44 S. H. Konrath, E. H. O'Brien, and C. Hsing, "Changes in Dispositional Empathy in American College Students Over Time: A Meta-Analysis," *Personality and Social Psychology Review* 15, no. 2 (2010): 180–198, DOI: 10.1177/1088868310377395.

45 S. Milgram, "Behavioral Study of Obedience," *Journal of Abnormal and Social Psychology* 67, no. 4 (1963): 371–378.

46 N. Eisenberg-Berg and P. Mussen, "Empathy and Moral Development in Adolescence," *Developmental Psychology* 14, no. 2 (1978): 185–186.

47 C. Zahn-Waxler, M. Radke-Yarrow, and R. A. King, "Child Rearing and Children's Prosocial Initiations toward Victims of Distress," *Child Development* 50, no. 2 (1979): 319–330.

48 J. Metcalfe and A. P. Shimamura, eds., *Metacognition: Knowing about Knowing* (Cambridge, MA: MIT Press, 1996).

49 L. S. Vygotsky and A. Kozulin, *Thought and Language*, 2nd ed. (Cambridge, MA: MIT Press, 1986).

50 J. H. Flavell, F. L. Green, and E. R. Flavell, "Young Children's Knowledge about Thinking," *Monographs of the Society for Research in Child Development* 60, no. 1: 1–96, discussion 97–114 (Chicago: University of Chicago Press, 1995); R. Fisher, "Thinking about Thinking: Developing Metacognition in Children," *Early Child Development and Care* 141 (1998): 1–15; R. Ritchhart, M. Church, and K. Morrison, *Making Thinking Visible: How to Promote Engagement, Understanding, and Independence for All Learners* (San Francisco: Jossey-Bass/Wiley, 2011).

51 R. Kestenbaum, E. A. Farber, and L. A. Sroufe, "Individual Differences in Empathy among Preschoolers: Relation to Attachment History," in N. Eisenberg, ed., *Empathy and Related Emotional Responses*, New Directions for Child Development, no. 44 (San Francisco: Jossey-Bass, 1989).

52 C. Zahn-Waxler, M. Radke-Yarrow, and R. A. King, "Child Rearing and Children's Prosocial Initiations toward Victims of Distress," *Child Development* 50, no. 2 (1979): 319–330.

53 N. Eisenberg-Berg and P. Mussen, "Empathy and Moral Development in Adolescence," *Developmental Psychology* 14, no. 2 (1978): 185–186.

54 L. Van Boven et al., "Changing Places: A Dual Judgment Model of Empathy Gaps in Emotional Perspective Taking," in J. M. Olson and M. P. Zanna, eds., *Advances in Experimental Social Psychology*, vol. 48, 117–171 (Amsterdam: Academic Press/Elsevier, 2013), DOI: 10.1016/B978-0-12-407188-9.00003-X.

55 D. C. Kidd and E. Castano, "Reading Literary Fiction Improves Theory of Mind," *Science* 342, no. 6156 (2013): 377–380.

56 P. Varkey, D. S. Chutka, and T. G. Lesnick, "The Aging Game: Improving Medical Students' Attitudes toward Caring for the Elderly," *Journal of the American Medical Directors Association* 7, no. 4 (2006): 224–229.

57 J. Decety and P. L. Jackson, "The Functional Architecture of Human Empathy," *Behavioral and Cognitive Neuroscience Review* 3 (2004): 71–100.

58 C.-C. Ni, "Loving Others' Rejects," *Los Angeles Times*, July 27, 2005, https://articles.latimes.com/2005/jul/27/world/fg-castaways27.

59 W. H. Cottingham, "The Greatest Game in the World: III Purpose and Plan," *System: The Magazine of Business* 14, no. 6 (December 1908): 570. https://www.google.com/books/edition/The_Magazine_of_Business/zF0kAQAAIAAJ?gbpv=1.

60 L. J. Sanna and N. Schwarz, "Metacognitive Experiences and Hindsight Bias: It's Not Just the Thought (Content) That Counts!," *Social Cognition* 25, no. 1 (2007): 185–202.

61 A. Tversky and D. Kahneman, "Availability: A Heuristic for Judging Frequency and Probability," *Cognitive Psychology* 5, no. 2 (1973): 207–232.

62 D. E. Haines and G. A. Mihailoff, *Fundamental Neuroscience for Basic and Clinical Applications*, 5th ed. (Amsterdam: Elsevier, 2017).

63 W. Mischel, E. B. Ebbesen, and A. R. Zeiss, "Cognitive and Attentional Mechanisms in Delay of Gratification," *Journal of Personality and Social Psychology* 21, no. 2 (1972): 204–218; W. Mischel, Y. Shoda, and M. L. Rodriguez, "Delay of Gratification in Children," *Science* 244, no. 4907 (1989): 933–938.

64 R. F. Baumeister and J. J. Exline, "Virtue, Personality, and Social Relations: Self-Control as the Moral Muscle," *Journal of Personality* 67 (1999): 1165–1194; S. J. Hayton et al., "Target-Specific Encoding of Response Inhibition: Increased Contribution of AMPA to NMDA Receptors at Excitatory Synapses in the Prefrontal Cortex," *Journal of Neuroscience* 30 (2010): 11493–11500.

65 F. B. Bryant and J. Veroff, *Savoring: A New Model of Positive Experience* (London: Psychology Press, 2006).

66 D. Goleman, *Emotional Intelligence: Why It Can Matter More Than IQ* (New York: Bantam, 1997).

67 H. Keller, *Helen Keller's Journal, 1936-1937* (London: Forgotten Books, 2018).

68 B. Lewis and D. Linder, "Thinking about Choking? Attentional Processes and Paradoxical Performance," *Personality and Social Psychology Bulletin* 23 (1997): 937–944.

69 S. L. Beilock and T. H. Carr, "When High-Powered People Fail: Working Memory and 'Choking under Pressure' in Math," *Psychological Science* 16, no. 2 (2005): 101–105.

70 A. Hirschi and D. Spurk, "Striving for Success: Towards a Refined Understanding and Measurement of Ambition," *Journal of Vocational Behavior* 127 (2021): 103577, ISSN 0001-8791.

71 R. J. Sternberg and J. C. Kaufman, eds., *The Nature of Creativity* (Cambridge: Cambridge University Press, 2018).

72 B. Baird et al., "Inspired by Distraction: Mind Wandering Facilitates Creative Incubation," *Psychological Science* 23, no. 10 (2012): 1117–1122, DOI: 10.1177/0956797612446024.

73 A. Koestler, *The Act of Creation* (London: Penguin, 1964); M. Turner and G. Fauconnier, *The Way We Think: Conceptual Blending and the Mind's Hidden Complexities* (New York: Basic Books, 2002); S. Helie and R. Sun, "Incubation, Insight, and Creative Problem Solving: A Unified Theory and a Connectionist Model," *Psychological Review* 117 (2010): 994–1024; L. Gabora and A. Saab, "Creative Interference and States of Potentiality in Analogy Problem Solving," in L. Carlson, C. Hoelscher, and T. Shipley, eds., *Proceedings of the 33rd Annual Meeting of the Cognitive Science Society*, 3506–3511 (Austin, TX: Cognitive Science Society, 2011).

74 G. J. Feist, "A Meta-Analysis of the Impact of Personality on Scientific and Artistic Creativity," *Personality and Social Psychological Review* 2 (1998): 290–309.

75 S. M. Fleming et al., "Relating Introspective Accuracy to Individual Differences in Brain Structure," *Science* 329, no. 5998 (2010): 1541–1543; R. E. Passingham and S. P. Wise, *The Neurobiology of the Prefrontal Cortex: Anatomy, Evolution, and the Origin of Insight* (Oxford: Oxford University Press, 2012).

76 C. Martindale and D. Hines, "Creativity and Cortical Activation during Creative, Intellectual, and EEG Feedback Tasks," *Biological Psychology* 3 (1975): 71–80; G. Lozanov, "Accelerated Learning and Individual Potential," *Prospects: Quarterly Review of Education* 9, no. 4 (1979): 414–425.

77 G. R. Fink et al., "Where in the Brain Does Visual Attention Select the Forest and the Trees?," *Nature* 382, no. 6592 (1996): 626–628.

78 G. Wallas, *The Art of Thought* (London: Jonathan Cape, 1926).

79 A. Kozbelt, R. A. Beghetto, and M. A. Runco, "Theories of Creativity," in James C. Kaufman and Robert J. Sternberg, eds., *The Cambridge Handbook of Creativity* (Cambridge: Cambridge University Press, 2010).

80 F. E. Williams, *Creativity Assessment Packet (CAP)* (Buffalo, NY: D. O. K. Publishers, 1980); D. J. Treffinger, "Research on Creativity Assessment," in S. G. Isaksen, ed., *Frontiers of Creativity Research: Beyond the Basics*, 103–119 (Buffalo, NY: Bearly, 1987); E. P. Torrance, "The Nature of Creativity as Manifest in Its Testing," in R. J. Sternberg, ed., *The Nature of Creativity*, 43–73 (New York: Cambridge University Press, 1988); J. Piirto, *Talented Children and Adults: Their Development and Education*, 3rd ed. (Waco, TX: Prufrock Press, 2007).

81 J. P. Guilford, *The Nature of Human Intelligence* (New York: McGraw-Hill, 1967); E. P. Torrance, *The Torrance Tests of Creative Thinking Norms—Technical Manual Figural (Streamlined) Forms A & B* (Bensenville, IL: Scholastic Testing Service, 1998); Williams, *Creativity Assessment Packet (CAP)*.

82 International Baccalaureate, *The IB Learner Profile*, 2022, https://ibo.org/benefits/learner-profile/.

83 K. H. Kim, B. Cramond, and D. L. Bandalos, "The Latent Structure of Scores on the Torrance Tests of Creativity-Figural," *Educational and Psychological Measurement* 66, no. 3 (2006): 459–477.

84 L. Zeng, R. W. Proctor, and G. Salvendy, "Can Traditional Divergent Thinking Tests Be Trusted in Measuring and Predicting Real-World Creativity?," *Creativity Research Journal* 23, no. 1 (2011): 24–37.

85 M. D. Mumford, "Where Have We Been, Where Are We Going? Taking Stock in Creativity Research," *Creativity Research Journal* 15 (2003): 107–120; P. Meusburger, "Milieus of Creativity: The Role of Places, Environments and Spatial Contexts," in P. Meusburger, J. Funke, and E. Wunder, eds., *Milieus of Creativity: An Interdisciplinary Approach to Spatiality of Creativity* (Dordrecht, The Netherlands: Springer, 2009).

86 R. J. Sternberg, "The Nature of Creativity," *Creativity Research Journal* 18, no. 1 (2006): 87–98 (quote on 87).

87 S. Estes, "The Real Reason Schools Are Failing: They're Boring and Lack 'Edutainment,'" *Huffington Post*, October 2, 2012, https://www.huffingtonpost.com/stephen-estes/the-real-reason-schools-a_b_1924437.html.

88 G. Carlson, *Child of Wonder: Nurturing Creative & Naturally Curious Children* (Eugene, OR: Common Ground Press, 2008).

89 S. Grantham-McGregor et al., "Developmental Potential in the First 5 Years for Children in Developing Countries," *The Lancet* 369, no. 9555 (2007): 60–70.

90 L. Y. Zhu, C. W. Bauman, and M. J. Young, "Unlocking Creative Potential: Reappraising Emotional Events Facilitates Creativity for Conventional Thinkers," *Organizational Behavior and Human Decision Processes* 174, no. 3 (2023): 104209, ISSN 0749-5978; A. Fletcher and M. Benveniste, "A New Method for Training Creativity: Narrative as an Alternative to Divergent Thinking," *Annals of the New York Academy of Sciences* 1512, no. 1 (2022): 29–45.

91 R. H. McKim, *Experiences in Visual Thinking*, 2nd ed. (Monterey, CA: Brooks/Cole, 1980), 89.

92 R. Gandhi, *Mohandas: A True Story of a Man, His People and an Empire* (London: Penguin, 2007), 328.

93 N. Luhmann, "What Is Communication?," *Communication Theory* 2, no. 3 (1992): 251–259.

94 D. Nevill, *Under Five Reigns* (London, Forgotten Books, 2018), 153.

6. Individualized Programs

1 F. Hooton, "Don't Judge a Scientist by Their Degree Grade," *The Biologist* 63, no. 1 (2016): 7. https://www.rsb.org.uk/images/biologist/2016_02_01_Vol63_No1_From_Smells_To_Signals.pdf.

2 A. Einstein, "Assails Education Today; Einstein Says 'It Is Miracle' Education Is Not 'Strangled'" *New York Times*, March 13, 1949: 34. https://www.nytimes.com/1949/03/13/archives/assails-education-today-einstein-says-it-is-miracle-inquiry-is-not.html.

3 J. F. Murphy, *Homeschooling in America: Capturing and Assessing the Movement* (Thousand Oaks, CA: Corwin/Sage, 2012).

4 J. Block, "Assimilation, Accommodation, and the Dynamics of Personality Development," *Child Development* 53, no. 2 (1982): 281–295; J. E. Ormrod and B. D. Jones, *Essentials of Educational Psychology: Big Ideas to Guide Effective Teaching*, 5th ed. (Boston: Pearson Education, 2018).

5 E. B. Bonawitz et al., "The Double-Edged Sword of Pedagogy: Teaching Limits Children's Spontaneous Exploration and Discovery," *Cognition* 120, no. 3 (2011): 322–330.

6 B. S. Bloom, "The 2 Sigma Problem: The Search for Methods of Group Instruction as Effective as One-to-One Tutoring," *Educational Researcher* 13, no. 6 (1984): 4–16.

7 C. S. Dweck, "The Power of Believing That You Can Improve," TEDx talk, December 17, 2014, https://www.ted.com/talks/carol_dweck_the_power_of_believing_that_you_can_improve?language=en; K. Spencer, "A New Kind of Classroom: No Grades, No Failing, No Hurry," *New York Times*, August 11, 2017, https://www.nytimes.com/2017/08/11/nyregion/mastery-based-learning-no-grades.html.

8 B. Gill and S. Schlossman, "History of Homework," *SFGATE*, December 19, 1999, https://www.sfgate.com/news/article/HISTORY-OF-HOMEWORK-3053660.php.

9 H. Cooper, "Synthesis of Research on Homework," *Educational Leadership* 47, no. 3 (1989): 85–91.

10 A. Kohn, *The Homework Myth: Why Our Kids Get Too Much of a Bad Thing* (Boston: Da Capo Press, 2007).

11 S. Bennett and N. Kalish, *The Case against Homework: How Homework Is Hurting Our Children and What We Can Do about It* (New York: Three Rivers Press, 2006).

12 While widely reported, see https://theysaidso.com/quote/donna-shalala-the-economic-dimension-is-very-clear-i-was-at-a-dinner-party-a-mot, for example, Ms. Shalala does not have a record of the source (personal correspondence).

13 L. Hillenbrand, "What Price Glory?," Beliefnet, May 21 2001, https://www.beliefnet.com/wellness/health/health-support/illness-and-recovery/what-price-glory.aspx.

14 F. Mosteller, "The Tennessee Study of Class Size in the Early School Grades," *The Future of Children* 5, no. 2 (1995): 113–127.

15 W. J. Fowler Jr., "School Size and Student Outcomes," in B. Levin, W. J. Fowler Jr., and H. J. Walberg, eds., *Advances in Educational Productivity, Vol. 5: Organizational Influences on Educational Productivity*, 3–25 (Greenwich, CT: JAI Press, 1995).

16 J. J. Heckman and D. V. Masterov, "The Productivity Argument for Investing in Young Children," lecture given as the T. W. Schultz Award Lecture at the Allied Social Sciences Association annual meeting, Chicago, January 5–7, 2007, https://jenni.uchicago.edu/human-inequality/papers/Heckman_final_all_wp_2007-03-22c_jsb.pdf.

17 M. Hohmann, D. P. Weikart, and A. S. Epstein, *Educating Young Children: Active Learning Practices for Preschool and Child Care Programs*, 3rd ed. (Ypsilanti, MI: HighScope Press, 2008).

18 A. S. Epstein, *Essentials of Active Learning in Preschool*, 2nd ed. (Ypsilanti, MI: HighScope Press, 2014).

19 A. J. Rolnick and R. Grunewald, "Early Childhood Development: Economic Development with a High Public Return," Federal Reserve Bank of Minneapolis, March 1, 2003, https://www.minneapolisfed.org/article/2003/early-childhood-development-economic-development-with-a-high-public-return.

20 F. A. Campbell et al., "Early Childhood Education: Young Adult Outcomes from the Abecedarian Project," *Applied Developmental Science* 6, no. 1 (2002): 42–57.

21 B. Stecher et al., "Class-Size Reduction in California: A Story of Hope, Promise, and Unintended Consequences," *Phi Delta Kappan* 82, no. 9 (2001): 670–674; L. W. Anderson, "Balancing Breadth and Depth of Content Coverage: Taking Advantage of the Opportunities Provided by Smaller Classes," in J. D. Finn and M. C. Wang, eds., *Taking Small Classes One Step Further*, 51–61 (Greenwich, CT: Information Age Publishing, 2002).

22 National Center on Intensive Intervention, *Data-Based Individualization: A Framework for Intensive Intervention* (Washington, DC: Office of Special Education, U.S. Department of Education, 2013).

23 L. Curry, "One Critique of the Research on Learning Styles," *Educational Leadership* 48 (1990): 50–56; S. A. Stahl, "Different Strokes for Different Folks? A Critique of Learning Styles," *American Educator* 23, no. 3 (1999): 27–31; H. Pashler et al., "Learning Styles: Concepts and Evidence," *Psychological Science in the Public Interest* 9 (2008): 105–119; L. Abbeduto and F. Symons, *Taking Sides: Clashing Views in Educational Psychology*, 7th ed. (New York: McGraw-Hill, 2014).

24 J. Henry, "Professor Pans 'Learning Style' Teaching Method," *The Telegraph*, July 29, 2007, https://www.telegraph.co.uk/news/uknews/1558822/Professor-pans-learning-style-teaching-method.html.

25 Khan Academy, *Annual Report*, 2021, https://s3.amazonaws.com/KA-share/2020+Khan+Academy+Inc.+Public+Disclosure+Client.pdf.

26 M. B. Horn and H. Staker, "The Rise of K–12 Blended Learning," Innosight Institute, January 2011, https://www.christenseninstitute.org/wp-content/uploads/2013/04/The-rise-of-K-12-blended-learning.pdf.

27 C. M. Christensen, M. B. Horn, and H. Staker, *Is K–12 Blended Learning Disruptive? An Introduction to the Theory of Hybrids* (San Mateo, CA: Clayton Christensen Institute, 2013), https://www.christenseninstitute.org/publications/hybrids/.

28 B. Means et al., *Evaluation of Evidence-Based Practices in Online Learning: A Meta-Analysis and Review of Online Learning Studies* (Washington, DC: US Department of Education, Office of Planning, Evaluation, and Policy Development, 2010), https://www2.ed.gov/rschstat/eval/tech/evidence-based-practices/finalreport.pdf.

29 Horn and Staker, "The Rise of K–12 Blended Learning."

30 A. Wang et al., "Authenticity, Interactivity, and Collaboration in Virtual Reality Games: Best Practices and Lessons Learned," *Frontiers in Virtual Reality* 2, no. 734083 (2021).

31 M. Prensky, *Digital Game-Based Learning* (St. Paul, MN: Paragon House, 2007); R. Van Eck, "Digital Game-Based Learning: It's Not Just the Digital Natives Who Are Restless," *EDUCAUSE Review* 41, no. 2 (2006): 16; D. Hamilton et al., "Immersive Virtual Reality as a Pedagogical Tool in Education: A Systematic Literature Review of Quantitative Learning Outcomes and Experimental Design," *Journal of Computers in Education* 8 (2021): 1–32.

32 J. Madden et al., "Ready Student One: Exploring the Predictors of Student Learning in Virtual Reality," *PLOS ONE* 15, no. 3 (2020): e0229788.

33 E. Jensen, "After 10 Years, Federal Money for Technology in Education," *New York Times*, January 25, 2010, https://www.nytimes.com/2010/01/25/technology/25center.html?_r=0.

34 J. Lew, "Making City Planning a Game," *New York Times*, June 15, 1989, https://www.nytimes.com/1989/06/15/garden/making-city-planning-a-game.html.

35 J. Hoppock, "Are Video Games the New Textbooks?," ABC News, June 13, 2008, https://abcnews.go.com/Technology/story?id=5063661&page=1.

36 B. Greteman, "ChatGPT Can Write Better Essays Than My College Students. That's a Good Thing," *Newsweek*, December 22, 2022, https://www.newsweek.com/chatgpt-can-write-better-essays-my-college-students-thats-good-thing-opinion-1769136.

7. A Labor of Love

1 E. C. Stuart Baker, "The Power of Scent in Wild Animals," *Bombay Natural History Society*, July 1920, https://archive.org/stream/journalofbombayn27192022bomb/journalofbombayn27192022bomb_djvu.txt.

2 R. M. Zingg, "Feral Man and Extreme Cases of Isolation," *American Journal of Psychology* 53, no. 4 (1940): 487–517, https://doi.org/10.2307/1417630; D. F. Bjorklund and C. H. Blasi, *Child and Adolescent Development: An Integrated Approach* (Boston: Cengage Learning, 2011); K. Dutta, "Raised in the Wild: Tales of Survival," *The Independent*, September 22, 2012, https://www.independent.co.uk/arts-entertainment/films/news/raised-in-the-wild-tales-of-survival-8165967.html.

3 Bjorklund and Blasi, *Child and Adolescent Development.*

4 L. Cockcroft, "Russian 'Bird-Boy' Discovered in Aviary," *The Telegraph*, February 28, 2008, https://www.telegraph.co.uk/news/worldnews/1580159/Russian-bird-boy-discovered-in-aviary.html.

5 W. Stewart, "Girl, 3, Raised by Dogs in Her Home After Her Alcoholic Mother Neglected Her," *Daily Mail*, February 25, 2009, https://www.dailymail.co.uk/news/article-1155351/Girl-3-raised-dogs-home-alcoholic-mother-neglected-her.html.

6 C. A. Nelson III et al., "Cognitive Recovery in Socially Deprived Young Children: The Bucharest Early Intervention Project," *Science* 318, no. 5858 (2007): 1937–1940, DOI: 10.1126/science.1143921, PMID: 18096809.

7 J. P. Shonkoff et al., "The Lifelong Effects of Early Childhood Adversity and Toxic Stress," *Pediatrics* 129, no. 1 (2012): e232–e246, DOI: 10.1542/peds.2011-2663, EPUB 2011 Dec 26, PMID: 22201156.

8 I. C. Weaver et al., "Epigenetic Programming by Maternal Behavior," *Nature Neuroscience* 7, no. 8 (2004): 847–854, DOI: 10.1038/nn1276, PMID: 15220929, S2CID: 1649281.

9 K. R. Kaneshiro, A. Rechtsteiner, and S. Strome, "Sperm-Inherited H3K27me3 Impacts Offspring Transcription and Development in *C. elegans*," *Nature Communications* 10 (2019): 1271, https://doi.org/10.1038/s41467-019-09141-w.

10 M. Slatkin, "Epigenetic Inheritance and the Missing Heritability Problem," *Genetics* 182, no. 3 (2009): 845–850, DOI:10.1534/genetics.109.102798, PMC 2710163, PMID 19416939.

11 E. C. Isbell et al., "Neuroplasticity of Selective Attention: Research Foundations and Preliminary Evidence for a Gene by Intervention Interaction," *Proceedings of National Academy of Sciences* 114, no. 35 (2017): 9247–9254.

12 K. Gibran, *The Prophet* (New York: Knopf, 1923).

13 Z. L. Hammond, *Culturally Responsive Teaching and the Brain: Promoting Authentic Engagement and Rigor among Culturally and Linguistically Diverse Students* (Thousand Oaks, CA: Corwin, 2014).

14 S. Suzuki, *Nurtured by Love: The Classic Approach to Talent Education*, trans. W. Suzuki, 2nd ed. (Van Nuys, CA: Alfred Music/Summy-Birchard, 2018).

15 T. Tunstall, *Changing Lives: Gustavo Dudamel, El Sistema, and the Transformative Power of Music* (New York: Norton, 2012).

8. Cultivating Growth Mindset

1 C. S. Dweck, *Mindset: The New Psychology of Success* (New York: Random House, 2006).

2 H. W. Stevenson and J. W. Stigler, *The Learning Gap: Why Our Schools Are Failing, and What We Can Learn from Japanese and Chinese Education* (New York: Summit Books, 1992).

3 F. L. Dyer and T. C. Martin, *Edison: His Life and Inventions*, vol. 2 (New York: Harper & Brothers), 615–616.

4 A. Bandura, "Self-Efficacy: Toward a Unifying Theory of Behavioral Change," *Psychological Review* 84, no. 2 (1977): 191–215.

5 F. Picard, P. Bossaerts, and F. Bartolomei, "Epilepsy and Ecstatic Experiences: The Role of the Insula," *Brain Sciences* 11, no. 11 (2021): 1384, DOI: 10.3390/brainsci11111384.

6 L. S. Vygotsky, *Mind in Society: The Development of Higher Psychological Processes* (Cambridge, MA: Harvard University Press, 1978).

7 S. H. Landry et al., "The Role of Early Parenting in Children's Development of Executive Processes," *Developmental Neuropsychology* 21 (2002): 15–41.

8 E. Young, "Lifting the Lid on the Unconscious," *New Scientist*, July 25, 2018, https://www.newscientist.com/article/mg23931880-400-lifting-the-lid-on-the-unconscious/.

9 R. Laibow, "Medical Applications of Neurobiofeedback," in J. R. Evans and A. Abarbanel, eds., *Introduction to Quantitative EEG and Neurofeedback*, 83–102 (Amsterdam: Academic Press/Elsevier, 1999).

10 R. Ader and N. Cohen, "Behaviorally Conditioned Immunosuppression," *Psychosomatic Medicine* 37, no. 4 (1975): 333–340, DOI: 10.1097/00006842-197507000-00007, PMID: 1162023.

11 L. N. Robins, *The Vietnam Drug User Returns: Final Report*, September 1973, Special Action Office monograph, ser. A, no. 2 (Washington, DC: US Government Printing Office, 1974); L. N. Robins, "Vietnam Veterans' Rapid Recovery from Heroin Addiction: A Fluke or Normal Expectation?," *Addiction* 88, no. 8 (1993): 1037–1167.

12 S. F. Brosnan and F. B. M. de Waal, "Monkeys Reject Unequal Pay," *Nature* 425, no. 6955 (2003): 297–299.

13 B. K. Hölzel et al., "Mindfulness Practice Leads to Increases in Regional Brain Gray Matter Density," *Psychiatry Research* 191, no. 1 (2011): 36–43.

14 M. P. Jensen et al., "New Directions in Hypnosis Research: Strategies for Advancing the Cognitive and Clinical Neuroscience of Hypnosis," *Neuroscience of Consciousness* 3, no. 1 (2017): 1–14, https://doi.org/10.1093/nc/nix004; M. Lifshitz, "Contemplative Experience in Context: Hypnosis, Meditation, and the Transformation of Consciousness," in A. Raz and M. Lifshitz, eds., *Hypnosis and Meditation: Towards an Integrative Science of Conscious Planes*, 3–16 (Oxford: Oxford University Press, 2016); P. W. Halligan and D. A. Oakley, "Hypnosis and Beyond: Exploring the Broader Domain of Suggestion," *Psychology of Consciousness: Theory, Research, and Practice* 1, no. 2 (2014): 105–122, https://doi.org/10.1037/cns0000019; Z. Dienes and S. Hutton, "Understanding Hypnosis Metacognitively: rTMS Applied to Left DLPFC Increases Hypnotic Suggestibility," *Cortex* 49, no. 2 (2013): 386–392, DOI: 10.1016/j.cortex.2012.07.009.

9. The Early Years

1 R. Fulghum, *All I Really Need to Know I Learned in Kindergarten: Uncommon Thoughts on Common Things* (New York: Villard Books, 1988).

2 C. Lopata, N. V. Wallace, and K. V. Finn, "Comparison of Academic Achievement between Montessori and Traditional Education Programs," *Journal of Research in Childhood Education* 20, no. 1 (2005): 5–13.

3 W. H. Kilpatrick, *The Montessori System Examined* (Boston: Houghton Mifflin, 1914).

4 Kilpatrick, *The Montessori System Examined.*

5 S. P. Suggate, E. A. Schaughency, and E. Reese, "Children Learning to Read Later Catch Up to Children Reading Earlier," *Early Childhood Research Quarterly* 28, no. 1 (2013): 33–48.

6 H. Hollingsworth, "US Parents Delaying Preschool and Kindergarten amid Pandemic," *Washington Post*, September 24, 2020, https://www.washingtonpost.com/health/us-parents-delaying-preschool-and-kindergarten-amid-pandemic/2020/09/24/ba6a6ce4-fe76-11ea-b0e4-350e4e60cc91_story.html.

10. Embracing the Three Pillars

1 S. Davies and H. Imai, *The Montessori Toddler: A Parent's Guide to Raising a Curious and Responsible Human Being* (New York: Workman, 2019); K. J. Payne and L. M. Ross, *Simplicity Parenting: Using the Extraordinary Power of Less to Raise Calmer, Happier, and More Secure Kids* (New York: Ballantine Books, 2009).

2 Sri Swami Satchidananda, *The Yoga Sutras of Patanjali*, rev. ed. (Yogaville, VA: Integral Yoga Publications, 2012).

3 T. Markham et al., *Project Based Learning Handbook: A Guide to Standards-Focused Project Based Learning for Middle and High School Teachers*, 2nd ed. (Novato, CA: Buck Institute for Education, 2003).

4 A. Datta, *Encyclopaedia of Indian Literature,* vol. 1 (Delhi, India: Sahitya Akademi, 1987), 292–293, ISBN 978-81-260-1803-1.

5 J. Hattie, *Visible Learning: The Sequel* (Abingdon: Routledge, 2023).

6 National Reading Panel, *Teaching Children to Read: An Evidence-based Assessment of the Scientific Research Literature on Reading and Its Implications for Reading Instruction* (Reports of the Subgroups, United States: National Institute of Child Health and Human Development, National Institutes of Health, 2000).

7 Hattie, *Visible Learning*, 89.

IV. Keeping the Faith

1 A. H. Aghababian, "The Kakawin Sutasoma: A Look at 'Bhinneka Tunggal Ika' and Perceptions of the Text's Religious Implications," *Inquiries Journal* 7, no. 9 (2015).

2 R. Wilkinson and K. Pickett, *The Spirit Level: Why Greater Equality Makes Societies Stronger* (New York: Bloomsbury Press, 2009).

11. Opportunity Costs

1 Millennium Development Goals, "United Nations General Assembly Resolution 2 Session 55 United Nations Millennium Declaration," UN General Assembly, September 8, 2000, https://www.un.org/en/development/desa/population/migration/generalassembly/docs/globalcompact/A_RES_55_2.pdf.

2 Inter-Agency and Expert Group on MDG Indicators, *The Millennium Development Goals Report: 2012*, UN Department of Economic and Social Affairs, 2012, https://www.un.org/millenniumgoals/pdf/MDG%20Report%202012.pdf.

3 UNICEF, "Annual Results Report. 2017. Education," 2018, https://www.unicef.org/media/47756/file/Annual_Results_Report_2017_Education.pdf.

4 World Bank, "Ending Learning Poverty: What Will It Take?," 2019, https://openknowledge.worldbank.org/bitstream/handle/10986/32553/142659.pdf?sequence=7&isAllowed=y.

5 S. Baum, J. Ma, and K. Payea, *Education Pays, 2010: The Benefits of Higher Education for Individuals and Society*, Trends in Higher Education Series (New York: College Board Advocacy & Policy Center, 2010).

6 L. Steer and G. Baudienville, *What Drives Donor Financing of Basic Education?* (London: Overseas Development Institute, 2010).

7 GPE, "2022-09-GPE-donor-contributions," Global Partnership for Education, February 15, 2023, https://www.globalpartnership.org/content/donor-contributions-gpe.

8 UNICEF, "The Investment Case for Education and Equity," 2015, https://www.unicef.org/reports/investment-case-education-and-equity.

9 UNICEF, "Addressing the Learning Crisis: An Urgent Need to Better Finance Education for the Poorest Children," UNICEF Education Section, 2020, https://www.unicef.org/media/63896/file/Addressing-the-learning-crisis-advocacy-brief-2020.pdf.

10 W. Yang, "China's Rural Education Challenge," Chinafocus.ucsd.edu, February 4, 2019, https://chinafocus.ucsd.edu/2019/02/04/chinas-rural-education-challenge/.

11 Pakistan Bureau of Statistics, "Key Findings Report: Pakistan Social and Living Standards Measurement Survey: 2019–20," 2020, https://www.pbs.gov.pk/sites/default/files//pslm/publications/pslm_district_2019-20/Key_Finding_Report_of_PSLM_District_Level_Survey_2019-20.pdf.

12 I. Lemberg and P. Colsey, "Ultra-Orthodox Jews in Israel Take to Streets over Court Ruling," CNN, June 18, 2010, https://www.cnn.com/2010/WORLD/meast/06/17/israel.demonstration/index.html.

13 UNESCO, "New Methodology Shows That 258 Million Children, Adolescents and Youth Are Out of School," Fact Sheet no. 56, UNESCO, September 2019, https://uis.unesco.org/sites/default/files/documents/new-methodology-shows-258-million-children-adolescents-and-youth-are-out-school.pdf.

14 Pakistan Bureau of Statistics, "Key Findings Report: Pakistan Social and Living Standards Measurement Survey: 2019–20."

15 UNESCO, "Building Bridges for Gender Equality," Global Education Monitoring Report, UNESCO, 2019, https://unesdoc.unesco.org/ark:/48223/pf0000368753/PDF/368753eng.pdf.multi.

16 BRAC, "BRAC at a Glance," 2023, https://www.brac.net/.

17 A. Hartwell, *Enhancing Girls' Education through Community Schools*, A Portfolio of Possibilities for Girls' Education, no. 1, 1998, USAID's Girls' and Women's Education Activity, https://pdf.usaid.gov/pdf_docs/PNACC492.pdf.

18 E. Mujahid-Mukhtar, "Poverty and Economic Vulnerability in South Asia: Does It Impact Girls' Education?," United Nations Girls' Education Initiative (UNGEI), 2008, https://www.researchgate.net/publication/265239338_Poverty_and_Economic_Vulnerability_in_South_Asia_Does_It_Impact_Girls'_Education.

19 K. T. Horning, M. V. Lindgren, and M. Schliesman, "A Few Observations on Publishing in 2012," Cooperative Children's Book Center, 2013, https://www.education.wisc.edu/ccbc/books/choiceintro13.asp.

20 N. Larrick, "The All-White World of Children's Books," *Saturday Review*, September 11, 1965, https://brichislitspot.files.wordpress.com/2017/08/384larrick.pdf.

21 S. N. Jarvis and J. A. Okonofua, "School Deferred: When Bias Affects School Leaders," *Social Psychological and Personality Science* 11, no. 4 (2020): 492–498, DOI: 10.1177/1948550619875150.

22 D. Vuri, "The Effect of Availability and Distance to School on Children's Time Allocation in Ghana and Guatemala," Understanding Children's Work Programme Working Paper, 2008, https://papers.ssrn.com/sol3/papers.cfm?abstract_id=1780142.

23 UNESCO, "Results of the Seventh Consultation of Member States on the Implementation of the Convention and Recommendation against Discrimination in Education," 34th General Conference, UNESCO, 2007, https://unesdoc.unesco.org/images/0015/001540/154007e.pdf.

24 Mujahid-Mukhtar, "Poverty and Economic Vulnerability in South Asia: Does It Impact Girls' Education?"

25 ILO, "Mobile Teachers Educate 'Seasonal Pupils,'" International Labour Organization, February 28, 2011, https://www.ilo.org/manila/whatwedo/projects/WCMS_153146/lang--en/index.htm.

26 "Govt School Teacher Ranjitsinh Disale Wins Global Teacher Prize, Makes History by Sharing Half with Other Finalists," *India Today*, December 4, 2020, https://www.indiatoday.in/education-today/news/story/govt-school-teacher-ranjitsinh-disale-wins-1-million-usd-global-teacher-prize-1746709-2020-12-04.

27 NCES, *Average Undergraduate Tuition, Fees, Room, and Board Rates Charged for Full-Time Students in Degree-Granting Postsecondary Institutions, by Level and Control of Institution: Selected Years, 1963–64 through 2020–21* (Washington, DC: National Center for Education Statistics, 2022).

28 J. Ma and P. Matea, *Trends in College Pricing and Student Aid* (New York: College Board, 2022).

29 NCES, *Public School Expenditures: Condition of Education* (Washington, DC: National Center for Education Statistics, Institute of Education Sciences, US Department of Education, 2022), https://nces.ed.gov/programs/coe/indicator/cmb.

30 G. C. Leef, "Why on Earth Do We Have a Student Loan Crisis? Student Loans Are Largely a Creature of Federal Intervention," Foundation for Economic Education (FEE), November 1, 2008, https://www.fee.org/the_freeman/detail/why-on-earth-do-we-have-a-student-loan-crisis#axzz2WRFktmwg.

31 A. Collinge, "Why College Prices Keep Rising," *Forbes*, March 19, 2012, https://www.forbes.com/sites/peterjreilly/2012/03/19/why-college-prices-keep-rising; M. Willie, "Taxing and Tuition: A Legislative Solution to Growing Endowments and the Rising Costs of a College Degree," *Brigham Young University Law Review* 2012, no. 5 (December 1, 2012): 1665–1702.

32 M. Kantrowitz, "Causes of Faster-Than-Inflation Increases in College Tuition," *College and University* 78, no. 2 (2002): 3–10; R. B. Archibald and D. H. Feldman, *Why Does College Cost So Much?* (New York: Oxford University Press, 2011).

33 Trachtenberg, "Why Is College So Expensive?"; A. Ripley, "Why Is College in America So Expensive? The Outrageous Price of a U.S. Degree Is Unique in the World," *The Atlantic*, September 11, 2018, https://www.theatlantic.com/education/archive/2018/09/why-is-college-so-expensive-in-america/569884/.

34 S. J. Trachtenberg, "Why Is College So Expensive?," *The Atlantic*, September 28, 2011, https://www.theatlantic.com/business/archive/2011/09/why-is-college-so-expensive/245839/.

35 R. Vedder and M. Denhart, "Why Does College Cost So Much?," CNN, December 2, 2011, https://www.cnn.com/2011/12/02/opinion/vedder-college-costs.

36 Archibald and Feldman, *Why Does College Cost So Much?*

37 J. J. Selingo, *College (Un)bound: The Future of Higher Education and What It Means for Students* (Las Vegas: Amazon Publishing, 2013).

38 R. Arum and J. Roksa, *Academically Adrift: Limited Learning on College Campuses* (Chicago: University of Chicago Press, 2011); B. D. Caplan, *The Case against Education: Why the Education System Is a Waste of Time and Money* (Princeton, NJ: Princeton University Press, 2018).

39 P. Attewell et al., "New Evidence on College Remediation," *Journal of Higher Education* 77 (2006): 886–924.

40 R. J. Samuelson, "Stronger Vocational Education Makes More Sense Than College for All," *Oregon Live*, May 29, 2012, https://www.oregonlive.com/opinion/index.ssf/2012/05/stronger_vocational_education.html.

41 J. Mitchell, *The Debt Trap: How Student Loans Became a National Catastrophe* (New York: Simon and Schuster, 2021).

42 M. John, *Children's Rights and Power: Charging Up for a New Century* (London: Jessica Kingsley Publishers, 2003); J. Elkington and P. Hartigan, *The Power of Unreasonable People: How Social Entrepreneurs Create Markets That Change the World* (Boston: Harvard Business Review Press, 2008).

43 B. Dogra, "50-Year Journey of the Barefoot College Celebrates Hidden Abilities and Great Potential of Ordinary People," *Mainstream* 60, no. 13 (2022), https://mainstreamweekly.net/article12154.html.

44 Barefoot College, *Annual Report 2020–2022*, Barefoot College International, 2023, https://www.barefootcollege.org/wp-content/uploads/2022/09/BCI-Annual-Report-2020-22.pdf.

45 G. Mortenson, "Sanjit 'Bunker' Roy," The 2010 TIME 100, *Time*, April 29, 2010, https://content.time.com/time/specials/packages/article/0,28804,1984685_1984745_1985478,00.html.

46 See https://en.wikiquote.org/wiki/Plato.

12. Excellence for Everyone

1 J. Coleman et al., *Equality of Educational Opportunity* (Washington, DC: US Government Printing Office, 1966).

2 H. S. Bloom et al., *Evaluating the Accelerated Schools Approach: A Look at Early Implementation and Impacts on Student Achievement in Eight Elementary Schools* (New York: Manpower Demonstration Research Corp., 2001).

3 J. S. Renzulli and S. M. Reis, *The Schoolwide Enrichment Model: A Comprehensive Plan for Educational Excellence* (Mansfield Center, CT: Creative Learning Press, 1985).

4 Education Opportunity Network, "An Education Declaration to Rebuild America," June 11, 2013, https://educationopportunitynetwork.org/declarationpress/; V. Strauss, "A New 'Education Declaration' for Genuine School Reform," *Washington Post*, June 11, 2013, https://www.washingtonpost.com/news/answer-sheet/wp/2013/06/11/a-new-education-declaration-for-genuine-school-reform/.

5 C. R. Torre-Halscott, *Extent to Which Selected Variables Predict Success among International Baccalaureate Students* (doctoral dissertation, University of Florida, 1992).

6 Hanover Research, *Current Trends in International Baccalaureate Programs*, October 2010, https://www.ibsom.org/uploads/9/0/6/3/9063770/current_trends_in_international_baccalaureate_programs_-_membership.pdf.

7 See, for example, International Baccalaureate, "Middle Years Programme Statistical Bulletin," 2022, https://www.ibo.org/about-the-ib/facts-and-figures/statistical-bulletins/middle-years-programme-statistical-bulletin/.

8 H. Gardner, *Frames of Mind: The Theory of Multiple Intelligences*, 2nd ed. (New York: Basic Books, 2011); R. J. Sternberg, *Beyond IQ: A Triarchic Theory of Human Intelligence* (New York: Cambridge University Press, 1985); J. S. Renzulli, "The Three-Ring Conception of Giftedness: A Developmental Model for Creative Productivity," in R. J. Sternberg and J. E. Davidson, eds., *Conceptions of Giftedness*, 53–92 (New York: Cambridge University Press, 1986); Reis et al., "Research on the Schoolwide Enrichment Model: Four Decades of Insights, Innovation, and Evolution"; H. M. Levin, "Accelerated Schools: A Decade of Evolution," in M. Fullan. ed., *Fundamental Change: International Handbook of Educational Change*, 137–160 (Dordrecht: Springer, 2005), https://doi.org/10.1007/1-4020-4454-2_9.

9 P. O. C. Ross et al., *National Excellence: A Case for Developing America's Talent* (Washington, DC: Office of Educational Research and Improvement, U.S. Department of Education, 1993).

10 E. P. Torrance, *The Torrance Tests of Creative Thinking Norms—Technical Manual Figural (Streamlined) Forms A & B* (Bensenville, IL: Scholastic Testing Service, 1998).

11 S. P. Marland Jr., *Education of the Gifted and Talented: Report to the Congress of the United States by the U.S. Commissioner of Education and Background Papers Submitted to the U.S. Office of Education*, 2 vols. (Washington, DC: U.S. Government Printing Office, 1972), Government Documents Y4.L 11/2: G36.

12 Gardner, *Frames of Mind.*

13 Ross et al., *National Excellence: A Case for Developing America's Talent.*

14 M. M. Fields, "Gifted and Talented Programs Dumb Down Our Students," *Time*, February 6, 2015, https://time.com/3698686/gifted-and-talented/.

15 L. S. Vygotsky, *Mind in Society: The Development of Higher Psychological Processes* (Cambridge, MA: Harvard University Press, 1978).

16 NCES, *Public School Expenditures: Condition of Education.*

17 S. G. Rivkin, E. A. Hanushek, and J. F. Kain, "Teachers, Schools, and Academic Achievement," *Econometrica* 73, no. 2 (2005): 417–458.

18 W. Durant, *The Story of Philosophy: The Lives and Opinions of the World's Greatest Philosophers*, 2nd ed. (New York: Pocket Books, 1991).

19 J. F. Westerlund et al., "Profiles of U.S. Science Teacher Candidates: Safeguards amidst the Gathering Storm," *International Journal of Environmental and Science Education* 6, no. 3 (2011): 213–227.

20 T. J. Kane, J. E. Rockoff, and D. O. Staiger, "What Does Certification Tell Us about Teacher Effectiveness? Evidence from New York City," *Economics of Education Review* 27, no. 6 (2008): 615–631.

21 Rivkin, Hanushek, and Kain, "Teachers, Schools, and Academic Achievement."

22 U.S. Bureau of Labor Statistics, "May 2022 National Occupational Employment and Wage Estimates: United States," Occupational Employment and Wage Statistics, April 25, 2023, https://www.bls.gov/oes/tables.htm.

23 C. Guarino, L. Santibanez, and G. Daley, "Teacher Recruitment and Retention: A Review of the Recent Empirical Literature," *Review of Educational Research* 72, no. 2 (2006): 173–208; R. Ingersoll, "Understanding Supply and Demand among Mathematics and Science Teachers," in J. Rhoton and P. Shane, eds., *Teaching Science in the 21st Century*, 197–211 (Arlington, VA: National Science Teachers Association, 2006).

24 NCES, *Estimated Average Annual Salary of Teachers in Public Elementary and Secondary Schools: Selected Years, 1959–60 through 2020–21* (Washington, DC: National Center for Education Statistics, 2021), https://nces.ed.gov/programs/digest/d21/tables/dt21_211.50.asp.

25 NEA, *Teacher Salary Benchmarks* (Washington, DC: National Education Association, April 26, 2022), https://www.nea.org/resource-library/teacher-salary-benchmarks.

26 OECD, *Education at a Glance 2022: OECD Indicators* (Paris: OECD Publishing, 2022), https://doi.org/10.1787/3197152b-en.

27 B. Auguste, P. Kihn, and M. Miller, *Closing the Talent Gap: Attracting and Retaining Top Third Graduates to a Career in Teaching* (New York: McKinsey & Company, September 2010), https://www.mckinsey.com/industries/education/our-insights/closing-the-teaching-talent-gap; D. Eggers and N. C. Calegari, "The High Cost of Low Teacher Salaries," *New York Times*, April 30, 2011, https://www.nytimes.com/2011/05/01/opinion/01eggers.html.

28 J. F. Kennedy, "Remarks in Nashville, Tennessee, at the 90th Anniversary Convocation of Vanderbilt University," May 18, 1963, https://www.jfklibrary.org/archives/other-resources/john-f-kennedy-speeches/vanderbilt-university-19630518.

29 from *Guru Gita* in the Uttarakhand section of *Skanda Purana* in the form of a dialogue between Shiva and Parvati

30 Eggers and Calegari, "The High Cost of Low Teacher Salaries."

31 H. F. Ladd, "Teacher Labor Markets in Developed Countries," *Future Child* 17, no. 1 (Spring 2007): 201–217.

32 R. Ingersoll, *Why Do High-Poverty Schools Have Difficulty Staffing Their Classrooms with Qualified Teachers? Report prepared for Renewing Our Schools, Securing Our Future, a National Task Force on Public Education.* (Washington, DC: Center for American Progress, Institute for America's Future, 2004). https://www.americanprogress.org/article/why-do-high-poverty-schools-have-difficulty-staffing-their-classrooms-with-qualified-teachers/.

33 W. Kopp with S. Farr, *A Chance to Make History: What Works and What Doesn't in Providing an Excellent Education for All* (New York: PublicAffairs/Perseus Books Group, 2011).

34 Tennessee Higher Education Commission, *2012 Report Card on the Effectiveness of Teacher Training Programs*, 2012, https://www.tntech.edu/education/pdf/performance-data/2012_State_of_TN_Report_Card.pdf.

35 P. Sahlberg, "Education Policies for Raising Student Learning: The Finnish Approach," *Journal of Education Policy* 22, no. 2 (2007): 147–171.

36 S. E. Abrams, "The Children Must Play: What the United States Can Learn from Finland about Education Reform," *New Republic*, January 28, 2011, https://www.newrepublic.com/article/politics/82329/education-reform-Finland-US#.

37 Abrams, "The Children Must Play"; Sahlberg, "Education Policies for Raising Student Learning."

38 V. Acker, *The French Educator Celestin Freinet (1896–1966): An Inquiry into How His Ideas Shaped Education* (Lanham, MD: Lexington Books, 2007).

39 J. Anderson, "From Finland, an Intriguing School-Reform Model," *New York Times*, December 12, 2011, https://www.nytimes.com/2011/12/13/education/from-finland-an-intriguing-school-reform-model.html?pagewanted=all&_r=0.

40 R. Jakku-Sihvonen and H. Niemi, eds., *Research Based Teacher Education in Finland: Reflections by Finnish Teacher Educators,* Research Report 25 (Turku: Finnish Educational Research Association, 2006).

41 F. Buchberger and I. Buchberger, "Problem-Solving Capacity of a Teacher Education System as a Condition of Success? An Analysis of the 'Finnish Case,'" in F. Buchberger and S. Berghammer, eds., *Education Policy Analysis in a Comparative Perspective*, 222–237 (Linz, Austria: Trauner, 2003).

42 Abrams, "The Children Must Play."

43 P. Sahlberg, "The Professional Educator: Lessons from Finland," *American Educator* 35, no. 2 (2011): 34–38.

44 P. Sahlberg, *Finnish Lessons 2.0: What Can the World Learn from Educational Change in Finland?* 2nd ed. (New York: Teachers College Press, 2015).

13. Gathering the Village

1 T. Kingkade, "How One Teacher's Black Lives Matter Lesson Divided a Small Wisconsin Town," NBC News, October 24, 2020, https://www.nbcnews.com/news/us-news/how-one-teacher-s-black-lives-matter-lesson-divided-small-n1244566.

2 H. Kurtz, "Educators Support Black Lives Matter, But Still Want Police in Schools, Survey Shows," *Education Week*, June 25, 2020, https://www.edweek.org/leadership/educators-support-black-lives-matter-but-still-want-police-in-schools-survey-shows/2020/06?cmp=eml-enl-eu-news2-rm&M=59604544&U=2391168&UUID=067a2edafd40c15bef0c7d3e56a4bb16.

3 G. Santayana, "Why I Am Not a Marxist," in A. Goldenweiser, G. Santayana, et al., *Modern Monthly: Volume 9 (April 1935)*, 77–79 (Whitefish, MT: Literary Licensing, 2013).

4 N. Mandela, "Address by President Nelson Mandela at the Launch of the Nelson Mandela Children's Fund, Pretoria," May 8, 1995, http://www.mandela.gov.za/mandela_speeches/1995/950508_nmcf.htm.

5 T. Tunstall, *Changing Lives: Gustavo Dudamel, El Sistema, and the Transformative Power of Music* (New York: Norton, 2012).

6 E. Strauss, "Maestro Dudamel Brings Sound, Spirit, and Star Power to Trenton," *Community News*, January 11, 2022, https://www.communitynews.org/towns/trenton-downtowner/maestro-dudamel-brings-sound-spirit-and-star-power-to-trenton/article_404db983-d782-506b-8b23-7c4d5e5a1512.html.

7 G. Baker, *El Sistema: Orchestrating Venezuela's Youth* (London: Oxford University Press, 2014).

8 M. J. Kreutzer and A. Teasdale, "The American Taxpayer Relief Act of 2012 ('ATRA')—Saved from the 'Fiscal Cliff,'" *National Law Review*, January 9, 2013, https://www.natlawreview.com/article/american-taxpayer-relief-act-2012-atra-saved-fiscal-cliff.

9 H. Evans, "A Place to Call Home: Dorothy Day Apts. Fine Example of Supportive Housing for Poor," *New York Daily News*, October 14, 2011, https://www.nydailynews.com/new-york/uptown/place-call-home-dorothy-day-apts-fine-supportive-housing-poor-article-1.960671.

10 J. M. Crotty, "In Philadelphia, Hockey Is Hook That Helps Inner City Kids Succeed," *Forbes*, December 6, 2011, https://www.forbes.com/sites/jamesmarshallcrotty/2011/12/06/in-philadelphia-hockey-is-the-hook-that-helps-inner-city-students-succeed/.

11 G. Marx and D. Jackson, "Small Town Succeeds Where Chicago Fails," *Chicago Tribune*, November 12, 2012, https://articles.chicagotribune.com/2012-11-12/news/ct-met-truancy-galesburg-20121112_1_truancy-hearings-school-attendance-outreach-workers.

12 G. M. Lamb, "Eric Schwarz and Citizen Schools Give Inner-City Kids a Leg Up," *Christian Science Monitor*, January 11, 2013, https://www.csmonitor.com/World/Making-a-difference/2013/0111/Eric-Schwarz-and-Citizen-Schools-give-inner-city-kids-a-leg-up.

13 S. R. Covey, "Our Children and the Crisis in Education," *Huffington Post*, June 20, 2010, https://www.huffpost.com/entry/our-children-and-the-cris_b_545034.

14 P. E. Davis-Kean, "The Influence of Parent Education and Family Income on Child Achievement: The Indirect Role of Parental Expectations and the Home Environment," *Journal of Family Psychology* 19, no. 2 (2005): 294–304.

15 V. J. Felitti, "The Relationship of Adverse Childhood Experiences to Adult Health: Turning Gold into Lead," *Zeitschrift für Psychosomatische Medizin und Psychotherapie* 48, no. 4 (2002): 359–369.

16 G. B. Shaw, *Everybody's Political What's What?* 2nd ed. (London: Constable, 1945).

17 L. Steinberg, *Beyond the Classroom: Why School Reform Has Failed and What Parents Need to Do* (New York: Simon and Schuster, 1997); A. Robbins, *The Teachers: A Year Inside America's Most Vulnerable, Important Profession* (New York: Dutton, 2023).

18 E. Wojcicki, *How to Raise Successful People: Simple Lessons for Radical Results* (Boston: Mariner Books, 2019).

19 P. Piff et al., "Higher Social Class Predicts Increased Unethical Behavior," *Proceedings of the National Academy of Sciences* 109 (2012): 4086–4091.

20 H. M. C. Schreier, K. A. Schonert-Reichl, and E. Chen, "Effect of Volunteering on Risk Factors for Cardiovascular Disease in Adolescents: A Randomized Controlled Trial," *JAMA Pediatrics* 167, no. 4 (2013): 327–332, DOI: 10.1001/jamapediatrics.2013.1100.

21 D. Juipe, "Deacon Jones Wants to Help Inner City Kids Succeed," *Las Vegas Sun*, April 20, 1998, https://www.lasvegassun.com/news/1998/apr/20/deacon-jones-wants-to-help-inner-city-kids-succeed/#axzz2WxLxityK.

22 N. Iqbal, "A Roadside School," *Indian Express*, November 11, 2012, https://archive.indianexpress.com/news/a-roadside-school/1029844/.

23 D. Moss, "My Kids Refused Their Inheritance: Here's How We're Giving It All Away," *Huffington Post*, February 20, 2021, https://www.huffpost.com/entry/covid-19-black-lives-matter-inheritance_n_602ad161c5b6f88289fdbd92.

Index

Page numbers followed by *f* indicate figures; those followed by *t* indicate tables.

B

C

D

E

F

G

H

I

J

K

L

M

N

O

P

Q

R

S

T

U

About the Author

Srinivas Jallepalli founded Sankalpa Academy, a growth-mindset school created to offer gifted-level education to all children. He is also the cofounder of Higher Orbit Foundation, a nonprofit that promotes educational equity. Jallepalli has an abiding passion for synthesizing the latest research findings in child development and understanding the challenges preventing us from bringing this research to our schools.

As an engineer and statistician, he has worked at AT&T's Bell Laboratories, Motorola, Freescale Semiconductor, and NXP. He is currently a technical director at NXP Semiconductors. Jallepalli holds four US patents and has contributed to more than forty-five papers in IEEE conferences and refereed journals. He has a Ph.D. in Electrical Engineering from the University of Texas at Austin.